NATIONAL SECURITY

ISSN 1543-5407

NATIONAL SECURITY

Kim Masters Evans

INFORMATION PLUS® REFERENCE SERIES
Formerly Published by Information Plus, Wylie, Texas

GALE
CENGAGE Learning·

Farmington Hills, Mich • San Francisco • New York • Waterville, Maine
Meriden, Conn • Mason, Ohio • Chicago

National Security

Kim Masters Evans

Kepos Media, Inc.: Steven Long and Janice Jorgensen, Series Editors

Project Editors: Tracie Moy, Laura Avery

Rights Acquisition and Management: Ashley M. Maynard

Composition: Evi Abou-El-Seoud, Mary Beth Trimper

Manufacturing: Rita Wimberley

For product information and technology assistance, contact us at
Gale Customer Support, 1-800-877-4253.
For permission to use material from this text or product,
submit all requests online at **www.cengage.com/permissions.**
Further permissions questions can be e-mailed to
permissionrequest@cengage.com

Cover photograph: © daughter/Shutterstock.com.

While every effort has been made to ensure the reliability of the information presented in this publication, Gale, a part of Cengage Learning, does not guarantee the accuracy of the data contained herein. Gale accepts no payment for listing; and inclusion in the publication of any organization, agency, institution, publication, service, or individual does not imply endorsement of the editors or publisher. Errors brought to the attention of the publisher and verified to the satisfaction of the publisher will be corrected in future editions.

Gale
27500 Drake Rd.
Farmington Hills, MI 48331-3535

ISBN-13: 978-0-7876-5103-9 (set)
ISBN-13: 978-1-57302-646-8

ISSN 1543-5407

This title is also available as an e-book.
ISBN-13: 978-1-57302-676-5 (set)
Contact your Gale sales representative for ordering information.

Printed in the United States of America
1 2 3 4 5   19 18 17 16 15

TABLE OF CONTENTS

PREFACE

National Security is part of the *Information Plus Reference Series*. The purpose of each volume of the series is to present the latest facts on a topic of pressing concern in modern American life. These topics include the most controversial and studied social issues of the 21st century: abortion, capital punishment, care for the elderly, crime, energy, gambling, gun control, health care, immigration, race and ethnicity, social welfare, women, youth, and many more. Although this series is written especially for high school and undergraduate students, it is an excellent resource for anyone in need of factual information on current affairs.

By presenting the facts, it is the intention of Gale, Cengage Learning, to provide its readers with everything they need to reach an informed opinion on current issues. To that end, there is a particular emphasis in this series on the presentation of scientific studies, surveys, and statistics. These data are generally presented in the form of tables, charts, and other graphics placed within the text of each book. Every graphic is directly referred to and carefully explained in the text. The source of each graphic is presented within the graphic itself. The data used in these graphics are drawn from the most reputable and reliable sources such as from the various branches of the U.S. government and from private organizations and associations. Every effort was made to secure the most recent information available. Readers should bear in mind that many major studies take years to conduct and that additional years often pass before the data from these studies are made available to the public. Therefore, in many cases the most recent information available in 2015 is dated from 2012 or 2013. Older statistics are sometimes presented as well, if they are landmark studies or of particular interest and no more-recent information exists.

Although statistics are a major focus of the *Information Plus Reference Series*, they are by no means its only content. Each book also presents the widely held positions and important ideas that shape how the book's subject is discussed in the United States. These positions are explained in detail and, where possible, in the words of their proponents. Some of the other material to be found in these books includes historical background, descriptions of major events related to the subject, relevant laws and court cases, and examples of how these issues play out in American life. Some books also feature primary documents or have pro and con debate sections that provide the words and opinions of prominent Americans on both sides of a controversial topic. All material is presented in an evenhanded and unbiased manner; readers will never be encouraged to accept one view of an issue over another.

HOW TO USE THIS BOOK

National security has been foremost in the minds of many Americans since the September 11, 2001, terrorist attacks. The United States has taken many major steps since that time, including the formation of the U.S. Department of Homeland Security, increased security measures at airports, the enactment of the Patriot Act of 2001, and the invasions of Afghanistan and Iraq. This book covers all these topics and more by providing the history of national security in the United States, descriptions of the various conventional and nonproliferation treaties and regimes, and information on countries of concern to the United States. Nuclear, chemical, and biological weapons are discussed in detail, as are domestic and international terrorism and Americans' feelings regarding national security after the September 11, 2001, terrorist attacks.

National Security consists of 10 chapters and three appendixes. Each chapter is devoted to a particular aspect of U.S. national security. For a summary of the information that is covered in each chapter, please see the synopses that are provided in the Table of Contents. Chapters generally begin with an overview of the basic facts and background information on the chapter's topic, then proceed to examine subtopics of particular interest. For example, Chapter 8: American Civil Liberties discusses the many complicated issues involved in balancing national security concerns during the so-called War on Terror against the rights granted to Americans by the U.S. Constitution. Historical events are examined that highlight government wartime decisions that have infringed on civil liberties. New laws, such as the Patriot Act, that were passed in the aftermath of the September 11, 2001, terrorist attacks are described. Although these laws were designed to advance the nation's counterterrorism efforts, they have also granted the government new or expanded powers that are very controversial. Whistleblowers from U.S. intelligence agencies have released classified information about troubling programs that collect data about Americans who have not been accused of criminal wrongdoing. The chapter also presents polls regarding U.S. public opinion on the government's perceived violation of civil liberties in the name of national security. Readers can find their way through a chapter by looking for the section and subsection headings, which are clearly set off from the text. They can also refer to the book's extensive Index, if they already know what they are looking for.

Statistical Information

The tables and figures featured throughout *National Security* will be of particular use to readers in learning about this topic. These tables and figures represent an extensive collection of the most recent and valuable statistics on national security, as well as related issues—for example, graphics cover the Geneva Conventions, U.S. casualties in the wars in Afghanistan and Iraq, organization charts for the various governmental departments and agencies that play a role in U.S. national security, and public opinion about the greatest threats to U.S. interests. Gale, Cengage Learning, believes that making this information available to readers is the most important way to fulfill the goal of this book: to help readers understand the issues and controversies surrounding national security in the United States and reach their own conclusions.

Each table or figure has a unique identifier appearing above it, for ease of identification and reference. Titles for the tables and figures explain their purpose. At the end of each table or figure, the original source of the data is provided.

To help readers understand these often complicated statistics, all tables and figures are explained in the text. References in the text direct readers to the relevant statistics. Furthermore, the contents of all tables and figures are fully indexed. Please see the opening section of the Index at the back of this volume for a description of how to find tables and figures within it.

Appendixes

Besides the main body text and images, *National Security* has three appendixes. The first is the Important Names and Addresses directory. Here, readers will find contact information for a number of government and private organizations that can provide further information on aspects of national security. The second appendix is the Resources section, which can also assist readers in conducting their own research. In this section, the author and editors of *National Security* describe some of the sources that were most useful during the compilation of this book. The final appendix is the Index. It has been greatly expanded from previous editions and should make it even easier to find specific topics in this book.

COMMENTS AND SUGGESTIONS

The editors of the *Information Plus Reference Series* welcome your feedback on *National Security*. Please direct all correspondence to:

Editors
Information Plus Reference Series
27500 Drake Rd.
Farmington Hills, MI 48331-3535

CHAPTER 1
A HISTORICAL OVERVIEW

Throughout its existence, the United States has faced several major external threats to its national security. The first and most enduring threat was the quest for land by other nations desiring to expand their empires. This threat persisted through the 1940s, culminating in World War II (1939–1945). Following the war, U.S. security was threatened by the spread of communism (an economic and political system completely in opposition to the principles of democracy and capitalism embraced by the United States). The Cold War period lasted into the early 1990s and pitted the United States against the world's only other superpower of the time: the Soviet Union. The U.S. government made many foreign policy decisions during the Cold War that affected its future national security.

Even before the Cold War ended, a new threat arose from political and ideological forces sweeping the planet. Terrorism gained prominence as a means for individuals with common grievances to challenge national governments. The United States has become a target for terrorist groups bent on destroying the political, economic, social, and military factors that have catapulted the United States to a position of dominance. At the same time, technological advances have allowed unfriendly nations to acquire new weapons that could inflict mass destruction on the United States. There is a real threat that such weapons could fall into the hands of terrorist groups that would not hesitate to use them against the United States.

Protecting U.S. national security means protecting its key assets: people, territory, infrastructure, economy, and sovereignty (supreme and independent political authority). Since its birth as a nation in 1776, the United States has developed a massive array of systems, tools, and weapons to safeguard these assets. However, national security is not just about defending the homeland and reacting to attacks. The U.S. government also takes a proactive approach, meaning that it anticipates future threats and uses its power to try to manipulate world affairs to its own political and economic benefit. U.S. goals for self-preservation and prosperity in the 21st century revolve around maintaining military supremacy, eliminating terrorism and weapons of mass destruction, and spreading democratic principles throughout the world. To understand how the United States arrived at this juncture, it is necessary to review the historical factors that have shaped U.S. foreign policy since the nation was founded.

REVOLUTIONARY WAR

Even before the Revolutionary War (1775–1783), the North American colonies had formed militias (groups of private citizens devoted to military missions). Some of the colonial militias gained valuable military experience fighting with the British against French and Native American forces during the French and Indian War (1754–1763). Among these fighters was a young officer named George Washington (1732–1799), who would be named commander in chief of the colonists' Continental army at the onset of the Revolutionary War.

The Continental army overcame enormous obstacles to defeat the professional British army, which was supplemented with thousands of Hessians (German mercenary soldiers). The colonists were aided in their struggle by a variety of European nations, particularly France, Britain's longtime enemy. In 1778 the colonists signed the Treaty of Alliance with France; it was the last bilateral (two-party) military agreement the United States would make for nearly two centuries. The military operations of the Revolutionary War ended in 1781, when the last British troops surrendered. The war was officially declared over two years later with the signing of the Treaty of Paris.

THE 19TH CENTURY

During the 1800s the new United States grew tremendously in terms of territory, population, and economic might. More than two dozen states were added to the Union. Expansionism was accompanied by violent conflicts with Great Britain (the War of 1812), Mexico (the Mexican War, 1846–1848), and Spain (the Spanish-American War, 1898). In addition, the so-called Indian Wars were waged for many years against Native American tribes.

The U.S. military matured throughout the 19th century as it secured and seized territory from Europe's colonial powers and Mexico. The growth of the U.S. Navy was driven in part by threats from the Barbary pirates—bands of pirates positioned around the Mediterranean Sea, primarily in North Africa, who terrorized and captured sailing ships and demanded ransom payments from the hostages' governments for their safe return. Some nations, including the United States, paid annual fees to the pirates to ensure the safe passage of their ships through the region. The U.S. government, however, tired of this arrangement in 1801 and launched military attacks against the pirates. The U.S. Navy eventually prevailed, and a treaty ended the threat to U.S. sailing ships.

Meanwhile in the United States, deep divisions developed between northern and southern states and territories on the morality of slavery and associated political and economic issues. In 1861 a devastating civil war erupted between Union (northern) and Confederate (southern) forces. When the war ended in 1865, hundreds of thousands of military personnel had died. (See Table 1.1.) Over the following decades the nation was consumed with reconstruction and internal affairs. The U.S. government vowed to stay out of territorial disputes simmering in Europe and the rest of the world.

THE WORLD WARS

In 1914 World War I began in Europe. It pitted Britain, France, Italy, and Russia (collectively known as the Allied powers) against Germany, Austria-Hungary, and the Ottoman Empire (collectively known as the Central powers). The United States was reluctant to get involved, but it eventually entered the war in April 1917 on the side of the Allies and fought until the war ended in November 1918. The Allies were victorious: Austria-Hungary and the Ottoman Empire were divided into a number of separate nations, and severe economic sanctions were imposed against Germany. Reacting to the tremendous loss of life and devastation caused by the war, the United States developed during the 1920s an isolationist stance, in that it was determined to stay out of any future European conflicts. This position was to be short-lived.

During the 1930s Germany, Japan, and Italy began aggressive military campaigns against their neighbors. In 1939, after years of aggressive expansion, Germany invaded Poland. In response, Britain, France, and Canada declared war on Germany, thereby marking the beginning of World War II. The German blitzkrieg (bombing raids that resembled a so-called lightning war) was incredibly successful. By 1941 German forces had defeated and occupied France and invaded the Soviet Union. War had spread throughout Europe, North Africa, parts of China, and the North Atlantic and South Pacific oceans. In the United States President Franklin D. Roosevelt (1882–1945) publicly adhered to the isolationist sentiment of the American public; however, as early as 1939 he began quietly expanding the nation's military capabilities.

On December 7, 1941, Japanese forces staged a surprise attack on the U.S. naval base at Pearl Harbor, Hawaii. Within days, the United States was at war with Japan, Germany, and Italy. A flood of U.S. goods and military might turned the tide of the war. By early 1945 Germany and Italy had been defeated. In August of that year Japan surrendered after two of its cities were devastated by U.S. atomic bombs. World War II was over, and a new world order had been established. The United States abandoned its isolationist stance and assumed an active role in international affairs.

THE UNITED NATIONS

Only months after World War II ended, the representatives of dozens of nations met in the United States and drafted a constitution for a new world organization called the United Nations (UN). The UN's purpose was twofold. First, it was to provide a medium through which international disagreements could be settled peacefully. Second, the UN would tackle vexing humanitarian issues, such as world hunger and disease. A similar organization, called the League of Nations, had sprung up after World War I, but fell apart soon afterward for a variety of reasons, including the United States' refusal to join the organization. The ravages of World War II, however, had convinced Americans that such a body was needed. In late 1945 Congress overwhelmingly ratified the UN Charter. The UN Security Council would play a major role in determining the course of future conflicts around the world. The Security Council was set up so that five nations (the so-called permanent members) have special veto powers over UN resolutions. The permanent members are China, France, Russia (formerly the Soviet Union), the United Kingdom, and the United States.

UN programs are funded through assessed and voluntary contributions by member countries. Assessments are based on each country's financial assets. In *United Nations System Funding: Congressional Issues* (January 15, 2013, https://www.fas.org/sgp/crs/row/RL33611.pdf),

TABLE 1.1

U.S. military personnel and casualties in major wars, 1775–1991

War/conflict	Branch of service	Number serving	Casualties			
			Total deaths	Battle deaths	Other deaths	Wounds not mortal[a]
Revolutionary War 1775–1783	Total	—[b]	4,435	4,435	—	6,188
War of 1812 1812–1815	Total	286,730[c]	2,260	2,260	—	4,505
Mexican War 1846–1848	Total	78,718[c]	13,283	1,733	11,550	4,152
Civil War (Union forces only)[d] 1861–1865	Total	2,213,363	364,511	140,414	224,097	281,881
Spanish-American War	Total	306,760	2,446	385	2,061	1,662
World War I 1917–1918	Total	4,734,991	116,516	53,402	63,114	204,002
World War II 1941–1946[e]	Total	16,112,566	405,399	291,557	113,842	670,846
Korean War 1950–1953[f]	Total	5,720,000	36,574	33,739	2,835	103,284
Vietnam conflict 1964–1973[g]	Total	8,744,000	58,220	47,434	10,786	Hosp. care reqd. 153,303
						No hospital care 150,341
Persian Gulf War 1990–1991[h]	Total	2,225,000	383	148	235	467

Notes: Data prior to World War I are based on incomplete records in many cases. Casualty data are confined to dead and wounded and, therefore, exclude personnel captured or missing in action who were subsequently returned to military control.

[a]Marine Corps data for World War II, the Spanish-American War, and prior wars represent the number of individuals wounded, whereas all other data in this column represent the total number (incidence) of wounds.

[b]Not known, but estimates range from 184,000 to 250,000.

[c]As reported by the Commissioner of Pensions in the annual report for fiscal year 1903.

[d]Authoritative statistics for the Confederate forces are not available. Estimates of the number who served range from 600,000 to 1,500,000. The final report of the Provost Marshal General, 1863–1866, indicated 133,821 Confederate deaths (74,524 battle and 59,297 other) based upon incomplete returns. In addition, an estimated 26,000 to 31,000 Confederate personnel died in Union prisons.

[e]Data are for the period December 1, 1941, through December 31, 1946, when hostilities were officially terminated by Presidential Proclamation, but a few battle deaths or wounds not mortal were incurred after the Japanese acceptance of the Allied peace terms on August 14, 1945. Number serving from December 1, 1941, through August 31, 1945, were: Total–14,903,213.

[f]Worldwide military deaths during the Korean War totaled 54,246. In-theater casualty records are updated annually.

[g]Number serving covers the period August 5, 1964 ("Vietnam era" begins) through January 27, 1973 (date of cease-fire). Deaths include the period November 1, 1955 (commencement date for the Military Assistance Advisory Group) through May 15, 1975 (date last American servicemember left Southeast Asia). Casualty records are updated annually, including current deaths that are directly attributed to combat in the Vietnam Conflict. Additional detail now on table shows number of WIA (Wounded in Action) servicemembers not requiring hospital care.

[h]Report does not include one POW (Prisoner of War)(Speicher). Casualty records are updated annually.

SOURCE: Adapted from "Principal Wars in Which the United States Participated—U.S. Military Personnel Serving and Casualties (1775–1991)," in *Defense Casualty Analysis System*, U.S. Department of Defense, Defense Manpower Data Center, 2014, https://www.dmdc.osd.mil/dcas/pages/report_principal_wars.xhtml (accessed June 4, 2014)

Marjorie Ann Browne of the Congressional Research Service notes that the United States has been the single largest financial contributor since the UN was founded. Public opinion polls, however, reveal lackluster support by Americans for the UN and its role in world affairs. In February 2014 a quarter (25%) of the respondents in a Gallup Organization poll said the UN should take the "leading role" in world affairs, down from 29% in 2007. (See Figure 1.1.) Another 37% of those asked in 2014 thought the UN should play a "major role," while 32% said the UN should have a "minor role" in world affairs. As shown in Figure 1.2, just over half (57%) of respondents in 2014 rated the job performance of the UN as "bad," whereas 35% said it was "good." The remainder had no opinion on the matter. The UN's rating among Americans has generally declined since the mid-1950s.

COMMUNISM AND THE COLD WAR

The Soviet Union had been a wartime ally of the United States, but relations became strained after World War II ended. During the war the Soviet army "liberated" a large part of eastern Europe from Nazi occupation. Through various means, the Union of Soviet Socialist Republics (USSR) took political control over these nations. The USSR assumed a major role in international affairs, placing it in direct conflict with the only other superpower of the time: the United States. A cold war began between two rich and powerful nations with completely different political, economic, and social goals for the world. The war was called "cold" because it was fought mostly by politicians and diplomats. A direct and large-scale military conflict (or hot war) between U.S. and Soviet forces never occurred.

Although a massive military conflict between U.S. and Soviet forces never took place, an expensive arms race began in which both sides produced and stockpiled large amounts of weapons as a show of force and to deter a first strike by the enemy. In addition, both sides provided financial and military support to countries around the world in an attempt to influence the political leanings of those populations. Communist China joined the Cold War during the 1950s and often partnered with the Soviet Union against U.S. interests.

Containment

U.S. political and military reaction to the threat posed by the Soviet Union was a policy called containment. The gist of containment was explained by President Harry S. Truman (1884–1972; August 29, 2001, http://www.nato.int/docu/speech/1947/s470312a_e.htm) in a speech to

FIGURE 1.1

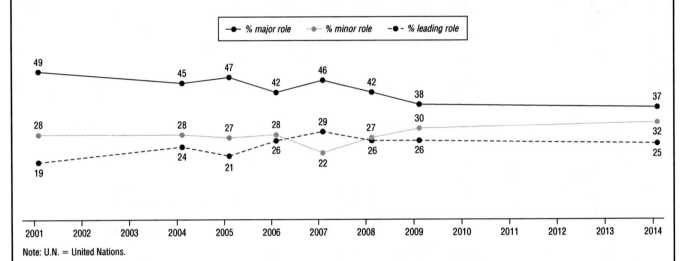

Public opinion on the role of the United Nations, 2001–14

NOW THINKING MORE SPECIFICALLY, WHICH OF THE FOLLOWING ROLES WOULD YOU LIKE TO SEE THE UNITED NATIONS PLAY IN WORLD AFFAIRS TODAY—SHOULD IT PLAY—[ROTATED: A LEADING ROLE WHERE ALL COUNTRIES ARE REQUIRED TO FOLLOW U.N. POLICIES, A MAJOR ROLE, WHERE THE U.N. ESTABLISHES POLICIES, BUT WHERE INDIVIDUAL COUNTRIES STILL ACT SEPARATELY WHEN THEY DISAGREE WITH THE U.N., (OR SHOULD IT PLAY) A MINOR ROLE, WITH THE U.N. SERVING MOSTLY AS A FORUM FOR COMMUNICATION BETWEEN NATIONS, BUT WITH NO POLICYMAKING ROLE]?

Note: U.N. = United Nations.

SOURCE: Andrew Dugan and Nathan Wendt, "The Role of U.N. in World Affairs, Today," in *Solid Majority of Americans Say UN Doing a Poor Job*, The Gallup Organization, February 25, 2014, http://www.gallup.com/poll/167576/solid-majority-americans-say-doing-poor-job.aspx (accessed June 4, 2014). Copyright © 2014 Gallup, Inc. All rights reserved. The content is used with permission; however, Gallup retains all rights of republication.

FIGURE 1.2

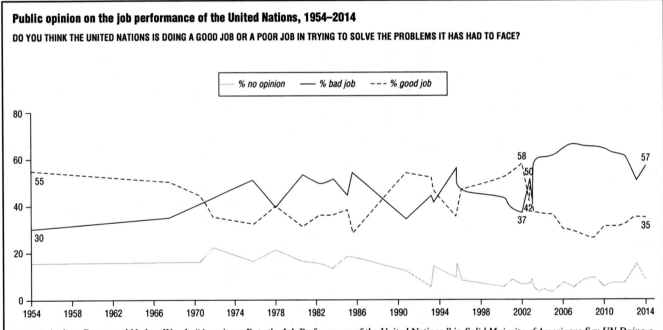

Public opinion on the job performance of the United Nations, 1954–2014

DO YOU THINK THE UNITED NATIONS IS DOING A GOOD JOB OR A POOR JOB IN TRYING TO SOLVE THE PROBLEMS IT HAS HAD TO FACE?

SOURCE: Andrew Dugan and Nathan Wendt, "Americans Rate the Job Performance of the United Nations," in *Solid Majority of Americans Say UN Doing a Poor Job*, The Gallup Organization, February 25, 2014, http://www.gallup.com/poll/167576/solid-majority-americans-say-doing-poor-job.aspx (accessed June 4, 2014). Copyright © 2014 Gallup, Inc. All rights reserved. The content is used with permission; however, Gallup retains all rights of republication.

Congress on March 12, 1947, and came to be known as the Truman Doctrine: "It must be the policy of the United States to support free peoples who are resisting attempted subjugation by armed minorities or by outside pressures." The Truman Doctrine marked an important change in U.S. foreign policy, which up to that time had mostly taken a hands-off approach to the internal affairs of other nations.

At the end of World War II, the United States was in sound economic shape. All other major nations had suffered great losses during the war in their infrastructure, financial stability, and populations. Hoping to instill an atmosphere that was conducive to peace and the spread of capitalism, the United States invested heavily in the postwar economies of Western Europe and Japan. U.S. barriers to foreign trade were relaxed to build new markets for U.S. exports and to allow some war-ravaged nations to make money by selling goods to U.S. consumers. Meanwhile, the United States enacted the Marshall Plan (1948–1952), which was designed to rebuild the allied nations of Europe and combat communism. Hundreds of millions of dollars in U.S. aid were transmitted to the governments of Greece and Turkey to help them stave off communist-led insurgencies (rebellions). Billions more went to the war-torn nations of Western Europe.

Nervousness in Western Europe about the closeness of Soviet military forces led to the creation in 1949 of the North Atlantic Treaty Organization (NATO)—a military coalition between the United States and 11 other nations. The NATO alliance provided added security for all the nations involved, because an attack against one was considered to be an attack against all. In 1958 the United States and Canada formed the North American Aerospace Defense Command to provide a warning and defense system against aircraft, missiles, and space vehicles entering North American air space.

In 1962 the United States and the Soviet Union came to the brink of nuclear war when U.S. intelligence agencies discovered that the Soviets had installed nuclear missile facilities in Cuba. In response, President John F. Kennedy (1917–1963) imposed a blockade to prevent Soviet ships from bringing new supplies to Cuba. He demanded that the nuclear facilities be removed and publicly warned the Soviets that any attack from Cuba on the United States would spur retaliation against the Soviet Union. After a suspenseful 12-day standoff, the Soviets backed down and removed the missiles. The Cuban missile crisis was a turning point in the Cold War. Negotiations began between the two superpowers on treaties to limit the testing and proliferation (growth or multiplication) of nuclear weapons. These talks would proceed sporadically for decades.

Korea and Vietnam

In 1950 North Korean forces backed by the Soviet military invaded South Korea, setting off the Korean War. Caught off guard by the invasion, the United States rushed to defend South Korea from a communist takeover. Over the next three years U.S. and allied forces under the UN fought against North Korean and Chinese troops that were supported by the Soviet Union. The war ended in a stalemate, with both sides back where they had

started: on either side of the 38th parallel (a line of latitude). In 1953 a cease-fire agreement ended the armed conflict in Korea. North Korea remained under communist control, whereas South Korea became a democracy protected by UN troops (primarily U.S. forces).

Also during the 1950s the U.S. military became involved in a conflict between communist North Vietnam and noncommunist South Vietnam. In an effort to bolster the defenses of the country, the United States sent thousands of military advisers to South Vietnam during the late 1950s and early 1960s. In 1964 the conflict escalated into full-scale civil war. Once again, the United States found itself in a remote Asian country trying to prevent the spread of communism.

The fight in Vietnam turned out to be a long and difficult one in which U.S. forces, assisted by a handful of other countries, were pitted against highly motivated forces equipped and backed by the Soviet Union and China. During the 1960s the United States was preoccupied with explosive social problems. Furthermore, there were widespread protests against the Vietnam War (1954–1975). By 1968 there were half a million U.S. troops in Vietnam. Nightly television coverage provided a bleak picture of the war's progress and helped turn public opinion against the war and President Lyndon B. Johnson (1908–1973). The United States was engaged in the war for more than a decade before withdrawing the last of its troops in 1975 and leaving South Vietnam to a communist takeover.

In both the Korean and Vietnam Wars the United States chose to fight in a limited manner without using its arsenal of nuclear weapons or engaging Chinese and Soviet troops directly for fear of sparking another world war.

Fighting for Influence

The Cold War firmly divided dozens of nations into two military coalitions or blocs. The western bloc included the United States and its NATO allies. The eastern or Soviet bloc included the Soviet Union and numerous central and east European countries. In addition, the Soviet Union enjoyed relatively good political relations with other nations around the world that embraced or leaned toward communist or socialist rule, such as Afghanistan, Cambodia, and Cuba.

Throughout the Cold War the United States and the Soviet Union sought to wield political influence in nations that were not strongly aligned with either side. Both countries used diplomacy, commercial trade, foreign aid, and the sales of military hardware as tools to promote political alliances. During the 1970s these efforts were focused on countries in and around the Middle East (i.e., North Africa and Southwest Asia). The importance of the region in terms of oil production and strategic location (e.g., sea access) became abundantly clear to both sides. The Soviet Union watched uneasily as the United States forged relations with the Middle Eastern countries of Saudi Arabia and Egypt (a former Soviet ally) and began playing a larger political role in the region's affairs.

The Afghanistan Invasion

In 1979 the Soviet Union invaded Afghanistan because the Soviets feared the communist Afghan government would fall due to widespread revolt within the country. The United States strongly condemned the invasion and worried that the Soviets were trying to extend their territory into the Middle East to control the flow of oil from that region.

President Jimmy Carter (1924–) implemented economic sanctions, including a grain embargo, against the Soviet Union. He and his successor, President Ronald Reagan (1911–2004), funneled large amounts of money to Afghanistan's neighbor Pakistan, because it was helping to arm and train Afghan rebel factions known collectively as the mujahideen (holy warriors). Meanwhile, the Soviets became mired down in Afghanistan as they fought against the mujahideen. Unable to achieve military victory, the Soviet Union withdrew the last of its troops from Afghanistan in 1989.

The End of the Cold War

Throughout the 1980s the Soviet Union was suffering from numerous domestic problems. These problems were exacerbated by the long war in Afghanistan. Meanwhile, the United States was conducting a massive and expensive buildup in military strength, forcing the Soviet Union to do likewise. In addition, Reagan began a new space-based military defense program that was intended to protect the United States from any incoming Soviet missiles.

In 1985 the newly elected Soviet premier Mikhail Gorbachev (1931–) began implementing political reforms that he hoped would quell growing discontent among his people. Gorbachev's new policy, called *glasnost* (which is Russian for "openness"), marked a historic change for the communist government. However, the reforms appeared to be too little and too late, as dissent (political opposition) and unrest continued to spread across many Soviet territories. The unrelenting weight of economic and sociopolitical problems precipitated a breakup of the Soviet Union during the late 1980s and early 1990s into individually governed republics. The Cold War was over, but its effects on U.S. national security and world politics would be long lasting.

U.S. POST-VIETNAM MILITARY

The Vietnam War severely dampened the United States' willingness to commit U.S. troops to foreign conflicts. The long war had not saved South Vietnam from a communist takeover and had been costly in terms of money and human suffering. Over 8.7 million U.S. military personnel served during the Vietnam conflict. (See Table 1.1.) U.S. casualties included 58,220 killed and 303,644 wounded. In addition, the war brought death and misery to millions of Vietnamese civilians. As a result, the American public and U.S. politicians were not eager to commit U.S. forces to future foreign conflicts.

During the 1980s the U.S. military had additional setbacks. An attempt to rescue hostages from the U.S. embassy in Iran in 1980 had to be aborted after a helicopter crash killed eight U.S. military personnel. (See Table 1.2.) U.S. Marines sent to Lebanon as part of a UN peacekeeping effort suffered a calamitous terrorist attack in 1983. More than 250 of them were killed. U.S. troops did conduct successful operations in Grenada and Panama during the decade, but these were small and limited in scope. These incidents did not indicate to the American public or the world at large the full capabilities of the maturing U.S. military.

An influx of money during the 1970s and 1980s from the Carter and Reagan administrations financed the development of sophisticated weapons and computer technology. Training was also a priority, as was the reorganization of the military hierarchy at the top levels.

TABLE 1.2

U.S. military deaths worldwide in selected military operations, selected years 1980–96

Military operation/incident	Casualty type	Total
Iranian Hostage Rescue Mission April 25, 1980	Nonhostile	8
Lebanon peacekeeping, August 25, 1982–February 26, 1984*	Hostile	256
	Nonhostile	9
	Total	265
Urgent Fury, Grenada, 1983	Hostile	18
	Nonhostile	1
	Total	19
Just Cause, Panama, 1989	Hostile	23
Persian Gulf War, 1990–1991		
Desert Shield	Nonhostile	84
Desert Storm	Hostile	148
	Nonhostile	151
	Total	299
Desert Shield/Storm	Total	383
Restore Hope/UNOSOM, Somalia, 1992–1994	Hostile	29
	Nonhostile	14
	Total	43
Uphold Democracy, Haiti, 1994–1996	Nonhostile	4

*Place of casualty, Lebanon   Note: UNOSOM = United Nations Operations in Somalia.

SOURCE: Adapted from "Worldwide U.S. Active Duty Military Deaths—Selected Military Operations (1980–1996)," in *Defense Casualty Analysis System*, U.S. Department of Defense, Defense Manpower Data Center, 2014, https://www.dmdc.osd.mil/dcas/pages/report_operations.xhtml (accessed June 4, 2014)

FIGURE 1.3

Map including the Middle East, Northeast Africa, and Southwest Asia

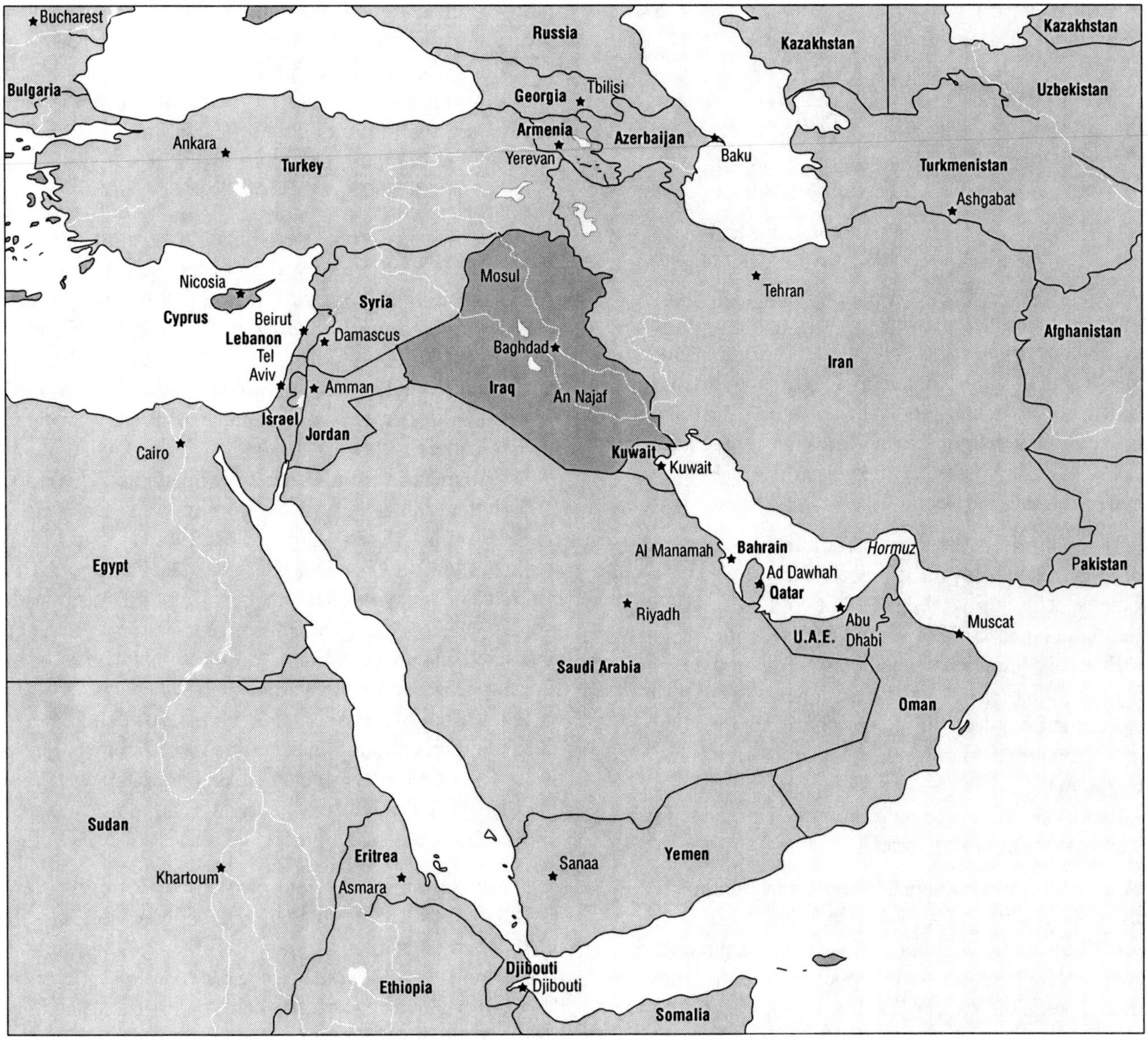

SOURCE: Christopher M. Blanchard et al., "Figure 1. Iraq and Its Neighbors," in *Iraq: Regional Perspectives and U.S. Policy*, Congressional Research Service, October 6, 2009, http://assets.opencrs.com/rpts/RL33793_20091006.pdf (accessed June 4, 2014)

As a result, U.S. forces performed extremely well in 1991, when a UN coalition was formed to drive Iraqi troops from Kuwait during Operation Desert Storm. It was the first of several major conflicts that would take place in the Middle East.

THE MIDDLE EAST

Geographically, the Middle East is a region at the intersection of Asia, Africa, and Europe. There is no official designation of the countries that make up the Middle East. The term is largely a sociopolitical one used by those in the Western world to collectively describe a group of countries in and around the Arabian Peninsula. This group is often thought to extend from Iran in the east to the northwestern coast of Africa. Some observers include other nearby countries, such as Turkey, Afghanistan, and Pakistan. (See Figure 1.3.) In a historical context, most of the region now known as the Middle East was once the core of the Ottoman Empire, which was splintered into individual nations following World War I.

Peoples and Religions

Westerners tend to describe all Middle Eastern people as Arabs. The term *Arab* is actually an ethnic designation applied to certain tribes descended from Shem (or Sem), the oldest son of Noah in biblical history. The descendants of Shem are called Semites; they include the Babylonians and Phoenicians and the Hebrew tribes of ancient times. The Hebrews embraced the religion of Judaism and settled the kingdom of Israel. Arab tribes were scattered throughout the region and were governed by various kings and tribal rulers. During the seventh century a new Arab leader emerged named Muhammad (c. 570–632), who would change the world by introducing a new religion called Islam.

The followers of Islam are called Muslims. They worship one God (whom they call Allah) and believe that Allah's messages were passed by the angel Gabriel to the prophet Muhammad in what is now modern-day Saudi Arabia. Allah's messages are called the Koran. This term is also used to refer to the messages in written form, which make up Islam's holy book. Most Muslims consider Islam much more than a religious practice; they believe it encompasses all areas of life, including economic, political, and social aspects.

By far, Islam is the most predominant religion in the Middle East. As with most religions, however, there are diverse sects within Islam. The two largest sects are called Sunni and Shia; their respective followers have historical disagreements about issues related to governance and theological interpretations. These disagreements sometimes lead to violent confrontations between fellow Muslims. Many other religions are practiced throughout the region but by small populations in most countries. The notable exception is Judaism, which is the predominant religion of Israel.

Ethnically, the modern Middle East is dominated by Arab peoples who reside mostly in Saudi Arabia, Jordan, Lebanon, Syria, Iraq, Egypt, and parts of northern Africa. There are, however, substantial pockets of non-Arabs; for example, Persians descended from tribes in Southwest Asia predominate in Iran, Turks in Turkey, Kurds in northern Iraq, and Jewish descendants of the ancient Hebrew tribes in Israel.

Thus, the Middle East is a complicated mosaic of societies in which some widely shared characteristics provide grounds for unity among much of the population. However, cultural, political, and religious differences within the region are a source of often violent confrontations between peoples. One such confrontation has grown to dominate the sociopolitical affairs of the Middle East and has become a source of great concern to U.S. national security interests: the Israeli-Palestinian conflict.

Israel and Palestine

Following World War I the League of Nations placed some territories of the former Ottoman Empire under the administration of Great Britain and France.

Iraq and Palestine were administered by Great Britain, and Syria and Lebanon by France. This arrangement was called the Mandates System and was designed to be temporary, lasting only until the territories could mature into independent nations ruled by their own governments. The populations of the administered countries greatly resented foreign intervention in their affairs and viewed the arrangement as colonialism. As a result, there was much political and social unrest in these countries. Eventually, Iraq, Syria, and Lebanon did gain their independence.

Palestine was supposed to become a nation called the Palestinian Arab State. A variety of factors prevented this from happening as described by the UN in *The Question of Palestine and the United Nations* (2008, http://unispal .un.org/pdfs/DPI2499.pdf). The UN indicates that the Palestinian Mandate was in effect from 1922 to 1947. However, the British government had already promised Jewish leaders a "national home" for the Jewish people in Palestine. That promise had been made in a November 1917 letter from the British foreign secretary Arthur James Balfour (1848–1930) to Lord Lionel Walter Rothschild (1868–1937). The Balfour Declaration (2012, http://avalon.law.yale.edu/20th_century/balfour.asp) stated in part: "His Majesty's Government view with favour the establishment in Palestine of a national home for the Jewish people, and will use their best endeavours to facilitate the achievement of this object, it being clearly understood that nothing shall be done which may prejudice the civil and religious rights of existing non-Jewish communities in Palestine, or the rights and political status enjoyed by Jews in any other country."

The Balfour Declaration pleased Zionists—Jews around the world seeking an independent Jewish state on the land inhabited in ancient times by the Hebrew tribes, that is, the Land of Israel. Most Jews had been driven from Palestine by the end of the second century. The land was subsequently ruled by the Byzantine Empire, the Persians, a series of Muslim rulers, and the Ottoman Empire. The many non-Jewish people (primarily Arab Muslims) inhabiting Palestine during the early 20th century did not want to lose their own chance at statehood and give up land their ancestors had inhabited for centuries.

STATE OF ISRAEL. The Balfour Declaration spurred mass migrations of Jews from around the world to Palestine. The UN explains in *Question of Palestine and the United Nations* that migrations were particularly heavy during the 1930s from Nazi Germany and eastern Europe—areas where Jews were subject to harsh persecution and even extermination. Violence grew between the Arab Palestinians and the incoming Jewish peoples— both of whom claimed the land as their own. In 1947 the British government turned the problem over to the UN, which proposed splitting Palestine into two approximately even-sized states, one Jewish and one Arab. Jerusalem, a city considered sacred to both Jews and Muslims, was to be ruled under a Special International Regime. The partition plan did not please Arab rulers, and the violence in Palestine escalated.

In 1948 the Jewish population of Palestine declared itself a nation—the State of Israel—and found itself immediately at war with the armies of Palestine's neighbors and Arab supporters. During the war Israeli forces captured more than three-fourths of the original territory of Palestine and most of Jerusalem. The remainder of the territory was held by the governments of Egypt and Jordan. These areas are called the Gaza Strip and the West Bank, respectively. (See Figure 1.4.) In the Six-Day War of 1967, Israel captured both of these areas and all of Jerusalem. In response, the UN issued Resolution 242, which called on Israel to withdraw from the areas it had just captured and for all states in the region to cease their "belligerency" and live in peaceful coexistence. This did not occur.

PALESTINIAN TERRITORIES. In 1964 the Palestine Liberation Organization (PLO) was appointed by a group of Arab nations to represent the political aspirations of Palestine. The PLO was an umbrella organization for a variety of Palestinian groups with varying views on the use of politics and violence to achieve their goals. The main group was al Fatah, which was led by Yasir Arafat (1929–2004). During its early years the PLO was often associated with acts of violence against Israeli civilians and soldiers. PLO splinter groups have been linked to many acts of terrorism around the world, including the killing of Israeli athletes at the 1972 Olympic Games in Munich, Germany. Meanwhile, Palestinian refugees fleeing wars and other violence spread throughout the world. They have played a substantial role in raising money and eliciting sympathy and support for the Palestinian cause.

During the 1990s the PLO achieved a measure of legitimacy as the United States worked to obtain a peace agreement in the decades-old dispute over Palestine. In 1993 the PLO and Israel reached an agreement called the Oslo Accords that laid out a plan for limited Palestinian control over some of its territories by a new government called the Palestinian National Authority (PNA). Full implementation of the plan was thwarted by continued violence between the Palestinians and the Israelis. In 2005, however, Israel did withdraw its troops from the Gaza Strip.

Arafat died in 2004 and was replaced by a close associate, Mahmoud Abbas (1935–), who was elected president of the PNA in 2005. In 2006 Palestinian voters gave members of the organization Hamas majority control of the PNA, relegating al Fatah to a minority position. The United States considers Hamas a foreign terrorist organization

FIGURE 1.4

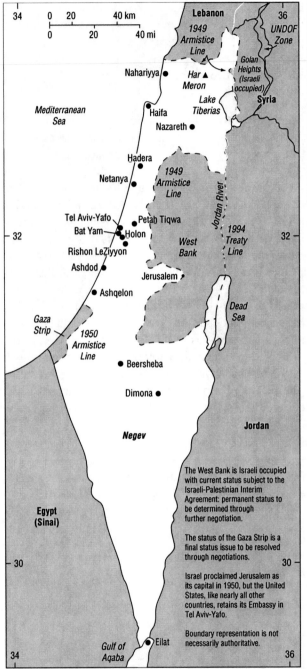

Map of Israel, the West Bank, the Gaza Strip, and the Golan Heights, 2014

The West Bank is Israeli occupied with current status subject to the Israeli-Palestinian Interim Agreement: permanent status to be determined through further negotiation.

The status of the Gaza Strip is a final status issue to be resolved through negotiations.

Israel proclaimed Jerusalem as its capital in 1950, but the United States, like nearly all other countries, retains its Embassy in Tel Aviv-Yafo.

Boundary representation is not necessarily authoritative.

SOURCE: "Map of Israel" in "Middle East: Israel," in *The World Factbook*, Central Intelligence Agency, March 27, 2014, https://www.cia.gov/library/publications/the-world-factbook/geos/is.html (accessed June 4, 2014)

under U.S. law. The United States and al Fatah refused to recognize Hamas as the legitimate leading party in Palestine. Furthermore, the U.S. government forbade direct economic aid to Palestine following the Hamas elections. Abbas began an internal political battle with the elected prime minister, Ismail Haniyeh (1962–), a member of Hamas. A near civil war erupted between Palestinian peoples allied with either side. In June 2007 Abbas declared a state of emergency and officially dissolved Haniyeh's government after Hamas forces routed al Fatah forces and seized military and political control of the Gaza Strip. Abbas appointed a new prime minister, Salam Fayyad (1952–), but the appointment was largely ignored by Hamas leaders and supporters. The United States lifted its earlier sanctions to encourage development of the Abbas government.

Egypt controls one land crossing on the border between its territory and the Gaza Strip. Following the Hamas takeover in 2006, Israel requested that Egypt begin blocking most of the people and cargo that cross at that border. Israel conducted its own much wider blockade to prevent the transport of certain goods into the Gaza Strip, because the latter was the source of frequent missile attacks on settlements in southern Israel. Despite the blockades, Hamas continued to launch missiles into Israel, prompting Israel to invade the Gaza Strip in January 2009. After three weeks of fighting, Israel declared a cease-fire, withdrew its troops, and imposed a near-total blockade on ground and sea transports of materials and supplies to the Gaza Strip. In May 2010 a flotilla of ships manned by foreign activists attempting to defy the blockade was boarded by Israeli forces, resulting in the deaths of nine of the activists. The Israeli action drew international condemnation, even from the United States. Israel and Egypt began relaxing their blockades to allow more shipments into the Gaza Strip; however, conflicts continued to rise between Hamas and Israel over rockets fired into Israel. In July 2014 tensions boiled over and the two sides engaged in armed conflict for weeks. As of August 2014, an uneasy cease-fire was in effect, and Israel and Egypt continued to limit the flow of people and goods into the Gaza Strip.

U.S. Connection to the Middle East

Since World War I, U.S. political, economic, and military affairs have become greatly entangled with circumstances in the Middle East. During the first decade of the 21st century U.S. military forces occupied two nations in the region: Afghanistan and Iraq. (See Figure 1.3.) Both invasions were driven by perceived threats to U.S. national security. In addition, there were ongoing issues related to the United States' alliance with Israel and U.S. dependence on petroleum from oil-rich nations of the Middle East.

The United States has been a staunch ally of Israel since that nation was founded. U.S. political and financial support for Israel—one of the few true democracies in the region—has continued for decades and is a source of deep resentment among the predominantly Muslim peoples of the Middle East.

Israel also enjoys popular support among the American people. Figure 1.5 shows the results of polling conducted

FIGURE 1.5

Poll respondents' sympathies in the Israeli-Palestinian conflict, 1988–2014

IN THE MIDDLE EAST SITUATION, ARE YOUR SYMPATHIES MORE WITH THE ISRAELIS OR MORE WITH THE PALESTINIANS?

SOURCE: Lydia Saad, "Americans' Sympathies Mideast Conflict," in *Americans Still Doubt Mideast Peace Is in the Cards*, The Gallup Organization, February 27, 2014, http://www.gallup.com/poll/167657/americans-doubt-mideast-peace-cards.aspx (accessed June 4, 2014). Copyright © 2014 Gallup, Inc. All rights reserved. The content is used with permission; however, Gallup retains all rights of republication.

FIGURE 1.6

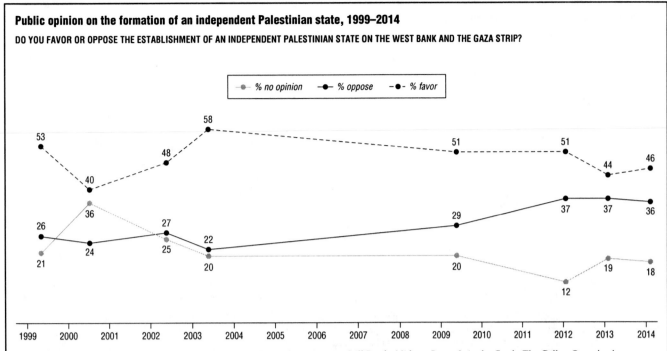

Public opinion on the formation of an independent Palestinian state, 1999–2014

DO YOU FAVOR OR OPPOSE THE ESTABLISHMENT OF AN INDEPENDENT PALESTINIAN STATE ON THE WEST BANK AND THE GAZA STRIP?

SOURCE: Lydia Saad, "Support for Independent Palestinian State," in *Americans Still Doubt Mideast Peace Is in the Cards*, The Gallup Organization, February 27, 2014, http://www.gallup.com/poll/167657/americans-doubt-mideast-peace-cards.aspx (accessed June 4, 2014). Copyright © 2014 Gallup, Inc. All rights reserved. The content is used with permission; however, Gallup retains all rights of republication.

by the Gallup Organization between 1988 and 2014 regarding American sympathies in the Israeli-Palestinian conflict. In 2014, 62% of Americans expressed sympathy for Israel. Only 18% of Americans expressed sympathy for the Palestinians. Strong support for Israel has persisted in the United States for more than two decades. As shown in Figure 1.6, nearly half (46%) of Americans said in 2014 that they favor establishment of an independent Palestinian state on the West Bank and the Gaza Strip. However, Americans are pessimistic about the chances for peace in the Middle East. Only 33% of respondents agreed in 2014 that "Israel and the Arab nations will be able to settle their differences and live in peace." (See Figure 1.7.)

Oil is another important connection between the United States and the Middle East. The United States and other industrialized nations consume much more oil than they produce and need a steady supply at low prices for their economies to function. Saudi Arabia, Iran, Iraq, Kuwait, and other nations along the Persian Gulf are all rich in oil, and significant deposits are found elsewhere in the Middle East as well. This means that Middle Eastern oil producers can influence the United States and other nations by manipulating, or threatening to manipulate, the supply of oil. Furthermore, anything that endangers the flow of oil from the Middle East, such as war or political instability in the region, threatens U.S. national security and may motivate a response.

The United States faces a challenging problem in trying to maintain both its alliance with Israel and good relations with the oil-rich Middle Eastern countries, where anti-Israel sentiment festers and threatens to boil over into full-fledged war.

COST OF NATIONAL SECURITY

The United States spends a great deal of money to protect its national security. Tasks within this area fall to a number of federal agencies, primarily the U.S. Department of Defense (DOD), the U.S. Department of Homeland Security, and the Central Intelligence Agency (CIA). Certain components and resources of other agencies, such as the U.S. Department of State (DOS) and the Federal Bureau of Investigation (FBI), are also devoted to national security interests. The specific roles and budgets of the individual agencies are described in subsequent chapters. Federal budgeting is conducted along a fiscal year (FY) that extends from October through September. For example, FY 2015 covers October 1, 2014, through September 30, 2015.

The U.S. government divides its total spending into categories called functions. In "Functional Classification" (2014, http://www.whitehouse.gov/tax-receipt/functions), the Office of the President of the United States explains that each function represents a "major purpose [that] the spending serves." As of 2014, there were 20 functions making up the federal budget. Although national security interests can fall across multiple functions, the three most crucial functions are national defense, international

FIGURE 1.7

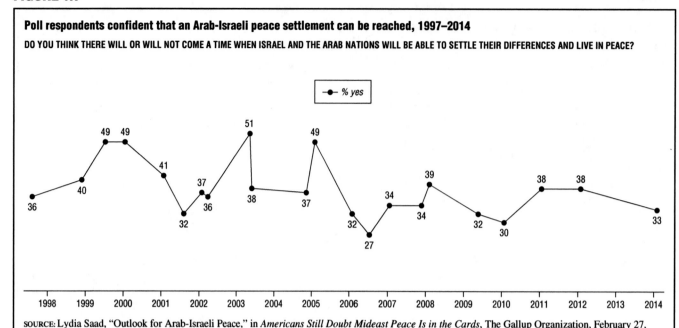

Poll respondents confident that an Arab-Israeli peace settlement can be reached, 1997–2014

DO YOU THINK THERE WILL OR WILL NOT COME A TIME WHEN ISRAEL AND THE ARAB NATIONS WILL BE ABLE TO SETTLE THEIR DIFFERENCES AND LIVE IN PEACE?

SOURCE: Lydia Saad, "Outlook for Arab-Israeli Peace," in *Americans Still Doubt Mideast Peace Is in the Cards*, The Gallup Organization, February 27, 2014, http://www.gallup.com/poll/167657/americans-doubt-mideast-peace-cards.aspx (accessed June 4, 2014). Copyright © 2014 Gallup, Inc. All rights reserved. The content is used with permission; however, Gallup retains all rights of republication.

affairs, and veterans benefits and services. Table 1.3 shows outlays for these three functions for FYs 2010 through 2013 and expected outlays for FYs 2014 and 2015. National defense is, by far, the most expensive undertaking.

National Defense

In "Budget Functions" (2014, http://budget.house.gov/budgetprocess/budgetfunctions.htm), the U.S. House of Representatives notes that national defense includes the following elements:

- Military activities of the DOD

- Nuclear weapons–related activities of the U.S. Department of Energy and the National Nuclear Security Administration

- National security activities of other agencies, such as the Selective Service System

- Portions of the activities of the U.S. Coast Guard and the FBI

National defense spending covers the following types of costs:

- Pay and benefits of military personnel

- DOD operations including training, maintenance of equipment, and facilities

- Health care for military personnel and dependents

- Weapons procurement

- Research and development

- Construction of military facilities, including housing

- Research on nuclear weapons

- Cleanup of nuclear weapons production facilities

Spending on national defense by the United States, particularly during wartime, has historically been high. It spiked during World War II, reaching nearly 90% of the nation's total outlays. (See Figure 1.8.) Since then, the portion of federal outlays devoted to national defense has declined dramatically. According to the Office of the President of the United States, in *Fiscal Year 2015 Historical Tables: Budget of the U.S. Government* (February 2014, http://www.whitehouse.gov/sites/default/files/omb/budget/fy2015/assets/hist.pdf), the total federal outlays in FY 2013 tallied $3.5 trillion, of which $633.4 billion (18%) was spent on national defense. (See Table 1.3.) The estimated annual spending in FYs 2014 and 2015 is expected to be lower as the U.S. military shrinks in size in response to the end of the war in Iraq and declining involvement in the war in Afghanistan. These topics are addressed in detail in Chapters 2 and 4.

The Gallup Organization surveys American attitudes about various national security issues. In *Gallup Poll Social Series: World Affairs* (February 6–9, 2014, http://www.gallup.com/file/poll/167654/Military_spending_140227.pdf), Jeff Jones and Lydia Saad report poll results from February 2014. At that time, 32% of respondents thought U.S. national defense and military spending was "about right." (See Table 1.4.) Another 37% considered it "too much," and 28% believed it was "too little." The remaining 3% had no opinion on the matter.

TABLE 1.3

Federal spending on national defense, international affairs, and veterans benefits and services, 2010–13 and estimated for 2014–15

[In millions of dollars]

Function and subfunction	2010	2011	2012	2013	2014 estimate	2015 estimate
050 National defense:						
051 Department of Defense-Military:						
Military personnel	155,690	161,608	152,266	150,825	154,268	141,632
Operation and maintenance	275,988	291,038	282,297	259,662	272,812	228,284
Procurement	133,603	128,003	124,712	114,912	92,090	91,387
Research, development, test, and evaluation	76,990	74,871	70,396	66,892	56,026	63,199
Military construction	21,169	19,917	14,553	12,318	13,110	10,077
Family housing	3,173	3,432	2,331	1,829	2,060	1,660
Other	90	−805	4,296	1,357	2,978	48,081
051 Subtotal, Department of Defense-Military	666,703	678,064	650,851	607,795	593,344	584,320
053 Atomic energy defense activities	19,308	20,410	19,246	17,573	18,447	20,837
054 Defense-related activities:						
Opportunity, growth, and security initiative (defense)	—	—	—	—	—	16,803
Other defense-related activities	7,474	7,080	7,755	8,017	8,771	9,320
054 Subtotal, defense-related activities	7,474	7,080	7,755	8,017	8,771	26,123
Total, national defense	**693,485**	**705,554**	**677,852**	**633,385**	**620,562**	**631,280**
150 International affairs:						
151 International development and humanitarian assistance	19,014	21,255	21,882	22,824	23,436	24,054
152 International security assistance	11,363	12,042	11,464	9,868	14,075	13,893
153 Conduct of foreign affairs	13,557	12,486	13,553	13,038	12,692	14,137
154 Foreign information and exchange activities	1,485	1,575	1,556	1,519	1,607	1,527
155 International financial programs	−224	−1,673	−1,266	−831	−3,338	−3,525
Total, international affairs	**45,195**	**45,685**	**47,189**	**46,418**	**48,472**	**50,086**
700 Veterans benefits and services:						
701 Income security for veterans	49,163	58,747	55,899	65,890	73,311	79,160
702 Veterans education, training, and rehabilitation	8,089	10,683	10,402	12,893	13,523	14,400
703 Hospital and medical care for veterans	45,714	50,062	50,588	52,544	55,404	57,353
704 Veterans housing	540	1,262	1,413	1,328	2,096	332
705 Other veterans benefits and services	4,878	6,435	6,293	6,283	6,831	7,279
Total, veterans benefits and services	**108,384**	**127,189**	**124,595**	**138,938**	**151,165**	**158,524**

SOURCE: Adapted from "Table 3.2—Outlays by Function and Subfunction: 1962–2019," in *Fiscal Year 2015 Historical Tables: Budget of the U.S. Government*, Office of the President of the United States, Office of Management and Budget, February 2014, http://www.whitehouse.gov/sites/default/files/omb/budget/fy2015/assets/hist.pdf (accessed June 7, 2014)

Gallup pollsters have also periodically questioned Americans about the strength of the U.S. military. As shown in Figure 1.9, more than half (53%) of the respondents in 2014 said the United States was "no. 1 in the world militarily." Forty-four percent thought the U.S. military was "only one of several leading military powers." Since the question was first asked in 1993, greater percentages of Americans have ranked the U.S. military as the world's best than have said it is one of several leading military powers.

International Affairs

National security encompasses more than military operations. The United States spends substantial amounts on international affairs, which the House of Representatives notes in "Budget Functions" include the following:

- Operating U.S. embassies and consulates (regional embassy offices) throughout the world

- Providing military assistance to allies

- Aiding developing nations

- Dispensing economic assistance to fledgling democracies

- Promoting U.S. exports abroad

- Making U.S. payments to international organizations

- Contributing to international peacekeeping efforts

The House of Representatives indicates that international affairs spending usually constitutes about 1% of the total federal outlays. Major agencies receiving funds in this category are the DOS, the U.S. Agency for International Development (USAID), the Millennium Challenge Corporation (MCC), the U.S. Department of Agriculture (USDA), and the U.S. Department of the Treasury. USAID and the MCC are agencies independent of the DOS that are devoted to providing foreign aid.

Table 1.3 shows international affairs funding for FYs 2010 through 2013 and estimated projections for FYs 2014 and 2015. The United States spent $46.4 billion on international affairs in FY 2013. This constituted 1% of the total federal outlays of $3.5 trillion.

FIGURE 1.8

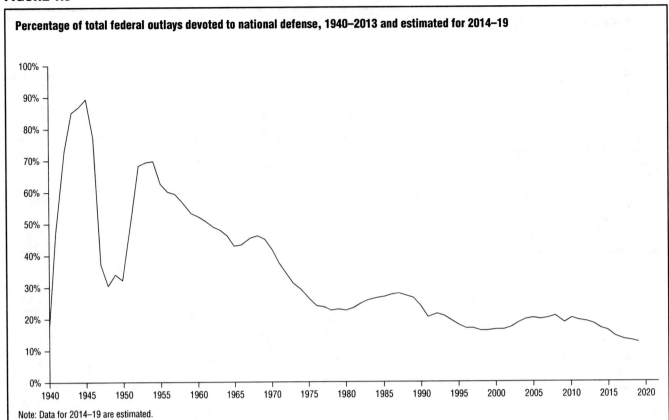

Percentage of total federal outlays devoted to national defense, 1940–2013 and estimated for 2014–19

Note: Data for 2014–19 are estimated.

SOURCE: Adapted from "Table 3.2—Outlays by Function and Subfunction: 1962–2019," in *Fiscal Year 2015 Historical Tables: Budget of the U.S. Government*, Office of the President of the United States, Office of Management and Budget, February 2014, http://www.whitehouse.gov/sites/default/files/omb/budget/fy2015/assets/hist.pdf (accessed June 7, 2014)

Most foreign aid is distributed by USAID and the DOS. The USDA, the MCC, and the Peace Corps are also significant donor agencies. In FY 2012 the United States distributed $31.2 billion in foreign economic assistance. (See Table 1.5.) Another $17.2 billion was spent on military assistance for foreign countries. Figure 1.10 lists the top-10 countries to which the United States made obligations (promises) in FY 2012 to provide future economic and military assistance. The largest obligations were made to Afghanistan ($12.9 billion), Israel ($3.1 billion), and Iraq ($1.9 billion). Figure 1.10 also lists the top-10 countries that received the most U.S. economic and military assistance in FY 2012. Afghanistan received, by far, the most money during this period: $9.9 billion. Other major recipients included Israel ($3.1 billion), Iraq ($1.9 billion), and Egypt ($1.5 billion).

Veterans Benefits and Services

According to the House of Representatives, in "Budget Functions," veterans benefits and services include medical care, compensation (e.g., for disabilities and burial expenses), pensions, education and rehabilitation benefits, and training, employment, and housing programs for veterans. In addition, the American Battle Monuments Commission is funded under this function. It administers and operates dozens of monuments and cemeteries in the United States and in foreign countries.

The amount spent on veterans benefits and services in FY 2013 was $138.9 billion. (See Table 1.3.) This constituted 4% of the total federal outlays of $3.5 trillion. In *Fiscal Year 2015 Historical Tables*, the Office of the President of the United States indicates that $45 billion was spent on veterans benefits and services in FY 2001, which ended only weeks after the September 11, 2001, terrorist attacks. The U.S. military vastly increased its force size during the subsequent wars in Afghanistan and Iraq. In addition, federal programs for veterans have been expanded. The result has been a dramatic increase in spending in this category.

Veterans benefits and services are primarily overseen by the U.S. Department of Veterans Affairs (VA). The VA indicates in "Department of Veterans Affairs: Statistics at a Glance" (April 2014, http://www.va.gov/vetdata/docs/Quickfacts/Homepage_slideshow_3_31_14.pdf) that there were nearly 22 million veterans in FY 2013. Around 8.9 million of these veterans were enrolled in the VA Health Care System, which as of April 2014 included 820 VA community-based outpatient clinics, 300 VA vet centers, and 150 VA hospitals. Just over 3.8 million

TABLE 1.4

Public opinion on U.S. national defense and military spending, 1969–2014

THERE IS MUCH DISCUSSION AS TO THE AMOUNT OF MONEY THE GOVERNMENT IN WASHINGTON SHOULD SPEND FOR NATIONAL DEFENSE AND MILITARY PURPOSES. HOW DO YOU FEEL ABOUT THIS? DO YOU THINK WE ARE SPENDING TOO LITTLE, ABOUT THE RIGHT AMOUNT, OR TOO MUCH?

	Too little	About right	Too much	No opinion
2014 Feb 6–9	28	32	37	3
2013 Feb 7–10	26	36	35	3
2012 Feb 2–5	24	32	41	3
2011 Feb 2–5	22	35	39	3
2010 Feb 1–3	27	36	34	2
2009 Feb 9–12	24	41	31	4
2008 Feb 11–14	22	30	44	3
2007 Feb 1–4	20	35	43	2
2006 Feb 6–9	25	40	32	3
2005 Feb 7–10	30	38	30	2
2004 Feb 9–12	22	45	31	2
2003 Feb 3–6	25	44	27	4
2002 Feb 4–6	33	48	17	2
2001 Feb 1–4	41	38	19	2
2000 Aug 24–27	40	34	20	6
2000 May 18–21	31	44	22	3
1999 May 7–9	28	35	32	5
1998 Nov 20–22	26	45	22	7
1993 Mar 29–31	17	38	42	3
1990 Jan 4–7	9	36	50	5
1987 Apr 10–13	14	36	44	6
1986 Mar 4–10	13	36	47	4
1985 Jan 25–28	11	36	46	7
1983 Sep 9–12	21	36	37	6
1982 Nov 5–8	16	31	41	12
1981 Jan 27	51	22	15	12
1976 Jan 23–26	22	32	36	10
1973 Sep 21–24	13	30	46	11
1971 Mar 11–14	11	31	50	8
1969 Nov 12–17	8	31	52	9

SOURCE: Jeff Jones and Lydia Saad, "11. There is much discussion as to the amount of money the government in Washington should spend for national defense and military purposes. How do you feel about this? Do you think we are spending too little, about the right amount, or too much?" in *Gallup Poll Social Series: World Affairs—Final Topline*, The Gallup Organization, February 6–9, 2014, http://www.gallup.com/file/poll/167654/Military_spending_140227.pdf (accessed May 9, 2014). Copyright © 2014 Gallup, Inc. All rights reserved. The content is used with permission; however, Gallup retains all rights of republication.

veterans were receiving VA disability compensation in FY 2013. Costs for VA medical care and disability compensation have skyrocketed as a result of the wars in Afghanistan and Iraq and are expected to continue to grow in the future as existing veterans age.

VA SCANDAL OF DELAYED TREATMENT. In November 2013 CNN publicized internal government reports that showed long delays at some VA facilities. In "Hospital Delays Are Killing America's War Veterans" (CNN.com, November 20, 2013), Scott Bronstein, Nelli Black, and Drew Griffin claim that military veterans "are dying needlessly because of long waits and delayed care at U.S. veterans hospitals." They note that the VA "is aware of the problems and has done almost nothing to effectively prevent veterans dying from delays in care." The scandal widened in April 2014, when it was revealed that at least 40 veterans had died while waiting for doctor

appointments at a VA hospital in Phoenix, Arizona. According to Scott Bronstein and Drew Griffin, in "A Fatal Wait: Veterans Languish and Die on a VA Hospital's Secret List" (CNN.com, April 23, 2014), a retired VA doctor alleged that the patients were on a "secret list" that the hospital maintained and kept hidden from VA authorities to cover up problems with long delays. Hospital officials denied this allegation.

Scott Bronstein and Tom Cohen report in "VA Controversy: White House Aide Heading to Phoenix" (CNN.com, May 23, 2014) that the VA's Office of Inspector General (OIG) announced in May 2014 that it was investigating dozens of VA facilities regarding treatment delay problems. The OIG's first report, an interim report on alleged problems at the Phoenix VA hospital, was released later that month. In *Veterans Health Administration—Interim Report: Review of Patient Wait Times, Scheduling Practices, and Alleged Patient Deaths at the Phoenix Health Care System* (May 28, 2014, http://www.va.gov/oig/pubs/VAOIG-14-02603-178.pdf), the OIG states, "While our work is not complete, we have substantiated that significant delays in access to care negatively impacted the quality of care at this medical facility." Eric Shinseki (1942–), the U.S. secretary of veterans affairs, resigned on May 30, 2014. The public furor over problems at the VA continued with calls from lawmakers for an investigation by the FBI into any criminal wrongdoing. In addition, the Obama administration and Congress announced plans to allow veterans in the VA medical system to receive care at private facilities.

U.S. INTERESTS AND STATUS

In February 2014 Gallup pollsters presented Americans with a list of possible threats to the "vital interests" of the United States over the next decade. Respondents were asked to rank the threats by their level of importance. As shown in Table 1.6, more than three-quarters (77%) of those asked rated international terrorism as a "critical threat" to the United States. Other high-ranking critical threats included development of nuclear weapons by Iran (76%), Islamic fundamentalism (57%), and the conflict between North Korea and South Korea (53%). All of these threats will be examined in detail in subsequent chapters.

Since 2000 the Gallup Organization has conducted polls in which it asks Americans about how they believe the United States is perceived by the rest of the world. In 2014 just over half (51%) of the respondents said the United States is viewed favorably; nearly half (47%) believed the United States is viewed unfavorably. (See Figure 1.11.) This breakdown has been fairly consistent since 2004. Prior to that year Gallup found that Americans felt the United States had a much better image in the eyes of the world. For example, in 2002 nearly eight out

FIGURE 1.9

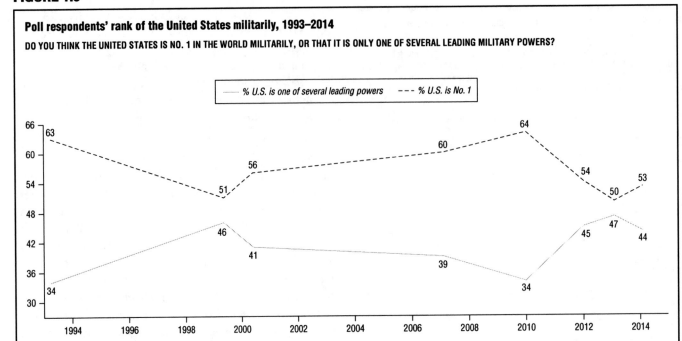

Poll respondents' rank of the United States militarily, 1993–2014

DO YOU THINK THE UNITED STATES IS NO. 1 IN THE WORLD MILITARILY, OR THAT IT IS ONLY ONE OF SEVERAL LEADING MILITARY POWERS?

······· % U.S. is one of several leading powers   - - - % U.S. is No. 1

of 10 (79%) of those asked thought the United States enjoyed a favorable reputation. In *Fewer Americans Think Obama Respected on World Stage* (February 24, 2014, http://www.gallup.com/poll/167534/fewer-americans-think-obama-respected-world-stage.aspx), Jeffrey M. Jones of the Gallup Organization notes that "opinions began to change in the lead-up to the 2003 Iraq war." The onset of the Iraq war also precipitated a change in American satisfaction with the United States' position in the world. As shown in Figure 1.12, one-third (33%) of Americans were dissatisfied with the United States' position in 2000; by 2014 this percentage had risen to 61%.

NATIONAL SECURITY STRATEGY

In May 2010 the administration of President Barack Obama (1961–) issued *National Security Strategy* (http://www.whitehouse.gov/sites/default/files/rss_viewer/national_security_strategy.pdf). The 52-page document outlines broad strategic measures and specific priorities for achieving what President Obama calls "four enduring national interests." They are as follows:

- Security—the security of the United States, its citizens, and U.S. allies and partners.

- Prosperity—a strong, innovative, and growing U.S. economy in an open international economic system that promotes opportunity and prosperity.

- Values—respect for universal values at home and around the world.

- International order—an international order advanced by U.S. leadership that promotes peace, security, and opportunity through stronger cooperation to meet global challenges.

The national security strategy encompasses many concerns; this book, however, focuses on the priorities that are listed for the security interest, as shown in Table 1.7. The measures that the United States has taken, is taking, and plans to take to achieve these priorities will be discussed in detail in the remaining chapters.

Cyberweapons

The United States has invested enormous amounts of money in developing and producing advanced military weapons, such as so-called smart bombs and stealth fighter jets. These weapons provide great tactical advantages to U.S. troops engaged in battle. Since the late 20th century a new form of war making has evolved that centers around cyberweapons. These are computer viruses, worms, and other forms of malware (malicious software) that can disable or disrupt computer-based systems. Example military targets include an enemy's radar or air defense systems and command and control communications systems. Cyberweapons can also be employed against industrial targets, such as power plants, to further national security goals.

In "Bush Wants Cyber Warfare Rules" (CBSNews.com, February 7, 2003), Jarrett Murphy claims that the

TABLE 1.5

Foreign economic and military assistance, 1946–2012

[In millions, historical $US]

| Program | Postwar relief period 1946–48 | Marshall Plan period 1949–52 | Mutual Security Act period 1953–61 | Foreign Assistance Act (FAA) period | | | | | | Total FAA period 1962–2012 | Total loans and grants 1946–2012 | Of which loans 1946–2012 | Outstanding amount as of September 30, 2012 |
				1962–2008	2009	2010	2011	2012					
Total economic assistance	12,482.0	18,634.3	24,050.0	487,046.6	34,088.8	37,171.5	30,712.8	31,204.8		620,224.5	675,390.9	66,302.7	9,452.9
Total military assistance	481.2	10,064.2	19,302.2	225,408.0	14,456.4	14,544.1	18,272.0	17,222.0		289,902.5	319,750.0	46,389.2	2,270.6
Total economic and military assistance	12,963.2	28,698.5	43,352.2	712,454.6	48,545.2	51,715.6	48,984.9	48,426.8		910,127.0	995,140.9	112,691.8	11,723.5

SOURCE: Adapted from "Summary of All Countries: Fiscal Year 2012 U.S. Overseas Loans and Grants—Obligations and Loan Authorizations," in *U.S. Overseas Loans and Grants: Obligations and Loan Authorizations, July 1, 1945–September 30, 2012*, U.S. Agency for International Development, 2014, http://pdf.usaid.gov/pdf_docs/PNAEC300.pdf (accessed May 30, 2014)

FIGURE 1.10

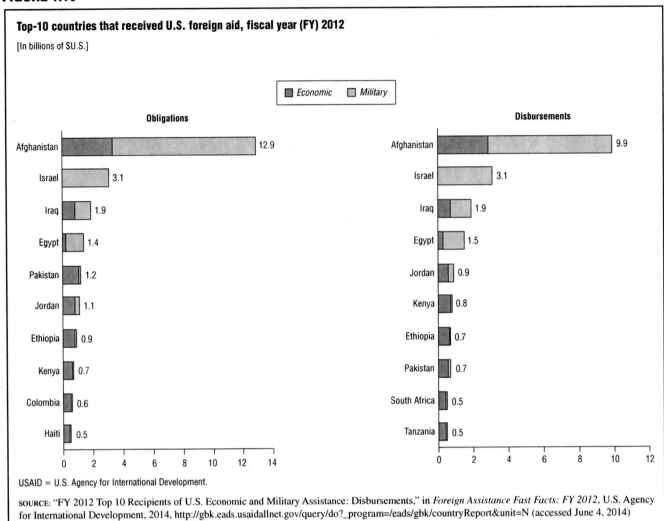

Top-10 countries that received U.S. foreign aid, fiscal year (FY) 2012

[In billions of $U.S.]

USAID = U.S. Agency for International Development.

SOURCE: "FY 2012 Top 10 Recipients of U.S. Economic and Military Assistance: Disbursements," in *Foreign Assistance Fast Facts: FY 2012*, U.S. Agency for International Development, 2014, http://gbk.eads.usaidallnet.gov/query/do?_program=/eads/gbk/countryReport&unit=N (accessed June 4, 2014)

United States has operated a cyberweapons program since at least 1998. Like other types of weapons, malware can cause collateral damage (unintended negative consequences to innocent nontargeted parties). Murphy cites as an example a cyberattack on the electrical network of an enemy's antiaircraft system that inadvertently knocks out power to nearby civilian facilities, including hospitals.

The U.S. military follows specific rules of engagement to limit collateral damage when it deploys conventional weapons. According to Murphy, in February 2003 President George W. Bush (1946–) ordered his administration to develop similar rules for the use of cyberweapons. The following month U.S. forces invaded Iraq in a conflict that is described in detail in Chapter 4. John Markoff and Thom Shanker indicate in "Halted '03 Iraq Plan Illustrates U.S. Fear of Cyberwar Risk" (NYTimes .com, August 1, 2009) that prior to the invasion the United States considered but abandoned plans to use malware to sabotage the Iraqi government's financial system. It was feared that the malware might spread via the Internet and

cause "worldwide financial havoc." The U.S. military, however, reportedly did use cyberweapons to disable Iraqi military and government communications systems.

In "Researchers Say Stuxnet Was Deployed against Iran in 2007" (Reuters.com, February 26, 2013), Jim Finkle notes that the Bush administration also developed cyberweapons for use against Iran after that nation embarked on a suspected campaign to develop nuclear weapons. As early as 2007, the U.S. government, in concert with Israel, deployed malware that was designed to attack Iranian nuclear facilities. The U.S. cyberweapons program was expanded by President Obama and continued to be used against Iran during the first half of the second decade of the 21st century. As described in Chapter 6, malware attacks have also been considered against government targets in Syria, which has been roiled by a revolution. The advent of cyberweapons represents a profound change in war making. David E. Sanger notes in "Syria War Stirs New U.S. Debate on Cyberattacks" (NYTimes .com, February 24, 2014) that "it is a transformation analogous to what happened when the airplane was first used in combat in World War I, a century ago."

TABLE 1.6

Public opinion on the threats to the United States over the next decade, February 2014

I AM GOING TO READ YOU A LIST OF POSSIBLE THREATS TO THE VITAL INTERESTS OF THE UNITED STATES IN THE NEXT 10 YEARS. FOR EACH ONE, PLEASE TELL ME IF YOU SEE THIS AS A CRITICAL THREAT, AN IMPORTANT BUT NOT CRITICAL THREAT, OR NOT AN IMPORTANT THREAT AT ALL.

	% Critical threat	% Important, not critical
International terrorism	77	19
Development of nuclear weapons by Iran	76	18
Islamic fundamentalism	57	27
Conflict between North Korea and South Korea	53	36
Economic power of China	52	36
Military power of China	46	41
Conflict between Israel and the Palestinians	46	42
Military power of Russia	32	49
Conflict between India and Pakistan	28	48

SOURCE: Art Swift, "Threats to the Vital Interests of the United States in Next 10 Years," in *Terrorism, Iranian Nukes Considered Greatest Threats to U.S.*, The Gallup Organization, February 28, 2014, http://www.gallup.com/poll/167672/terrorism-iranian-nukes-considered-greatest-threats.aspx (accessed June 7, 2014). Copyright © 2014 Gallup, Inc. All rights reserved. The content is used with permission; however, Gallup retains all rights of republication.

FIGURE 1.11

Public opinion on how the United States is viewed by rest of the world, 2000–14

IN GENERAL, HOW DO YOU THINK THE UNITED STATES RATES IN THE EYES OF THE WORLD—VERY FAVORABLY, SOMEWHAT FAVORABLY, SOMEWHAT UNFAVORABLY, OR VERY UNFAVORABLY?

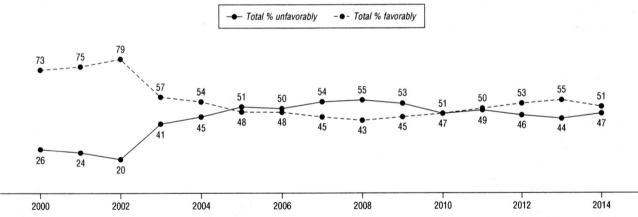

SOURCE: Jeffrey M. Jones, "Americans' Perceptions of How U.S. Rates in the Eyes of the World," in *Fewer Americans Think Obama Respected on World Stage*, The Gallup Organization, February 24, 2014, http://www.gallup.com/poll/167534/fewer-americans-think-obama-respected-world-stage.aspx (accessed June 4, 2014). Copyright © 2014 Gallup, Inc. All rights reserved. The content is used with permission; however, Gallup retains all rights of republication.

FIGURE 1.12

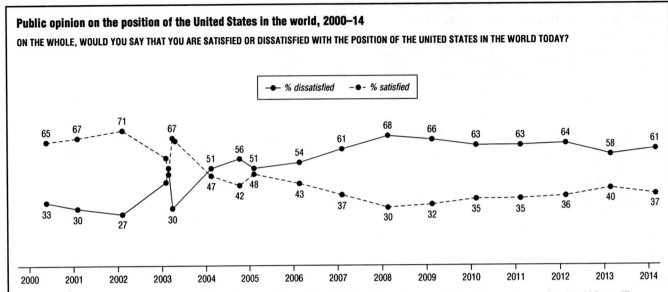

Public opinion on the position of the United States in the world, 2000–14

ON THE WHOLE, WOULD YOU SAY THAT YOU ARE SATISFIED OR DISSATISFIED WITH THE POSITION OF THE UNITED STATES IN THE WORLD TODAY?

SOURCE: Jeffrey M. Jones, "Satisfaction with United States' Position in the World," in *Fewer Americans Think Obama Respected on World Stage*, The Gallup Organization, February 24, 2014, http://www.gallup.com/poll/167534/fewer-americans-think-obama-respected-world-stage.aspx (accessed June 4, 2014). Copyright © 2014 Gallup, Inc. All rights reserved. The content is used with permission; however, Gallup retains all rights of republication.

TABLE 1.7

U.S. national security strategic goals, 2010

Strengthen security and resilience at home

Enhance security at home
Effectively manage emergencies
Empowering communities to counter radicalization
Improve resilience through increased public-private partnerships
Engage with communities and citizens

Disrupt, dismantle and defeat Al-Qa'ida and its violent extremist affiliates in Afghanistan, Pakistan, and around the world

Prevent attacks on and in the homeland
Strengthen aviation security
Deny terrorists weapons of mass destruction
Deny Al-Qa'ida the ability to threaten the American people, our allies, our partners and our interests overseas
Deny safe havens and strengthen at-risk states
Deliver swift and sure justice
Resist fear and overreaction
Contrast Al-Qa'ida's intent to destroy with our constructive vision

Reverse the spread of nuclear and biological weapons and secure nuclear materials

Pursue the goal of a world without nuclear weapons
Strengthen the nuclear non-proliferation treaty
Present a clear choice to Iran and North Korea
Secure vulnerable nuclear weapons and material
Support peaceful nuclear energy
Counter biological threats

Advance peace, security, and opportunity in the greater Middle East

Complete a responsible transition as we end the war in Iraq
Pursue Arab-Israeli peace
Promote a responsible Iran

Invest in the capacity of strong and capable partners

Foster security and reconstruction in the aftermath of conflict
Pursue sustainable and responsible security systems in at-risk states
Prevent the emergence of conflict

Secure cyberspace

Investing in people and technology
Strengthening partnerships

SOURCE: Adapted from *National Security Strategy*, Office of the President of the United States, May 27, 2010, http://www.whitehouse.gov/sites/default/files/rss_viewer/national_security_strategy.pdf (accessed June 7, 2014)

CHAPTER 2

THE ORGANIZATION OF NATIONAL SECURITY

The U.S. national security framework consists of government agencies and offices with responsibilities in various disciplines: policy making, military activities, intelligence gathering and analysis, diplomacy, criminal investigation, immigration control, and law enforcement. Interaction and cooperation between separate government entities and disciplines is crucial to ensure that U.S. goals are met for foreign policy and homeland security. Coordination of all functions is ultimately the responsibility of the president of the United States, who is the commander in chief of the nation's military forces and the chief decision maker for matters related to national security.

NATIONAL SECURITY COUNCIL

The National Security Council (NSC) is the top entity in the U.S. national security structure. It lies within the executive office of the president and includes decision makers at the highest levels of government. Table 2.1 lists the regular members and occasional attendees who are associated with the NSC. It was created following World War II (1939–1945) by the National Security Act of 1947, which was amended in 1949.

The NSC provides a forum for the president to discuss national security issues with his top advisers. The decisions and policies resulting from these meetings are implemented by the department heads within the government, chiefly the secretaries of the U.S. Departments of State (foreign affairs), Defense (military affairs), and the Treasury (economic affairs). The chair of the Joint Chiefs of Staff is the highest ranking officer within the U.S. military and advises the president on military issues. The director of national intelligence heads a collection of agencies that are devoted to intelligence gathering and analysis. The assistant to the president for national security affairs is more commonly called the national security adviser. This person is not a member of a particular department or branch within the

government but is chosen by the president to offer an independent viewpoint on national security matters.

U.S. DEPARTMENT OF DEFENSE

The U.S. Department of Defense (DOD) traces its history back to 1789, when it was created as the Department of War under the administration of President George Washington (1732–1799). Some branches of the nation's armed forces (U.S. Army, Navy, and Marine Corps) were already in operation, having been established in 1775 for the Revolutionary War (1775–1783). Following World War II Congress created a civilian (nonmilitary) agency within the government, led by a secretary of defense who had direct control over the armed forces including the newly created U.S. Air Force. This agency was eventually called the Department of Defense.

Figure 2.1 lists the main entities that are organized under the DOD. The Joint Chiefs of Staff are planners and advisers on issues of national security. They advise the president, the secretary of defense, and the NSC.

Besides the regular forces of the U.S. military, there is an additional contingency force that makes up the reserve components. These personnel are part time, meaning that they are technically civilians but can be called to service when needed. Many reservists are former members of the regular armed forces.

Military Budget and Sequestration

The federal government operates on a fiscal year (FY) that extends from October through September; thus, FY 2015 covers October 1, 2014, through September 30, 2015. Each year around February, the president submits to Congress a budget request for the upcoming fiscal year. Over subsequent months congressional committees debate the request and finalize the amounts devoted to specific agencies and programs. The amounts to be appropriated

TABLE 2.1

Membership of the National Security Council, 2014

Chair	President
Regular attendees	Vice President
	Secretary of State
	Secretary of the Treasury
	Secretary of Defense
	Assistant to the President for National Security Affairs
Military advisor	Chairman of the Joint Chiefs of Staff
Intelligence advisor	Director of National Intelligence
Invited to any meeting	The Chief of Staff to the President
	Counsel to the President
	Assistant to the President for Economic Policy
Attend meetings pertaining to their responsibilities	The Attorney General
	Director of the Office of Management and Budget
Attend meetings when appropriate	The heads of other executive departments and agencies, as well as other senior officials.

SOURCE: Adapted from "National Security Council," in *National Security Council*, Office of the President of the United States, 2014, http://www.whitehouse.gov/administration/eop/nsc/ (accessed May 26, 2014)

are specified in bills that must be passed by the U.S. House of Representatives and the U.S. Senate and signed by the president to become law. If the appropriations bills are not enacted by the beginning of October (the beginning of the fiscal year), then Congress adopts continuing resolutions that generally keep funding around the previous year's level until the final appropriation bills are enacted. During the first half of the second decade of the 21st century reliance on continuing resolutions increased dramatically because of partisan fighting in Congress over spending priorities.

Typically, an agency's budget is expected to rise annually to counteract the effects of inflation on the value of money. Table 2.2 shows the total budget amounts appropriated to the DOD for FYs 2001 through 2014 and requested for FY 2015. Following the terrorist attacks of September 11, 2001, the United States initiated wars in Afghanistan and Iraq. These operations, along with related anti-terrorism operations, are collectively called the Overseas Contingency Operations (OCO). The U.S. military greatly increased its size and budget for the OCO. As shown in Table 2.2, the DOD's funding peaked in FY 2010 at $691 billion, which included $527.9 billion for the base budget and $162.4 billion for the OCO. U.S. military operations in Iraq ceased in December 2011, and U.S. military involvement in Afghanistan began to decline dramatically. As a result, the DOD received fewer funds for the OCO in FYs 2011 and 2012. However, the agency's base budgets for these years increased by small amounts. In FY 2013 the DOD's base budget declined sharply due to funding cuts laid out in the Budget Control Act of 2011 (BCA).

In *Approaches for Scaling Back the Defense Department's Budget Plans* (March 2013, http://www.cbo.gov/

sites/default/files/cbofiles/attachments/43997_Defense _Budget.pdf), the Congressional Budget Office notes, "The BCA initially created a set of caps that limited funding for discretionary programs and activities for each year over the 2012–2021 period. That act also established procedures that led to automatic spending reductions, which lowered those initial caps for 2014 to 2021 and cut funding for 2013 through a process known as sequestration." When the BCA was passed in 2011, the future spending caps were much lower than the amounts that the DOD had expected to receive in its annual base budgets. Karen Parrish explains in "Panetta, Dempsey: Sequestration Would Defeat Defense Strategy" (February 16, 2012, http://www.defense.gov/News/NewsArticle.aspx?ID=67226) that the BCA essentially required the agency to cut $487 billion in planned defense spending over a decade.

In 2013, after Congress failed to achieve the overall BCA spending targets, automatic across-the-board spending cuts were triggered in domestic and defense programs. However, Congress provided some temporary relief in the Bipartisan Budget Act of 2013, which raised the spending caps for FYs 2014 and 2015, but extended sequestration through FY 2023.

Cutting DOD spending was particularly controversial and spurred political debate about possible detrimental effects on national security. The FY 2014 budget process was also complicated by partisan disagreements in Congress over spending and the nation's debt. As a result, the budget for FY 2014 (October 2013 through September 2014) did not become final until January 2014. It was enacted through passage of an omnibus spending bill (a single bill that encompasses multiple appropriations bills). Legislators eased some of the sequestration cuts affecting the DOD over the short term. In "Department of Defense Press Briefing with Rear Admiral John Kirby" (January 16, 2014, http://www.defense.gov/Transcripts/Transcript.aspx?TranscriptID=5353), a DOD spokesperson notes, "While the bipartisan budget act provides funding for fiscal year '15 above sequestration levels it will still be $40 billion less than projected last year and without further compromise, sequestration will remain the law of the land for the next decade."

The DOD's budget request for FY 2015 was $575 billion. (See Table 2.2.) This included $495.6 billion for the base budget and $79.4 billion for the OCO. However, the latter figure was a rough estimate because a final OCO request had not been finalized. As will be explained in Chapter 4, the United States' future military involvement in Afghanistan was uncertain at that time. The Afghan president Hamid Karzai (1957–) refused to allow U.S. troops to stay beyond year-end 2014. However, a presidential election was scheduled for mid-2014, and there was the possibility that the new Afghan president would allow U.S. military forces to remain beyond 2014. As a result, future OCO budgetary needs were indeterminate.

FIGURE 2.1

Department of Defense (DOD) organization chart in effect as of April 2014

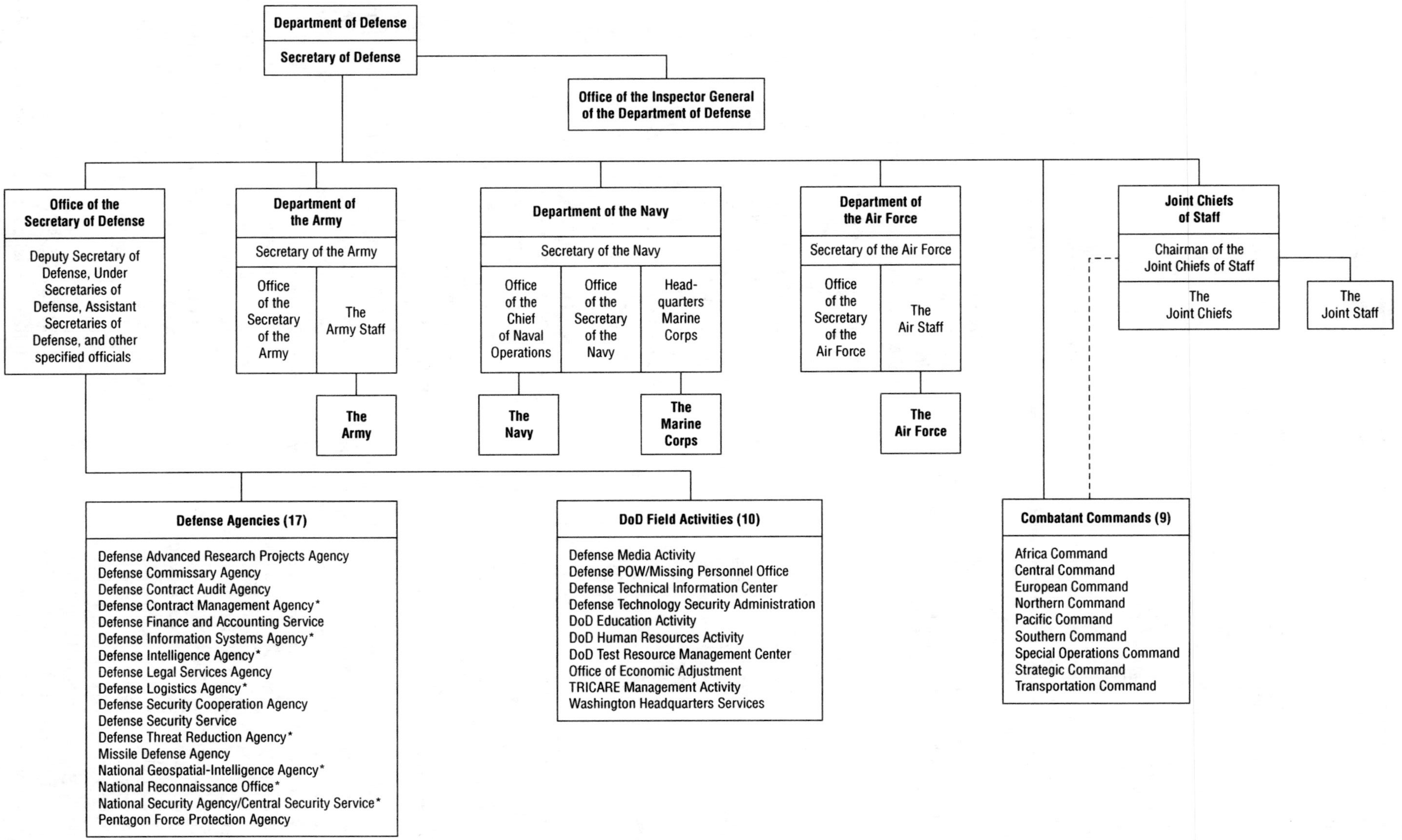

Department of Defense

Secretary of Defense

Office of the Secretary of Defense

Deputy Secretary of Defense, Under Secretaries of Defense, Assistant Secretaries of Defense, and other specified officials

Office of the Inspector General of the Department of Defense

Department of the Army

Secretary of the Army

Office of the Secretary of the Army | The Army Staff

The Army

Department of the Navy

Secretary of the Navy

Office of the Chief of Naval Operations | Office of the Secretary of the Navy | Head-quarters Marine Corps

The Navy | The Marine Corps

Department of the Air Force

Secretary of the Air Force

Office of the Secretary of the Air Force | The Air Staff

The Air Force

Joint Chiefs of Staff

Chairman of the Joint Chiefs of Staff | The Joint Chiefs

The Joint Staff

Combatant Commands (9)

Africa Command
Central Command
European Command
Northern Command
Pacific Command
Southern Command
Special Operations Command
Strategic Command
Transportation Command

Defense Agencies (17)

Defense Advanced Research Projects Agency
Defense Commissary Agency
Defense Contract Audit Agency
Defense Contract Management Agency*
Defense Finance and Accounting Service
Defense Information Systems Agency*
Defense Intelligence Agency*
Defense Legal Services Agency
Defense Logistics Agency*
Defense Security Cooperation Agency
Defense Security Service
Defense Threat Reduction Agency*
Missile Defense Agency
National Geospatial-Intelligence Agency*
National Reconnaissance Office*
National Security Agency/Central Security Service*
Pentagon Force Protection Agency

DoD Field Activities (10)

Defense Media Activity
Defense POW/Missing Personnel Office
Defense Technical Information Center
Defense Technology Security Administration
DoD Education Activity
DoD Human Resources Activity
DoD Test Resource Management Center
Office of Economic Adjustment
TRICARE Management Activity
Washington Headquarters Services

*Identified as a Combat Support Agency (CSA)

SOURCE: "Organization of the Department of Defense (DoD)," in *Other OSD Resources and References,* U.S. Department of Defense, March 2012, http://odam.defense.gov/Portals/43/Documents/Functions/Organizational%20Portfolios/Organizations%20and%20Functions%20Guidebook/DoD_Organization_March_2012.pdf (accessed June 7, 2014)

TABLE 2.2

U.S. Department of Defense (DOD) budget, fiscal years 2001–14 and requested for fiscal year 2015

[Dollars in billions]

	FY01	FY02	FY03	FY04	FY05	FY06	FY07	FY08	FY09	FY10	FY11	FY12	FY13	FY14	FY15
Base	287.4	328.2	364.9	376.5	400.1	410.6	431.5	479.0	513.2	527.9	528.2	530.4	495.5	496.0	495.6
OCO	22.9	16.9	72.5	90.8	75.6	115.8	166.3	186.9	145.7	162.4	158.8	115.1	82.0	85.2	79.4*
Other	5.8	—	—	0.3	3.2	8.2	3.1	—	7.4	0.7	—	—	0.1	—	—
Total	**316.2**	**345.1**	**437.5**	**467.6**	**478.9**	**534.5**	**600.9**	**665.9**	**666.3**	**691.0**	**687.0**	**645.5**	**577.6**	**581.2**	**575.0**

*The FY 2015 OCO figure is a placeholder pending submission of a final OCO request.
FY = fiscal year. OCO = Overseas Contingency Operations.
Discretionary budget authority. FY 2013 includes the sequestration of funds under the Budget Control Act of 2013.
Notes: Numbers may not add due to rounding.

SOURCE: "Figure 1-2. Department of Defense Topline since September 11th Attacks," in *Overview: United States Department of Defense Fiscal Year 2015 Budget Request*, U.S. Department of Defense, March 2014, http://comptroller.defense.gov/Portals/45/Documents/defbudget/fy2015/fy2015_Budget_Request_ Overview_ Book.pdf (accessed June 7, 2014)

TABLE 2.3

U.S. Department of Defense (DOD) budget by appropriation title, fiscal year 2014 and requested for fiscal year 2015

[Dollars in thousands]

Base budget	FY 2014 enacted	FY 2015 request	Delta FY14–FY15
Military personnel	135,924,801	135,193,685	−731,116
Operation and maintenance	192,822,692	198,726,096	5,903,404
Procurement	92,439,558	90,358,540	−2,081,018
RDT&E	62,805,956	63,533,947	727,991
Revolving and management funds	2,222,427	1,234,468	−987,959
Defense bill	**486,215,434**	**489,046,736**	**2,831,302**
Military construction	8,392,244	5,366,912	−3,025,332
Family housing	1,415,764	1,190,535	−225,229
Military construction bill	**9,808,008**	**6,557,447**	**−3,250,561**
Total	**496,023,442**	**495,604,183**	**−419,259**

RDT&E = research, development, testing, and evaluation. FY = fiscal year.
Note: Reflects Discretionary Budget Authority, FY 2014 includes $4,205,938 in prior year rescissions. Numbers may not add due to rounding.

SOURCE: "Table A-6. DoD Base Budget by Appropriation Title," in *Overview: United States Department of Defense Fiscal Year 2015 Budget Request*, U.S. Department of Defense, March 2014, http://comptroller.defense.gov/Portals/ 45/Documents/defbudget/fy2015/fy2015_Budget_Request_Overview_Book .pdf (accessed June 7, 2014)

Table 2.3 provides a breakdown of the DOD budgets for FYs 2014 (enacted) and 2015 (requested) by appropriation title. During both years the largest single budgeted item was operation and maintenance, followed by the costs for military personnel.

BUDGET CUT IMPACTS. Sequestration has deeply impacted the DOD. In *Estimated Impacts of Sequestration-Level Funding* (April 2014, http://www.defense.gov/ pubs/2014_Estimated_Impacts_of_Sequestration-Level _Funding_April.pdf), the DOD states that the annual cuts through the FY 2015 budget request totaled nearly $600 billion. According to the agency, if sequestration continues through FY 2021 the total reductions will exceed $1 trillion. The DOD warns that "if sequestration-level cuts persist, our forces will assume substantial additional risks

in certain missions and will continue to face significant readiness and modernization challenges. These impacts would leave our military unbalanced and eventually too small to meet the needs of our strategy fully."

During the second decade of the 21st century, the DOD began reducing its force size in response to declining wartime needs. Deeper cuts have been spurred by sequestration. Table 2.4 indicates that active duty military forces were expected to number nearly 1.35 million at the end of FY 2014 and drop to almost 1.31 million at the end of FY 2015. Table 2.5 shows that the reserve component end strength was expected to be 830,700 in FY 2014 and decline to 820,800 in FY 2015.

The DOD's civilian workforce has also been slated for reduction. Leo Shane III notes in "Union Decries Proposed DOD Civilian Cuts" (MilitaryTimes.com, March 18, 2014) that the agency's civilian workforce numbered around 775,000 in March 2014 but is expected to lose around 40,000 workers by 2017.

SECTION 1206 FUNDS. DOD funds are not devoted solely to U.S. military forces. Section 1206 of the Fiscal Year 2006 National Defense Authorization Act authorized the DOD to use some of its allocated funds to train and equip the military forces of what are called "partner nations" to conduct counterterrorism activities or related military operations. According to Nina M. Serafino of the Congressional Research Service, in *Security Assistance Reform: "Section 1206" Background and Issues for Congress* (April 4, 2014, http://www.fas.org/sgp/crs/natsec/ RS22855.pdf), as of April 2014 approximately $2.2 billion of DOD funds had been allotted or promised to more than 40 other countries. The largest recipient was Yemen, which had received $400 million.

THE INTELLIGENCE COMMUNITY

Intelligence is information, specifically information with strategic importance. Reliable intelligence helps

TABLE 2.4

Active duty military personnel, estimated for fiscal years (FY) 2014 and 2015

[In thousands]

Service	Fiscal year 2014 estimate	Fiscal year 2015	Delta Fiscal years 14–15
Army[b]	510.4	490.0	−20.4
Navy	323.9	323.6	−0.3
Marine Corps	188.8	184.1	−4.7
Air Force	322.2	310.9	−11.3
Total[c]	**1,345.3**	**1,308.6**	**−36.7**

[a]Fiscal year 2014 projected end strength levels.
[b]Fiscal year 2015 the Army funds a baseline ES of 490K with-no OCO funded end strength.
[c]President's invoking of emergency authorities permits end strength to vary from authorized levels.
Notes: Numbers may not add due to rounding. OCO = Overseas Contingency Operations. ES = end strength.

SOURCE: "Table A-4. Active Component End Strength—Base + OCO Budget (in Thousands)," in *Overview: United States Department of Defense Fiscal Year 2015 Budget Request*, U.S. Department of Defense, March 2014, http://comptroller.defense.gov/Portals/45/Documents/defbudget/fy2015/fy2015_Budget_Request_Overview_ Book.pdf (accessed June 7, 2014)

TABLE 2.5

Military reserve personnel, estimated for fiscal years 2014 and 2015

[In thousands]

Service	FY 2014 estimate*	FY 2015	Delta FY14–FY15
Army Reserve	202.0	202.0	—
Navy Reserve	59.1	57.3	−1.8
Marine Corps Reserve	39.6	39.2	−0.4
Air Force Reserve	70.4	67.1	−3.3
Army National Guard	354.2	350.2	−4.0
Air National Guard	105.4	105.0	−0.4
Total	**830.7**	**820.8**	**−9.9**

*Authorized end strengths are shown for all services except the Army Reserve.
Notes: Numbers may not add due to rounding. FY = fiscal year.

SOURCE: "Table A-5. Reserve Component End Strength (in Thousands)," in *Overview: United States Department of Defense Fiscal Year 2015 Budget Request*, U.S. Department of Defense, March 2014, http://comptroller.defense.gov/Portals/45/Documents/defbudget/fy2015/fy2015_Budget_Request_ Overview_Book.pdf (accessed June 7, 2014)

policy makers make sound decisions, plan effective strategies, and set reasonable priorities for the nation. Thus, intelligence is useful across many areas of national security, including military activities, foreign affairs, and law enforcement.

Counterintelligence is a related field in which the goal is to thwart the intelligence gathering and hostile acts of one's enemies. The National Security Act of 1947 defines counterintelligence as "information gathered, and activities conducted, to protect against espionage, other intelligence activities, sabotage, or assassinations conducted by or on behalf of foreign governments or elements thereof, foreign organizations, or foreign persons, or international terrorist activities." Both intelligence and counterintelligence are areas in which secrecy and espionage (spying) play important roles.

The U.S. intelligence community (IC) consists of 17 federal agencies and departments that are engaged in intelligence activities. (See Table 2.6.) The director of national intelligence oversees the IC, specifically the agency program managers, the departments, and the five military intelligence services. (See Figure 2.2.) The Office of the Director of National Intelligence (ODNI) notes in *ODNI Fact Sheet* (2014, http://www.dni.gov/files/documents/ODNI%20Fact%20Sheet_2011.pdf) that it began operating in 2005 following passage of the Intelligence Reform and Terrorism Prevention Act of 2004. The Central Intelligence Agency (CIA) is the primary agency concerned with U.S. intelligence and is self-contained. All other agencies are part of larger organizations, such as the DOD. Cooperation and sharing of information between IC components is considered critical to protecting national security.

IC activities are divided into two broad categories: the National Intelligence Program (NIP) and the Military Intelligence Program (MIP). In *Intelligence Spending and Appropriations: Issues for Congress* (September 18, 2013, http://www.fas.org/sgp/crs/intel/R42061.pdf), Marshall C. Erwin and Amy Belasco of the Congressional Research Service define the programs as follows:

- NIP—IC programs, projects, and activities that are oriented toward the strategic needs of decision makers

- MIP—intelligence activities that are intended to support tactical military operations and priorities

Erwin and Belasco indicate that for decades intelligence spending was considered secret. The terrorist attacks of September 11, 2001, spurred intense interest in U.S. intelligence gathering and funding. Later that decade, the director of national intelligence and the secretary of defense began publicly announcing their respective budget amounts. Figure 2.3 shows total intelligence spending for FYs 1980 through 2013 in constant 2014 dollars (i.e., assuming the buying power of a 2014 dollar). The data through FY 2006 are estimates compiled by Erwin and Belasco. After 2001 intelligence spending skyrocketed, reaching a peak of $86.6 billion in FY 2010. Spending then declined through FY 2013, when the requested amount was $73.2 billion. This latter number does not reflect any cuts that are related to sequestration.

Figure 2.4 provides an estimated breakdown of intelligence spending for FYs 2007 through 2013 by OCO and non-OCO activities. Spending for OCO intelligence peaked in FY 2010 at nearly $14 billion and then decreased.

Central Intelligence Agency

In 1946 President Harry S. Truman (1884–1972) created a new civilian intelligence agency called the

TABLE 2.6

Components of the U.S. intelligence community

The intelligence community consists of the following:

The Office of the Director of National Intelligence
Central Intelligence Agency (CIA)
Bureau of Intelligence and Research, Department of State (INR)
Defense Intelligence Agency (DIA)
National Security Agency (NSA)
National Reconnaissance Office (NRO)
National Geospatial-Intelligence Agency (NGA)
The National Security Branch, Federal Bureau of Investigation (FBI)
Army Intelligence
Navy Intelligence
Air Force Intelligence
Marine Corps Intelligence
Coast Guard Intelligence
The Office of Intelligence and Analysis, Department of the Treasury
The Office of Intelligence, Department of Energy
The Office of National Security Intelligence, Drug Enforcement Administration (DEA)
The Office of Intelligence and Analysis, Department of Homeland Security

SOURCE: Marshall Curtus Erwin, "Intelligence Community," in *Intelligence Issues for Congress*, Congressional Research Service, April 23, 2013, http://www.fas.org/sgp/crs/intel/RL33539.pdf (accessed June 7, 2014)

Central Intelligence Group. It was tasked with detecting strategic threats to the United States via the operation of clandestine (secret) activities around the world. The National Security Act of 1947 created a new intelligence structure in which the CIA operated under the direction of a National Security Council and the president. However, the scope of the CIA was limited to matters outside of law enforcement and outside U.S. borders. Over the decades, the agency has been accused of violating these restrictions, particularly by spying on Americans in the United States. These controversies are explored in detail in Chapter 8. In addition, in 2014 accusations arose in Congress that the CIA had been spying on congressional members who were investigating questionable tactics used by the agency to interrogate accused terrorists. Those allegations are addressed in Chapter 9.

The CIA headquarters are located in Langley, Virginia, at the George Bush Center for Intelligence. In "CIA Vision, Mission, Ethos & Challenges" (December 16, 2013, https://www.cia.gov/about-cia/cia-vision-mission-values/index.html), the CIA states that its mission is to "preempt

FIGURE 2.2

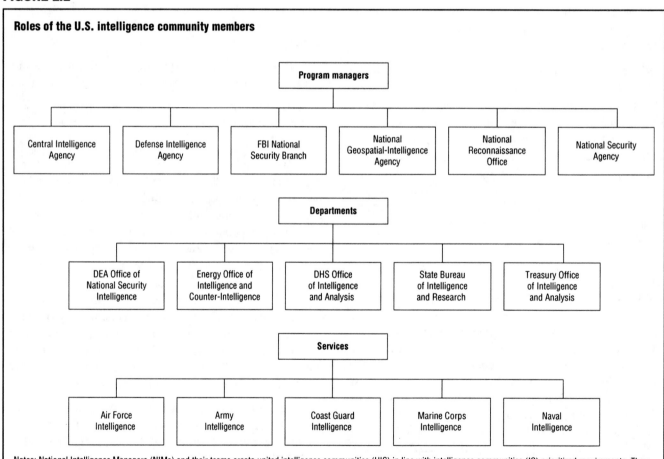

Roles of the U.S. intelligence community members

Notes: National Intelligence Managers (NIMs) and their teams create united intelligence communities (UIS) in line with intelligence communities (IS) prioritized requirements. They are thus charged with leading integration across the IC by geography and topic. DEA = Drug Enforcement Agency. DHS = Department of Homeland Security.

SOURCE: "National Intelligence Managers (NIMs) and Their Teams Create UISs in Line with the IC Prioritized Requirements," in *U.S. National Intelligence: An Overview, 2013*, Office of the Director of National Intelligence, 2013, http://www.dni.gov/files/documents/USNI%202013%20Overview_web.pdf (accessed June 7, 2014)

FIGURE 2.3

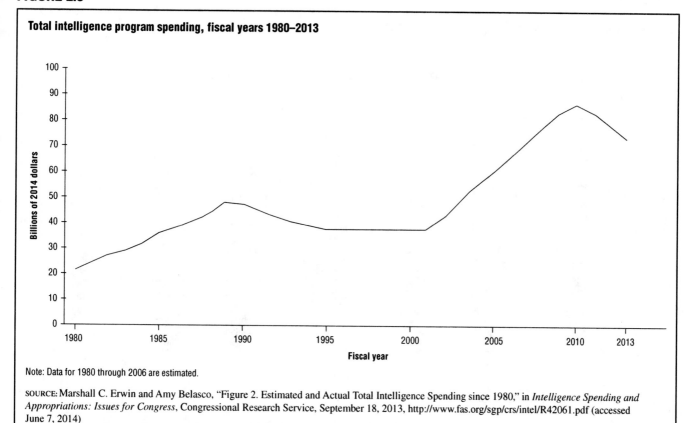

Total intelligence program spending, fiscal years 1980–2013

Note: Data for 1980 through 2006 are estimated.

SOURCE: Marshall C. Erwin and Amy Belasco, "Figure 2. Estimated and Actual Total Intelligence Spending since 1980," in *Intelligence Spending and Appropriations: Issues for Congress*, Congressional Research Service, September 18, 2013, http://www.fas.org/sgp/crs/intel/R42061.pdf (accessed June 7, 2014)

threats and further US national security objectives by collecting intelligence that matters, producing objective all-source analysis, conducting effective covert action as directed by the President, and safeguarding the secrets that help keep our Nation safe."

DRONE WARS. Following the terrorist attacks of September 11, 2001, the United States drastically increased its counterterrorism operations. One means it has embraced is the use of unmanned aerial vehicles (UAVs), which are commonly called drones. They are small, reusable, robotic aircraft used for a variety of purposes including conducting reconnaissance and collecting intelligence. Both the U.S. military and the CIA operate drone programs. Armed drones are capable of firing short-range missiles with great precision. The use of drones to kill targeted individuals in foreign countries has become quite controversial.

The U.S. military is somewhat transparent about its armed drone program, meaning that it publicly acknowledges having conducted drone strikes. In contrast, the CIA's drone program has been cloaked in secrecy since it began in 2001. At that time, George W. Bush (1946–) was president. According to Jane Mayer, in "The Predator War" (NewYorker.com, October 26, 2009), Bush signed a secret Memorandum of Notification that gave the CIA "the right to kill members of Al Qaeda and their

confederates virtually anywhere in the world. Congress endorsed this policy, passing a bill called the Authorization for Use of Military Force."

When Barack Obama (1961–) became president in 2009, he continued the so-called drone wars as part of his administration's counterterrorism program. The killings are controversial from a legal standpoint because they are extrajudicial, meaning they are conducted without judicial (court) approval. In essence, the targets are executed without trial. Critics claim these assassinations violate international law. Complicating matters, American citizens alleged to be terrorists have been killed in drone attacks in foreign countries. Such killings raise questions about the due process rights afforded American citizens by the U.S. Constitution. This issue is addressed in Chapter 8.

In addition, critics claim that innocent people have been killed and wounded in drone attacks. Investigating these claims is difficult, because the strikes often take place in remote areas of Yemen and Pakistan. According to Craig Whitlock, in "Drone Strikes Killing More Civilians Than U.S. Admits, Human Rights Groups Say" (WashingtonPost.com, October 22, 2013), a United Nations investigation estimated in 2013 that 2,200 people in Pakistan had been killed by U.S. drone strikes. Whitlock states, "Estimates of drone-related casualties vary

FIGURE 2.4

Intelligence program spending, by category, fiscal years 2007–13

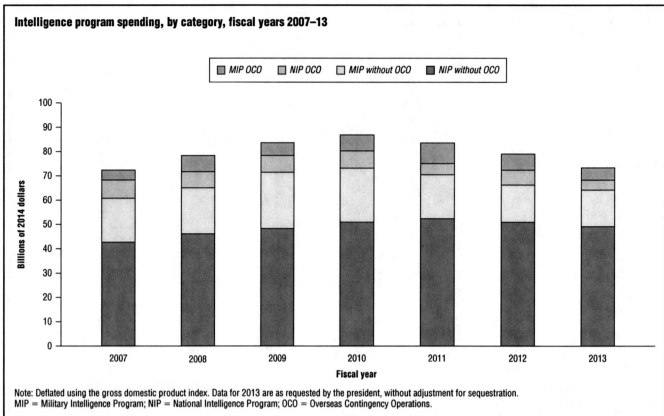

Note: Deflated using the gross domestic product index. Data for 2013 are as requested by the president, without adjustment for sequestration.
MIP = Military Intelligence Program; NIP = National Intelligence Program; OCO = Overseas Contingency Operations.

SOURCE: Marshall C. Erwin and Amy Belasco, "Figure 1. Total Intelligence Spending, FY 2007–FY 2013," in *Intelligence Spending and Appropriations: Issues for Congress*, Congressional Research Service, September 18, 2013, http://www.fas.org/sgp/crs/intel/R42061.pdf (accessed June 7, 2014)

wildly. Sorting out how many people were legitimate targets under the laws of war and how many were bystanders is an even greater challenge."

Nevertheless, polls conducted in the United States show public approval for drone attacks. In March 2013 the Gallup Organization asked Americans their opinion about the practice. As shown in Table 2.7, nearly two-thirds (65%) of those asked said it is acceptable to "launch [drone] airstrikes in other countries against suspected terrorists." There was less support for targeting U.S. citizens who are allegedly performing terrorist activities in other countries; 41% of respondents said this is acceptable. A quarter (25%) approved of drone strikes on suspected terrorists located within the United States. Only 13% specifically supported the targeting of U.S. citizens within the United States who are suspected terrorists.

In December 2013 numerous media outlets reported that a U.S. drone had struck a convoy of vehicles in Yemen carrying a wedding procession and killed around a dozen people. In "Debate Grows over Proposal for CIA to Turn over Drones to Pentagon" (LATimes.com, May 11, 2014), Ken Dilanian notes that the attack was carried out by the DOD, which insisted that "everyone killed or wounded in the attack was an Al Qaeda militant and

therefore a lawful military target." However, Dilanian states that CIA operatives in Yemen were opposed to the strike, because they "did not have confidence in the underlying intelligence."

Public outcry about civilian casualties during U.S. drone attacks has spurred the Obama administration to impose more restrictive conditions under which the attacks can be conducted. In mid-2013 the president indicated that he wanted to transfer the CIA's drone program to the DOD. That plan proved unpopular in Congress. Greg Miller reports in "Lawmakers Seek to Stymie Plan to Shift Control of Drone Campaign from CIA to Pentagon" (WashingtonPost.com, January 15, 2014) that some influential members of Congress believe the CIA is better able than the DOD to conduct accurate drone strikes. As of August 2014, no final decision on the move had been reached.

MIP Agencies

As noted earlier, MIP agencies are tasked with supporting tactical military operations and priorities. A summary of the activities of the eight MIP agencies is included in Table 2.8. Four of these agencies fall directly under the DOD: the Defense Intelligence Agency (DIA), the National Geospatial-Intelligence Agency, the

TABLE 2.7

Public opinion on the use of drones against suspected terrorists, March 2013

DO YOU THINK THE U.S. GOVERNMENT SHOULD OR SHOULD NOT USE DRONES TO—?

[Among national adults]

	% Yes, should	% No, should not	% No opinion
Launch airstrikes in other countries against suspected terrorists[a]	65	28	8
Launch, airstrikes in other countries against U.S. citizens living abroad who are suspected terrorists[a]	41	52	7
Launch airstrikes in the U.S. against suspected terrorists living here[b]	25	66	9
Launch airstrikes in the U.S. against U.S. citizens living here who are suspected terrorists[b]	13	79	7

[a]Based on Sample A of 502 national adults.
[b]Based on Sample B of 518 national adults.

SOURCE: Alyssa Brown and Frank Newport, "Do you think the U.S. government should or should not use drones to...?" in *In U.S., 65% Support Drone Attacks on Terrorists Abroad*, The Gallup Organization, March 25, 2013, http://www.gallup.com/poll/161474/support-drone-attacks-terrorists-abroad.aspx (accessed May 13, 2014). Copyright © 2013 Gallup, Inc. All rights reserved. The content is used with permission; however, Gallup retains all rights of republication.

TABLE 2.8

Intelligence agencies within the Department of Defense (DOD)

Defense Intelligence Agency

Produces and manages foreign military intelligence to provide assessments of foreign military intentions and capabilities to U.S. military commanders and civilian policymakers.

National Geospatial-Intelligence Agency

Collects and generates information about the Earth, which is used for navigation, national security, U.S. military operations, and humanitarian aid efforts.

National Reconnaissance Office

Staffed by detailees from CIA, the Air Force and other IC agencies and elements. The NRO is our nation's eyes and ears in space. They design, build, and operate the nation's signals and imagery reconnaissance satellites. Information from these satellites is used to warn of potential foreign military aggression, monitor weapons programs, enforce arms control and environmental treaties, and assess the impact of natural and manmade disasters.

National Security Agency

Our nation's cryptologic organization charged with protecting the government's information systems and producing foreign signals intelligence information. Their work includes cryptanalysis, cryptography, mathematics, computer science, and foreign language analysis.

U.S. Air Force, Intelligence, Surveillance and Reconnaissance

Conducts surveillance and reconnaissance to provide a tactical advantage to our troops.

U.S. Army, Army Military Intelligence

Supplies relevant and timely information, pertaining to ground troops and movements, to Army and other military personnel at all levels.

U.S. Marine Corps, Marine Corps Intelligence Activity

Responsible for intelligence, counterintelligence, terrorism, classified information, security review, and cryptologic activities.

U.S. Navy, Office of Naval Intelligence

Support maritime operations worldwide and defend U.S. naval borders. Naval intelligence professionals are deployed throughout the Navy as well as the Department of Defense.

SOURCE: Adapted from *Our Strength Lies in Who We Are*, U.S. Intelligence Community and Office of the Director of National Intelligence, 2014, http://www.intelligence.gov/mission/member-agencies.html (accessed June 7, 2014)

National Reconnaissance Office, and the National Security Agency (NSA)/Central Security Service. (See Figure 2.1.) In addition, the four military branches—the army, navy, marine corps, and air force—each have an intelligence agency.

The DIA coordinates the overall performance of military intelligence for the MIP. The agency is headquartered at the Pentagon, which is located in Arlington, Virginia, but it has a Washington, D.C., address. Other major DIA facilities include the Defense Intelligence Analysis Center at Bolling Air Force Base in Washington, D.C.; the National Center for Medical Intelligence at Fort Detrick in Frederick, Maryland; and the Missile and Space Intelligence Center at Redstone Arsenal in Huntsville, Alabama.

Like the CIA, MIP agencies have been criticized over the decades for spying on law-abiding Americans within the United States. This criticism was especially true during the Vietnam War (1954–1975), when American protesters against the war were kept under surveillance. This issue is addressed in Chapter 8. Around the same time, allegations began emerging that the NSA was conducting a massive surveillance program, including listening to the private phone calls of Americans. As explained in Chapter 8, the government denied these claims until 2013, when incriminating documents were leaked to the press by Edward Snowden (1983–), a former intelligence analyst.

IC workers take oaths not to divulge information about intelligence activities. In addition, various U.S. laws, including the Espionage Act of 1917, forbid the disclosure of classified information. Snowden chose to risk prosecution because he thought the NSA's actions violate the U.S. Constitution. Likewise, disillusionment with U.S. foreign policy spurred Bradley Manning (1987–), a U.S. Army intelligence analyst, to leak classified information to WikiLeaks in 2010. WikiLeaks is a private organization that uses a website (https://wikileaks.org) to disseminate sensitive information collected from various anonymous sources. In "WikiLeaks Fast Facts" (CNN.com, April 23, 2014), CNN explains that WikiLeaks began releasing hundreds of thousands of documents and videos in 2010. Most of this information concerned U.S. military operations in Iraq and Afghanistan. The U.S. government launched an investigation of the WikiLeaks founder Julian Assange (1971–) and soon arrested Manning and charged him with making the leaks. In 2013 Manning was sentenced to 35 years in prison following his court-martial (military trial). The following year he announced his desire to undergo a sex-change operation to become female and legally changed his name to Chelsea Manning.

The Federal Bureau of Investigation's National Security Branch

The Federal Bureau of Investigation (FBI) is the nation's premier agency devoted to law enforcement and operates under the U.S. Department of Justice (DOJ). John F. Fox Jr. explains in "The Birth of the Federal Bureau of Investigation" (July 2003, http://www.fbi.gov/about-us/history/highlights-of-history/articles/birth) that the FBI was created in 1908. Its primary focus was the investigation of a handful of federal crimes, such as land fraud. Over the decades, the agency acquired new responsibilities in intelligence gathering and counterintelligence, particularly the prevention of espionage and sabotage.

In 1986 Congress gave the FBI jurisdiction over terrorist acts that were committed against American citizens outside U.S. borders. The agency played a crucial role in investigating the bombings at the Khobar Towers (a housing facility for U.S. military personnel) in Saudi Arabia in 1996, the bombings at two U.S. embassies in East Africa in 1998, and a terrorist attack against the USS *Cole* in Yemen in 2000. The FBI also played a major role in investigating the terrorist bombing of the World Trade Center in 1993 and the terrorist attacks of September 11, 2001.

The Uniting and Strengthening America by Providing Appropriate Tools Required to Intercept and Obstruct Terrorism (USA PATRIOT) Act of 2001 (which is known simply as the Patriot Act) greatly expanded the FBI's role in counterterrorism. In 2005 President Bush directed the FBI to combine all of its intelligence and counterterrorism elements into one organization under the direction of a high-ranking FBI official. The result was the FBI's National Security Branch (NSB; November 2013, http://www.fbi.gov/about-us/nsb/nsb-brochure-2013). The organizational structure of the NSB is shown in Figure 2.5. Its major components are as follows:

- Counterintelligence Division—prevents and investigates foreign intelligence activities conducted within the United States
- Counterterrorism Division—uses an "intelligence-driven approach" to investigate domestic and international terrorism
- Directorate of Intelligence—provides a workforce that is devoted to collecting intelligence; its agents work at the FBI headquarters and are embedded in Field Intelligence Groups spread throughout the country
- Terrorist Screening Center—maintains a comprehensive watch list of known or suspected terrorists that is made available to federal, state, and local authorities
- Weapons of Mass Destruction Directorate—leads U.S. efforts to prevent countries and subnational entities (groups and individuals) from obtaining materials and technologies related to weapons of mass destruction, such as nuclear bombs and chemical and biological weapons

OTHER INTELLIGENCE AGENCIES

Besides the ODNI, the CIA, the eight MIP intelligence agencies, and the NSB, the IC includes six other members whose roles are described by the ODNI in "Our Strength Lies in Who We Are" (2014, http://www.intelligence.gov/mission/member-agencies.html). The following is a brief summary of the six agencies:

- U.S. Department of Energy (DOE), Office of Intelligence and Counterintelligence—provides technical intelligence regarding energy issues and foreign nuclear weapons and materials.
- U.S. Department of Homeland Security (DHS), Office of Intelligence and Analysis—collects intelligence related to terrorist threats within the United States. DHS activities are described in detail in Chapter 5.
- U.S. Coast Guard Intelligence—an agency of the DHS that collects intelligence related to maritime security and homeland defense.
- U.S. Department of State, Bureau of Intelligence and Research—conducts intelligence activities to support diplomatic goals.
- U.S. Department of the Treasury, Office of Intelligence and Analysis—collects intelligence related to domestic and international financial matters. It lies within the Treasury Department's Office of Terrorism and Financial Intelligence, which is described later in this chapter.
- Drug Enforcement Administration, Office of National Security Intelligence—conducts drug enforcement activities. Any intelligence relevant to national security that is obtained during these activities is shared with the IC.

U.S. DEPARTMENT OF STATE

As noted earlier, the DOS Bureau of Intelligence and Research is part of the IC; however, that bureau represents just a small part of the role that the DOS plays in national security. The DOS is the primary agency tasked with representing U.S. interests abroad through the use of diplomacy. Diplomacy is defined by Merriam-Webster (2014, http://www.merriam-webster.com/dictionary/diplomacy) as "the art and practice of conducting negotiations between nations" and "skill in handling affairs without arousing hostility." In a modern political sense, diplomacy can be defined as any foreign policy action short of armed aggression, such as a trade embargo imposed on another nation to punish it for some transgression.

FIGURE 2.5

Federal Bureau of Investigation's National Security Branch organization chart, 2014

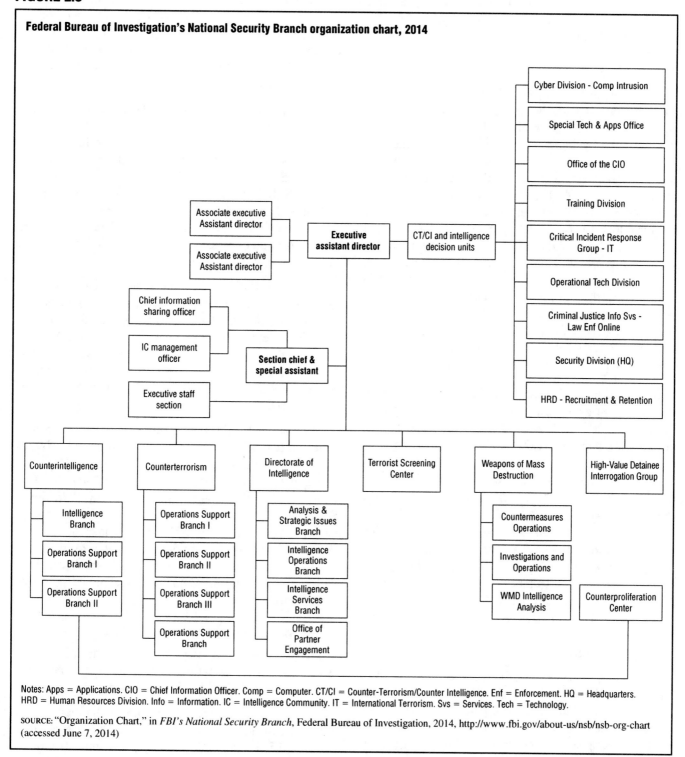

Notes: Apps = Applications. CIO = Chief Information Officer. Comp = Computer. CT/CI = Counter-Terrorism/Counter Intelligence. Enf = Enforcement. HQ = Headquarters. HRD = Human Resources Division. Info = Information. IC = Intelligence Community. IT = International Terrorism. Svs = Services. Tech = Technology.

SOURCE: "Organization Chart," in *FBI's National Security Branch*, Federal Bureau of Investigation, 2014, http://www.fbi.gov/about-us/nsb/nsb-org-chart (accessed June 7, 2014)

History

The DOS was created in 1789 from a previous agency known as the Department of Foreign Affairs. Historians consider Benjamin Franklin (1706–1790) to be the nation's first diplomat. In 1778 he was pivotal in securing two treaties with France: the Treaty of Amity and Commerce (which promoted trade) and the Treaty of Alliance (which formed a military alliance between the two nations). Franklin was called a plenipotentiary, a word derived from a Latin phrase meaning "full power." In other words, he had been granted full power to represent the U.S. government abroad.

The Treaty of Amity and Commerce was the first of many treaties the United States would forge with other nations regarding peaceful relations, commerce, travel, navigation, extradition of criminals, and other nonmilitary affairs. The Treaty of Alliance would be the only bilateral military agreement assumed by the United States for nearly two centuries.

Organization and Personnel

At the highest level, DOS officials craft U.S. foreign policy in concert with the president and negotiate with the leaders and foreign ministers of other nations. The DOS is headed by the secretary of state, who is a member of both the president's cabinet and the NSC. Figure 2.6 shows the organization chart for the main components of the DOS as of 2014. The two positions located underneath and to the left of the secretary of state are the administrators of the U.S. Agency for International Development (USAID) and the U.S. Mission to the United Nations. The latter is more widely known as the U.S. ambassador to the United Nations. This person is appointed by the president and confirmed by the U.S. Senate to represent the United States at the United Nations. USAID is the principal agency through which the federal government provides financial assistance to foreign nations and peoples.

In *Congressional Budget Justification: Department of State, Foreign Operations, and Related Programs, Fiscal Year 2015* (March 2014, http://www.state.gov/documents/organization/222898.pdf), the DOS indicates that the budget request for the DOS and USAID for FY 2015 was $46.2 billion. This included $40.3 billion for the regular budget and $5.9 billion for OCO spending. These values were down from FYs 2013 and 2014, when the two agencies had combined budgets of $48.9 billion and $46.8 billion, respectively. The DOS notes in *United States Department of State: Fiscal Year 2013 Agency Financial Report* (December 2013, http://www.state.gov/documents/organization/217939.pdf) that it had approximately 71,000 employees at the end of FY 2013.

U.S. Diplomatic Relations

According to the DOS, in the fact sheet "Independent States in the World" (December 9, 2013, http://www.state.gov/s/inr/rls/4250.htm), the United States recognized 195 independent states around the world in 2013. An independent state is defined by the DOS as "politically organized into a sovereign state with a definite territory recognized as independent by the US." The DOS indicates that as of December 2013 the United States had official diplomatic relations with all but four of the 195 recognized independent states. Those four nations were:

- Bhutan

- Cuba

- Iran

- North Korea

Bhutan is a tiny mountainous country located between India and Tibet. For decades, Bhutan has chosen to remain isolated from the outside world to protect its deeply religious Buddhist society. The United States conducts informal relations with Bhutan through the U.S. embassy in India.

In January 1961 the United States broke diplomatic ties with Cuba after it became obvious that Fidel Castro (1926–), the new Cuban leader, intended to form a communist government. In 1977 the United States opened an Interests Section office in Havana, Cuba. Although it is staffed by U.S. Foreign Service personnel, the office is officially a part of the Swiss embassy. The U.S. Interests Section handles requests for visas and performs other diplomatic functions. Cuba maintains a similar office at the Swiss embassy in Washington, D.C.

In April 1980 the United States broke diplomatic relations with Iran after the Iranian government refused to intervene on behalf of the U.S. diplomats who were taken hostage by Iranian militants at the U.S. embassy. A U.S. Interests Section office was later opened at the Swiss embassy in Tehran, Iran. Likewise, Iran maintains an Interests Section office at the Pakistani embassy in Washington, D.C.

Following World War II the Korea Peninsula was split into two occupied territories: the north under Soviet control and the south under U.S. control. This was intended to be a temporary arrangement until the two halves could be reunited as one nation. In 1948 South Korea adopted a constitution and became a sovereign nation. However, Cold War politics and the Korean War (1950–1953) prevented reunification from occurring. The United States did not form diplomatic relations with the communist government that assumed power in North Korea.

Travel Documents: Passports and Visas

One of the functions performed by the DOS is the issuance of international travel documents: passports for U.S. citizens and visas for foreign citizens.

A passport is an official travel document that verifies a person's identity and nationality. The DOS issues passports to U.S. citizens. Most foreign governments require U.S. visitors to possess a passport and show it when entering and leaving their countries. Likewise, a passport is typically required for U.S. citizens to reenter the United States after traveling abroad.

A visa is a document that indicates permission has been given by a government for a person of foreign nationality to travel to that country. DOS offices at U.S. embassies and consulates (regional embassy offices) can grant visas to foreign nationals to travel to the United States. A U.S.-granted visa indicates a person is eligible

FIGURE 2.6

U.S. Department of State (DOS) organization chart, 2014

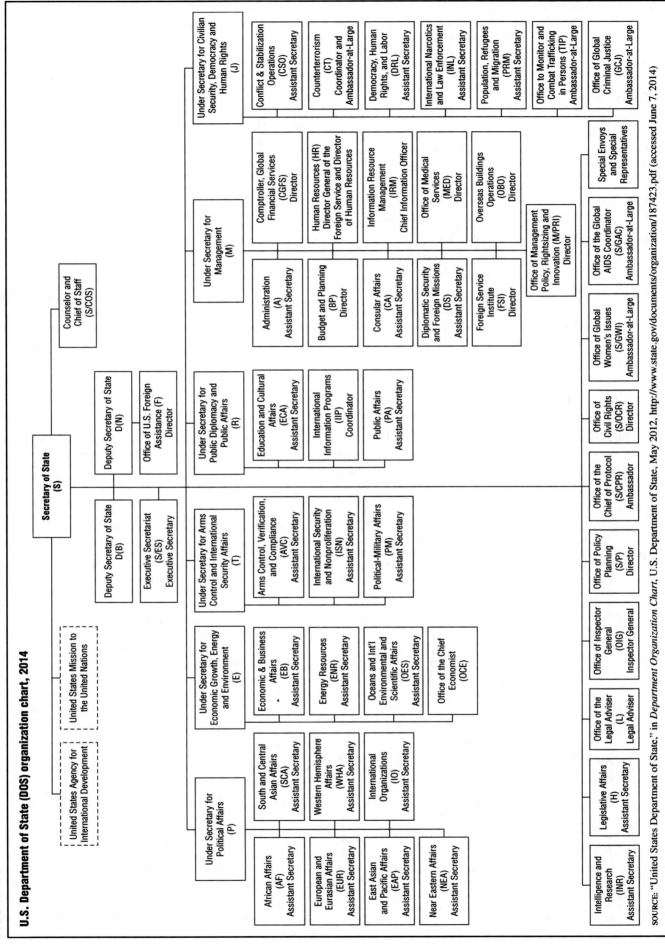

SOURCE: "United States Department of State," in *Department Organization Chart*, U.S. Department of State, May 2012, http://www.state.gov/documents/organization/187423.pdf (accessed June 7, 2014)

to enter the United States for a specific purpose. However, the determination of whether or not to grant entry is made by immigration officers at U.S. ports of entry (airports and land border crossings).

FOREIGN ECONOMIC ASSISTANCE

One of the historic diplomatic policies of the United States has been foreign aid. As noted in Chapter 1, there are two major types of foreign aid: economic assistance and military assistance. Foreign economic assistance includes humanitarian aid that is designed to generate goodwill for the United States. Since the terrorist attacks of September 11, 2001, foreign economic assistance has been increasingly viewed as a tool of national security.

Figure 2.7 provides a breakdown of the U.S. economic assistance that was obligated for FY 2012 by funding agency. The DOS and USAID together accounted for 75% of the aid. Other federal agencies, including the Treasury Department and the U.S. Department of Agriculture, accounted for smaller percentages of the total.

PUBLIC DIPLOMACY

Public diplomacy is diplomacy directed toward the foreign public at large, rather than just toward foreign governments. Public diplomacy projects are conducted by various entities within the U.S. government, including

FIGURE 2.7

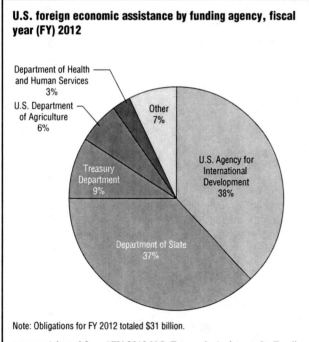

U.S. foreign economic assistance by funding agency, fiscal year (FY) 2012

Department of Health and Human Services 3%

U.S. Department of Agriculture 6%

Other 7%

U.S. Agency for International Development 38%

Treasury Department 9%

Department of State 37%

Note: Obligations for FY 2012 totaled $31 billion.

SOURCE: Adapted from "FY 2012 U.S. Economic Assistance by Funding Agency," in *Foreign Assistance Fast Facts: FY 2012*, U.S. Agency for International Development, 2014, http://gbk.eads.usaidallnet.gov/query/do?_program=/eads/gbk/countryReport&unit=N (accessed June 4, 2014)

the DOS, the DOD, USAID, and the Broadcasting Board of Governors (BBG). The projects are designed in accordance with guidance that is provided by the White House and the NSC (specifically the deputy national security adviser for strategic communications and global outreach).

Broadcasting Board of Governors

The BBG oversees government and government-sponsored international broadcasting services, including both radio and television. Although these services have a variety of different audiences, they have the common goal of delivering information about U.S. actions, goals, culture, and opinions to people who might otherwise not have access to such data. According to the BBG, in *Broadcasting Board of Governors 2013 Annual Report* (January 2014, http://www.bbg.gov/wp-content/media/2014/01/BBGAnnualReport_2013.pdf), its broadcasting services reached an estimated 206 million people weekly in 2013. The International Broadcasting Bureau (2014, http://www.bbg.gov/about-the-agency/organizational-chart) performs the administrative and marketing activities of the BBG and provides transmission services for the broadcasters. In 2014 there were five broadcasters:

- Voice of America (http://www.bbg.gov/broadcasters/voa)—this service includes programs in 45 languages via radio, television, and the Internet. It airs news, information, and educational and cultural shows.

- Radio Free Europe/Radio Liberty (http://www.bbg.gov/broadcasters/rferl)—this service can be heard across eastern Europe and central and southwestern Asia. The broadcasts are in 28 languages and are available over the radio, television, and Internet.

- Radio and TV Martí (http://www.bbg.gov/broadcasters/ocb)—these two services are broadcast in Cuba and operated by the Office of Cuba Broadcasting from its headquarters in Miami, Florida.

- Radio Free Asia (http://www.bbg.gov/broadcasters/rfa)—this service is operated out of Washington, D.C., and is funded by a grant from the BBG. Radio Free Asia broadcasts in nine languages via radio and the Internet to Burma (Myanmar), Cambodia, China, Laos, North Korea, and Vietnam.

- Middle East Broadcasting Networks, Inc. (http://www.bbg.gov/broadcasters/mbn)—this nonprofit organization operates Alhurra Television and Radio Sawa in the Middle East under a grant from the BBG.

U.S. DEPARTMENT OF ENERGY

As will be explained in Chapter 7, one of the greatest threats to U.S. national security is the proliferation (growth or multiplication) of weapons, particularly weapons of mass destruction, such as nuclear bombs. The DOE has long held responsibility for nuclear weapons development and production within the United States. In 2000 Congress established within the DOE the National Nuclear Security Administration (NNSA). According to the NNSA (2014, http://www.nnsa.energy.gov/aboutus/ourhistory), its responsibilities are as follows:

Managing and ensuring the security of the nation's nuclear weapons stockpile

Nuclear nonproliferation, that is, stemming the growth or multiplication of nuclear weapons around the world

Supporting work on naval reactors, for example, nuclear-powered submarines and aircraft carriers

Responding to nuclear and radiological emergencies within the United States and around the world

Providing "safe and secure" transportation of nuclear weapons, components, and materials

U.S. LAW ENFORCEMENT AGENCIES

U.S. law enforcement agencies play an important part in defending national security through counterintelligence operations, which have already been described, and through counterterrorism activities. Law enforcement agencies attempt to detect potential terrorists or other foreign agents and prevent them from carrying out harmful actions. If spying or a terrorist attack does occur, they investigate the incident and help capture those responsible.

After the September 11, 2001, terrorist attacks on the United States, lawmakers quickly put together the Patriot Act, which was designed to help the United States fight the terrorist threat. One of the purposes of the act is to facilitate better cooperation and information sharing between government agencies, particularly between the IC and law enforcement agencies. This act is described in detail in Chapter 8.

The law enforcement agencies engaged in counterterrorism activities include the DOJ, the DHS, and the Treasury Department. The primary DOJ agency devoted to counterterrorism and counterintelligence is the FBI, which was described earlier in this chapter. Major agencies within the DHS include the Transportation Security Administration, the Coast Guard, the U.S. Customs and Border Protection, the U.S. Immigration and Customs Enforcement, and the U.S. Secret Service. The roles of these agencies are discussed at length in Chapter 5. The Treasury Department operates the Office of Intelligence and Analysis within its Office of Terrorism and Financial Intelligence. The latter office combines intelligence and enforcement functions to protect the U.S. financial system against foreign threats, including rogue nations, narcotics traffickers, terrorist financiers, and money launderers.

CHAPTER 3
TERRORISM

During the late 20th century terrorism replaced the Cold War as the United States' greatest national security concern. Terrorism is not new. It has plagued the world for centuries. What is different is the scope and reach of terrorist acts. In the past the vast majority of terrorist acts were committed by people with domestic or regional grievances. The terrorists had narrow agendas and limited resources for achieving them. This is no longer true. The goals and means of some terrorist groups have broadened considerably. The technological advancements that have made international travel and communication possible have made it easier for terrorists to extend their reach to all parts of the world. Likewise, their weapons and methods are much more sophisticated and deadly. The combination of all these factors has made the U.S. homeland a viable and attractive target for terrorism.

As will be explained in this chapter, many of the terrorist groups that threaten U.S. national security are based in the Middle East, North Africa, and Southwest Asia. (See Figure 3.1.) Most of the terrorists and groups from this region have names in Arabic, which uses an alphabet completely different from that of English. Transliteration is a means for rendering words in one alphabet into another alphabet. Nevertheless, it is not an exact or universally agreed on process. Information sources, such as U.S. government agencies and news organizations, have differing transliteration practices. For example, the Arabic name of the terrorist group al Qaeda is also transliterated as "al Qa'ida," "al-Qaida," "al-Qaeda," and "Al Qaeda." Note that throughout this book transliterated Arabic words may appear in different forms between the graphics and the text, depending on the sources from which the information was obtained. However, the text will consistently maintain the same transliteration for the name of each group or individual mentioned.

There are also difficulties with translating certain Arabic words into English. For example, in 2013 the group known as al Qaeda in Iraq began calling itself al-Dawla al-Islamiya fil-Iraq wa al-Sham. According to Patrick J. Lyons and Mona El-Naggar, in "What to Call Iraq Fighters? Experts Vary on S's and L's" (NYTimes.com, June 18, 2014), this was translated by some media sources as "Islamic State in Iraq and Syria," or "ISIS" for short. Other analysts, however, insist the Arabic word *al-Sham* does not refer merely to Syria. Lyons and El-Naggar note, "Al-Sham is the classical Arabic term for Damascus and its hinterlands, and over time, it came to denote the area between the Mediterranean and the Euphrates, south of the Taurus Mountains and north of the Arabian desert." The U.S. government translated the group's name as "Islamic State in Iraq and the Levant" or "ISIL." The term *Levant* refers to the region along the eastern Mediterranean Sea and encompasses Syria, Lebanon, Israel, and Jordan. (See Figure 3.2.) In June 2014 the group shortened its name to al-Dawla al-Islamiya, or Islamic State (IS). That name will be used in this book to refer to the terrorist group that evolved from al Qaeda in Iraq. However, note that as of late 2014 many sources continued to refer to the group as ISIS or ISIL.

WHAT IS TERRORISM?

Terrorism is not easily defined. Within U.S. law and government agencies there are differing definitions of terrorism; however, for the purposes of this chapter, only one of these definitions will be used. In the U.S. Code, Title 22 (2014, http://www.law.cornell.edu/uscode/text/22) focuses on foreign relations. Chapter 38, Section 2656f(d) of that code defines terrorism as "premeditated, politically motivated violence perpetrated against noncombatant targets by subnational groups or clandestine agents."

One of the key components defining terrorism is its political nature. This excludes violence committed solely for financial gain, personal reasons, or other nonpolitical

FIGURE 3.1

Map of the Middle East and North Africa

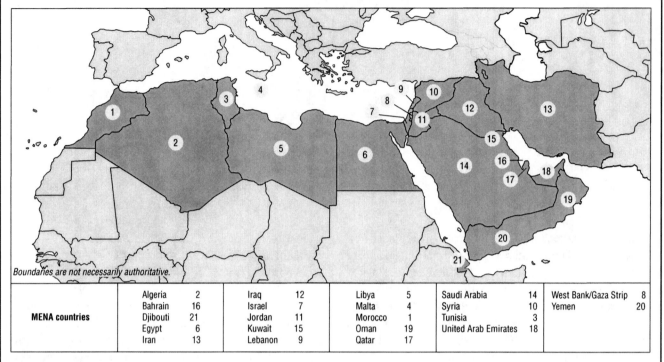

Boundaries are not necessarily authoritative.

MENA countries									
	Algeria	2	Iraq	12	Libya	5	Saudi Arabia	14	West Bank/Gaza Strip	8
	Bahrain	16	Israel	7	Malta	4	Syria	10	Yemen	20
	Djibouti	21	Jordan	11	Morocco	1	Tunisia	3		
	Egypt	6	Kuwait	15	Oman	19	United Arab Emirates	18		
	Iran	13	Lebanon	9	Qatar	17				

Note: MENA = Middle East and North Africa.

SOURCE: Shayerah Ilias Akhtar, Mary Jane Bolle, and Rebecca M. Nelson, "Figure 1. Map of Middle East and North Africa (MENA)," in *U.S. Trade and Investment in the Middle East and North Africa: Overview and Issues for Congress*, Congressional Research Service, March 4, 2013, http://www.fas.org/sgp/crs/misc/R42153.pdf (accessed June 7, 2014)

purposes. A second major component of terrorism is that noncombatants (civilians) are targeted. This distinguishes terrorism from traditional war making, in which official military forces are pitted against one another. Subnational means less than (or lower than) national. Clandestine means secret. By this definition, terrorism is not perpetrated openly (as war would be) by the governments of nations. Instead, it is associated with lesser groups or with secret national agents.

The subnational nature of terrorism makes it difficult, if not impossible, to thwart using U.S. military might alone. In essence, terrorists are criminals. They do not openly act on behalf of foreign governments. Nevertheless, it is well known that some terrorist groups receive direct or indirect support from foreign governments, particularly nations that are not politically allied with the United States. In addition, terrorist groups find safe harbor in countries with governments that lack the means (or the will) to police activities within their own borders. These factors make combating terrorism a difficult international challenge. The U.S. government uses a combination of diplomatic, military, financial, and intelligence (information) gathering measures to thwart terrorists. These efforts are collectively known as counterterrorism.

The overall organization of the U.S. national security framework was described in Chapter 2. The military, the intelligence community, and the U.S. Department of State (DOS) play vital counterterrorism roles.

TERRORISM STATISTICS

The National Counterterrorism Center (NCTC) is part of the Office of the Director of National Intelligence (ODNI), which was described in Chapter 2. Until 2012 the NCTC maintained a publicly available database called the Worldwide Incidents Tracking System that included statistics gathered by U.S. agencies on the number, location, and type of terrorist incidents committed around the world each year and the number of people killed, injured, or kidnapped during these incidents. The statistics were reported and discussed by the DOS's Bureau of Counterterrorism (CT) in an annual report to Congress called *Country Reports on Terrorism*.

In 2012 the NCTC ceased operating its tracking system. The DOS contracted with the National Consortium for the Study of Terrorism and Responses to Terrorism (START) at the University of Maryland to produce a statistical appendix for the CT's annual report. START

FIGURE 3.2

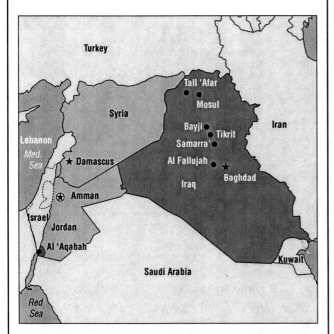

Map of Iraq and surrounding countries

SOURCE: "Al-Qa'ida in Iraq (AQI)/Islamic State of Iraq and the Levant (ISIL)," in *Counterterrorism 2014 Calendar*, National Counterterrorism Center, September 16, 2013, http://www.nctc.gov/site/pdfs/ct_calendar_2014.pdf (accessed June 7, 2014)

operates the Global Terrorism Database (http://www.start.umd.edu/gtd), an online collection of data about attacks that have been blamed on terrorists based on publicly available information such as news stories and unclassified government reports.

As of August 2014, the CT's most recently published annual report was *Country Reports on Terrorism 2013* (April 2014, http://www.state.gov/documents/organization/225886.pdf). The CT broadly reviews terrorist activities that occurred during 2013 and describes specific terrorist groups and global counterterrorism efforts. In the appendix *Annex of Statistical Information: Country Reports on Terrorism 2013* (April 2014, http://www.state.gov/documents/organization/225043.pdf), START provides statistical data on terrorist attacks that occurred in 2013. The organization notes that it uses three criteria to classify incidents as terrorist attacks in the appendix:

1. The violent act was aimed at attaining a political, economic, religious, or social goal

2. The violent act included evidence of an intention to coerce, intimidate, or convey some other message to a larger audience (or audiences) other than the immediate victims

3. The violent act was outside the precepts of International Humanitarian Law insofar as it targeted non-combatants

START estimates that 9,707 terrorist attacks occurred worldwide in 2013 that killed more than 17,800 people and wounded 32,500 others. The countries with the most terrorist attacks in 2013 were Iraq (2,495 attacks), Pakistan (1,920 attacks), and Afghanistan (1,144 attacks). These three countries accounted for more than half (57%) of the known terrorist attacks in 2013. Long-running wars and civil conflicts in Iraq and Afghanistan and conflicts in Pakistan, which neighbors Afghanistan, will be described in detail in Chapter 4. According to START, nearly 12,000 people were killed by terrorist violence in these three countries, accounting for almost two-thirds of the total deaths attributed to terrorism in 2013.

Perpetrators were identified in around one-third (32%) of the total terrorist attacks tracked by START in 2013. Overall, more than 220 organizations were specifically blamed. The known perpetrators with the largest numbers of attacks were the Taliban (641 attacks), the Islamic State (401 attacks), and Boko Haram (213 attacks). Each of these groups is described in detail later in this chapter.

FOREIGN TERRORIST ORGANIZATIONS

Throughout history various violent groups have been called terrorist organizations. During the late 20th century the U.S. government established a process by which a foreign organization is officially deemed to be a terrorist group. In 1996 Congress passed the Antiterrorism and Effective Death Penalty Act, which authorizes the U.S. secretary of state to officially designate groups as foreign terrorist organizations (FTOs). This is a legal process, so any group that is deemed to be an FTO can challenge the designation in court. To be designated as an FTO, an organization must meet the following criteria:

- Be a foreign organization

- Engage in terrorist activity or terrorism as defined by federal law or retain the capability and intent to engage in terrorist activity or terrorism

- Threaten the security of Americans or the national defense, foreign relations, or economic interests of the United States through terrorist activity

As of May 2014, the most recent list of FTOs contained 59 organizations. (See Table 3.1.) It is illegal for any person who is in the United States or subject to U.S. jurisdiction to knowingly provide "material support or resources" to a designated FTO. U.S. financial institutions are required to take control over any funds in their possession that were deposited by an FTO or one of its agents and report the funds to the U.S. Department of the Treasury. Finally, alien members or representatives of an FTO are not allowed to enter the United States and, in some cases, can be deported.

TABLE 3.1

Listing status of foreign terrorist organizations designated by the U.S. government, as of May 2014

Listed Date designated	Name
10/8/1997	Abu Nidal Organization (ANO)
10/8/1997	Abu Sayyaf Group (ASG)
10/8/1997	Aum Shinrikyo (AUM)
10/8/1997	Basque Fatherland and Liberty (ETA)
10/8/1997	Gama'a al-Islamiyya (Islamic Group) (IG)
10/8/1997	HAMAS
10/8/1997	Harakat ul-Mujahidin (HUM)
10/8/1997	Hizballah
10/8/1997	Kahane Chai (Kach)
10/8/1997	Kurdistan Workers Party (PKK) (Kongra-Gel)
10/8/1997	Liberation Tigers of Tamil Eelam (LTTE)
10/8/1997	National Liberation Army (ELN)
10/8/1997	Palestine Liberation Front (PLF)
10/8/1997	Palestinian Islamic Jihad (PIJ)
10/8/1997	Popular Front for the Liberation of Palestine (PFLP)
10/8/1997	PFLP-General Command (PFLP-GC)
10/8/1997	Revolutionary Armed Forces of Colombia (FARC)
10/8/1997	Revolutionary Organization 17 November (17N)
10/8/1997	Revolutionary People's Liberation Party/Front (DHKP/C)
10/8/1997	Shining Path (SL)
10/8/1999	al-Qa'ida (AQ)
9/25/2000	Islamic Movement of Uzbekistan (IMU)
5/16/2001	Real Irish Republican Army (RIRA)
9/10/2001	United Self Defense Forces of Colombia (AUC)
12/26/2001	Jaish-e-Mohammed (JEM)
12/26/2001	Lashkar-e Tayyiba (LeT)
3/27/2002	Al-Aqsa Martyrs Brigade (AAMB)
3/27/2002	Asbat al-Ansar (AAA)
3/27/2002	al-Qaida in the Islamic Maghreb (AQIM)
8/9/2002	Communist Party of the Philippines/New People's Army (CPP/NPA)
10/23/2002	Jemaah Islamiya (JI)
1/30/2003	Lashkar i Jhangvi (LJ)
3/22/2003	Ansar al-Islam (AAI)
7/13/2004	Continuity Irish Republican Army (CIRA)
12/17/2004	Libyan Islamic Fighting Group (LIFG)
12/17/2004	Islamic State of Iraq and the Levant (ISIL), formerly al-Qaida in Iraq (AQI)
6/17/2005	Islamic Jihad Union (IJU)
3/5/2008	Harakat ul-Jihad-i-Islami/Bangladesh (HUJI-B)
3/18/2008	al-Shabaab
5/18/2009	Revolutionary Struggle (RS)
7/2/2009	Kata'ib Hizballah (KH)
1/19/2010	al-Qa'ida in the Arabian Peninsula (AQAP)
8/6/2010	Harakat ul-Jihad-i-Islami (HUJI)
9/1/2010	Tehrik-e Taliban Pakistan (TTP)
11/4/2010	Jundallah
5/23/2011	Army of Islam (AOI)
9/19/2011	Indian Mujahedeen (IM)
3/13/2012	Jemaah Anshorut Tauhid (JAT)
5/30/2012	Abdallah Azzam Brigades (AAB)
9/19/2012	Haqqani Network (HQN)
3/22/2013	Ansar al-Dine (AAD)
11/14/2013	Boko Haram
11/14/2013	Ansaru
12/19/2013	al-Mulathamun Battalion
1/13/2014	Ansar al-Shari'a in Benghazi
1/13/2014	Ansar al-Shari'a in Darnah
1/13/2014	Ansar al-Shari'a in Tunisia
4/10/2014	Ansar Bayt al-Maqdis
5/15/2014	al-Nusrah Front

TABLE 3.1

Listing status of foreign terrorist organizations designated by the U.S. government, as of May 2014 [CONTINUED]

Delisted Date removed	Name	Date originally designated
10/8/1999	Democratic Front for the Liberation of Palestine-Hawatmeh Faction	10/8/1997
10/8/1999	Khmer Rouge	10/8/1997
10/8/1999	Manuel Rodriguez Patriotic Front Dissidents	10/8/1997
10/8/2001	Japanese Red Army	10/8/1997
10/8/2001	Tupac Amaru Revolution Movement	10/8/1997
5/18/2009	Revolutionary Nuclei	10/8/1997
10/15/2010	Armed Islamic Group (GIA)	10/8/1997
9/28/2012	Mujahedin-e Khalq Organization (MEK)	10/8/1997
5/28/2013	Moroccan Islamic Combatant Group (GICM)	10/11/2005

SOURCE: "Designated Foreign Terrorist Organizations," in *Foreign Terrorist Organizations*, U.S. Department of State, Bureau of Counterterrorism, May 2014, http://www.state.gov/j/ct/rls/other/des/123085.htm (accessed May 25, 2014)

forces. Many of the group's leaders, including its head Mohammed Omar (1959?–), fled to Pakistan. From there the Afghan Taliban has carried out an armed insurgency against the newly installed Afghan government and U.S. and coalition troops. The Afghan Taliban is widely considered to be a terrorist group, but as of May 2014 it had not been officially designated as an FTO by the United States. Observers speculate the U.S. government fears that such a designation might jeopardize ongoing efforts to negotiate a peace agreement in Afghanistan. More information about U.S. interactions with the Afghan Taliban is provided in Chapter 4.

MOTIVATIONS OF TERRORISM

As defined under U.S. law, terrorism is "politically motivated violence." One common political motivation is a desire for political autonomy (self-governance). For example, during the 20th century the Irish Republican Army waged a violent campaign to gain independence for Ireland from the United Kingdom. In the Middle East the Palestinian cause has long been a rallying point for many militant radicals. Some disillusioned Palestinians and their supporters have used terrorism against Israel and the world at large to push their agenda for statehood. Palestinians are largely of the Muslim faith, while Israelis are predominantly of the Jewish faith. Although religion is not the driving factor in the conflict, it is an element in which the two sides differ. In reality, religious and/or ethnic identity often intertwine with the political motivations for terrorism. This is particularly true in the Middle East, where the vast majority of the population is Muslim. As will be explained in Chapter 10, many followers of Islam believe their religion provides a method for governing nations and maintaining law and order. In other words, there is not a separation between "church and state" as is common in the West.

The FTO designation process is sometimes criticized for being influenced by political considerations. Critics complain that the DOS has failed to designate or has delayed the designation of some groups that clearly meet the FTO definition. The most obvious example is the Afghan Taliban, which ruled Afghanistan from 1996 until its ouster in 2001 by U.S. and coalition military

TABLE 3.2

Public opinion on the threat of Islamic fundamentalism to U.S. interests, selected years, 2004–14

	% Critical threat	% Important, not critical
Feb 6–9, 2014	46	42
Feb 7–10, 2013	44	44
Feb 1–3, 2010	47	41
Feb 9–12, 2004	58	32

Islamic Connection

A majority of the FTOs listed in Table 3.1 support causes or people that are associated with the Islamic faith, particularly the most conservative and fundamentalist elements of the religion. As noted in Table 1.6 in Chapter 1, Gallup pollsters found in February 2014 that more than half (57%) of Americans considered Islamic fundamentalism a "critical threat" to the vital interests of the United States over the next 10 years. Table 3.2 shows that the percentage of respondents with this viewpoint has stayed the same since 2004, when 58% of those asked deemed Islamic fundamentalism to be a "critical threat." Terrorists who espouse Islamic fundamentalism are typically labeled as Islamic extremists. Many advocate for the formation of an Islamist society (a society in which the government operates in strict accordance with Islamic law). One goal is the creation of an Islamic state or a caliphate. A caliphate is a geopolitical area spanning the territory of many countries, all under the rule of an Islamic leader called a caliph.

Another key goal for Islamists is the implementation of Sharia. In "What Is *Sharia* Law" (June 2011, http://www.loc.gov/law/help/sharia-law.php), Issam M. Saliba of the Library of Congress explains, "In its Islamic context, *Sharia* may be defined as the totality of God's commands and exhortations, intended to regulate all aspects of human conduct and guide believers on the path of eternal salvation." Saliba notes that Sharia covers behaviors related to worship, such as prayer and fasting, and "transactional dealings," which are interactions between people. Sharia law, as it is known, is interpreted and applied differently throughout the Muslim world. According to Saliba, "Some provisions of *Sharia* law are difficult to reconcile with western concepts of personal freedom and equality between the sexes." Islamists believe their nations should strictly follow rigid interpretations of Sharia and reject alternative legal systems.

Thus, FTOs devoted to achieving an Islamic state (or caliphate) operated in accordance with Sharia law are motivated by both political and religious ideology.

Within the Sunni branch of Islam there is a belief system called Salafism that has been closely associated with some of the most violent terrorist organizations. Salafism is variously described as a fundamentalist, traditionalist, or orthodox approach to Islam. Salafists seek to practice Islam as it was practiced by its earliest followers during the eighth century. There is a minority within this faction that champions a revolutionary style of Salafism in which violence is considered justifiable to re-create the Islamic caliphates of ages past.

Revolutionary Salafism has its roots in an organization called the Muslim Brotherhood that began in Egypt in 1928. Originally dedicated to education and social reform, it evolved into a political organization that embraced terrorism during the 1940s. Over the following decades the Muslim Brotherhood adopted as its spiritual leader the Egyptian intellectual Sayyid Qutb (1906–1966), who was a major proponent of Islamism. He briefly attended college in the United States during the 1940s and was highly critical of the "debauchery" of American society. Qutb advocated the use of violence, particularly against non-Muslims, in the quest for an Islamist society. This violence has been called a jihad (holy war) by the Western media. FTOs such as al Qaeda have embraced the concept of revolutionary Salafism and the use of violent jihad, even against fellow Muslims deemed to be less than true believers. Al Qaeda and other FTOs that strike at targets outside their regional base, such as at targets in the West, are said to be global jihadists. However, it should be noted that the Arabic term *jihad* translates more accurately as "struggle" and has a variety of meanings within Islamic tradition.

THE ARAB SPRING

Nearly all the nations in the Middle East have autocratic governments in which one person, family, or entity (such as the military) has wielded near-total power for decades. In 2010 the status quo began to crumble as restless people started demanding democratic reforms. Civil unrest and antigovernment demonstrations began in Tunisia in December 2010 and had spread to Egypt, Libya, and Yemen by the spring of 2011. Long-ruling autocrats in these countries were ousted from power. Zine el Abidine Ben Ali (1936–) was chased from Tunisia, Hosni Mubarak (1928–) was arrested in Egypt, Muammar al-Qadhafi (1942–2011) was killed in Libya, and Ali Abdullah Saleh (1942–) was forced from the presidency in Yemen. An uprising also began in Syria to oust President Bashar al-Assad (1965–); however, as will be explained in Chapter 6, it evolved into a civil war that still raged in 2014.

These series of revolutions were dubbed the "Arab Spring" by the media because many of the events transpired during the spring of 2011. However, revolutionary fever has continued to thrive in some Middle Eastern countries. Thus, the generic term *Arab Spring* does not describe a defined period, but rather a movement away from the political status quo in the region.

The Arab Spring uprisings presented opportunities for long-oppressed people to engage in democracy and choose their own leaders. Many Western observers were surprised (and concerned) when these populations voted Islamists into office. John M. Owen IV notes in the editorial "Why Islamism Is Winning" (NYTimes.com, January 6, 2012) that "a revolution's consequences need not follow from its causes. Rather than bringing secular revolutionaries to power, the Arab Spring is producing flowers of a decidedly Islamist hue. More unsettling to many, Islamists are winning fairly: religious parties are placing first in free, open elections in Tunisia, Morocco and Egypt." The political power of Islamists in Egypt proved to be short lived, however. Mohamed Morsi (1951–), the nation's first democratically elected leader and a member of the Muslim Brotherhood, was ousted from office in July 2013 by the Egyptian military following massive public protests. New elections held in Egypt in May 2014 saw Abdel Fattah el-Sisi (1954–), Egypt's former military chief, chosen as the nation's president.

MAJOR TERRORIST ORGANIZATIONS

Some terrorist organizations that were active during the 20th century have ceased to be major participants in terrorist attacks in the 21st century. In some cases this is because of cease-fires or other political agreements that have lessened violent opposition. For example, terrorist groups operating in Ireland have been relatively inactive since the late 1990s because of peace agreements accepted by most parties involved in the conflict. In other cases extremely hierarchal terrorist organizations have diminished in power following the deaths of their leaders.

In *Country Reports on Terrorism 2013*, the CT singles out several FTOs for their influence on political events in 2013 and for threatening U.S. interests. These groups are described in the following pages.

Al Qaeda and Affiliates

The FTO called al Qaeda, meaning "the foundation" or "the base," gained prominence during the 1990s as a sophisticated and well-funded organization that was capable of conducting terrorist attacks around the world, including on U.S. soil. Its members are predominantly Sunni and include some devoted adherents of Salafism.

Al Qaeda was founded in 1988 by Osama bin Laden (1957?–2011), a wealthy man from a prominent Saudi family. He followed the precepts of the Muslim Brotherhood and believed that violence was a necessary tool for ridding Muslim lands of unbelievers. During the 1980s he fought against the Soviet forces that occupied Afghanistan. Following the Soviet withdrawal, he united and trained his fighters to wage war against regional regimes he considered non-Islamist and against Israel and the United States. Bin Laden and al Qaeda's rise to power are described at length by the National Commission on Terrorist Attacks upon the United States in *The 9/11 Commission Report* (July 2004, http://www.9-11commission.gov/report/911Report.pdf).

In 1991 bin Laden left Saudi Arabia to set up his organization in Sudan in northern Africa. From there he moved to Afghanistan in 1996. Throughout the 1990s bin Laden issued statements urging Muslims around the world to kill Americans and their allies. In 1998 he and his cohorts published a fatwa in an Arabic-language newspaper in London. (A fatwa is an interpretation of Islamic law usually written by a scholar or religious authority.) Al Qaeda's fatwa declared war on the United States.

By 1998 bin Laden and al Qaeda had raised sufficient funds to launch carefully planned and directed attacks against U.S. interests. The organization was not strictly hierarchal in structure but featured a network of semi-independent cells of followers. Between 1998 and 2001 al Qaeda conducted a series of stunning terrorist attacks: in 1998 bombings at two U.S. embassies in Africa killed more than 200 people and injured another 5,000; in 2000 the bombing of the USS *Cole* in Yemen killed 17 Americans and wounded 39 others; and in 2001 over 2,700 people were killed when hijackers crashed two airplanes into both towers of the World Trade Center in New York City and a third airplane into the Pentagon in Arlington, Virginia, just outside Washington, D.C. A fourth airplane was brought down in Pennsylvania.

Following the September 11, 2001 (9/11), terrorist attacks, the U.S. military invaded Afghanistan and killed, captured, or chased into hiding many of al Qaeda's leaders, with the exception of bin Laden. The invasion initially disrupted al Qaeda's organization and capabilities; however, the FTO regained some of its strength with help from friendly tribal leaders across the border in western Pakistan. The effects of these events on the war in Afghanistan are described in detail in Chapter 4.

Bin Laden eluded detection for 10 years, but was finally killed by U.S. special forces in May 2011 in Pakistan. Following bin Laden's death, al Qaeda's leadership was taken over by Ayman al-Zawahiri (1951–), a former physician from Egypt. However, the power of the core al Qaeda organization has decreased significantly since bin Laden's death. In *Country Reports on Terrorism 2013*, the CT assesses al-Zawahiri's role in 2013 and explains that he "experienced difficulty in maintaining influence throughout the AQ [al Qaeda] organization and was rebuffed in his attempts to mediate a dispute among AQ affiliates operating in Syria." In addition, the CT states, "Guidance issued by Zawahiri in 2013 for AQ affiliates to avoid collateral damage was routinely disobeyed, notably in increasingly violent attacks by these affiliates against civilian populations." In fact, the CT indicates there is growing concern in the United States about terrorist groups affiliated with or inspired by the core al Qaeda. According to the CT, "2013 saw the rise of increasingly aggressive and autonomous AQ affiliates and like-minded groups in the Middle East and Africa who took advantage of the weak governance and instability in the region to broaden and deepen their operations."

ISLAMIC STATE. Numerous terrorist groups affiliated themselves with al Qaeda after the September 11, 2001, attacks. One such group formed in 2004 and was called Al Qaeda in Iraq (AQI). The group was founded by Abu Musab al-Zarqawi (1966–2006), a Jordanian and a Sunni extremist. During the war in Iraq the AQI waged a massive campaign of violence against allied troops, foreign workers and journalists, and Iraqi civilians. The AQI conducted many kidnappings, beheadings, and suicide bombings as part of the insurgency (resistance) movement and succeeded in fomenting near civil war between the Sunnis and Shiites in Iraq.

The killing of al-Zarqawi in a U.S. bombing raid in 2006 temporarily dampened the power and capabilities of the AQI. Nevertheless, the group remained a troublesome presence in Iraq and conducted several terrorist attacks against Shiites and Iraqi security forces. The NCTC notes in *Counterterrorism 2014 Calendar* (September 16, 2013, http://www.nctc.gov/site/pdfs/ct_calendar_2014.pdf) that AQI suicide bombers and car bombs killed approximately 1,000 Iraqis during the first half of 2013 alone. In April of that year the group's leader, Abu Bakr al-Baghdadi (1971–), changed its name to what would later be called the Islamic State (IS).

According to the CT, in *Country Reports on Terrorism 2013*, the IS was expelled from the al Qaeda network in February 2014 and began operating independently. In "Al-Qaeda Disavows Any Ties with Radical Islamist ISIS Group in Syria, Iraq" (WashingtonPost.com, February 3, 2014), Liz Sly indicates that al Qaeda and IS first fought together against the Assad government in the Syrian civil war; however, their relationship quickly deteriorated. According to Sly, al-Zawahiri could not mediate disputes between IS and Jabhat al-Nusra (or the al-Nusrah Front)— al Qaeda's official affiliate in Syria—after the two groups began battling with each other. Sly notes that IS is considered "the most extreme of the Islamist groups fighting in Syria" and states "the group's brutal tactics, including beheadings, floggings and bans on smoking, music and

other perceived un-Islamic behaviors, have incurred the wrath of many ordinary Syrians."

In early 2014 IS insurgents made substantial gains in neighboring Iraq when they seized control of the cities of Fallujah, Mosul, and Tikrit. News reports indicated that Iraqi security forces abandoned their posts and weapons to the terrorists. As will be explained in Chapter 4, Iraq has been torn by infighting between Sunnis and Shiites since the United States withdrew its military forces in 2011. The IS, a Sunni group, enjoys some support from the nation's Sunni minority who have become deeply unhappy with the Shiite-led government. By the end of June 2014 the IS controlled huge swaths of territory across both Syria and Iraq. The terror group issued a proclamation declaring that it had established a caliphate led by al-Baghdadi.

Over the next several weeks IS forces fought the Iraqi military and continued to gain ground. The militants enforced a strict fundamentalist version of Islam and waged a terror campaign against ethnic and religious minorities, which forced them to flee from their homes in large numbers. The U.S. government became concerned that tens of thousands of minorities faced extermination in northern Iraq. In addition, IS militants were fighting their way toward Erbil, a city that contained a U.S. consulate (a regional embassy office). In early August 2014 President Barack Obama (1961–) ordered the U.S. military to conduct air strikes on IS positions, send advisers to help the Iraqi military forces, and airdrop humanitarian supplies for fleeing civilians. As of late August 2014, these operations continued and are described in more detail in Chapter 4.

AL QAEDA IN THE ISLAMIC MAGHREB. In 2006 an Algerian Sunni jihadist group called the Salafist Group for Preaching and Combat aligned with al Qaeda and renamed itself Al Qaeda in the Islamic Maghreb (AQIM). *Maghreb* is a term used to collectively describe the Arab-majority countries of northern Africa, chiefly Algeria, Libya, Mali, Mauritania, Morocco, and Tunisia. Figure 3.3 shows the geographical area in which the AQIM was most active as of September 2013. Mali, in particular, has become a hot spot for terrorist activities since its democratic government was dissolved following a military coup in 2012. According to the CT, in *Country Reports on Terrorism 2013*, the AQIM and allied fighters attempted to seize northern Mali in 2013 but were driven back by French and African forces. Mali held elections in late 2013 and formed a new government. The CT notes that the AQIM funds itself largely through kidnapping-for-ransom activities.

The AQIM is suspected of playing a role in the violent attack on the U.S. consulate in Benghazi, Libya. On September 11, 2012, J. Christopher Stevens (1960–2012), the U.S. ambassador to Libya, and three of his staffers were

FIGURE 3.3

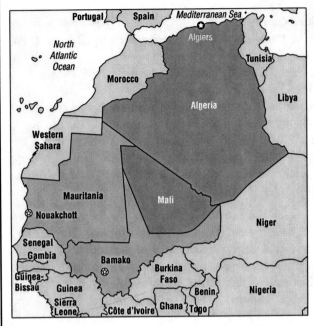

Map of area in which U.S. officials believed that al Qaeda in the Islamic Maghreb was most active, as of September 2013

SOURCE: "Al-Qa'ida in the Lands of the Islamic Maghreb (AQIM)," in *Counterterrorism 2014 Calendar*, National Counterterrorism Center, September 16, 2013, http://www.nctc.gov/site/pdfs/ct_calendar_2014 .pdf (accessed June 7, 2014)

FIGURE 3.4

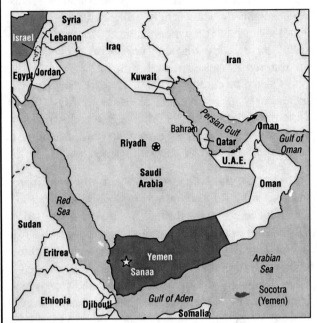

Map of area in which U.S. officials believed that al Qaeda in the Arabian Peninsula was most active, as of September 2013

SOURCE: "Al-Qa'ida in the Arabian Peninsula (AQAP)," in *Counterterrorism 2014 Calendar*, National Counterterrorism Center, September 16, 2013, http://www.nctc.gov/site/pdfs/ct_calendar_2014 .pdf (accessed June 7, 2014)

killed after armed militants stormed the U.S. compound. Initially, media reports linked the attack to ongoing protests in the Middle East over an anti-Muslim video that originated in the United States and sparked outrage after being posted on the Internet. However, attention soon turned to terrorists with ties to al Qaeda.

In January 2014 the U.S. Senate Select Committee on Intelligence published its findings in *Review of the Terrorist Attacks on U.S. Facilities in Benghazi, Libya, September 11–12, 2012* (http://www.intelligence.senate.gov/ benghazi2014/benghazi.pdf). The committee notes that "individuals affiliated with terrorist groups, including AQIM, Ansar al-Sharia, AQAP [Al Qaeda in the Arabian Peninsula], and the Mohammad Jamal Network, participated in the September 11, 2012, attacks. Intelligence suggests that the attack was not a highly coordinated plot, but was opportunistic." The committee goes on to say, "It remains unclear if any group or person exercised overall command and control of the attacks or whether extremist group leaders directed their members to participate."

AL QAEDA IN THE ARABIAN PENINSULA. In 2009 Sunni terrorist groups based in Yemen and Saudi Arabia united to form Al Qaeda in the Arabian Peninsula (AQAP). Figure 3.4 shows a map of the Arabian Peninsula and the countries in which the AQAP was believed

to be most active as of September 2013. U.S. officials are particularly concerned about the group because of the violent history of the AQAP's predecessor group Al Qaeda in Yemen, the extremely unsecure status of the Yemeni government, and the terrorist attacks that AQAP operatives have made or attempted on U.S. targets, including the Benghazi attack described earlier.

The AQAP is also blamed for the so-called underwear bomber, who failed to detonate explosives on a commercial airliner that landed in Detroit, Michigan, in December 2009. In October 2010 AQAP-planted explosives hidden aboard cargo airplanes traveling to the United States were intercepted and disabled following tips from Saudi intelligence. In May 2012 the Saudi government announced that it had thwarted another AQAP attempt to blow up a U.S.-bound airliner. That same month an AQAP suicide bomber killed more than 90 Yemeni soldiers in Sanaa, the capital of Yemen. Ibrahim al-Asiri (1982–), a Saudi citizen, is believed to be the mastermind behind the AQAP's sophisticated bombing operations. Nasir al-Wahishi, a Yemeni citizen and former aide to bin Laden, is frequently mentioned as the overall leader of the AQAP. According to the CT, in *Country Reports on Terrorism 2013*, in 2013 al-Zawahiri named al-Wahishi as one of his deputies, which indicates there are close ties between the two groups.

The AQAP is known for its propaganda, which includes the online English-language magazine *Inspire* that was launched in 2010. The magazine was spearheaded by the AQAP recruiters Anwar al-Awlaki (1971–2011) and Samir Khan (1986–2011), two young web-savvy men who were U.S. citizens and grew up in the United States. They specialized in recruiting Westerners, particularly Americans, to join the AQAP. In September 2011 al-Awlaki and Khan were killed by a U.S. drone attack in Yemen. However, the AQAP continued to publish the magazine. In March 2014 various media sources announced that a new issue of *Inspire* had been released. Lee Faran indicates in "Al Qaeda's Latest Magazine: Notes from Dead American Terrorists" (ABCNews.com, March 15, 2014) that the publication included instructions for building car bombs and urged followers to detonate the bombs in major U.S. cities.

Harakat al-Shabaab al-Mujahidin

The terrorist group Harakat al-Shabaab al-Mujahidin (commonly called al-Shabaab) operates in Somalia along the northeastern coast of Africa. (See Figure 3.5.) The country has been wracked by years of civil war and famine. It has not had a functioning central government since the early 1990s. Thus, Somalia provides an excellent place of refuge for terrorist organizations. According to the NCTC, in *Counterterrorism 2014 Calendar*, al-Shabaab has focused most of its attacks against government figures, peacekeepers from the African Union, and aid workers. In 2010 it conducted terrorist attacks against multiple targets within and outside Somalia. The most notable was a pair of suicide bombings in Kampala, Uganda, that killed more than 70 people. In 2013 al-Shabaab was blamed for attacks against a United Nations (UN) compound in Somalia and a mall in Kenya. More than 80 people were killed in the attacks.

The group has drawn the U.S. government's attention because it has successfully recruited Westerners, including Americans, to its ranks and because some of its top commanders have expressed allegiance to al Qaeda's goals for global jihad. However, the NCTC notes that al-Shabaab's members "come from disparate clans, and the group is susceptible to clan politics, internal divisions, and shifting alliances."

Boko Haram

In *Counterterrorism 2014 Calendar*, the NCTC notes that Boko Haram is a nickname for the Nigerian terrorist group Jama'atu Ahl as-Sunnah li-Da'awati wal-Jihad (Group of the Sunni People for the Calling and Jihad). The Arabic word *haram* means "forbidden"; thus, the group's nickname roughly translates as "Western education is forbidden." According to the NCTC, the group's goal is to "overthrow the current Nigerian Government and replace it with a regime based on Islamic law."

FIGURE 3.5

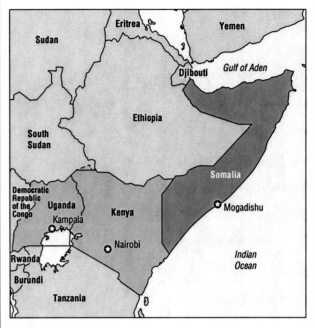

Map of area in which U.S. officials believed that al-Shabaab was most active, as of September 2013

SOURCE: "Al-Shabaab," in *Counterterrorism 2014 Calendar*, National Counterterrorism Center, September 16, 2013, http://www.nctc.gov/site/pdfs/ct_calendar_2014.pdf (accessed June 7, 2014)

Figure 3.6 shows the areas of western Africa in which Boko Haram was most active as of September 2013.

The group made headlines in 2011, when it attacked a UN compound in Abuja, Nigeria's capital, and killed nearly two dozen people. The NCTC indicates that Boko Haram has targeted Christians, Nigerian security and police forces, media personnel, politicians, and schools. In April 2014 Boko Haram militants attacked a school in Chibok in northeastern Nigeria and kidnapped more than 200 girls. The act roused international outrage and focused attention on the Nigerian government's security weaknesses. In desperation, the government asked for help from other nations, including the United States, to free the schoolgirls. As of August 2014, the girls had not been freed, although negotiations were ongoing.

According to Robert Windrem, in "Bloody Toll: Boko Haram behind Deadliest Killing Spree since 9/11" (NBCNews.com, June 12, 2014), in the two months following the kidnapping Boko Haram killed more than 1,000 Nigerians during multiple terrorist attacks. Windrem quotes an unnamed U.S. counterterrorism official as saying, "The group's ability to conduct high-casualty attacks has evolved to an unprecedented level." In addition, Boko Haram is believed to have kidnapped dozens more schoolgirls.

FIGURE 3.6

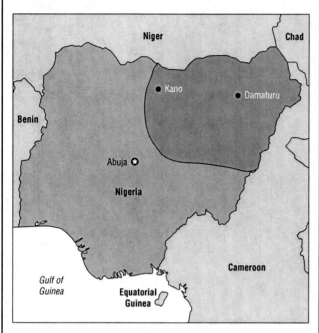

Map of Nigeria showing areas in which U.S. officials believed that Boko Haram terrorists were most active, as of September 2013

SOURCE: "Boko Haram," in *Counterterrorism 2014 Calendar*, National Counterterrorism Center, September 16, 2013, http://www.nctc.gov/site/pdfs/ct_calendar_2014.pdf (accessed June 7, 2014)

FIGURE 3.7

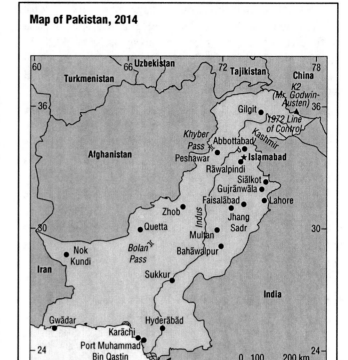

Map of Pakistan, 2014

SOURCE: "South Asia: Pakistan," in *The World Factbook*, Central Intelligence Agency, April 14, 2014, https://www.cia.gov/library/publications/the-world-factbook/geos/pk.html (accessed May 25, 2014)

Pakistan-Based Terrorist Groups

In *Country Reports on Terrorism 2013*, the CT singles out three Pakistan-based terrorist groups for special notice: Lashkar-e Tayyiba, Tehrik-e Taliban Pakistan (which is more commonly called the Pakistani Taliban), and the Haqqani Network. (Figure 3.7 shows a map of Pakistan.) The three groups are worrisome because they have forged ties with terrorist groups, such as al Qaeda, and with insurgents that are fighting against U.S. and UN military forces in Afghanistan.

The United States has had a shaky political alliance with Pakistan since 2001, when the war in Afghanistan began. As will be explained in Chapter 4, that alliance has been weakened considerably by U.S drone attacks inside Pakistani territory and by the U.S. incursion into Pakistan to kill bin Laden. In addition, there are claims that some elements within the Pakistani government have conspired with terrorist groups or allowed them to operate with impunity to further particular political goals. The CT indicates that in 2013 the Pakistani military undertook operations against groups, such as the Pakistani Taliban, that want to overthrow the Pakistani government. The CT, however, claims that Pakistan "did not take action against other groups such as Lashkar-e-Tayyiba, which continued to operate, train, rally, and

fundraise in Pakistan during the past year." In addition, the CT notes, "Afghan Taliban and HQN [Haqqani Network] leadership and facilitation networks continued to find safe haven in Pakistan, and Pakistani authorities did not take significant military or law enforcement action against these groups."

TEHRIK-E TALIBAN PAKISTAN. Tehrik-e Taliban Pakistan (or the Pakistani Taliban) is described by the NCTC in *Counterterrorism 2014 Calendar* as "an alliance of militant groups" that formed in 2007. The FTO actively fights against Pakistani troops in the largely lawless area of western Pakistan along the border with Afghanistan. According to the NCTC, the group "has repeatedly threatened to attack the US homeland." A failed car bombing attempt in 2010 in New York City's Times Square was blamed on a Pakistani Taliban operative. In addition, the group claimed responsibility for numerous retaliatory terrorist attacks that occurred in Pakistan following the U.S. killing of bin Laden in May 2011. The NCTC notes that the leaders of the Pakistani Taliban "hope to impose a strict interpretation of Qur'anic instruction throughout Pakistan and to expel Coalition troops from Afghanistan."

In 2012 the Pakistani Taliban took credit for the attempted assassination of Malala Yousafzai (1997–), a teenaged schoolgirl who lived in northern Pakistan. She was an outspoken proponent of education for girls, which the Taliban opposes. Yousafzai was shot three times but survived and as of 2014 continued to advocate for educational rights for girls.

LASHKAR-E TAYYIBA. Lashkar-e Tayyiba translates as "Army of the Good" or "Army of the Righteous." According to the CT, in *Country Reports on Terrorism 2013*, the group formed during the late 1980s in the Pakistani part of Kashmir, a disputed territory that spans northern Pakistan, northern India, and southern China. The FTO is blamed for a series of terrorist attacks in Mumbai, India, in 2008 that killed 174 people, including six Americans. U.S. authorities charged David Headley (1960–), a U.S. citizen, with aiding and abetting the FTO in the Mumbai attacks. In 2013 he was sentenced to 35 years in prison for his role. In "Planner of Mumbai Attacks Is Given a 35-Year Sentence" (NYTimes.com, January 24, 2013), Steven Yaccino notes that the sentence was relatively light because Headley cooperated with U.S. authorities after his capture and provided valuable intelligence about Lashkar-e Tayyiba.

THE HAQQANI NETWORK. The Haqqani Network is a Sunni Islamist militant group based in Pakistan. In *Counterterrorism 2014 Calendar*, the NCTC states that the group formed during the 1980s in the lawless mountains of northwestern Pakistan and is named after its founder Jalaluddin Haqqani (c. 1950–). His son, Sirajuddin Haqqani (c. 1973–), is the current leader of the group, which seeks to reinstate the Afghan Taliban to power in Afghanistan. The NCTC notes that the Haqqani Network is "considered the most lethal insurgent group targeting Coalition and Afghan forces in Afghanistan." The terrorist group is blamed for several high-profile attacks in Afghanistan, including an assault in June 2011 at a hotel in Kabul, the capital of Afghanistan. In September 2011 Haqqani operatives staged a day-long attack on the U.S. embassy and the North Atlantic Treaty Organization's headquarters in Kabul. Although the attackers were repelled, their success at gaining close access to these heavily secured buildings indicated sophisticated planning and coordination.

In "Brutal Haqqani Crime Clan Bedevils U.S. in Afghanistan" (NYTimes.com, September 24, 2011), Mark Mazzetti, Scott Shane, and Alissa J. Rubin call the network "a ruthless crime family that built an empire out of kidnapping, extortion, smuggling, even trucking. They have trafficked in precious gems, stolen lumber and demanded protection money from businesses building roads and schools with American reconstruction funds." Media reports describe the group as a network of mercenaries that work at the behest of elements within the Pakistani government, particularly the Inter-Services Intelligence Agency.

Although active for years, the Haqqani Network was not designated as an FTO by U.S. officials until September 2012. (See Table 3.1.) Many observers believe the U.S. government was reluctant to do so for fear of further alienating the Pakistani government. The latter has its own regional agenda that overwhelmingly focuses on India, its arch enemy. Observers allege that the Pakistani government uses heavily armed terrorist groups, such as the Haqqani Network, as proxies (agents acting on someone else's behalf). Mazzetti, Shane, and Rubin state, "American officials who were once optimistic they could change Pakistani behavior through cajoling and large cash payments now accept a sober reality: as long as Pakistan sees its security under threat by India's far larger army, it will rely on militant groups like the Haqqanis, the Taliban and Lashkar-e-Taiba as occasional proxy forces."

Hamas

Hamas is an acronym for Harakat al-Muqawama al-Islamiya, meaning "Islamic Resistance Movement." Its primary area of operation is in the Palestinian territories of Israel, where it seeks to install an Islamic state. (See Figure 3.8.) Hamas formed during the 1980s and created a charter outlining its mission. In *Hamas: Background and Issues for Congress* (December 2, 2010, http://fas.org/sgp/crs/mideast/R41514.pdf), Jim Zanotti of the

FIGURE 3.8

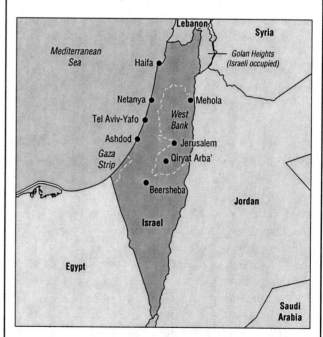

Map of area in which U.S. officials believed that Hamas was most active, as of September 2013

SOURCE: "HAMAS," in *Counterterrorism 2014 Calendar*, National Counterterrorism Center, September 16, 2013, http://www.nctc.gov/site/pdfs/ct_calendar_2014.pdf (accessed June 7, 2014)

Congressional Research Service states, "The 1988 charter commits Hamas to the destruction of Israel and the establishment of an Islamic state in all of historic Palestine. It calls for the elimination of Israel and Jews from Islamic holy land and portrays Jews in decidedly negative terms, citing anti-Semitic texts and conspiracies."

Hamas uses both political and terrorist methods to pursue its goals. These two functions are carried out by different divisions within the organization. Terrorist activities are associated with paramilitary fighters (civilians organized to function like a military unit) in the Izz al-Din al-Qassam Brigades. According to the CT, in *Country Reports on Terrorism 2013*, the Hamas brigades have conducted many terrorist attacks, including suicide bombings, against civilian and military targets in Israel but have not directly attacked U.S. interests.

Hamas is believed to have tens of thousands of supporters and sympathizers. Its activities are chiefly funded through donations collected from Palestinians living around the world and from wealthy private individuals in Saudi Arabia and other Arab countries. The FTO's popularity in Palestine is attributed in large part to its social and charitable works, including schools, medical clinics, and youth camps. As mentioned in Chapter 1, Hamas members were elected in sufficient numbers during the January 2006 elections to take over majority control of the Palestinian National Authority (PNA), the existing governing body of the Palestinian territories.

Hamas attacks against Israel decreased dramatically following the election, until June 2006, when Hamas forces attacked a group of Israeli soldiers, killing two and kidnapping another. In response, Israel imposed strict travel and economic sanctions against Palestinians in the Gaza Strip. (See Figure 3.9.) Israel controls the airspace above the Gaza Strip, its ports, and all of its land border crossings, except those along the Egyptian border. The latter are controlled by Egypt.

In 2007 a military-type coup by Hamas forces routed the PNA from the Gaza Strip. Hamas unofficially seized control of the area and continued to wage bomb and rocket attacks against Israeli targets. Israel responded by implementing a strict blockade on the passage of many goods into the Gaza Strip. Egypt also implemented a blockade at the border crossings it controlled; however, Hamas had already dug many tunnels between Egypt and the Gaza Strip to facilitate the inflow of prohibited goods—particularly rockets and other arms. Hamas expanded its tunnel network after the blockade began and even constructed tunnels into Israeli territory, allowing militants to engage in cross-border raids and kidnappings. The Israeli military has responded with air strikes and raids targeting the militants. A near-continuous cycle of violence and retribution has resulted in numerous deaths including many among Gazan civilians. Their

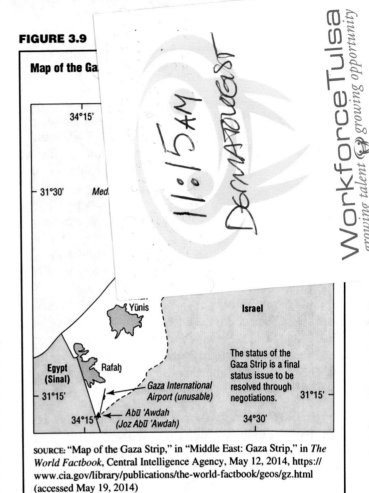

FIGURE 3.9

Map of the Ga...

SOURCE: "Map of the Gaza Strip," in "Middle East: Gaza Strip," in *The World Factbook*, Central Intelligence Agency, May 12, 2014, https://www.cia.gov/library/publications/the-world-factbook/geos/gz.html (accessed May 19, 2014)

deaths and suffering arouse sympathy around the world and elicit criticism of Israeli military actions. Israel and its supporters, however, argue that Hamas terrorizes the Israeli people and operates its tunnels and rocket launchers in densely populated areas of Gaza, putting its own civilians at risk.

As of August 2014, the Israel military had conducted three major operations against the Hamas in Gaza:

- December 2008–January 2009—during Operation Cast Lead Israeli ground forces invaded Gaza. After three weeks of fighting Israel announced a unilateral cease-fire. Unilateral means "one-sided." In other words, Israel declared a cease-fire without negotiating the terms with Hamas. The article "UN Condemns 'War Crimes' in Gaza" (BBC.com, September 16, 2009) indicates that approximately 1,200 to 1,400 Palestinians were killed, along with three Israeli civilians and 10 Israeli soldiers.

- November 2012—during Operation Pillar of Defense Israel killed the Hamas commander Ahmed Jaabari (1960–2012). Eight days of fighting included numerous cross-border skirmishes, but no full-out ground invasion. The operation ended with a truce that was brokered by Egypt and the United States. David D.

Kirkpatrick and Jodi Rudoren note in "Israel and Hamas Agree to a Cease-Fire, after a U.S.-Egypt Push" (NYTimes.com, November 21, 2012) that at least 150 Palestinians and five Israelis were killed during the conflict.

- July–August 2014—during Operation Protective Edge the Israeli military undertook a massive air and ground campaign to destroy the tunnel network and rocket-launching facilities in Gaza. Numerous Hamas leaders were also targeted. The operation was precipitated, in part, by the murder of three Israeli teens in the West Bank, which the Israeli government blamed on Hamas. In "The Toll in Gaza and Israel, Day by Day" (NYTimes.com, August 8, 2014), Karen Yourish and Josh Keller report that nearly 3,000 rockets were launched at Israel during the operation. An estimated 1,881 Palestinians and 67 Israelis were killed before Israel withdrew its forces from Gaza in early August. Various cease-fire agreements brokered by Egypt went into effect while the two sides tried to negotiate a lasting truce. As of late August 2014, those negotiations continued.

Hezbollah

Hezbollah is an FTO based in Lebanon. Figure 3.10 shows the areas of Lebanon in which the CT believes that Hezbollah was most active as of September 2013. The FTO is unique in that unlike nearly all of its Middle Eastern counterparts, Hezbollah consists of Shiites rather than Sunnis. As will be explained in Chapter 10, Shia make up only about 10% to 15% of the world's Muslim population. They are mostly concentrated in India, Iran, Iraq, and Pakistan; relatively large numbers are also found in Azerbaijan, Lebanon, Turkey, Saudi Arabia, and Syria.

In English *Hezbollah* means "Party of God." The group also calls itself Islamic Jihad or Islamic Jihad for the Liberation of Palestine. It emerged in Lebanon following Israel's invasion of that nation in 1982. The FTO has close ties to Iran and Syria.

Hezbollah is blamed for a number of terrorist attacks against Israeli and U.S. interests, including some of the most notorious incidents of the 1980s and 1990s. U.S. officials believe Hezbollah agents bombed the U.S. embassy and marine barracks in Lebanon in 1983, killing over 300 Americans; hijacked TWA Flight 847 in 1985 and killed a U.S. Navy diver aboard the plane; and participated in the 1996 bombing of the Khobar Towers (a housing facility for U.S. military personnel) in Saudi Arabia, during which 19 Americans were killed and 515 injured.

Lebanon bounds Israel to the north. In about 2005 the Lebanese government allowed Hezbollah militants essentially to take control of southern Lebanon, ostensibly to

FIGURE 3.10

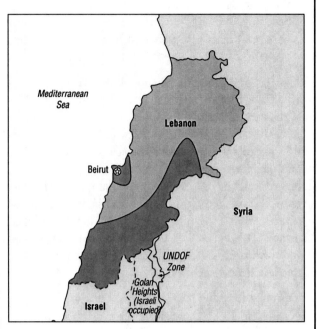

Map of area in which U.S. officials believed that Hezbollah was most active, as of September 2013

SOURCE: "Hizballah," in *Counterterrorism 2014 Calendar*, National Counterterrorism Center, September 16, 2013, http://www.nctc.gov/site/pdfs/ct_calendar_2014.pdf (accessed June 7, 2014)

guard against an Israeli attack. There were many skirmishes between Hezbollah militants and Israeli military forces. In July 2006 Hezbollah agents crossed the border and kidnapped two Israeli soldiers. In response, Israel conducted air strikes and fired missiles against a variety of targets in Lebanon, before launching a ground invasion. Likewise, Hezbollah fired hundreds of rockets into Israel. Following approximately a month of fighting, a cease-fire was brokered by the UN. In August 2006 the UN Security Council passed Resolution 1701, which called for the withdrawal of Israeli troops from Lebanon and the disarming of Hezbollah fighters. In *Country Reports on Terrorism 2013*, the CT notes that "according to the Government of Israel, Hizballah has stockpiled some 60–70,000 missiles in Lebanon since the 2006 Lebanon War, some of which are capable of striking anywhere in Israel, including population centers."

Hezbollah is a focal point of diplomatic tension between Israel and Iran. As will be explained in Chapter 6, that relationship became even more strained during the first half of the second decade of the 21st century over Iran's alleged program to develop nuclear weapons.

MAJOR TERRORIST ACTS AND ATTEMPTS

Palestinian resistance groups have been responsible for many acts of terrorism since the founding of Israel in

1948. Until the 1960s these acts were largely restricted to areas within Israel and the Palestinian territories. The emergence of the Palestine Liberation Organization and various splinter groups changed the dynamics of terrorism, giving it a more international reach. Airline hijackings became a vexing problem throughout the region. Palestinian militants also ventured frequently into Western Europe to carry out terrorist acts.

Except for diplomatic personnel, Americans were not usually the target of terrorist attacks before the 1980s. This changed dramatically after the 1982 invasion of Lebanon by Israel. Israeli forces withdrew in 1983 and were replaced by international forces that included U.S. troops. This precipitated a number of deadly attacks against Americans in Lebanon and other nations. Kidnappings of U.S. citizens in Lebanon also became common; however, most victims were eventually released unharmed. By the end of the decade airline hijackings around the world had largely been eliminated because of heightened airport security.

During the early 1990s terrorists began striking on U.S. soil. In 1993 there were two such attacks: an ambush at CIA headquarters in Virginia by a lone gunman and a bombing at the World Trade Center in New York City. Within the next few years the al Qaeda terrorist network under bin Laden became a major force in terrorism and began targeting U.S. interests worldwide. On September 11, 2001, members of this network hijacked and commandeered four U.S. airliners. Three of the airplanes were purposely flown into buildings: the Pentagon in Arlington, Virginia, and both towers of the World Trade Center in New York City. The fourth plane crashed in Pennsylvania, after a struggle between the hijackers and the passengers. In total, over 2,700 people were killed in the one-day attacks. As of August 2014, the 9/11 attack was the most recent terrorist attack by an FTO on U.S. soil.

The Most Serious Terrorist Incidents

Various media sources, private organizations, and government agencies maintain lists of some of the thousands of terrorist acts that have occurred around the world over the past few decades. The DOS features a listing in "Significant Terrorist Incidents, 1961–2003: A Brief Chronology" (March 2004, http://www.fas.org/irp/threat/terror_chron.html). The following are only a few of the events mentioned by the DOS that have had major effects in terms of U.S. casualties or influence on U.S. foreign policy and public opinion:

- Olympic Games, Munich, Germany (1972)—Palestinian terrorists seized 11 Israeli athletes, nine of whom were subsequently killed. West German authorities launched a bungled rescue attempt as the terrorists tried to leave the country with their hostages. The Black September group was blamed for this terrorist incident.

- Air France Airliner, Entebbe, Uganda (1976)—terrorists hijacked a plane containing 258 passengers and forced it to land in Entebbe. Israeli commandos infiltrated Uganda and rescued the hostages. The terrorists were members of the German left-wing organization Baader-Meinhof and the Popular Front for the Liberation of Palestine.

- U.S. embassy, Tehran, Iran (1979–1981)—66 American diplomatic personnel were held hostage in the embassy by militant Iranian students, who were supported by the conservative Islamic government of Ruhollah Khomeini (1902?–1989). All hostages were eventually released unharmed.

- U.S. embassy, Beirut, Lebanon (1983)—Hezbollah claimed responsibility for bombing the embassy. The attack killed 63 people and injured 120.

- U.S. Marine Barracks, Beirut, Lebanon (1983)—Hezbollah claimed responsibility for a bombing that killed 242 Americans. Fifty-eight French troops were killed the same day in a similar attack on a French military compound.

- Restaurant, Torrejon, Spain (1984)—Hezbollah claimed responsibility for a bomb that killed 18 U.S. military personnel and injured 83.

- TWA Flight 847 (1985)—Hezbollah terrorists hijacked the flight and held it for 17 days, forcing it to fly to and from various airports around the Middle East. The terrorists killed an American hostage, a U.S. Navy sailor.

- *Achille Lauro* Cruise Liner (1985)—Palestine Liberation Front terrorists seized the cruise liner on the Mediterranean Sea with more than 700 hostages aboard. An American passenger in a wheelchair was thrown overboard.

- Pan Am Flight 103 (1988)—Libyan terrorists placed a bomb on the plane that exploded in flight over Lockerbie, Scotland. All 259 passengers and 11 people on the ground were killed.

- World Trade Center (1993)—a car bomb explosion in the underground garage killed six people and injured approximately 1,000. U.S. authorities blamed the followers of an Egyptian cleric living in the United States: Umar Abdel Rahman (1938–).

- Khobar Towers, Dhahran, Saudi Arabia (1996)—several terrorist groups claimed responsibility for bombing a housing facility for U.S. troops. Nineteen U.S. military personnel were killed and 515 were wounded.

- U.S. embassies, Nairobi, Kenya, and Dar es Salaam, Tanzania (1998)—bombs exploded nearly simultaneously at the embassies, killing 301 people and injuring thousands. Al Qaeda and bin Laden were blamed for the attacks.

- USS *Cole*, Aden, Yemen (2000)—a small explosives-laden boat rammed the U.S. destroyer and killed 17 American personnel and wounded 39. Al Qaeda was blamed for the incident.

- World Trade Center, New York City, and Pentagon, Arlington, Virginia (2001)—three hijacked planes piloted by terrorists were flown into these buildings. A fourth plane crashed before reaching its target, and all aboard were killed. In total, over 2,700 people, primarily Americans, were killed. Al Qaeda was blamed for the attacks.

- Nightclubs in Bali, Indonesia (2002)—an FTO linked to al Qaeda conducted bombings that killed 202 people, mostly foreign tourists.

More recent terrorist events include the following:

- Trains in Madrid, Spain (2004)—the Moroccan Islamic Combatant Group, an FTO linked to al Qaeda, bombed several commuter trains during morning rush hour. Nearly 200 people were killed and hundreds more were injured.

- Subway and bus in London, England (2005)—suicide bombers struck the mass transit system in different locations during morning rush hour. Over 50 people were killed and hundreds more were injured. According to the British government, in *Report of the Official Account of the Bombings in London on 7th July 2005* (May 11, 2006, http://www.official-documents .co.uk/document/hc0506/hc10/1087/1087.pdf), the bombings were carried out by four young Muslim men with extremist views.

- Multiple targets in Mumbai, India (2008)—10 heavily armed men stormed numerous facilities, including hotels, a hospital, a railway station, a Jewish center, and a café, leaving 174 dead and hundreds more wounded. Six Americans were among the dead. The attack was blamed on Lashkar-e Tayyiba.

- U.S. consulate in Benghazi, Libya (2012)—four Americans, including the U.S. ambassador to Libya, died after armed militants stormed the consulate on the 11th anniversary of the September 11, 2001, terrorist attacks. As noted earlier in this chapter, the attackers were believed to be members of the AQIM, Ansar al-Sharia, the AQAP, and the Mohammad Jamal Network.

THWARTED ATTEMPTS. Besides the completed terrorist acts described in this chapter, there have been several major unsuccessful attempts since the 1990s in which the terrorists were thwarted by law enforcement or otherwise failed to complete their missions. The following are a few of the unsuccessful attacks:

- In 1994 a terrorist cell in the Philippines led by the Pakistani Ramzi Ahmed Yousef (1969–) was preparing to bomb nearly a dozen airliners bound from Asia to the United States and to assassinate Pope John Paul II (1920–2005). Yousef was the mastermind behind the 1993 bombing of the World Trade Center and the nephew of Khalid Shaikh Mohammed (1964–), a top al Qaeda figure believed to have overseen the 9/11 terrorist attacks. Both men were eventually captured by law enforcement.

- In December 1999 Ahmed Ressam (1967–) was caught trying to enter Port Angeles, Washington, near a Canadian border crossing, with a car full of explosives. Authorities believe the man was acting under al Qaeda orders to bomb targets during New Year's Eve celebrations.

- In December 2001 a Briton named Richard Colvin Reid (1973–) was on a commercial airliner flying from Paris to Miami, Florida, when he tried to set off explosives hidden in his shoes. He was thwarted and overpowered by people aboard the plane and turned over to authorities. Reid was dubbed by the media as the "shoe bomber."

- In August 2006 British police captured two dozen suspects in England who were accused of planning to blow up as many as 10 planes bound from Europe to the United States. The plot centered on the use of liquid explosives hidden in carry-on items, such as sports drinks.

- In December 2009 Umar Farouk Abdulmutallab (1986–) was on a commercial airliner flying from Amsterdam, Netherlands, to Detroit, Michigan, when he tried to ignite explosives hidden in his underwear as the plane came in for a landing. The explosives did not detonate, and he was subdued by passengers and crew members. The Nigerian-born conspirator allegedly had ties to al Qaeda operatives in Yemen. Abdulmutallab's father had warned U.S. officials in Nigeria only a month before that his son had radical Islamic beliefs.

- In May 2010 street vendors alerted police to a smoking sport-utility vehicle that was parked in the busy Times Square area of New York City. The vehicle was packed with explosives, which failed to detonate. Officials arrested Faisal Shahzad (1979–) as he tried to flee the country and charged him with the attempted attack. Born in Pakistan, Shahzad had become an American citizen in 2009 and reportedly had been trained by terrorist operatives in Pakistan.

9/11 Terrorist Attacks

For many Americans and people around the globe, the events of September 11, 2001, were the most stunning terrorist attacks. In one day 19 individuals managed to

FIGURE 3.11

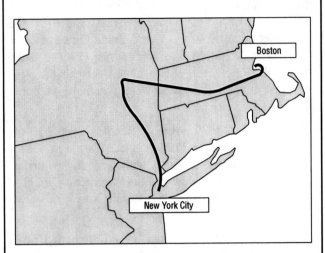

Path of American Airlines Flight 11 on September 11, 2001

SOURCE: Adapted from "American Airlines Flight 11," in *The 9/11 Commission Report*, National Commission on Terrorist Attacks upon the United States, July 22, 2004, http://www.9-11commission.gov/report/911Report.pdf (accessed June 7, 2014)

FIGURE 3.12

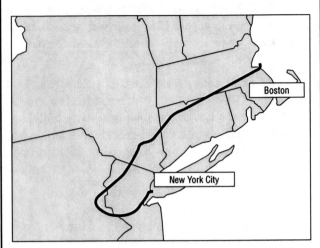

Path of United Airlines Flight 175 on September 11, 2001

SOURCE: Adapted from "United Airlines Flight 175," in *The 9/11 Commission Report*, National Commission on Terrorist Attacks upon the United States, July 22, 2004, http://www.9-11commission.gov/report/911Report.pdf (accessed June 7, 2014)

kill more than 2,700 people and completely destroy the World Trade Center—a center of international commerce and a symbol of U.S. economic power. In July 2004 the National Commission on Terrorist Attacks upon the United States published its findings on the attack in the *9/11 Commission Report*.

The report uses data and information collected from a variety of sources to re-create the events leading up to and occurring on and after 9/11. On the morning of the attacks the 19 terrorists boarded four separate commercial airliners bound from the East Coast to the West Coast. Less than an hour after takeoff of each plane, the hijackers overpowered the cockpit crews and assumed piloting control. Figure 3.11, Figure 3.12, Figure 3.13, and Figure 3.14 show the flight paths of each commandeered plane. American Airlines Flight 11 and United Airlines Flight 175 crashed into the twin towers of the World Trade Center in New York City. American Airlines Flight 77 was flown into the Pentagon in Arlington, Virginia. United Airlines Flight 93 crashed into a field near Shanksville, Pennsylvania, after passengers stormed the cockpit. The hijackers' target for that plane is believed to have been the U.S. Capitol in Washington, D.C.

All the hijackers were from the Middle East; 16 of them were Saudi nationals. According to the report, six of the men were "lead operatives" who represented the most intelligent and best trained of the team. Four of these men piloted the hijacked planes after having studied for months at American flight schools. The lead operatives lived in the United States for up to a year before the day of the attacks. Thirteen of the men were so-called

muscle hijackers, who were selected to assist in overpowering the flight crew and passengers. They arrived in the United States only months before the attacks after undergoing extensive training at al Qaeda terrorist camps in Afghanistan.

All the terrorists were selected for the operation because of their willingness to martyr themselves for the Islamist cause espoused by bin Laden. However, the commission found that only a handful of people within al Qaeda knew the details and scope of the hijack plan before it was carried out.

Domestic Counterterrorism Cases

Domestic counterterrorism cases involve terrorist crimes that were attempted or committed against targets and/or people within the United States. The following are a few of the major cases:

• 1993 World Trade Center Bombers—the Federal Bureau of Investigation (FBI) investigated the 1993 bombing of the World Trade Center, which resulted in the convictions of six terrorists, including the ringleader, Ramzi Ahmed Yousef. In 1998 Yousef was sentenced to life in prison plus 240 years for his role in the bombing. Yousef had also put a bomb aboard a Filipino airliner in 1994 and masterminded a foiled plot that same year to blow up nearly a dozen airliners bound from Asia to the United States.

• Zacarias Moussaoui (1968–)—in August 2001 the FBI arrested Moussaoui for an immigration violation. He had been attending flight school in Minnesota and

FIGURE 3.13

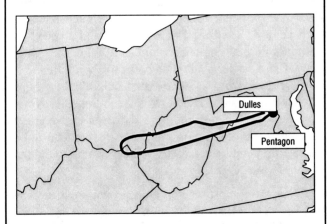

Path of American Airlines Flight 77 on September 11, 2001

SOURCE: Adapted from "American Airlines Flight 77," in *The 9/11 Commission Report*, National Commission on Terrorist Attacks upon the United States, July 22, 2004, http://www.9-11commission.gov/report/911Report.pdf (accessed June 7, 2014)

FIGURE 3.14

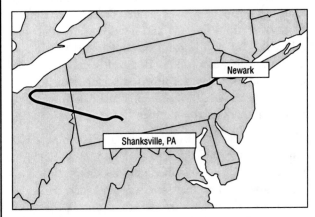

Path of United Airlines Flight 93 on September 11, 2001

SOURCE: Adapted from "United Airlines Flight 93," in *The 9/11 Commission Report*, National Commission on Terrorist Attacks upon the United States, July 22, 2004, http://www.9-11commission.gov/report/911Report.pdf (accessed June 9, 2014)

had aroused suspicions by his odd behavior. After 9/11 the FBI held Moussaoui as a material witness, believing that he was supposed to be the so-called 20th hijacker. He was charged with conspiring to commit terrorist acts. In May 2006 he was sentenced to life in prison.

- Lackawanna Six—this group of American citizens of Yemeni descent was accused of going to Afghanistan in early 2001 to support the Taliban and receive terrorist training at al Qaeda camps. In 2002 they were arrested by the FBI in Lackawanna, New York, and subsequently tried and convicted of supporting an FTO. Each received a sentence of between seven and 10 years in prison. A seventh conspirator was eventually arrested in Yemen and sentenced to prison.

- Portland Seven—this cell operated out of Portland, Oregon, and included six men and one woman accused of conspiring against U.S. troops in Afghanistan. All the men had tried to enter Afghanistan in 2001, but only one was successful. He was subsequently killed by Pakistani troops at an al Qaeda training camp. The remaining six were arrested in the United States in 2002 and received varying sentences. Most of the cell members were American citizens.

- Iyman Faris (1969–)—Faris was a naturalized American citizen born in Kashmir. In 2003 he was arrested and charged with conspiring with al Qaeda to commit terrorism in the United States. He worked as a truck driver in Ohio and is believed to have been scoping out potential targets for terrorist attacks. Faris pleaded guilty and was sentenced to 20 years in prison.

- Northern Virginia Jihad—this network included 11 men of varying nationalities who were accused of operating a terrorist network in northern Virginia that supported the Taliban and Lashkar-e Tayyiba and conspired to wage war against the United States. A series of trials in 2004 resulted in convictions and sentences of various lengths for nine of the men. Two of the accused were acquitted.

- Lodi network—soon after 9/11 the FBI began investigating a mosque in Lodi, California, for alleged links between two Pakistani imams (spiritual leaders) and their followers with al Qaeda. The two imams were detained on immigration violations and ultimately left the country under threat of deportation. In early 2006 two members of the Lodi community, a father and son, were tried for terrorism charges. The father pleaded guilty to a lesser immigration charge. The son was convicted for attending a terrorist training camp in Pakistan and lying about it to the FBI.

- Fort Dix Conspirators—in May 2007 six Muslim men from New Jersey and Pennsylvania were arrested and charged with planning a terrorist attack against Fort Dix, a U.S. Army base in New Jersey. The men had collected an arsenal of weapons and hoped to kill as many soldiers as possible during the attack. In December 2008 five of the men were convicted of conspiracy to commit terrorism, but were acquitted of attempted murder charges. Four of the five received life sentences; the fifth man received a sentence of 33 years in prison. The sixth man pleaded guilty in early 2008 to firearms charges and was sentenced to 20 months in prison. He was released from prison in March 2009.

- JFK Terror Plot—in June 2007 four men were arrested for conspiring to blow fuel supply lines and tanks at the John F. Kennedy International Airport in New York City. One of the men, an American citizen from Guyana, formerly worked at the airport. His conspirators were from Guyana and Trinidad. All four were allegedly part of a Muslim extremist network. In June 2010 one of the conspirators pleaded guilty to lesser charges in exchange for a prison sentence of no more than 15 years. In 2011 and early 2012 the other three men were convicted and given life sentences.

- New York City Subway Plot—in September 2009 authorities arrested three Afghan natives and charged them with plotting suicide bombings on the New York City subway. The men allegedly planned to set off backpack bombs on crowded trains during the morning rush hour. The plot was reportedly ordered by senior al Qaeda leaders in Pakistan who were later killed by U.S. drones. In early 2010 two of the accused pleaded guilty to the charges; the third man pleaded not guilty, but was convicted in May 2012 based on the testimony of his coconspirators.

- Fort Hood Shooting—in November 2009 Nidal Malik Hasan (1970?–), a U.S. Army psychiatrist, was arrested for allegedly shooting over 40 people during a rampage at the Fort Hood Army Base in Killeen, Texas. Thirteen of the victims died. Hasan was shot by military police officers. He survived but was paralyzed from the chest down. In August 2013 he was convicted on 45 counts of premeditated murder and sentenced to death. As of August 2014, he was appealing the sentence.

- Boston Marathon—in April 2013 two bombs exploded near the finish line of the Boston Marathon killing three people and injuring more than 200 others. One of the alleged perpetrators, Tamerlan Tsarnaev (1987?–2013), was killed during the ensuing manhunt. His brother, Dzhokhar Tsarnaev (1993–), was eventually apprehended by authorities. The brothers were of Chechnyan ethnicity, although neither ever lived in Chechnya, which is a troubled Russian republic located in the northern Caucasus region. According to Michael Cooper, Michael S. Schmidt, and Eric Schmitt, in "Boston Suspects Are Seen as Self-Taught and Fueled by Web" (NYTimes.com, April 23, 2013), U.S. officials believe the brothers "were motivated by extremist Islamic beliefs but were not acting with known terrorist groups." As of August 2014, Dzhokhar Tsarnaev's trial was scheduled to begin in November 2014. If convicted, he faced the death penalty.

HOMEGROWN TERRORISTS. Before 2009 very few U.S. citizens were accused or convicted of terrorist attacks against American people or targets. A notable exception was Timothy McVeigh (1968–2001), a New York native and antigovernment zealot who was executed in 2001 for the 1995 bombing of a federal building in Oklahoma that killed more than 160 people and wounded hundreds more. Beginning in 2009 a number of people who were either born in the United States or had become U.S. citizens were charged and arrested for plotting or committing terrorist attacks within the United States. These suspects are often collectively referred to as "homegrown terrorists." Dozens of individuals, groups, and terrorist plots and attacks have been linked to homegrown terrorists. Some of these terrorists converted to Islam from other religions and became radicalized—meaning they embraced a very radical Islamic view that condones violence.

Perhaps the most wanted homegrown terrorist as of 2014 was Adam Gadahn (1978–). He grew up in California in a Catholic and Jewish family. During the mid-1990s he converted to Islam and moved to Pakistan, where he became affiliated with al Qaeda. He appeared in numerous al Qaeda videos calling on Muslims to wage violent jihad against Jews and their supporters. In 2006 Gadahn was indicted in the United States for treason and for providing material support to al Qaeda. A charge of treason is very serious and very rare. Prior to 2006 it had been more than 50 years since anyone has been charged with treason. As of August 2014, Gadahn remained at large. There was a $1 million reward for information leading to his capture.

U.S. PUBLIC OPINION ON TERRORISM

As shown in Table 1.6 in Chapter 1, a poll conducted by the Gallup Organization in February 2014 found that Americans rated international terrorism the most critical threat to the vital interests of the United States. More than three-quarters (77%) of those asked shared this opinion. Table 3.3 compares these results with those obtained during earlier Gallup polls. Since 2004 large majorities

TABLE 3.3

Public opinion on the threat of international terrorism to the United States over the next decade, February 2014

	% Critical threat	% Important, not critical
Feb 6–9, 2014	77	19
Feb 7–10, 2013	81	17
Feb 1–3, 2010	81	16
Feb 9–12, 2004	82	16

SOURCE: Jeff Jones and Lydia Saad, "21. Next, I am going to read you a list of possible threats to the vital interests of the United States in the next 10 years. For each one, please tell me if see this as a critical threat, an important but not critical threat, or not an important threat at all: International terrorism," in *Gallup Poll Social Series: World Affairs—Final Topline*, The Gallup Organization, February 6–9, 2014, http://www.gallup.com/file/poll/167678/Americas_Greatest_Threats_140228%20.pdf (accessed June 7, 2014). Copyright © 2014 Gallup, Inc. All rights reserved. The content is used with permission; however, Gallup retains all rights of republication.

FIGURE 3.15

Public perceptions about the likelihood of terrorism in the United States, 2001–13

HOW LIKELY IS IT THAT THERE WILL BE ACTS OF TERRORISM IN THE UNITED STATES OVER THE NEXT SEVERAL WEEKS—VERY LIKELY, SOMEWHAT LIKELY, NOT TOO LIKELY, OR NOT AT ALL LIKELY?

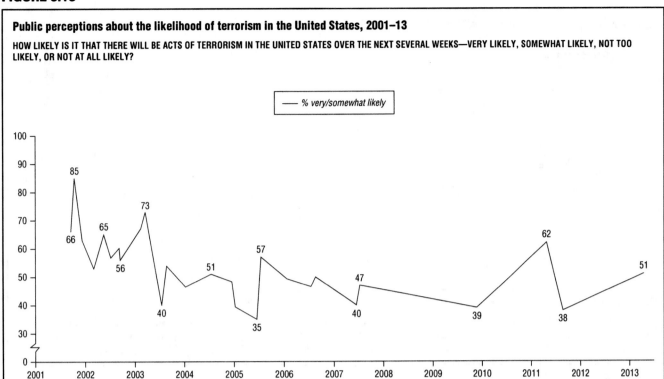

SOURCE: Lydia Saad, "Perceived Likelihood of Acts of Terrorism Occurring in Next Few Weeks," in *Post-Boston, Half in U.S. Anticipate More Terrorism Soon*, The Gallup Organization, April 26, 2013, http://www.gallup.com/poll/162074/post-boston-half-anticipate-terrorism-soon.aspx (accessed June 7, 2014). Copyright © 2013 Gallup, Inc. All rights reserved. The content is used with permission; however, Gallup retains all rights of republication.

of respondents have deemed international terrorism a critical threat to U.S. interests.

Since 9/11 the possibility of new terrorist attacks on U.S. soil has been a source of concern for many Americans. Polling, however, shows that this concern has decreased over time as no new large-scale attack has been successfully completed. Figure 3.15 shows the results of a Gallup poll in which respondents were asked "how likely is it that there will be acts of terrorism in the United States over the next several weeks." In late 2001, 85% of those asked felt that such attacks are very or somewhat likely to occur. By September 2011 that percentage had dropped to 38%. Nevertheless, it rose to 51% in April 2013 following the Boston Marathon bombing, which was described earlier.

The Gallup Organization also asks Americans how they feel about the nation's security from terrorism. As shown in Figure 3.16, in April 2013 a majority (70%) of those asked expressed a "great deal/fair amount" of confidence that the U.S. government can protect its citizens from future acts of terrorism. This value was down from a high of 88% in late 2001.

FIGURE 3.16

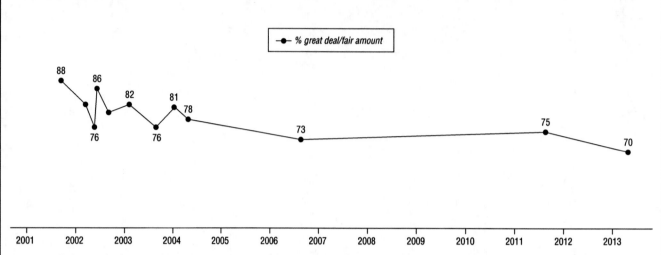

Public confidence in the U.S. government's ability to protect its citizens from terrorism, 2001–13

HOW MUCH CONFIDENCE DO YOU HAVE IN THE U.S. GOVERNMENT TO PROTECT ITS CITIZENS FROM FUTURE ACTS OF TERRORISM—A GREAT DEAL, A FAIR AMOUNT, NOT VERY MUCH, OR NONE AT ALL?

SOURCE: Lydia Saad, "Confidence in U.S. Government to Protect Citizens from Terrorism," in *Post-Boston, Half in U.S. Anticipate More Terrorism Soon*, The Gallup Organization, April 26, 2013, http://www.gallup.com/poll/162074/post-boston-half-anticipate-terrorism-soon.aspx (accessed June 7, 2014). Copyright © 2013 Gallup, Inc. All rights reserved. The content is used with permission; however, Gallup retains all rights of republication.

CHAPTER 4
THE WARS IN AFGHANISTAN AND IRAQ

The United States' immediate response to the terrorist attacks of September 11, 2001 (9/11), was to invade Afghanistan. The goal was twofold: capture or kill Osama bin Laden (1957?–2011; the mastermind of the attacks) and the other members of the al Qaeda terrorist organization and overthrow the Taliban government, which was harboring and supporting al Qaeda. The invasion was a resounding military success. The repressive Taliban government was defeated and replaced by a more liberal, U.S.-friendly regime. Major terrorist training camps were destroyed and many members of al Qaeda were captured or forced to flee. The victory was not complete, however, because bin Laden was neither captured nor killed right away. Furthermore, the Taliban and its supporters remained active and continued to wage a surprisingly strong insurgency (resistance) against the occupying forces. As of August 2014, U.S. troops continued to serve as part of an international military force intended to help bring stability to the war-torn country.

In 2003 the United States invaded Iraq. One of the drivers was assessments from the U.S. intelligence community that Iraq had collaborated with al Qaeda and was amassing weapons of mass destruction (WMDs). These claims were later proved to be inaccurate. The U.S. military operation in Iraq was at first successful. The longtime Iraqi dictator Saddam Hussein (1937–2006) was ousted from power, and a new, more democratic government was slowly installed. A fierce insurgency, however, erupted, driven by Hussein supporters and militant elements opposed to the occupation. The violence soon widened into a bitter and deadly civil struggle between Iraqi factions divided by religious and political differences. By 2008 the worst of the insurgency was over, and the United States withdrew all of its combat troops from Iraq by the end of 2011. However, the security situation has deteriorated dramatically since then with the country plagued by civil unrest and terrorist activities.

AFGHANISTAN

Afghanistan is a landlocked country in south-central Asia. Its largest neighbors are Pakistan to the east and south and Iran to the west. (See Figure 4.1.) Turkmenistan, Uzbekistan, and Tajikistan border Afghanistan to the north. Its capital is Kabul. The Central Intelligence Agency (CIA) indicates in *The World Factbook: Afghanistan* (June 24, 2014, https://www.cia.gov/library/publications/the-world-factbook/geos/af.html) that Afghanistan covers 251,800 square miles (652,230 square km) and is slightly smaller than the state of Texas. Its population was estimated at 31.8 million in 2014. According to the CIA, the largest ethnic groups are the Pashtun (42%) and Tajik (27%). Approximately 80% of Afghans are Sunni Muslims, 19% are Shia Muslims, and the remaining 1% practice other religions. The official name of the country is the Islamic Republic of Afghanistan. It includes dozens of provinces, as shown in Figure 4.2.

A Legacy of War

The history of Afghanistan revolves around an ancient group of people called the Pashtun. As described by the article "Peoples: Pashtun" (NationalGeographic.com, July 2005), the Pashtun have lived in this region for centuries and have survived conquest by many invaders, including the Persians, Macedonians, Turks, and Mongols. They have earned a reputation as being fierce fighters. However, the Pashtun are also known for in-fighting and waging blood feuds among themselves. They are a group of tribes that together make up the largest surviving tribal society in the world. They adhere to an ancient strict code of conduct called *pakhtunwalimale* that specifies rules for all areas of society and everyday life. The Pashtun were known by the Persian term *Afghan* long before their land was called Afghanistan.

Afghanistan's Islamic history dates back to the seventh century and is described by the Library of Congress

FIGURE 4.1

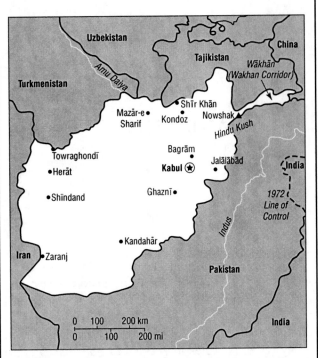

Map of Afghanistan, 2014

SOURCE: "Map of Afghanistan," in "South Asia: Afghanistan," *The World Factbook*, Central Intelligence Agency, April 11, 2014, https://www.cia.gov/library/publications/the-world-factbook/geos/af.html (accessed June 7, 2014)

(LOC) in *A Country Study: Afghanistan* (March 22, 2011, http://lcweb2.loc.gov/frd/cs/aftoc.html). In 637 Muslims from the Arab empire invaded the region and maintained power for several centuries. The LOC notes that "from the seventh through the ninth centuries, most inhabitants of what is present-day Afghanistan, Pakistan, southern parts of the former Soviet Union, and areas of northern India were converted to Sunni Islam."

In *World Factbook: Afghanistan*, the CIA reports that the founding of modern Afghanistan occurred in 1747, when warring Pashtun tribes were united under one leader. At that time the British Empire ruled the land to the east (India and modern-day Pakistan) and the Russians controlled Turkmenistan, Uzbekistan, and Tajikistan to the north. British and Afghan rulers warred over control of Afghanistan until 1919, when the country won its independence. What followed was a series of monarchies that culminated in a coup in 1978, which led to the installation of a highly unpopular communist government. In 1979 the Soviet Union invaded Afghanistan to prevent a brewing revolution and preserve communist rule. The Soviets waged a decade-long war but were driven out by well-armed rebels who called themselves the mujahideen (holy warriors).

Mujahideen and bin Laden

The mujahideen were young Muslims who came from around the world to fight against the Soviet forces as part of a jihad (holy war). In 1980 a wealthy young man named Osama bin Laden traveled from his homeland in Saudi Arabia to help the mujahideen. His role is described at length by the National Commission on Terrorist Attacks upon the United States in *The 9/11 Commission Report* (July 2004, http://www.9-11commission.gov/report/911Report.pdf). Bin Laden's specialty was raising money and recruiting volunteers, who came to be known as the Arab Afghans. He excelled at organizing fund-raising networks that included charities and wealthy donors throughout the world. These funds were used to buy arms and provide training for the Arab Afghans.

The United States, anxious to see its communist enemy defeated in Afghanistan, supported the mujahideen in its efforts. The *9/11 Commission Report* notes that the United States and Saudi Arabia secretly supplied billions of dollars' worth of weapons and equipment to the mujahideen through Pakistani military intelligence. However, there is no record of U.S. involvement with bin Laden or the Arab Afghans, who had their own funding sources. In 1988 the Soviets decided to withdraw from Afghanistan in the face of unrelenting resistance from the mujahideen. Bin Laden and his compatriots were reluctant to dismantle their well-funded and highly trained organization, so they decided to maintain it for future jihads. They began calling it al Qaeda, which means "the base" or "the foundation." In 1991 they set up operations in Sudan at the invitation of that country's leader and maintained camps in Afghanistan and Pakistan to train young militant Muslims as jihadists.

The Taliban and bin Laden

The demise of the communist government in Afghanistan left a power vacuum. Rival mujahideen factions began fighting for control. In *A Country Study: Afghanistan*, the LOC describes these events and notes that during the Soviet occupation the mujahideen were often described in the Western press as "'freedom fighters'— as if their goal were to establish a representative democracy in Afghanistan—in reality these groups each had agendas of their own that were often far from democratic." Civil war wracked the country until the mid-1990s, when a new political-military force—the Taliban—achieved power. The LOC points out that most members of the Taliban were Pashtun who attended or had recently graduated from religious schools called madrassas in southern Afghanistan and Pakistan.

According to the *9/11 Commission Report*, madrassas are privately funded religious schools that teach strict fundamentalist forms of Islam. Beginning in the 1970s the schools started appearing in southern Pakistan because

FIGURE 4.2

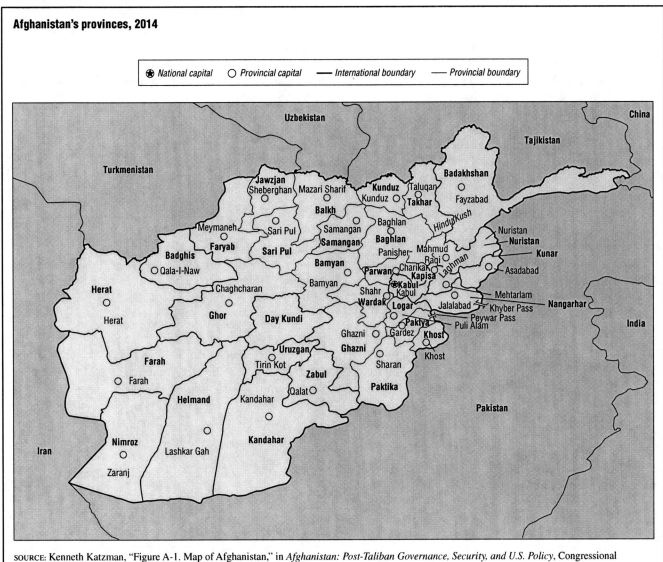

⊛ National capital   ○ Provincial capital   — International boundary   — Provincial boundary

SOURCE: Kenneth Katzman, "Figure A-1. Map of Afghanistan," in *Afghanistan: Post-Taliban Governance, Security, and U.S. Policy*, Congressional Research Service, April 9, 2014, https://www.fas.org/sgp/crs/row/RL30588.pdf (accessed June 7, 2014)

the government could not afford to educate the many Afghan refugees who had fled there to escape the violence in their own country. The report notes that "these schools produced large numbers of half-educated young men with no marketable skills but with deeply held Islamic views." Eventually, Pakistan became concerned about the presence of so many militant young men within its borders, so it encouraged them to return to Afghanistan and restore order there.

By 1996 the Taliban had seized control over most of Afghanistan. In May of that year bin Laden moved the bulk of his al Qaeda organization from Sudan back to Afghanistan. By this time he had enlarged his focus from regional Islamic causes to what the *9/11 Commission Report* calls "hatred of the United States." This development could be traced back to the 1990 Iraqi invasion of Kuwait. At that time bin Laden reportedly approached Saudi rulers and offered to organize a mujahideen force to drive out the Iraqis, but was turned down. Saudi Arabia allied with the United States during the subsequent Persian Gulf War (1990–1991) and allowed U.S. troops to deploy from Saudi soil. This decision infuriated Islamic fundamentalists because they opposed the presence of nonbelievers in Saudi Arabia, the birthplace of Muhammad (c. 570–632). After criticizing Saudi leaders, bin Laden had his passport taken away. However, he managed to leave the country in 1991 and eventually turned up in Afghanistan, where he enjoyed the protection of the Taliban leader Mohammed Omar (1959?–). The two men had long-standing ties, as both had fought against the Soviet occupation of Afghanistan during the 1980s.

Throughout the 1990s bin Laden expanded his al Qaeda network with the blessing of the Afghan Taliban regime. In 1998 he publicly announced his intention to wage a jihad against the United States by issuing a fatwa (an interpretation of Islamic law usually written by a scholar or religious authority) that was published in an Arabic-language newspaper in London. As described in Chapter 3, al Qaeda operatives then carried out a series of attacks against U.S. interests, including the 1998 bombings at two U.S. embassies in Africa, the 2000 bombing of the USS *Cole* in Yemen, and 9/11.

THE INVASION OF AFGHANISTAN

According to the *9/11 Commission Report*, on the evening of the 9/11 attacks President George W. Bush (1946–) addressed the nation about the tragedy and warned, "We will make no distinction between the terrorists who committed these acts and those who harbor them." The United States quickly identified the 9/11 hijackers as al Qaeda operatives under the control of bin Laden and determined that Afghanistan was harboring them.

U.S. View of the Taliban

Peter L. Bergen claims in *Holy War, Inc.: Inside the Secret World of Osama bin Laden* (2001) that the U.S. government was optimistic about the Taliban when it first seized power in Afghanistan, but quickly became disillusioned. Bergen notes the Taliban imposed laws that blended "ultrapurist" Islam with traditional Pashtun customs. The result was a society in which men were forbidden to shave or trim their beards. All forms of entertainment, such as listening to the radio or flying a kite, were outlawed. Women were forced to cover themselves with thick head-to-toe cloaks called burkas and were not allowed in public unless accompanied by a male relative. Most women were forbidden to work or obtain an education. Taliban laws were enforced by religious police who roamed the streets and beat violators with sticks. By this time the Afghan people had suffered from decades of war that had destroyed most of the country's infrastructure; their economy was in shambles and food was in short supply.

In 1999 and 2000 the United Nations (UN) Security Council imposed economic sanctions against Afghanistan for a variety of infractions, including providing sanctuary to and training international terrorists, particularly bin Laden and his associates. In December 2000 the UN demanded that bin Laden be surrendered and that all terrorist training camps be closed within a month. The Taliban angrily refused to comply, insisting that there was no evidence against bin Laden and that the sanctions were motivated by anti-Islamic sentiment.

Operation Enduring Freedom Begins

Within days after 9/11, the United States had decided to target Afghanistan. In an address to Congress on September 20, 2001, President Bush publicly blamed al Qaeda and bin Laden for the attacks and demanded that the Taliban hand over bin Laden and his top lieutenants

or the United States would strike. According to the *9/11 Commission Report*, the demands had already been privately passed to the Taliban through the Pakistani government, which the United States had warned "would be at risk" unless it helped the United States against Afghanistan. As expected, Afghanistan refused to comply with U.S. demands.

By October 2001 a U.S. war plan had been compiled that was originally called Infinite Justice. However, fears about offending religious sensibilities prompted a quick name change to Operation Enduring Freedom (OEF) when U.S. officials learned that Muslims associate the term *infinite justice* with God's power. The *9/11 Commission Report* indicates that the OEF had four phases:

- Phase one—deploy U.S. forces to Afghanistan's neighbors in readiness for an invasion. This step was begun almost immediately and entailed the cooperation of Pakistan and Uzbekistan.

- Phase two—conduct air strikes on Afghan targets and pair special operations teams with Taliban opposition groups to conduct damaging raids on al Qaeda strongholds. Even before this time, the CIA had been collaborating with opposition groups in northern Afghanistan known collectively as the Northern Alliance. Phase two began on October 7, 2001, and proceeded quickly with the help of United Kingdom (UK) military forces. By the end of the month most of the objectives of this phase had been achieved.

- Phase three—launch a ground invasion of Afghanistan to "topple the Taliban regime and eliminate al Qaeda's sanctuary." By early December 2001 the coalition of U.S. and Northern Alliance forces, with the assistance of UK military forces, had captured all major Afghan cities. However, bin Laden and Omar escaped.

- Phase four—the United States called this phase "security and stability operations." It began on December 22, 2001, when Hamid Karzai (1957–; an Afghani Pashtun) was installed as the head of the nation's interim government. U.S. and allied forces began training the Afghan National Security Forces (ANSF) to provide national security for the country.

Insurgency Drags out the War

As Afghanistan initiated a series of democratic reforms, it was plagued by violence waged by Taliban fighters and their supporters. The insurgents proved tenacious and found safe harbor and support in the desolate mountainous regions of eastern Afghanistan and western Pakistan.

According to the LOC, in *Country Profile: Afghanistan* (August 2008, http://lcweb2.loc.gov/frd/cs/profiles/Afghanistan.pdf), Taliban fighters involved in the insurgency were crossing in and out of neighboring Pakistan to elude U.S. and allied forces. The U.S. Government Accountability Office (GAO) explains in *Afghanistan's Security Environment* (May 5, 2010, http://www.gao.gov/new.items/d10613r.pdf) that "the insurgency [was] facilitated by several factors, including the porous nature of the Afghanistan-Pakistan border region, the ineffective nature of governance and services in various parts of Afghanistan, assistance from militant groups outside of Pakistan and Afghanistan, and continued financial support in the form of narcotics trafficking revenue and funds from outside of the region."

Meanwhile, the UN had spearheaded the formation of a multinational military force called the International Security Assistance Force (ISAF). U.S. troops made up the vast majority of the ISAF and also continued to operate the OEF in Afghanistan. In 2003 the North Atlantic Treaty Organization (NATO) assumed control of the ISAF under UN mandate and at the request of the Afghan government. In 2004 the first Afghan presidential election put Karzai in power for a five-year term. Although the election itself was relatively violence-free, the country continued to struggle with internal problems. In 2006 there was an upswing in militant violence in Afghanistan, particularly in the southern part of the country. Insurgent attacks on ISAF, OEF, and ANSF forces and on civilians increased dramatically. By 2009 the attacks had reached a wartime high. During that year Karzai was reelected; however, there were widespread allegations of voter fraud and intimidation.

The United States responded to the growing insurgency by sending several thousand more troops to Afghanistan, both under the auspices of the ISAF and the OEF. The forces engaged in more air strikes and raids against suspected insurgent camps and hideouts. However, this aggressive approach resulted in highly publicized deaths of Afghan civilians. For example, the article "NATO Strike Kills 27 Afghanistan Civilians" (BBCNews.com, February 22, 2010) lists a series of "botched" air raids that occurred between July 2008 and September 2009 and reportedly killed nearly 350 civilians. Although U.S. and NATO leaders claimed the number of civilian deaths in these strikes was lower than the numbers reported by the media, Afghan officials insisted that the numbers were even higher.

The situation in Afghanistan continued to worsen. In August 2009 General Stanley A. McChrystal (1954–), the commander of the ISAF and the OEF, presented a bleak outlook in his assessment report *Commander's Initial Assessment* (http://media.washingtonpost.com/wp-srv/politics/documents/Assessment_Redacted_092109.pdf?hpid=topnews). McChrystal noted, "Although considerable effort and sacrifice have resulted in some progress, many indicators suggest the overall effort is deteriorating." He cited numerous problems including the growing insurgency, corruption in the Afghan government, poor performance by the ISAF, and lack of confidence of the general population in the national government. McChrystal called for more troops to be sent to the battlefield.

President Barack Obama (1961–) was under pressure from his liberal supporters to end U.S. involvement in the war and from conservatives to escalate the war. In December 2009 he attempted to appease both sides by announcing that 30,000 additional U.S. troops would be deployed to Afghanistan by the summer of 2010. However, he also said that the United States would begin withdrawing its forces in July 2011.

The 2014 Deadline

On June 7, 2010, the 104-month war in Afghanistan became the longest-running war in U.S. history. In *Afghanistan Index* (May 16, 2012, http://www.brookings.edu/~/media/programs/foreign%20policy/afghanistan%20index/index20120516.pdf), Ian S. Livingston and Michael O'Hanlon of the Brookings Institution track the number of foreign troops deployed to Afghanistan over time. Troop strength grew gradually between 2001 and mid-2009 to around 70,000. Over the next two years this number skyrocketed, reaching an estimated 140,000 foreign troops by mid-2011. Approximately 100,000 of these troops were from the United States. The enormous troop presence brought a measure of stability to Afghanistan. Talks between NATO and Afghan leaders culminated in a plan to fully transfer responsibility for the nation's security to the ANSF by the end of 2014. Meanwhile, the United States and Afghanistan reached a separate agreement allowing U.S. military forces to have access to Afghan facilities through year-end 2014.

The ISAF's role in Afghanistan began to change dramatically as the 2014 deadline approached. In July 2013 the U.S. Department of Defense (DOD) stated in *Progress toward Security and Stability in Afghanistan* (http://www.defense.gov/pubs/Section_1230_Report_July_2013.pdf) that the "ISAF's primary focus has largely transitioned from directly fighting the insurgency to training, advising and assisting the Afghan National Security Forces (ANSF)." Foreign troop levels in Afghanistan began declining dramatically. According to NATO, in "International Security Assistance Force (ISAF): Key Facts and Figures" (http://www.isaf.nato.int/images/media/20140603_isaf-placemat-final.pdf), as of June 1, 2014, there were 49,902 troops from 48 nations in the ISAF. The largest contingents were from the United States (32,800 troops), the United Kingdom (5,200 troops), and Italy (2,000 troops).

In 2013 the United States and Afghanistan negotiated an agreement that would allow U.S. military troops to operate within Afghanistan after 2014. Officially called the Security and Defense Cooperation Agreement between the United States of America and the Islamic Republic of Afghanistan, it is more commonly known as the Bilateral Security Agreement (BSA). In *Report on Progress toward Security and Stability in Afghanistan* (April 2014, http://www.defense.gov/pubs/April_1230 _Report_Final.pdf), the DOD notes that the BSA received the "overwhelming endorsement" of a Loya Jirga (an Afghan assembly of decision makers) in November 2013. However, President Karzai refused to sign the agreement. He argued that the decision should be left to his predecessor who was to be elected in 2014. This unexpected development caused much consternation for the U.S. government, which strongly desired a troop presence in Afghanistan beyond 2014 for counterterrorism purposes.

The U.S. government believes the ANSF needs further foreign support to succeed. The DOD states, "Although the International Security Assistance Force (ISAF) continues to develop capabilities, ANSF requires more time and effort to close four key high-end capability gaps that will remain after the ISAF mission ends on December 31, 2014: air support; intelligence enterprise; special operations; and Afghan security ministry capacity. International funding and coalition force assistance will be critical to sustaining the force after 2014." Table 4.1 provides some statistics about the security situation in Afghanistan as of 2014. Although Afghan security force numbers were approaching their target sizes, there were still as many as 25,000 Taliban fighters with which they had to contend.

In April 2014 Afghanistan held its presidential election. Two candidates—Abdullah Abdullah and Ashraf Ghani—each captured enough votes to trigger a runoff election that occurred in June 2014. Both men have said they will sign the BSA if elected. Although there were deep concerns about the ANSF's ability to prevent high-profile attacks during the June election, it proceeded rather smoothly. Ernesto Londoño and Kevin Sieff report in "Afghans Vote in Historic Election amid Attacks, Allegations of Fraud" (WashingtonPost.com, June 14, 2014) that the election was not impeded by "massive attacks," but was "marred by scattered deadly attacks and mounting reports of fraud." Dozens of people were killed, and 11 voters reportedly had their fingers cut off by insurgents.

Soon after the runoff election, allegations arose from both candidates that widespread election fraud had taken place. As tensions mounted, the U.S. secretary of state John Kerry (1943–) brokered a deal that allowed the UN to oversee a recount of the estimated 8 million votes that were cast. Both candidates agreed to abide by the results of the audit. It was hoped the recount would be finished quickly; however, as of August 2014 it had not been completed.

TABLE 4.1

Security statistics for Afghanistan, 2014

Force	Current level
Afghan National Army (ANA)	About 185,000, close to the 195,000 target size that was planned by November 2012. 5,300 are commando forces, trained by U.S. Special Forces.
Afghan National Police (ANP)	About 152,000, close to the target size of 157,000. 21,000 are Border Police; 3,800+ counter-narcotics police; 14,400 Civil Order Police (ANCOP).
ANSF salaries	About $1.6 billion per year, paid by donor countries bilaterally or via trust funds
Al Qaeda in Afghanistan	Between 50–100 members in Afghanistan, according to U.S. commanders. Also, small numbers of Lashkar-e-Tayyiba, Islamic Movement of Uzbekistan, and other Al Qaeda affiliates.
Number of Taliban fighters	Up to 25,000, including about 3,000 Haqqani network and 1,000 HIG.

ANSF = Afghanistan National Security Forces; HIG = Hizb-e-Islam Gulbuddin, an Islamist political faction.

SOURCE: Adapted from Kenneth Katzman, "Table 5. Major Security-Related Indicators," in *Afghanistan: Post-Taliban Governance, Security, and U.S. Policy,* Congressional Research Service, April 9, 2014, https://www.fas.org/sgp/crs/row/RL30588.pdf (accessed June 7, 2014)

Casualties in Afghanistan

FOREIGN MILITARY PERSONNEL. NATO (2014, http://www.isaf.nato.int/article/casualty-report/index.php) publishes a brief notification statement following the death of any ISAF member in Afghanistan. However, the organization does not provide statistics regarding overall ISAF casualties. Some media sources and private organizations do track such statistics. For example, the website iCasualties.org estimates in "Coalition Military Fatalities by Year" (http://icasualties.org/oef) that as of August 2014 there had been 2,341 U.S. deaths, 453 UK deaths, and 672 deaths of military personnel from other countries for a grand total of 3,466 deaths. These figures include deaths from all causes, including accidents.

Table 4.2 is a record of DOD casualties associated with OEF and ISAF operations. As of May 21, 2014, 2,320 personnel had died, including 2,184 troops in Afghanistan. Another 19,772 personnel had been wounded in action. Of the total deaths, 1,818 deaths were attributed to hostile action. Table 4.3 provides demographic details about the personnel who were killed. Most of the deaths were among white male soldiers on active duty. Table 4.4 provides an annual breakdown of the casualty statistics as of May 20, 2014. The years 2010 and 2011 were the most lethal with 437 and 360 deaths, respectively. As noted earlier, these years saw the massive troop surge that the United States implemented to stem the insurgency in Afghanistan.

One of the most disturbing trends in Afghanistan has been the killing of foreign troops by Afghan security forces. The U.S. military calls these "insider attacks."

TABLE 4.2

U.S. Department of Defense (DoD) casualties associated with Operation Enduring Freedom (OEF) as of May 21, 2014

OEF U.S. military casualties	Total deaths	KIA	Non-hostile	Pending	WIA
Afghanistan only[a]	2,184	1,806	378	0	19,600
Other locations[b]	133	11	122	0	172
OEF U.S. DoD civilian casualties	3	1	2		
Worldwide total	**2,320**	**1,818**	**502**	**0**	**19,772**

KIA = killed in action; WIA = wounded in action.
[a]Operation Enduring Freedom (Afghanistan only), includes casualties that occurred in Afghanistan only.
[b]Operation Enduring Freedom (Other locations), includes casualties that occurred in Guantanamo Bay (Cuba), Djibouti, Eritrea, Ethiopia, Jordan, Kenya, Kyrgyzstan, Pakistan, Philippines, Seychelles, Sudan, Tajikistan, Turkey, Uzbekistan, and Yemen. WIA cases in this category include those without a casualty country listed.

SOURCE: Adapted from *Operation Enduring Freedom (OEF) U.S. Casualty Status: Fatalities as of: May 21, 2014, 10 a.m. EDT*, U.S. Department of Defense, May 21, 2014, http://www.defense.gov/news/casualty.pdf (accessed May 21, 2014)

TABLE 4.3

U.S. military deaths in Afghanistan, by category, 2001– May 20, 2014

Casualty type	Total
Hostile	1,817
Non-hostile	500
Total	**2,317**
Gender	
Female	50
Male	2,267
Total	**2,317**
Age	
<22	507
22–24	533
25–30	718
31–35	257
>35	302
Total	**2,317**
Race	
American Indian/Alaska Native	29
Asian	62
Black or African American	189
Native Hawaiian or other Pacific Islander	7
White	1,970
Multiple races	30
Unknown	30
Total	**2,317**

Note: Data are through May 20, 2014.

SOURCE: Adapted from "U.S. Military Casualties—Operation Enduring Freedom (OEF) Military Deaths (as of May 20, 2014)," in *Defense Casualty Analysis System*, U.S. Department of Defense, May 20, 2014, https://www.dmdc.osd.mil/dcas/pages/report_oef_deaths.xhtml (accessed May 21, 2014)

Insider attacks make media headlines, dampen foreign troop morale, and stir foreign public resentment against the war. In *Progress toward Security and Stability in Afghanistan*, the DOD notes that as of March 31, 2013, there had been 102 insider attacks against ISAF personnel resulting in 144 deaths. Another 208 personnel were wounded. Roughly two-thirds of those killed or wounded were U.S. soldiers. The number of insider attacks peaked in 2012, when 48 took place. However, the DOD indicates in *Report on Progress toward Security and Stability in Afghanistan* that the number of insider attacks declined to 15 in 2013. Insider attacks are attributed to a variety of causes. The DOD estimates that about half of the 2012 attacks involved "some level of insurgent links." Other motivators are believed to be "personal grievances, broad cultural conflicts, psychological distress and social pressures."

AFGHAN MILITARY AND SECURITY PERSONNEL. In *Afghanistan Casualties: Military Forces and Civilians* (February 29, 2012, http://assets.opencrs.com/rpts/R41084_20120229.pdf), Susan G. Chesser of the Congressional Research Service (CRS) provides estimates gleaned from various sources about the number of casualties among Afghan military and security personnel. Between 2007 and January 2012 an estimated 2,184 members of the Afghan National Army were killed and 3,568 were wounded. The Afghan police forces (national, local, and border) suffered 3,945 deaths and 4,746 injured.

CIVILIANS. It is difficult to determine the total number of civilians that have been killed or wounded during the long-running war in Afghanistan. The UN, NATO, and U.S. government all publish statistics on civilian casualties; however, the Afghan government and human rights groups generally insist that these estimates are too low. Nevertheless, the statistics provide at least a partial glimpse of the war's toll on the Afghan people.

According to the UN Assistance Mission in Afghanistan (UNAMA) and the UN Office of the High Commissioner for Human Rights, in *Afghanistan Annual Report 2013 Protection of Civilians in Armed Conflict* (February 2014, http://unama.unmissions.org/Portals/UNAMA/human%20rights/Feb_8_2014_PoC-report_2013-Full-report-ENG.pdf), the UNAMA documented 8,615 civilian casualties in Afghanistan in 2013. Of that total, 2,959 people died and 5,656 were injured. These numbers were up from 2012, when the UNAMA documented 7,589 total civilian casualties (2,768 killed and 4,821 injured). Overall, 14,064 civilians lost their lives between 2009 and 2013 due to the war in Afghanistan. The UNAMA attributes 74% of the civilian casualties in 2013 to anti-government elements (insurgents). Another 10% resulted from battles between pro-government and anti-government forces, while 8% were blamed on the ANSF and 3% on international forces. The remaining 5% of the civilian casualties were attributed to encounters by victims with unexploded ordnance.

One of the greatest dangers to civilians (and troops) in Afghanistan is improvised explosive devices (IEDs), which are basically "homemade" bombs planted by

TABLE 4.4

U.S. military casualties in Afghanistan, by year, 2001–May 20, 2014

Year	Hostile deaths	Non-hostile/ pending deaths	All deaths	Wounded in action
2001	3	8	11	33
2002	18	31	49	74
2003	17	28	45	99
2004	25	27	52	217
2005	66	32	98	269
2006	65	33	98	403
2007	83	34	117	749
2008	132	23	155	795
2009	271	40	311	2,146
2010	437	62	499	5,250
2011	360	55	415	5,222
2012	237	76	313	2,966
2013	91	41	132	1,353
2014	12	10	22	196
Totals	**1,817**	**500**	**2,317**	**19,772**

Note: Data for 2014 are through May 20, 2014.

SOURCE: Adapted from "U.S. Military Casualties—Operation Enduring Freedom (OEF) Casualty Summary by Month and Service (as of May 20, 2014)," in *Defense Casualty Analysis System*, U.S. Department of Defense, May 20, 2014, https://www.dmdc.osd.mil/dcas/pages/report_oef_month .xhtml# (accessed May 21, 2014)

insurgents. Like traditional landmines, IEDs are triggered by movement and are typically placed beneath or beside roads. The UNAMA notes that IEDs were the leading single cause of civilian casualties in 2013.

It should be noted that foreign civilians in Afghanistan have also been casualties of the war. For example, as shown in Table 4.2, three civilian employees of the DOD had died as part of the OEF as of May 21, 2014. Other foreign civilians in the country include people working for commercial enterprises and humanitarian organizations. In February 2014 the U.S. Department of State (http://travel.state.gov/content/passports/english/alertswarn ings/afghanistan-travel-warning.html) issued a travel warning for Afghanistan, stating, "Travel to all areas of Afghanistan remains unsafe due to ongoing military combat operations, landmines, banditry, armed rivalry between political and tribal groups, and the possibility of insurgent attacks, including attacks using vehicle-borne or other improvised explosive devices."

THE PAKISTAN PROBLEM

When the war in Afghanistan began in 2001, the U.S. goal was to rout the Taliban from power and to prevent terrorists from having safe harbor there. As of August 2014, the United States and NATO were partially successful in achieving this goal because the Taliban had been removed from power. As described in Chapter 3, bin Laden's death in 2011 and more than 10 years of military and counterterrorism activities have weakened al Qaeda. However, the Taliban and al Qaeda have survived. They continue to pose a threat to the future stability of Afghanistan and the

FIGURE 4.3

Areas of Afghanistan and Pakistan under Taliban influence or with Taliban presence as of 2014

SOURCE: "Taliban Presence in Afghanistan," in *Counterterrorism 2014 Calendar*, National Counterterrorism Center, September 16, 2013, http://www.nctc.gov/site/pdfs/ct_calendar_2014.pdf (accessed June 7, 2014)

national security interests of the United States. This is due in part to the actions (or inactions) of Pakistan. In *In Brief: Next Steps in the War in Afghanistan? Issues for Congress* (June 15, 2012, http://fpc.state.gov/documents/organiza tion/193693.pdf), Catherine Dale of the CRS points out that to completely defeat an insurgency, it needs to be "smother[ed] within a closed environment." This has proven impossible in Afghanistan.

Figure 4.3 shows the areas within Pakistan and Afghanistan in which the U.S. government believes the Afghan Taliban still had influence and presence as of 2014. The region labeled "FATA" (Federally Administered Tribal Areas) lies within Pakistan along its western border with Afghanistan. The FATA is one of the poorest and most rugged regions of the country and has a separate legal structure that makes it difficult to control by the central Pakistani government. As a result, the FATA has long been accused of providing safe haven for Afghan Taliban and al Qaeda fighters.

The United States has had an inconstant relationship with Pakistan since the beginning of the war in Afghanistan. One technique widely employed by the U.S. military against al Qaeda in Pakistan has been drone attacks. According to media reports, hundreds of U.S. drone attacks have occurred in Pakistan, mostly targeting senior al Qaeda leaders. Although the attacks are praised by military leaders, they are criticized by social activists for allegedly killing innocent civilians. For example, according to Craig Whitlock, in "Drone Strikes Killing More Civilians Than U.S. Admits, Human Rights Groups Say" (WashingtonPost.com, October 22, 2013), the UN estimated in 2013 that approximately 2,200 Pakistani civilians had been killed by U.S. drone strikes. The continued use of drones within Pakistani territory has been a source of controversy between the U.S. and Pakistani governments.

In 2011, two events occurred that severely weakened the alliance between the United States and Pakistan. In May 2011 U.S. special forces secretly entered Pakistan to kill bin Laden at his compound in Abbottabad, a city about 30 miles (48 km) north of Islamabad, the capital of Pakistan. (See Figure 4.3.) Pakistan was angry that the United States had entered its territory to conduct the raid; the United States was angry that bin Laden had been living with impunity in Pakistan. Dale notes this action also "left many in the U.S. with the view that bin Laden could not have found sanctuary for so long without some official Pakistani knowledge or support." In November 2011 tensions spiked again when more than 20 Pakistani troops were killed at a border checkpoint after being fired on by ISAF helicopters. NATO insisted the helicopters were responding to gunfire that came from the area; Pakistan contended the attack was unprovoked. Widespread outrage spurred the Pakistani government to close down NATO supply lines that ran through the country. The Pakistani government demanded an apology from the United States, which was provided by the U.S. secretary of state Hillary Rodham Clinton (1947–). Shortly thereafter, the NATO supply lines were reopened.

Chapter 3 describes the continuing political tensions between Pakistan and the United States and the latter's claims that some members of the Pakistani government work against U.S. interests in Afghanistan. This sentiment is echoed by the DOD in *Report on Progress toward Security and Stability in Afghanistan*, in which it sums up security developments in Afghanistan through March 31, 2014. The DOD claims that "elements of Pakistan's government continued to tolerate Afghan-focused insurgent groups attacking U.S. and coalition forces." These developments are particularly troubling given the large amount of money the United States has given Pakistan.

In *Pakistan: U.S. Foreign Assistance* (July 1, 2013, http://www.fas.org/sgp/crs/row/R41856.pdf), Susan B. Epstein and K. Alan Kronstadt of the CRS estimate that direct overt U.S. aid and military reimbursements to Pakistan between fiscal years (FY) 2002 and 2013 totaled $25.9 billion.

AFGHANISTAN AND ITS FUTURE

Various sources provide mixed analyses on the effects of the war on Afghanistan and the nation's future prospects. In some respects, economic and social conditions have improved dramatically for Afghans since the war began in 2001. Kenneth Katzman of the CRS provides in *Afghanistan: Post-Taliban Governance, Security, and U.S. Policy* (July 11, 2014, http://fas.org/sgp/crs/row/RL30588.pdf) a comprehensive overview of Afghan and U.S. interests. One measure of a country's economic condition is its gross domestic product (GDP; the total market value of final goods and services that are produced within an economy in a given year). As shown in Table 4.5, Afghanistan's GDP was $33.6 billion in 2012, up from around $10 billion during the last year of Taliban rule. However, Katzman notes that "donor aid accounts for more than 95% of Afghanistan's GDP."

The United States has been, by far, the largest contributor of aid since the war began. Figure 4.4 shows U.S. assistance to Afghanistan between FYs 2002 and 2014 and estimates for FY 2015. The total amount over this period is $100.4 billion. This total does not include the costs associated with U.S. combat operations, which are discussed later in this chapter. Many other countries and organizations have also provided financial assistance to Afghanistan. Katzman notes that between 2002 and 2012 approximately $24.9 billion had been pledged, of which $19.7 billion had been disbursed through early 2014. The largest non-U.S. donors were Japan ($13.2 billion), the European Union ($2.9 billion), and Germany ($2.7 billion).

Despite the huge influx of money, Afghanistan remains a very poor country. The UN's World Food Programme (WFP) highlights in the press release "On World Food Day, WFP Says Investment in Nutrition Is Key to Unlocking a Better Future" (October 21, 2013, http://www.wfp.org/node/3191/3237/585746) the nation's problem with hunger and malnutrition. According to the WFP, 60.5% of Afghan children under the age of five years suffer from chronic malnutrition. However, some social and economic statistics show that conditions in Afghanistan have improved since the Taliban era. (See Table 4.5.) It must be noted that these gains were achieved with a heavy presence of foreign troops in Afghanistan.

ISAF operations are scheduled to cease at the end of 2014. Some military personnel—a residual force—may remain beyond that time, depending on BSA finalization.

TABLE 4.5

Economic and social statistics about Afghanistan, 2014

Literacy rate	28% of population over 15 years of age. 43% of males; 12.6% of females.
GDP, and GDP growth and unemployment rates	$33.55 billion purchasing power parity (PPP) in 2012. 109th in the world. Per capita: $1,000 purchasing power parity. 212th in the world. Growth has averaged about 9% per year every year since Taliban rule, but fell to 3.1% in 2013. Growth is forecast at about 5% for 2014 by the IMF. GDP was about $10 billion (PPP) during last year of Taliban rule. Unemployment rate is about 8%, but underemployment rate may be nearly 50%.
Children in school/schools built since 2002	8 million, of which 40% are girls. Up from 900,000 boys in school during Taliban era. 4,000 schools built (all donors) and 140,000 teachers hired since Taliban era. 17 universities, up from 2 in 2002. 75,000 Afghans in universities in Afghanistan (35% female); 5,000 when Taliban was in power.
Afghans with access to health coverage	85% with basic health services access, compared to 9% during Taliban era. Infant mortality down 22% since Taliban to 135 per 1,000 live births. 680 clinics built.
Roads built	About 3,000 miles paved post-Taliban, including repaving of "Ring Road" (78% complete) that circles the country. Kabul-Qandahar drive reduced to 6 hours. About 1,500 additional miles still under construction.
Judges/courts	Over 1,000 judges (incl. 200 women) trained since fall of Taliban.
Banks operating	17, including branches in some rural areas, but about 90% of the population still use hawalas (informal money transfer services). No banks existed during Taliban era. Some limited credit card use. Some Afghan police now paid by cell phone (E-Paisa).
Access to electricity	15%–20% of the population. Much of its electricity imported from neighboring states.
Government revenues (excl. donor funds)	About $2 billion in 2012 compared to $200 million in 2002. Total Afghan budget is about $4.5 billion (including development funds)—shortfall covered by foreign donors, including through Afghanistan Reconstruction Trust Fund.
Financial reserves/debt	About $4.4 billion, up from $180 million in 2002. Includes amounts due Central Bank. $8 billion bilateral debt, plus $500 million multilateral. U.S. forgave $108 million in debt in 2004, and $1.6 billion forgiven by other creditors in March 2010.
Foreign/private investment	About $500 million to $1 billion per year. Four Afghan airlines: Ariana (national) plus at least two privately owned: Safi and Kam. Turkish Air and India Air fly to Kabul.
Legal exports/agriculture	80% of the population is involved in agriculture. Self-sufficiency in wheat production as of May 2009 (first time in 30 years). Exports: $400 million+ (2011): fruits, raisins, melons, pomegranate juice (Anar), nuts, carpets, lapis lazuli gems, marble tile, timber products (Kunar, Nuristan provinces).
Oil proven reserves	3.6 billion barrels of oil, 36.5 trillion cubic feet of gas. Current oil production negligible, but USAID funding project to revive oil and gas facilities in the north.
Cell phones/tourism	About 18 million cell phone subscribers, up from neglibile amounts during Taliban era. Tourism: National park opened in Bamiyan June 2009. Increasing tourist visits.

GDP = gross domestic product; IMF = International Monetary Fund; USAID = U.S. Agency for International Development.

SOURCE: Adapted from Kenneth Katzman, "Table 8. Comparative Social and Economic Statistics," in *Afghanistan: Post-Taliban Governance, Security, and U.S. Policy*, Congressional Research Service, April 9, 2014, https://www.fas.org/sgp/crs/row/RL30588.pdf (accessed June 6, 2014)

FIGURE 4.4

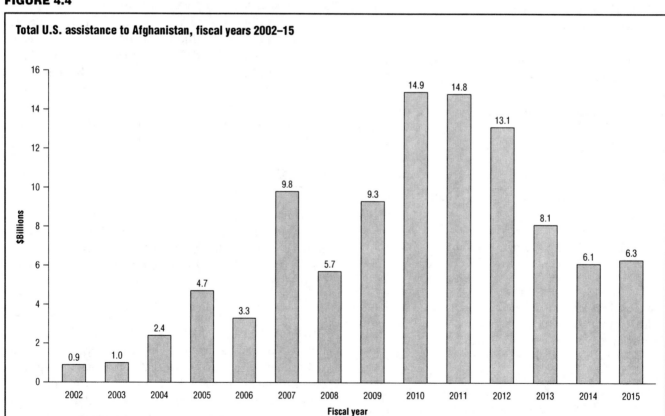

Total U.S. assistance to Afghanistan, fiscal years 2002–15

Note: Amount for 2015 is estimated.

SOURCE: Adapted from Kenneth Katzman, "Table 12. Post-Taliban U.S. Assistance to Afghanistan," in *Afghanistan: Post-Taliban Governance, Security, and U.S. Policy*, Congressional Research Service, April 9, 2014, https://www.fas.org/sgp/crs/row/RL30588.pdf (accessed June 7, 2014)

In May 2014 President Obama announced that he would like to keep 9,800 U.S. troops and an undetermined number of allied troops in Afghanistan through 2015. In "Obama to Cut Troops, Says Afghanistan 'Will Not Be a Perfect Place'" (CNN.com, May 27, 2014), Tom Cohen reports the president planned to reduce U.S. troop levels in 2015 and 2016, leaving only enough troops in 2017 to secure the U.S. embassy in Afghanistan.

In *Afghanistan: Post-Taliban Governance, Security, and U.S. Policy*, Katzman discusses the debate over how Afghanistan will fare without a large foreign troop presence to stabilize the country. He states, "Some assert that the ANSF will not be able to secure Afghanistan if left almost completely on its own by 2016, and that there could be substantial Taliban gains and even a full political collapse after international forces depart." However, Katzman notes that more optimistic observers believe the Taliban does not enjoy widespread popular support in Afghanistan and can be fended off by the ANSF.

One controversial strategy the United States has championed as a possible solution for Afghanistan is a negotiated settlement between the Afghan government and the Taliban. Katzman indicates that some meetings between the warring parties have taken place, but to little avail. The talks did result in the release in June 2014 of Bowe Bergdahl (1986–), the only U.S. soldier held by the Taliban. In return, the United States released five Taliban members from the Guantánamo Bay detention facility in Cuba. They were transported to Qatar, a small country in the Middle East. Qatari negotiators helped mediate the exchange and reportedly assured U.S. authorities that the Taliban members would not be allowed to leave Qatar for at least one year.

The prisoner swap caused a political uproar for the Obama administration, which had kept the deal secret from Congress. In December 2013 the president signed into law the National Defense Authorization Act for Fiscal Year 2014. Section 1035 of the law requires the U.S. secretary of defense to notify "the appropriate committees of Congress" at least 30 days before a Guantánamo prisoner is transferred or released to a foreign country. Some legislators have complained that the Obama administration violated the law by failing to provide congressional notification prior to the swap. In addition, a public debate has raged about the possible future threats to national security posed by the five released detainees. Bergdahl's conduct prior to being captured in 2009 has also come under fire amid allegations from soldiers who served with him that he deserted his post. As of August 2014, it was uncertain how these various issues would play out.

There are numerous concerns that allowing Taliban members into the Afghan government will reverse the human rights gains that have been achieved in Afghanistan.

Katzman explains, "The minority communities in the north, women, intellectuals, and others remain skeptical that their freedoms can be preserved if there is a political settlement with the Taliban—a settlement that might involve Taliban figures obtaining ministerial posts, seats in parliament, or even control over territory." The threat to women is particularly keen. Taliban militants have killed high-profile women in Afghanistan, including the author Sushmita Banerjee (1964–2013) and three senior female police officials, all of whom were assassinated in 2013.

The existing Afghan government's protection of human rights has also come under fire, particularly in regard to women's rights. As shown in Table 4.5, females accounted for 40% of schoolchildren and 35% of university students as of 2014. These percentages are a substantial improvement compared to when the Taliban was in power. However, critics complain that the government has slowly chipped away at women's rights. In *Report on Progress toward Security and Stability in Afghanistan*, the DOD indicates that some members of the Afghan parliament have tried to weaken a law that prohibits violence against women. The DOD notes that "women face entrenched societal discrimination and limits to their freedom. Violence against women is widespread, but underreported."

THE WAR IN AFGHANISTAN: PUBLIC OPINION

Since the start of the war in 2001, the Gallup Organization has asked Americans whether sending military forces to Afghanistan has been "a mistake." Figure 4.5 shows the poll results for this question. In late 2001 and in early 2002 only a small portion of respondents (9% and 6%, respectively) said the United States had made a mistake in sending military forces to Afghanistan. Over time, support for the war faded considerably. By 2014 Americans were nearly evenly split on the question, with 49% saying the United States had made a mistake and 48% saying it had not made a mistake.

IRAQ

Iraq is bordered on the east by Iran, on the north by Turkey, on the west by Syria and Jordan, and on the south by Saudi Arabia. (See Figure 4.6.) The tiny nation of Kuwait also lies to the south and abuts Iraq's small stretch of coastline on the Persian Gulf. The capital of Iraq is Baghdad. According to the CIA, in *The World Factbook: Iraq* (June 22, 2014, https://www.cia.gov/library/publications/the-world-factbook/geos/iz.html), Iraq covers 169,200 square miles (438,317 square km) and is slightly larger than the state of Idaho doubled. Iraq is crossed by two large rivers—the Tigris and the Euphrates—whose waters provide a broad fertile plain in the center of the country. The remainder of the landscape is primarily desert. In 2014 the population was estimated

FIGURE 4.5

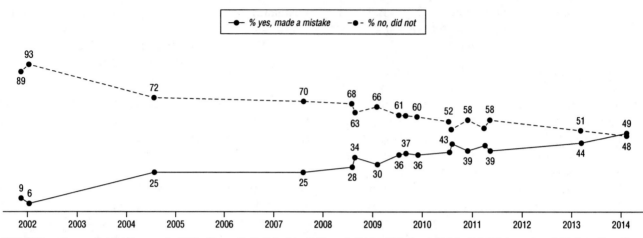

Public opinion on whether the U.S. made a mistake in sending troops to Afghanistan, 2001–14

LOOKING BACK, DO YOU THINK THE UNITED STATES MADE A MISTAKE SENDING TROOPS TO FIGHT IN AFGHANISTAN IN 2001?

—●— % yes, made a mistake   –●– % no, did not

2001–2011 question wording: Thinking now about U.S. military action in Afghanistan that began in October 2001, do you think the United States made a mistake in sending military forces to Afghanistan, or not?

SOURCE: Frank Newport, "Looking back, do you think the United States made a mistake sending troops to fight in Afghanistan in 2001?" in *More Americans Now View Afghanistan War As a Mistake*, The Gallup Organization, February 19, 2014, http://www.gallup.com/poll/167471/americans-view-afghanistan-war-mistake.aspx (accessed June 7, 2014). Copyright © 2014 Gallup, Inc. All rights reserved. The content is used with permission; however, Gallup retains all rights of republication.

FIGURE 4.6

Map of Iraq, 2014

SOURCE: "Map of Iraq," in "Middle East: Iraq," *The World Factbook*, Central Intelligence Agency, April 11, 2014, https://www.cia.gov/library/publications/the-world-factbook/geos/iz.html (accessed June 7, 2014)

at nearly 32.6 million. Most of the population is Arab (75% to 80%) but includes a Kurdish sector (15% to 20%) and other ethnic minorities. The Kurds are an ethnic group found mostly in the mountainous regions of northern Iraq. They see themselves as a distinct group and have long pursued their own independent nation. Nearly all Iraqis are Muslim (99%), with 60% to 65% Shiite and 32% to 37% Sunni.

The United States has fought two wars with Iraq. The first war, which is commonly called the Persian Gulf War, spanned several months between 1990 and 1991. The second war began in 2003, but its roots lie within the earlier war.

The Persian Gulf War

Saddam Hussein was a brutal dictator who first took power in Iraq during the early 1970s. In 1990 Iraqi military forces invaded Kuwait. The article "On This Day: 1990—Iraq Invades Kuwait" (BBC.co.uk, 2010) notes that Hussein accused the Kuwaitis of taking oil from an oil field near the border between the two countries. The international community almost universally condemned Iraq's actions. The UN imposed strict economic sanctions that would remain in place for many years. President George H. W. Bush (1924–) put together a U.S.-led coalition of international military forces for Operation Desert Storm, which began in January 1991 with the bombing of strategic targets within Iraq. By the end of February the coalition had liberated Kuwait and seriously damaged Iraq's infrastructure and military capabilities. As shown in Table 1.1 in Chapter 1, the United States lost 383 troops during the Persian Gulf War. Over 2.2 million U.S. military personnel served during the war.

THE KURDS. The struggle of the Iraqi Kurds against Hussein and the Iraqi government is reviewed by Frank Viviano in "The Kurds in Control" (NationalGeographic.com, January 2006). During the 1980s and early 1990s Hussein's government killed an estimated 100,000 to 180,000 Kurds and destroyed thousands of their villages. Much of the killing occurred near the end of the Iran-Iraq War (1980–1988) as punishment for Kurdish support of Iran. The genocide included the use of chemical weapons against the Kurds during the so-called Anfal Campaign. (For more information about this campaign, see the Human Rights Watch report *Genocide in Iraq: The Anfal Campaign against the Kurds* [July 1993, http://www.hrw.org/reports/1993/iraqanfal/].)

According to Viviano, the United States chose at first to ignore the genocide so as not to antagonize Hussein, a would-be American ally during the late 1980s. This attitude changed following Iraq's invasion of Kuwait in 1990. Immediately after the Persian Gulf War, U.S., British, and French military forces began enforcing a no-fly zone over the Kurdish territories in northern Iraq to prevent Hussein from attacking the Kurds with aircraft. In addition, a no-fly zone was established over southern Iraq to protect the largely Shiite population, which was repressed by Hussein's predominantly Sunni Muslim government.

In April 1991 the UN Security Council passed Resolution 687 (http://www.iaea.org/OurWork/SV/Invo/resolutions/res687.pdf), which set forth the terms of the cease-fire between Iraq and Kuwait. It also called on Iraq to "agree not to acquire or develop nuclear weapons" or any related technology and to declare the "locations, amounts, and types" of all existing nuclear weapons and usable materials within Iraq and turn them over to the International Atomic Energy Agency (IAEA) for destruction. For the remainder of the decade Iraq followed a pattern of denial and deception with IAEA inspectors and refused to abide by Resolution 687 and subsequent UN resolutions. In 1998 a defiant Hussein had the IAEA inspectors kicked out of the country. (For a timeline of events, see the IAEA's "In Focus: IAEA and Iraq" [2014, http://www.iaea.org/NewsCenter/Focus/IaeaIraq/index.shtml].)

The 2003 War in Iraq

By the time of the September 11, 2001, terrorist attacks, the United States had experienced an entire decade of problems with Iraq. Iraq denounced the no-fly zones within its borders as illegal and often fired at U.S. and British warplanes that enforced them. Hussein's continuing defiance of UN resolutions was worrying to U.S. officials, who feared that Iraq was hiding a program to build WMDs.

According to the *9/11 Commission Report*, President George W. Bush "wondered immediately after the [9/11] attack whether Saddam Hussein's regime might have had a hand in it." The U.S. intelligence community investigated possible connections and found no compelling case of Iraqi involvement. Nevertheless, some members of the Bush administration, particularly the U.S. deputy secretary of defense Paul D. Wolfowitz (1943–), thought the United States should strike Iraq as part of the ensuing War on Terror (which was later renamed the Overseas Contingency Operations). On January 29, 2002, during his annual State of the Union speech (http://georgewbush-whitehouse.archives.gov/stateoftheunion/2002), President Bush described Iraq as a member of an "axis of evil" in the world.

Throughout the remainder of the year the Bush administration worked to garner UN approval for a military strike against Iraq. These efforts were driven by reports from the U.S. intelligence community that Iraq was amassing WMDs and had restarted its nuclear weapons program. In February 2003 the U.S. secretary of state Colin Powell (1937–) addressed the UN and presented the U.S. case for military action against Iraq. The UN had already passed resolutions that condemned Iraq for its continuing defiance of previous UN resolutions and for refusing to allow IAEA inspectors back into the country. However, the United States was unable to convince the UN that a military response was necessary. Only the United Kingdom pledged to fully support the U.S. plan for war.

The coalition gathered by the United States for the impending war was smaller than the one garnered against Iraq in 1991. In 2003 only Great Britain pledged troops; however, many other nations contributed small military forces, money, or equipment (most notably Spain, Australia, and Israel). France, Russia, and China, in particular, were opposed to military action against Iraq.

WAR BEGINS IN IRAQ

Operation Iraqi Freedom (OIF) began on March 20, 2003, with a massive bombardment of Iraqi targets. By the end of April, the invasion was complete. According to the DOS, in *Patterns of Global Terrorism 2003* (April 2004, http://www.state.gov/documents/organization/31912.pdf), by the end of 2003 coalition forces had killed or captured 42 of the 55 most-wanted members of Iraq's former regime, including Hussein, who was captured in December 2003. In October 2005 Hussein stood trial in Iraq for war crimes committed against his people during his rule.

He was found guilty by a five-member Iraqi tribunal (group of judges) and hanged for his crimes in December 2006.

Although the military goals of the war were accomplished easily, the U.S.-led coalition forces were unable to achieve stability in Iraq. Following the invasion, mass looting and lawlessness broke out and many buildings were burned. U.S. troops were unsuccessful at restoring civil order. Looting and mayhem continued to be a problem in other occupied areas as well. Over the ensuing years a massive insurgency erupted that took the lives of many Iraqis, Americans, and other foreigners within Iraq. These attacks were carried out by a wide variety of individuals and groups with various grievances and agendas. In 2006 bloody sectarian violence escalated between Iraq's minority Sunni population and the majority Shiite population.

By early 2007 Iraq was in a state of near-total civil war. The American public was increasingly displeased with the course of the war. More than 3,000 U.S. military personnel had been killed during the OIF, and there was no end in sight to the hostilities. In an attempt to quell the violence in Iraq, the Bush administration responded with a troop surge.

According to the GAO, in *Securing, Stabilizing, and Rebuilding Iraq: Progress Report: Some Gains Made, Updated Strategy Needed* (June 2008, http://gao.gov/new.items/d08837.pdf), the number of U.S. forces increased by approximately 32,000 troops during the troop surge, peaking at around 169,000 troops in August 2007. Fierce fighting resulted in high U.S. military casualties—764 deaths in 2007, the highest since the start of the war. (See Table 4.6.) In 2008, however, the casualty rate dropped dramatically as insurgent attacks decreased. Likewise, the GAO reports there was a substantial decline in the number of deaths among Iraqi civilians and security forces.

U.S. INTELLIGENCE: "DEAD WRONG"

During and after the invasion of Iraq, U.S. forces searched the country for WMDs, but found none. An outcry in the American media spurred President Bush to establish a commission to investigate the situation. In March 2005 the Commission on the Intelligence Capabilities of the United States Regarding Weapons of Mass Destruction issued *Report to the President of the United States*. The commission's assessment was extremely critical, noting, "We conclude that the Intelligence Community was dead wrong in almost all of its pre-war judgments about Iraq's weapons of mass destruction." The commission learned that U.S. intelligence agents had obtained much false information from unreliable informants and poor data sources. In addition, intelligence officials had ignored information that did not support their

TABLE 4.6

U.S. military casualties as a result of Operation Iraqi Freedom, by year, as of May 20, 2014

Year	Hostile deaths Total	Non-hostile/ pending deaths Total	All deaths Total	Wounded in action Total
2003	315	171	486	2,422
2004	713	133	846	8,002
2005	673	171	844	5,944
2006	704	116	820	6,411
2007	764	139	903	6,119
2008	221	92	313	2,049
2009	74	74	148	678
2010	15	33	48	316
2011	0	0	0	0
2012	2	0	2	0
2013	0	0	0	0
Totals	**3,481**	**929**	**4,410**	**31,941**

SOURCE: Adapted from "U.S. Military Casualties—Operation Iraqi Freedom (OIF) Casualty Summary by Month and Service (as of May 20, 2014)," in *Defense Casualty Analysis System*, U.S. Department of Defense, May 20, 2014, https://www.dmdc.osd.mil/dcas/pages/report_oif_month.xhtml (accessed May 22, 2014)

preconceived notion about Iraq's guilt. The commission noted, "The harm done to American credibility by our all too public intelligence failings in Iraq will take years to undo." The commission's findings were embarrassing to the Bush administration, which had pressed the international community for the invasion.

THE BEGINNING OF THE END

Although the casualty rate declined significantly in 2008, widespread American public support for the war in Iraq had faded. When the war began in 2003, Americans were torn, but generally favorable, about invading Iraq. This support waned as the insurgency raged and the death toll rose. In 2003 the Gallup Organization (2014, http://www.gallup.com/poll/1633/Iraq.aspx) began conducting polls on American attitudes regarding the war in Iraq. Americans were asked whether the United States "made a mistake in sending troops to Iraq." In early 2003, 75% of respondents said it had not been a mistake to send U.S. troops to Iraq. However, over the following years support for the war dropped dramatically. In 2008 the percentage of respondents who thought the war had been a mistake increased to 63%, its highest point, and then declined somewhat. In June 2014 Gallup found that 57% of Americans thought the war was a mistake and 39% thought it had not been a mistake. Another 3% had no opinion on the matter.

Between 2007 and 2008 the Bush administration and the Iraqi government conducted negotiations that resulted in two important agreements: the Status of Forces Agreement (SOFA), which focused on security and military matters, and the Strategic Framework, which addressed the future cooperation between the two countries in areas

TABLE 4.7

U.S. military deaths as a result of Operation Iraqi Freedom, by category, as of May 20, 2014

Casualty type	Total
Hostile	3,481
Non-hostile	929
Total	**4,410**
Gender	
Female	110
Male	4,300
Total	**4,410**
Age	
<22	1,283
22–24	1,073
25–30	1,126
31–35	426
>35	502
Total	**4,410**
Component	
Active duty	3,501
Reserve	412
National Guard	497
Total	**4,410**
Race	
American Indian/Alaskan native	43
Asian	77
Black or African American	439
Native Hawaiian or other Pacific Islander	17
White	3,639
Multiple races	62
Unknown	133
Total	**4,410**

SOURCE: Adapted from "U.S. Military Casualties—Operation Iraqi Freedom (OIF) Military Deaths (as of May 20, 2014)," in *Defense Casualty Analysis System*, U.S. Department of Defense, May 20, 2014, https://www.dmdc.osd.mil/dcas/pages/report_oif_type.xhtml (accessed May 22, 2014)

TABLE 4.8

U.S. military casualties as a result of Operation New Dawn, by year, as of May 20, 2014

Year	Hostile deaths	Non-hostile/ pending deaths	All deaths	Wounded in action
2010	4	8	12	74
2011	34	20	54	221
2012	0	0	0	0
2013	0	0	0	0
2014	0	0	0	2
Totals	**38**	**28**	**66**	**297**

SOURCE: Adapted from "U.S. Military Casualties—Operation New Dawn (OND) Casualty Summary by Month and Service (as of May 20, 2014)," in *Defense Casualty Analysis System*, U.S. Department of Defense, May 20, 2014, https://www.dmdc.osd.mil/dcas/pages/report_ond_month.xhtml (accessed May 22, 2014)

not specifically covered by SOFA, chiefly diplomacy. In SOFA the United States agreed to withdraw all of its combat forces from Iraqi "urban areas" by June 30, 2009, and withdraw all U.S. troops by the end of 2011. However, the U.S. and Iraqi governments began negotiating the possibility of establishing permanent U.S. military bases in Iraq.

On June 30, 2009, Iraq celebrated a new holiday—National Sovereignty Day—as U.S. troops completed withdrawing from the nation's urban areas. Tim Cocks and Muhanad Mohammed report in "Iraqis Rejoice as U.S. Troops Leave Baghdad" (Reuters.com, June 29, 2009) that the Iraqi population was pleased about the withdrawal, but extremely frustrated that its quality of life had not improved after six years of U.S. occupation.

On August 31, 2010, the OIF officially ended in Iraq, marking a formal end to U.S. military combat actions. As of May 20, 2014, 4,410 U.S. military personnel had died as a result of the OIF. (See Table 4.6.) Most of the deaths (3,481) were due to hostile actions. The remainder were due to accidents or other causes. The largest number of deaths was among white male troops on active duty. (See Table 4.7.) Table 4.6 also shows that 31,941 U.S. military personnel were wounded in action during the OIF but survived their wounds.

Between September 1, 2010, and December 15, 2011, the U.S. military conducted Operation New Dawn (OND) in Iraq. The DOD explains in "Operation New Dawn" (August 31, 2010, http://www.army.mil/article/44526/Operation_New_Dawn) that the OND was dedicated to "advising, assisting and training Iraqi Security Forces." As shown in Table 4.8, 66 U.S. military personnel died as a result of the OND. Thirty-eight of the deaths were due to hostile actions. The largest number of deaths was among white male troops on active duty. (See Table 4.9.)

In October 2011 President Obama announced that his administration and the Iraqi government had failed to reach a consensus on the establishment of permanent U.S. military bases in Iraq. One of the major sticking points was the United States' insistence that its personnel would not be subject to prosecution by the Iraqi justice system for any off-base criminal activities. The rejection of the bases was a major disappointment to the DOD and some politicians who had hoped to station tens of thousands of U.S. troops in Iraq as a deterrent to neighboring Iran. In late December 2011 the U.S. military completed its troop withdrawals, leaving behind only a few hundred personnel as guards and training specialists at the U.S. embassy and related facilities in Iraq.

IRAQI CIVILIAN CASUALTIES DURING THE WAR AND OCCUPATION

Various organizations have estimated that tens of thousands to more than a million Iraqis were killed during the war and the occupation. In 2013 a team of U.S., Canadian, and Iraqi researchers published an estimate based on a survey of a representative sample of Iraqi

TABLE 4.9

U.S. military deaths as a result of Operation New Dawn, by category, as of May 20, 2014

Casualty type	Total
Hostile	38
Non-hostile	28
Total	**66**
Gender	
Male	66
Total	**66**
Age	
<22	11
22–24	15
25–30	25
31–35	5
>35	10
Total	**66**
Component	
Active duty	54
Reserve	6
National Guard	6
Total	**66**
Race	
Asian	1
Black or African American	5
Native Hawaiian or other Pacific islander	1
White	58
Multiple races	1
Total	**66**

SOURCE: Adapted from "U.S. Military Casualties—Operation New Dawn (OND) Military Deaths (as of May 20, 2014)," in *Defense Casualty Analysis System*, U.S. Department of Defense, May 20, 2014, https://www.dmdc.osd.mil/dcas/pages/report_ond_deaths.xhtml (accessed May 22, 2014)

households. The results are reported by Amy Hagopian et al. in "Mortality in Iraq Associated with the 2003–2011 War and Occupation: Findings from a National Cluster Sample Survey by the University Collaborative Iraq Mortality Study" (*PLoS Medicine*, October 15, 2013). The researchers estimate that 405,000 civilian deaths occurred due to the armed conflicts that raged in Iraq between 2003 and 2011. They attribute more than 60% of the deaths directly to violence and the rest to "the collapse of infrastructure and other indirect, but war-related, causes," such as health and sanitation system failures. According to Hagopian et al., "Violent deaths were attributed primarily to coalition forces (35%) and militia (32%)." They indicate that around 2 million Iraqis fled the country after the war began. Using secondary sources, the researchers estimate that the emigrant families likely incurred another 55,000 deaths due to war-related violence. Thus, the total estimate of civilians killed during the war and occupation is 460,000.

Since January 2008 the UN Assistance Mission for Iraq (UNAMI) has provided monthly data on the number of Iraqi civilians it has confirmed were killed or wounded due to armed violence and acts of terrorism. For the four-year period ending December 2011 (the end of the occupation) the UNAMI (May 2013, http://www.uniraq.org/images/documents/UNAMI_HRO_%20CIVCAS%202008-2012.pdf) estimates that 15,567 Iraqi civilians were killed and 49,343 were wounded.

IRAQ AND THE UNITED STATES FIGHT THE ISLAMIC STATE

The United States has expended a heavy investment in Iraq in terms of human lives and money. The Persian Gulf War, the OIF, and the OND resulted in over 4,800 U.S. troop deaths. In addition, more than 32,000 military personnel were injured. Figure 4.7 shows the annual amounts of U.S. assistance to Iraq between FYs 2003 and 2014 and estimated for FY 2015. The total is $57.7 billion, but it does not include combat costs, which are described later in this chapter.

The U.S. government wants a good diplomatic relationship with Iraq, in part to counter Iran's influence. Iraq and Iran have developed close political ties because both countries have predominantly Shiite populations. The United States also desires a stable Iraq. After U.S. troops left there in 2011 it was hoped that the Iraqi government could unite the nation's people behind it. However, these hopes have proved elusive as the nation has been torn by sectarian violence and political turmoil.

The UNAMI (May 2013, http://www.uniraq.org/images/documents/UNAMI_HRO_%20CIVCAS%202008-2012.pdf) estimates that in 2012, 3,238 Iraqi civilians were killed and 10,379 were wounded due to armed violence and acts of terrorism. The casualties grew even higher in 2013. In "UN Casualty Figures for December, 2013 Deadliest since 2008 in Iraq" (January 2, 2014, http://www.uniraq.org), the UNAMI states that an estimated 7,818 civilians (including police officers) were killed and 17,981 were wounded in 2013. Deadly sectarian violence continued in 2014. According to the UNAMI (August 1, 2014, http://www.uniraq.org/index.php?option=com_k2&view=itemlist&layout=category&task=category&id=159&Itemid=633&lang=en), 5,596 civilians were killed between January and July 2014 and another 9,495 were wounded.

Iraq's national government includes an elected parliament called the Council of Representatives whose 300-plus members choose a prime minister and a less powerful president. Nuri al-Maliki (1950–), a Shiite, was elected prime minister in 2006 and 2010. Thus, he led Iraq when the U.S. military withdrew its forces at the end of 2011. In *Iraq: Politics, Governance, and Human Rights* (August 12, 2014, http://www.fas.org/sgp/crs/mideast/RS21968.pdf), Katzman notes that al-Maliki came to be highly resented by Iraq's minority Sunni Arabs, who claimed they were oppressed by his government. In addition, relations deteriorated between al-Malaki's administration in Baghdad and the semi-autonomous Kurdish region in northern Iraq. The political tensions only worsened the

FIGURE 4.7

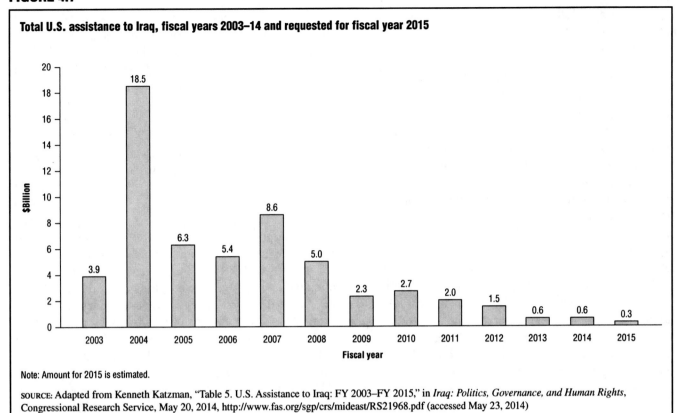

Total U.S. assistance to Iraq, fiscal years 2003–14 and requested for fiscal year 2015

Note: Amount for 2015 is estimated.

SOURCE: Adapted from Kenneth Katzman, "Table 5. U.S. Assistance to Iraq: FY 2003–FY 2015," in *Iraq: Politics, Governance, and Human Rights*, Congressional Research Service, May 20, 2014, http://www.fas.org/sgp/crs/mideast/RS21968.pdf (accessed May 23, 2014)

existing deep divides between Iraq's various religious and ethnic sects.

One aggravating factor was the bloody civil war in neighboring Syria. (See Figure 4.6.) The Syrian uprisings began in 2011 as part of the so-called Arab Spring. Various elements within Syria rebelled against Bashar al-Assad (1965–), who responded with a fierce military crackdown. Iraq was already troubled by Sunni-aligned militants, such as the terrorist group Al Qaeda in Iraq (AQI) before the Syrian insurrection began. As explained in Chapter 3, the AQI wreaked havoc in Iraq during the U.S. occupation and afterward and was blamed for the deaths of thousands of Iraqis. The group spread its influence by taking advantage of seething Sunni anger against the nation's Shiite-dominated government.

As the situation worsened, the United States became more involved militarily with Iraq. According to Katzman, the United States sold Iraq surveillance systems (including unarmed drones), F-16 combat aircraft, attack helicopters, HELLFIRE missiles, and other military hardware. In 2012, when Sunni protests became especially violent, the Iraqi government sought additional forms of U.S. military assistance. The DOD agreed to engage in cooperative military exchanges and joint exercises with the Iraqi military and to help it develop its defense intelligence and counterterrorism capabilities. Katzman notes that U.S. special forces and CIA "paramilitary" forces began deploying to Iraq to support these efforts.

In 2013 Abu Bakr al-Baghdadi (1971–), the leader of the AQI, changed the organization's name to what would later be called the Islamic State (IS). The IS was dropped from al Qaeda and began operating independently. In December 2013 IS attacks on Iraqi government security forces prompted al-Maliki to send troops to arrest Ahmed al-Alwani, a prominent Sunni politician. Al-Alwani's brother was killed during the raid. The incident greatly inflamed anti-government sentiment in Sunni areas and emboldened IS members to seize control of Ramadi and Fallujah near Baghdad and some smaller cities in western Iraq. The militants were joined by local Sunni militias who fought against government forces. Although the latter managed to retake Ramadi, other towns fell to the IS over the following months. In April 2014 al-Malaki's political party again won the most seats on the Council of Representatives, making him the likely candidate for prime minister. However, he faced fierce opposition within the council, and the vote was delayed while the government dealt with the insurgency. In June 2014 IS rebels captured Mosul in northern Iraq and Tikrit in central Iraq. The group declared al-Baghdadi as the leader of a new caliphate that encompassed large parts of Syria and Iraq.

The United States was greatly alarmed by these developments. President Obama began weighing options for bolstering the Iraqi army short of sending U.S. troops back into combat. In addition, his administration strongly pressured al-Malaki to resign in the hopes that a different government could win the support of the Sunni population.

Media reports arose about the strict form of fundamentalist Islam that was being enforced by the IS. The militants waged a terror campaign against Iraqi civilians, particularly ethnic and religious minorities, forcing them to flee their homes. In August 2014 a humanitarian crisis developed when tens of thousands of minority Yazidis were chased by the IS to a remote mountain location with little food and water. The U.S. and Iraqi military delivered humanitarian supplies to the desperate people. Meanwhile, IS forces had advanced to the outskirts of Erbil, an oil-rich Kurdish city that contained a U.S. consulate (a regional embassy office). The semi-autonomous Kurdish government had its own army called the Peshmerga that was aided by Kurdish civilian militias. Obama authorized U.S. air strikes that helped the Peshmerga drive back IS forces threatening the Yazidis and Erbil. Later that month U.S. air power assisted the Peshmerga in recapturing a large dam that had been seized by the IS near Mosul.

On August 14, 2014, al-Maliki formally resigned as Iraq's prime minister after it became obvious he no longer had the support of the Council of Representatives. An alternative candidate, Haider al-Abadi (1952–), also a Shiite, was nominated to be the new prime minister. As of late August 2014, the election had not taken place, but was expected to confirm al-Abadi as Iraq's new leader. It remained to be seen if the new administration could convince the nation's Sunni rebels to abandon their allegiance to the IS. There were also serious doubts about the abilities of the Iraqi army and the Peshmerga to defeat the militants without U.S. military help. This issue was highly controversial for the war-weary U.S. public. Throughout the summer of 2014 Obama reassured Americans that he had no plans to deploy U.S. combat troops to Iraq. However, hundreds of U.S. military advisers, marines, and special forces personnel had been sent to Iraq by the end of August 2014.

Meanwhile, human rights activists were concerned about the growing influence of Islamists on the Council of Representatives. For example, Suadad al-Salhy reports in "Iraqi Women Protest against Proposed Islamic Law in Iraq" (Reuters.com, March 8, 2014) that Iraqi law "enshrines women's rights regarding marriage, inheritance, and child custody, and has often been held up as the most progressive in the Middle East." However, Islamist lawmakers introduced a law in 2014 that would strip women of many of their rights. As of August 2014, the draft law had not been voted on by the parliament.

WAR COSTS AND BUDGETS

As noted in Chapter 2, the wars in Afghanistan and Iraq and related anti-terrorism operations are collectively called the Overseas Contingency Operations (OCO). The most costly OCO components have been the wars in Afghanistan and Iraq. Amy Belasco of the CRS details in *The Cost of Iraq, Afghanistan, and Other Global War on Terror Operations since 9/11* (March 29, 2011, http://www.fas.org/sgp/crs/natsec/RL33110.pdf) estimates of the yearly and cumulative OCO costs between FYs 2001 (when the war in Afghanistan began) and 2012. (See Table 4.10.) The total OCO costs were estimated at $1.4 trillion during this period, with $823.2 billion devoted to the war in Iraq, $557.1 billion spent on the war in Afghanistan, $28.7 billion spent on enhanced security at DOD bases, and $5.5 billion in unallocated funds (i.e., the CRS could not determine to which operation the money was devoted). Belasco also breaks down the $1.4 trillion total by government agency. The DOD accounted for the vast majority of the total at more than $1.3 trillion. The remainder was allocated to the DOS and U.S. Agency for International Development ($77.4 billion) and to the U.S. Department of Veterans Affairs' (VA) medical fund ($11.4 billion). The VA provides medical treatment and numerous other services and benefits to veterans.

In early 2014 President Obama presented to Congress his federal budget request for FY 2015. The details about the DOD funding are provided in Chapter 2. Table 4.11 shows the trends in OCO funding for FYs 2013 and 2014 and for the FY 2015 budget request. The total OCO cost for all three years was $270 billion, including $246.6 billion for the DOD and $23.4 billion in nondefense spending to support the OCO. (See Table 2.2 in Chapter 2.)

Based on these data, a conservative estimate of total OCO costs through FY 2015 is nearly $1.7 trillion, including both defense and nondefense spending. The economic cost of the two wars will escalate in the future for a variety of reasons. The United States borrowed money to fund wartime spending. The interest on this debt will be paid back in the future. In addition, the U.S. government is obligated to cover certain expenses for wartime veterans, including medical care, disability compensation, and pensions. These costs will be incurred for decades as the veterans age.

Medical care costs, in particular, are expected to be significant because of the serious nature of many of the injuries that were suffered during the wars. Figure 4.8 shows the number of major limb amputations that were conducted on combat veterans between 2001 and 2013. The peak number was 250 in 2011. Far more common were cases of traumatic brain injury (TBI). The Centers for Disease Control and Prevention notes in "Traumatic Brain Injury" (March 6, 2014, http://www.cdc.gov/Traumatic

TABLE 4.10

Estimated war funding, by operation, fiscal years 2001–11 and requested for fiscal year 2012

[CRS estimates in billions of dollars of budget authority]

Operation and source of funds	Fiscal year 2001 & 2002	Fiscal year 2003	Fiscal year 2004	Fiscal year 2005	Fiscal year 2006	Fiscal year 2007	Fiscal year 2008	Fiscal year 2009	Fiscal year 2010	Fiscal 2011 CRA P.L. 112-6*	Fiscal year 2012 request	Cumulative enacted, fiscal years 2001–2011 as of 3-18-11	Cum. total w/ fiscal year CRA & fiscal year 2012 request
Iraq	0.0	53.0	75.9	85.5	101.6	131.2	142.1	95.5	71.3	49.3	17.7	805.5	823.2
Afghanistan	20.8	14.7	14.5	20.0	19.0	39.2	43.5	59.5	93.8	118.6	113.7	443.0	557.1
Enhanced Security	13.0	8.0	3.7	2.1	0.8	0.5	0.1	0.1	0.1	0.1	0.1	28.6	28.7
Unallocated	0	5.5	0	0	0	0	0	0	0	0	0	5.5	5.5
Total	33.8	81.2	94.1	107.6	121.4	170.9	185.7	155.1	165.3	168.1	131.7	1,283.3	1,414.8
Annual change	NA	140%	16%	13%	13%	41%	9%	−16%	7%	2%	−22%	NA	NA
Change since fiscal year 2003	NA	NA	16%	33%	50%	111%	129%	91%	104%	107%	62%	NA	NA

CRS = Congressional Research Service.
CRA = Continuing Resolution Amendment.
P.L. = Public Law.
DOD = U.S. Department of Defense.
USAID = U.S. Agency for International Development.
Notes: NA = not applicable. Totals may not add due to rounding. Total includes $5.5 billion in fiscal year 2003 of DOD funds that cannot be allocated between Iraq and Afghanistan because DOD records are incomplete.
*The sixth fiscal year 2011 Continuing Resolution was signed by the president on March 18, 2011, and extended funding for all agencies till April 8, 2011 generally at the fiscal year 2010 enacted level. In the case of DOD and the Department of Veterans' Affairs, war funding was close to the administration's request, but for the State Department and USAID, fiscal year 2011 funding levels could be $1 billion lower than requested.

SOURCE: Amy Belasco, "Table 1. Estimated War Funding by Operation: FY2001–FY2012 War Request," in *The Cost of Iraq, Afghanistan, and Other Global War on Terror Operations since 9/11,* Congressional Research Service, March 29, 2011, http://www.fas.org/sgp/crs/natsec/RL33110.pdf (accessed June 7, 2014)

TABLE 4.11

Overseas Contingency Operations funding, fiscal years 2013–14 and requested for fiscal year 2015

[Billions of dollars]

	Actual, 2013	Enacted, 2014[a]	President's budget, 2015[b]	Percentage change	
				2013–2014	2014–2015
Defense					
Overseas contingency operations[c]	82	85	79	3.7	−7.0
Emergency requirements	*	0	0	−100.0	0
Other	518	520	550	0.5	5.6
Subtotal	**600**	**606**	**629**	**0.9**	**3.8**
Nondefense					
Overseas contingency operations[c]	11	7	6	−39.9	−9.3
Emergency requirements	48	0	−1	−100.0	n.a.
Other	481	521	529	8.3	1.5
Subtotal	**540**	**528**	**533**	**−2.3**	**1.1**
Total	**1,140**	**1,133**	**1,163**	**−0.6**	**2.6**

*Between zero and $500 million.
[a]The president does not propose any changes to appropriations for 2014.
[b]The president proposes to reduce budget authority by a total of $19 billion for certain mandatory programs through the appropriation process. In keeping with long-standing procedures, those changes are credited against discretionary spending and therefore are included in the figures for 2015. (For 2013 and 2014, any such effects appear in their normal mandatory accounts and are not shown here.)
[c]Overseas contingency operations consist of military operations and related activities in Afghanistan and other countries.
Notes: The numbers shown here do not include obligation limitations for certain transportation programs.

SOURCE: "Table 4. Discretionary Budget Authority Proposed by the President for 2015, Compared with Appropriations for 2013 and 2014," in *An Analysis of the President's 2015 Budget*, Congressional Budget Office, April 2014, http://www.cbo.gov/sites/default/files/cbofiles/attachments/45230-APB_0.pdf (accessed June 7, 2014)

FIGURE 4.8

Annual number of major-limb amputations due to battle injuries among U.S. military members and veterans, 2001–13

[As of December 21, 2013]

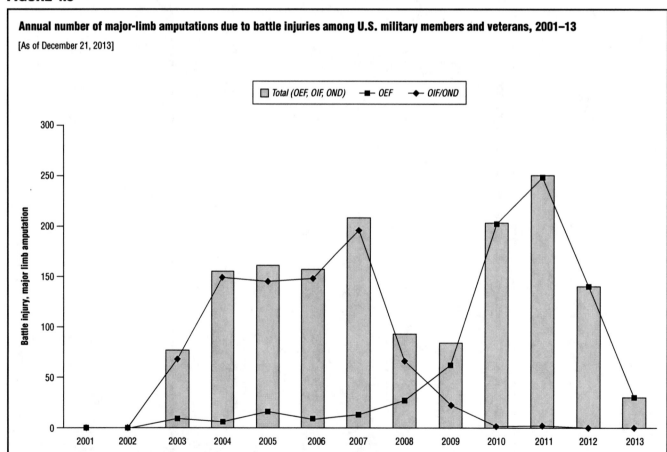

Notes: OEF = Operation Enduring Freedom. OIF = Operation Iraqi Freedom. OND = Operation New Dawn.

SOURCE: Hannah Fischer, "Figure 4. Major-Limb Amputations Due to Battle Injuries in OIF/OND and OEF, 2001–2013 (as of December 21, 2013)," in *A Guide to U.S. Military Casualty Statistics: Operation New Dawn, Operation Iraqi Freedom, and Operation Enduring Freedom*, Congressional Research Service, February 19, 2014, http://www.fas.org/sgp/crs/natsec/RS22452.pdf (accessed June 7, 2014)

FIGURE 4.9

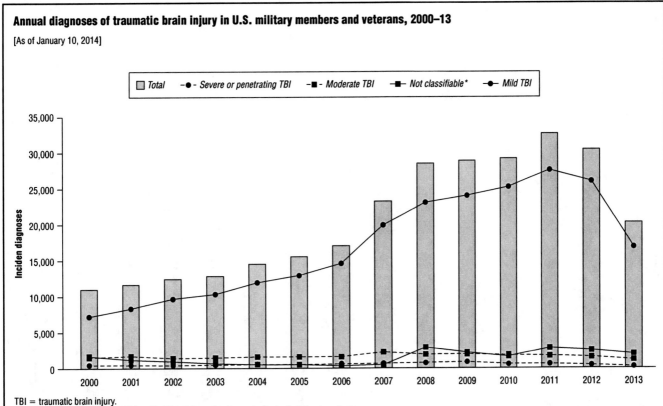

Annual diagnoses of traumatic brain injury in U.S. military members and veterans, 2000–13

[As of January 10, 2014]

TBI = traumatic brain injury.
*"Not Classifiable" indicates additional incident information is required prior to TBI categorization.

SOURCE: Hannah Fischer, "Figure 3. Traumatic Brain Injury (TBI) over Time, 2000–2013 Q3, Deployed and Not Previously Deployed Combined (as of January 10, 2014)," in *A Guide to U.S. Military Casualty Statistics: Operation New Dawn, Operation Iraqi Freedom, and Operation Enduring Freedom,* Congressional Research Service, February 19, 2014, http://www.fas.org/sgp/crs/natsec/RS22452.pdf (accessed June 7, 2014)

BrainInjury) that "a TBI is caused by a bump, blow or jolt to the head or a penetrating head injury that disrupts the normal function of the brain." As shown in Figure 4.9, TBI diagnoses among veterans more than tripled between 2000 and 2011.

Besides physical injuries, wartime experiences (like other traumatic experiences) can have lasting negative effects on mental health. In "Post-Traumatic Stress Disorder" (2014, http://www.mayoclinic.org/diseases-conditions/post-traumatic-stress-disorder/basics/definition/con-20022540), the Mayo Clinic defines post-traumatic stress disorder (PTSD) as "a mental health condition that's triggered by a terrifying event—either experiencing it or witnessing it. Symptoms may include flashbacks, nightmares and severe anxiety, as well as uncontrollable thoughts about the event." Figure 4.10 shows the number of PTSD diagnoses annually in veterans between 2000 and 2013. Tens of thousands of cases have been reported.

FIGURE 4.10

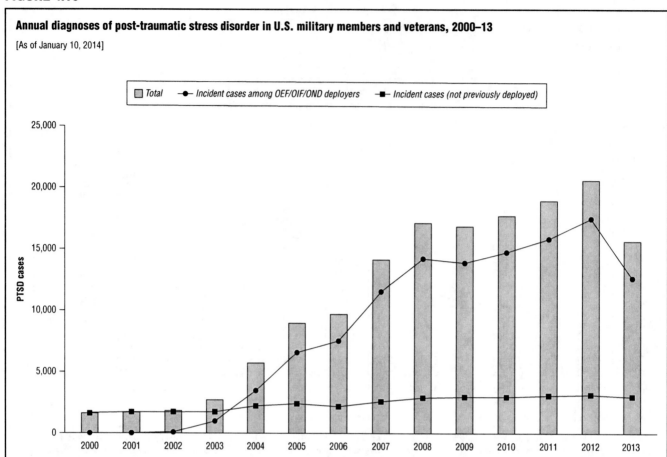

Annual diagnoses of post-traumatic stress disorder in U.S. military members and veterans, 2000–13

[As of January 10, 2014]

Legend: Total · Incident cases among OEF/OIF/OND deployers · Incident cases (not previously deployed)

Notes: OEF = Operation Enduring Freedom. OIF = Operation Iraqi Freedom. OND = Operation New Dawn. PTSD = post-traumatic stress disorder.

SOURCE: Hannah Fischer, "Figure 1. Annual Post-Traumatic Stress Disorder Diagnoses in All Services, 2000–2013 (as of January 10, 2014)," in *A Guide to U.S. Military Casualty Statistics: Operation New Dawn, Operation Iraqi Freedom, and Operation Enduring Freedom*, Congressional Research Service, February 19, 2014, http://www.fas.org/sgp/crs/natsec/RS22452.pdf (accessed June 7, 2014)

CHAPTER 5
HOMELAND SECURITY

Protecting the U.S. homeland from terrorist attacks is a formidable and challenging task. The scope is enormous. U.S. borders span more than 100,000 miles (160,000 km) and are difficult to protect against illegal entry. There are hundreds of land border crossings, seaports, and international airports that must be secured. The United States has vast air and rail transportation systems and many highly concentrated metropolitan areas, all of which are attractive targets for terrorists. American society is relatively open with little restriction on movement or access to public places, and foreign visitors are welcomed.

To counter the vulnerabilities inherent to American society, the U.S. government has developed a homeland security infrastructure that coordinates the efforts of many agencies at the federal, state, and local levels. The overall goal is threefold: to prevent terrorists from striking in the United States, to fortify U.S. defenses against an attack, and to prepare the American people and emergency responders in case an attack does occur.

U.S. DEPARTMENT OF HOMELAND SECURITY

The U.S. Department of Homeland Security (DHS) was established by President George W. Bush (1946–) in 2002 and began operating in 2003. It brought together dozens of agencies and offices that had previously operated as separate entities. The DHS works in concert with other federal entities devoted to national security, particularly the intelligence community (IC), the U.S. military, and the Federal Bureau of Investigation (FBI). Besides this horizontal cooperation, the DHS is also charged with coordinating homeland security efforts in a vertical manner—across federal, state, and local government levels. State and local officials are particularly important to the task of emergency response because they represent the first wave of government assistance in the event of a terrorist attack.

Figure 5.1 shows an organization chart for the DHS as of 2014. Major agencies within the department include the Transportation Security Administration, the U.S. Customs and Border Protection, the U.S. Citizenship and Immigration Services, the U.S. Immigration and Customs Enforcement, the U.S. Secret Service, the Federal Emergency Management Agency, and the U.S. Coast Guard.

The DHS's projected budget for fiscal year (FY) 2015 was $60.9 billion. (See Table 5.1.) This value was up slightly from FYs 2013 and 2014, when its budgets were $59.2 billion and $60.7 billion, respectively. Table 5.2 shows the number of full-time equivalent employees that were expected to be employed at each agency or in agency-wide functions in FY 2015. Overall, the DHS was projected to employ 224,642 full-time equivalent employees.

The following is a description of each appropriation and agency listed in Table 5.1 based on information contained in the DHS publication *Budget-in-Brief: Fiscal Year 2015* (March 2014, http://www.dhs.gov/sites/default/files/publications/FY15BIB.pdf):

- Departmental Operations—this appropriation funds leadership, direction, and management elements of the DHS, including executive management, administrative support, financial management, and information technology.

- Analysis and Operations—this appropriation funds resources that support the Office of Intelligence and Analysis (I&A) and the Office of Operations Coordination and Planning (OPS). The I&A is the DHS's representative in the national IC. The OPS (2014, http://www.dhs.gov/about-office-operations-coordination-and-planning) monitors homeland security "on a daily basis" and coordinates homeland security activities within the DHS and with state and local partners.

- Office of the Inspector General—serves as an independent and objective audit, inspection, and investigative

FIGURE 5.1

Department of Homeland Security (DHS) organization chart, 2014

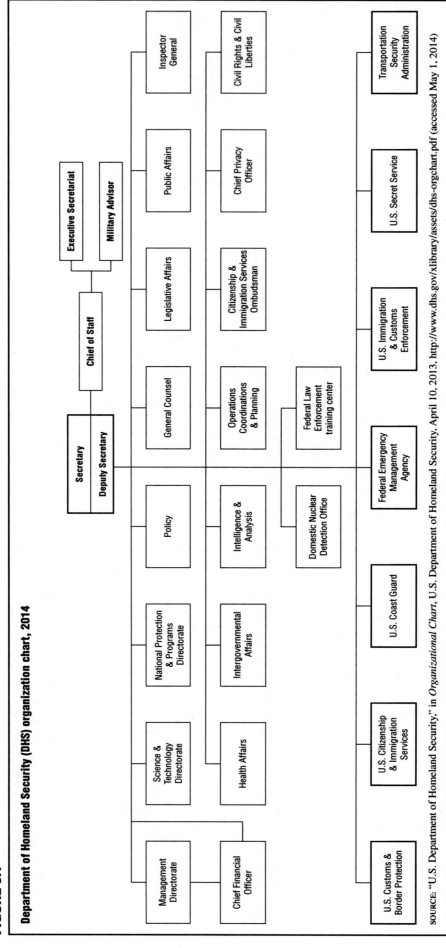

SOURCE: "U.S. Department of Homeland Security," in *Organizational Chart*, U.S. Department of Homeland Security, April 10, 2013, http://www.dhs.gov/xlibrary/assets/dhs-orgchart.pdf (accessed May 1, 2014)

TABLE 5.1

Department of Homeland Security (DHS) budgets for fiscal years 2013–14 and requested for fiscal year 2015, by agency

	FY 2013 Revised enacted	FY 2014 Enacted	FY 2015 Pres. budget	FY 2015 +/− FY 2014	FY 2015 +/− FY 2014
	$000	$000	$000	$000	%
Departmental operations*	$708,695	$728,269	$748,024	$19,755	2.7%
Analysis and Operations (A&O)	301,853	300,490	302,268	1,778	0.6%
Office of the Inspector General (OIG)	137,910	139,437	145,457	6,020	4.3%
U.S. Customs & Border Protection (CBP)	11,736,990	12,445,616	12,764,835	319,219	2.6%
U.S. Immigration & Customs Enforcement (ICE)	5,627,660	5,614,361	5,359,065	(255,296)	−4.5%
Transportation Security Administration (TSA)	7,193,757	7,364,510	7,305,098	(59,412)	−0.8%
U.S. Coast Guard (USCG)	9,972,425	10,214,999	9,796,995	(418,004)	−4.1%
U.S. Secret Service (USSS)	1,808,313	1,840,272	1,895,905	55,633	3.0%
National Protection and Programs Directorate (NPPD)	2,638,634	2,813,213	2,857,666	44,453	1.6%
Office of Health Affairs (OHA)	126,324	126,763	125,767	(996)	−0.8%
Federal Emergency Management Agency (FEMA)	11,865,196	11,553,899	12,496,517	942,618	8.2%
FEMA: Grant programs	2,373,540	2,530,000	2,225,469	(304,531)	−12.0%
U.S. Citizenship & Immigration Services (USCIS)	3,378,348	3,219,142	3,259,885	40,743	1.3%
Federal Law Enforcement Training Center (FLETC)	243,111	258,730	259,595	865	0.3%
Science & Technology Directorate (S&T)	794,227	1,220,212	1,071,818	(148,394)	−12.2%
Domestic Nuclear Detection Office (DNDO)	302,981	285,255	304,423	19,168	6.7%
Total budge authority:	**$59,209,964**	**$60,655,168**	**$60,918,787**	**$263,619**	**0.4%**
Less: Mandatory, fee, and trust funds:	(11,308,307)	(11,526,210)	(11,890,496)	(364,286)	3.2%

*Departmental Operations is comprised of the Office of the Secretary & Executive Management, DHS Headquarters Consolidation, the Office of the Undersecretary for Management, the Office of the Chief Financial Officer, and the Office of the Chief Information Officer.
Notes: DHS = Department of Homeland Security. FY = fiscal year. Pres. = President's.

SOURCE: Adapted from "Total Budget Authority by Organization," in *Budget-in-Brief Fiscal Year 2015 Department of Homeland Security*, Department of Homeland Security, 2014, http://www.dhs.gov/sites/default/files/publications/FY15BIB.pdf (accessed May 1, 2014)

body to promote economy, effectiveness, and efficiency in DHS programs and operations and to prevent and detect fraud, waste, and abuse.

- U.S. Customs and Border Protection—protects the U.S. borders at and between official ports of entry. Also protects the nation's economic security by regulating and facilitating the lawful movement of goods and people across U.S. borders.

- U.S. Immigration and Customs Enforcement—investigates the illegal introduction of goods, terrorists, and other criminals seeking to cross U.S. borders.

- Transportation Security Administration—protects the transportation system and ensures the freedom of movement for people and commerce.

- U.S. Coast Guard—principal federal agency responsible for maritime safety, security, and stewardship. Besides its nonhomeland security responsibilities (e.g., search and rescue), the Coast Guard conducts law enforcement and national defense missions to protect homeland security.

- U.S. Secret Service—protects the president, vice president, and other dignitaries and designated individuals; enforces laws relating to obligations and securities of the United States (e.g., counterfeiting); investigates financial and electronic crimes; and protects the White House and other buildings in the Washington, D.C., area.

- National Protection and Programs Directorate—protects against "terrorist attacks, natural disasters, and other catastrophic incidents," protects U.S. physical infrastructure and cyber (Internet) and communications infrastructure, performs risk management tasks, and coordinates partnerships within the DHS and between the DHS and outside partners.

- Office of Health Affairs—oversees medical and health preparedness for the DHS.

- Federal Emergency Management Agency—leading federal government agency that "manages and coordinates the Federal response to and recovery from major domestic disasters and emergencies of all types."

- U.S. Citizenship and Immigration Services—grants immigration and citizenship benefits and protects the integrity of the U.S. immigration system.

- Federal Law Enforcement Training Center—provides training of federal law enforcement personnel from various agencies.

- Science and Technology Directorate—provides technological resources to federal, state, tribal, and local officials.

- Domestic Nuclear Detection Office—develops and deploys detection techniques and equipment for nuclear materials, including nuclear materials that might be smuggled into and used against the United States.

TABLE 5.2

Expected employee counts for Department of Homeland Security agencies for fiscal year 2015, by agency

	Fiscal year 2015 president's budget
	Full time equivalent employees
Departmental Management and Operations	1,939
U.S. Customs and Border Protection	61,387
U.S. Immigration and Customs Enforcement	19,374
Transportation Security Administration	53,670
U.S. Coast Guard	49,547
U.S. Secret Service	6,572
National Protection & Programs Directorate	3,463
Office of Health Affairs	99
Federal Emergency Management Agency (FEMA)	12,134
Citizenship & Immigration Services	13,196
Federal Law Enforcement Training Center	1,092
Science & Technology	467
Domestic Nuclear Detection Office	127
Department of Homeland Security	224,642

Notes:
Fiscal year 2015 president's budget:
• Includes FEMA Disaster Relief base funds of $371.672 million and an additional $6.438 billion for major disasters declared pursuant to the Stafford Act and designated by the Congress as being for disaster relief pursuant to section 251 (b)(2)(D) of the Balance Budget and Emergency Deficit Control Act (BBEDCA) of 1985, as amended by the Budget Control Act of 2011.
• Total Budget Authority Request excluding DRF Major Disasters Cap Adjustment is: $54,480,994.
• Gross Discretionary Request excluding DRF Major Disasters Cap Adjustment is: $42,590,498.
• Net Discretionary Request excluding DRF Major Disasters Cap Adjustment is: $38,175,700.

SOURCE: Adapted from "Department of Homeland Security Total Budget Authority," in *Budget-in-Brief Fiscal Year 2015 Department of Homeland Security*, Department of Homeland Security, 2014, http://www.dhs.gov/sites/default/files/publications/FY15BIB.pdf (accessed May 1, 2014)

HOMELAND SECURITY STRATEGY AND GOALS

The terrorist attacks of September 11, 2001 (9/11), made U.S. leaders aware that the country lacked a coordinated strategy for protecting the U.S. homeland from terrorism. In July 2002 President Bush issued *National Strategy for Homeland Security* (https://www.hsdl.org/?view&did=856), which was updated in October 2007 (http://www.dhs.gov/xlibrary/assets/nat_strat_homeland security_2007.pdf). As of August 2014, this report was the most recent update. The strategy lists three primary goals of homeland security:

- Prevent and disrupt terrorist attacks

- Protect the American people, critical infrastructure, and key resources

- Respond to and recover from incidents

The DHS has outlined its specific strategies for meeting these goals in various documents, including *The 2014 Quadrennial Homeland Security Review* (June 2014, http://www.dhs.gov/sites/default/files/publications/qhsr/2014-QHSR.pdf). Another important document is *Department of Homeland Security Strategic Plan: Fiscal Years 2012–2016* (February 2012, http://www.dhs.gov/xlibrary/assets/dhs-strategic-plan-fy-2012-

2016.pdf). The remainder of this chapter is devoted to detailing the DHS's actions and operations in the context of its three primary goals for homeland security.

PREVENT AND DISRUPT TERRORIST ATTACKS

The goal to prevent and disrupt terrorist attacks focuses primarily on gathering and sharing intelligence, securing the nation's borders and transportation systems, and conducting law enforcement counterterrorism activities.

Role of Intelligence

As described in Chapter 2, intelligence is information with strategic importance. The *National Strategy for Homeland Security* calls for a highly coordinated and integrated framework for intelligence gathering and analysis. One of the roles of the IC is tactical threat analysis. This is the collection and analysis of reliable information about terrorist plots and plans. This task is led by the director of national intelligence (the head of the IC), the FBI, and the DHS. Intelligence achieved during this task allows the development of effective preventive action—that is, the disruption of planned terrorist plots and the capture of the terrorists. Preventive activities are spearheaded by the FBI through a collection of law enforcement entities called the joint terrorism task forces (JTTFs). The FBI describes in "Protecting America from Terrorist Attack" (2014, http://www.fbi.gov/about-us/investigate/terrorism/terrorism_jttfs) the JTTFs as "small cells of highly trained, locally based, passionately committed investigators, analysts, linguists, SWAT [special weapons and tactics] experts, and other specialists from dozens of U.S. law enforcement and intelligence agencies" and notes that there are more than 100 of them located throughout the country. The FBI also operates a national JTTF out of its headquarters in Washington, D.C.

A second important intelligence task is strategic analysis of the enemy. This is a deep and comprehensive delving into the history, motivations, workings, and structures of terrorist organizations to identify their members and means of financial support. The goal is to determine their vulnerabilities, intentions, and capabilities. This task is led by the director of national intelligence, the FBI, and the DHS.

Border Security

The U.S. Customs and Border Protection (CBP) is responsible for protecting U.S. borders from the illegal entry of people and goods. At the same time, it must ensure that legal visitors and cargo have relatively easy passage into and out of the United States. Since becoming a part of the DHS in 2003, the CBP has been given an important priority: detect terrorists and their weapons and prevent them from entering the United States. This is besides the CBP's many other responsibilities, including screening all traffic (people, vehicles, and cargo) into and out of the country for illegal activities or contraband. The task is enormous because U.S. borders are long, cross-border traffic is voluminous, and the country's economy is dependent on international trade. The CBP states in "On a Typical Day in 2013" (2014, http://www.cbp.gov/newsroom/stats/on-a-typical-day-fy2013) that in FY 2013 it managed 328 ports of entry, and on a typical day it processed 992,243 passengers and pedestrians and 67,337 truck, rail, and sea containers.

The security (or lack thereof) along the U.S. border with Mexico is a controversial political issue in terms of illegal immigration and Mexican-based criminal activities, particularly in illegal drugs and human trafficking. These problems are a prime concern to the U.S. states along the border, and their officials often accuse the federal government of failing to adequately secure the border. In 2006 President Bush deployed thousands of National Guard troops to the border to support CBP activities. In 2010 President Barack Obama (1961–) did likewise; however, both deployments were for limited durations and included tight restrictions on troop activities. The Posse Comitatus Act of 1878 forbids U.S. military forces from acting in a law enforcement role over civilians unless specifically authorized by the U.S. Constitution or Congress.

Aviation Security

The vulnerability of the nation's aviation system became painfully clear on 9/11. On that day 19 terrorists were able to board four commercial airliners as passengers, seize control of the cockpits during flight, and pilot the planes on missions of violent destruction. Three of the airliners were crashed into buildings: the twin towers of the World Trade Center in New York City and the U.S. Pentagon in Arlington, Virginia. The fourth plane crashed in a field in Pennsylvania after a revolt by the passengers. Its probable destination was the U.S. Capitol in Washington, D.C. The combined attacks left some 2,700 dead. Americans were stunned by the ease with which the terrorists were able to board and commandeer the planes. A variety of shortcomings and oversights in U.S. aviation security procedures had been exploited with disastrous results.

The events that transpired during the hijackings have been pieced together by investigators based largely on cell phone calls from crew members and passengers on the planes. A detailed chronology and description of these calls is included in *The 9/11 Commission Report* (July 2004, http://www.9-11commission.gov/report/911Report.pdf). The report was compiled by the National Commission on Terrorist Attacks upon the United States, an organization created by President Bush and Congress to investigate all the circumstances relating to the 9/11 terrorist attacks.

The commission believes the terrorists used small sharp items (e.g., box cutters) as weapons to attack and subdue crew members and passengers as the hijackings began. The terrorists were either allowed entry or forced their way into the cockpits, where they overcame and may have killed the cockpit crews. Before and during 9/11 it had been standard policy on commercial airliners for crew members to offer no resistance to armed hijackers. This policy evolved after a spate of hijackings in the United States during the late 1960s and early 1970s. In most of those events the hijackers demanded to be flown to a specific destination (often Cuba), and once there, they released the passengers and crew unharmed. The implementation of tougher security measures and x-ray screening at U.S. airports virtually eliminated hijacking aboard domestic U.S. flights. Thus, it had not been viewed as a serious threat to U.S. commercial aviation for some time. As a result, U.S. planes did not have fortified cockpit doors in 2001.

In 1988 Pan Am Flight 103 was en route from London to New York City when a bomb in the luggage compartment exploded, tearing apart the plane. It crashed near the small village of Lockerbie, Scotland, killing all 259 passengers and crew members and 11 people on the ground. It was later determined that terrorists had managed to hide a bomb inside a radio that was somehow tagged for placement aboard the plane, although it did not belong to a passenger. Following this incident, the United States implemented stricter regulations and inspection of passenger baggage.

According to the *9/11 Commission Report*, it was standard procedure in 2001 to hold a high-risk passenger's luggage until that person had boarded the plane. This was to prevent a terrorist from checking baggage containing explosives and then not boarding the plane. It was assumed that if both passenger and luggage were aboard, then there was no danger posed by the luggage. Mohamed Atta (1968–2001) is believed to have been the ringleader of the 9/11 hijackers. He piloted American Airlines Flight 11 into the first tower at the World Trade Center. Before boarding his flight in Boston, Atta had been picked by a computerized prescreening system for heightened security measures. As a result, his checked baggage was not loaded onto the plane until it had been confirmed that he was aboard the aircraft.

The 9/11 terrorist attacks changed many assumptions and conventions that had guided aviation security for decades. It became obvious that terrorists were willing to die as part of their missions. Thus, it was not inconceivable that a terrorist could both check in luggage containing explosives and board the plane.

NEW AVIATION SECURITY MEASURES. In November 2001 Congress passed the Aviation and Transportation Security Act. It created the Transportation Security

FIGURE 5.2

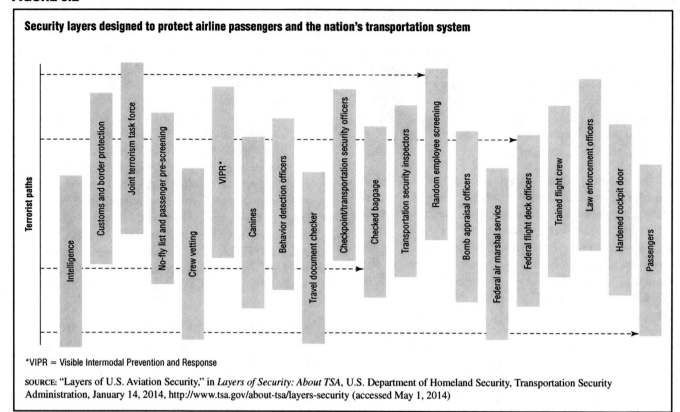

Security layers designed to protect airline passengers and the nation's transportation system

*VIPR = Visible Intermodal Prevention and Response

SOURCE: "Layers of U.S. Aviation Security," in *Layers of Security: About TSA*, U.S. Department of Homeland Security, Transportation Security Administration, January 14, 2014, http://www.tsa.gov/about-tsa/layers-security (accessed May 1, 2014)

Administration (TSA) within the U.S. Department of Transportation. In 2003 the TSA became part of the newly created DHS. The TSA is responsible for protecting the United States' transportation systems. However, numerous other agencies and organizations, such as the IC, the CBP, and the FBI, work with the TSA to provide multiple levels of security for U.S. aviation. (See Figure 5.2.)

One security level is the so-called No-Fly List. This TSA-compiled list purportedly contains the names of people with ties to terrorism who are forbidden to fly on aircraft originating in or coming to the United States. A second list is called the Secondary Security Screening Selection List, or the selectee list, for short. People on the selectee list undergo secondary screening before being allowed to fly. The names on the lists and the criteria used to select them are secret. Various media sources report that thousands of names are on the lists.

Until 2007 the TSA was prohibited by the Privacy Act of 1974 from maintaining records of certain personal information for people not accused of or suspected of criminal activity. However, the TSA explains in "Secure Flight Program" (June 7, 2014, http://www.tsa.gov/stakeholders/secure-flight-program) that in 2007 it issued a ruling exempting itself from certain provisions of the Privacy Act. The exemptions allowed the agency to begin implementing its Secure Flight Process for preflight passenger screening. The process requires airlines to

obtain identifying information about potential passengers, including their full name, date of birth, and gender. This information is relayed to the TSA and checked against the watch lists for possible matches. Cleared passengers can then be issued their boarding passes by the airlines.

The TSA also conducts preflight screening of passengers and baggage at airports and provides air marshals on selected flights. The Air Marshal Program began in 1970 in response to a rash of hijackings. At that time the program was overseen by the U.S. Customs Service (now the CBP). More than 1,000 agents were trained to thwart attempted hijackings. They flew undercover (dressed as passengers) on various flights and were armed. The program was discontinued in 1974. During the mid-1980s the program was restarted, but only for international flights of U.S. airlines.

In "Brief History: Air Marshals" (Time.com, January 18, 2010), Laura Fitzpatrick notes that there were only a few dozen air marshals in the program when the 9/11 terrorist attacks occurred. President Bush greatly expanded the program and placed it under the TSA. Several thousand new agents have been trained as air marshals. Besides flying undercover on domestic and international flights, these agents also staff positions in the National Counterterrorism Center and the JTTFs. Another program operated under the TSA allows certain airline crew members to fly armed. Federal flight deck officers are trained in firearm usage and taught other necessary skills to thwart a hijacker.

In December 2001 a man aboard a commercial airliner flying from Paris, France, to Miami, Florida, tried to detonate explosives hidden in his shoes. The so-called shoe bomber was overpowered by passengers aboard the plane and turned over to authorities. The incident prompted airport screeners to have passengers remove their footwear for closer inspection. Following the August 2006 discovery of a plot by British terrorists to use liquid explosives hidden in carry-on items, such as sports drinks and water bottles, the TSA temporarily banned the carrying on of all liquid and gel items. Eventually, a standard was adapted by the TSA (June 24, 2014, http://www.tsa.gov/traveler-information/make-your-trip-better-using-3-1-1) allowing each passenger to carry on only one quart-sized plastic bag holding containers of 3 ounces or less of liquids and gels.

In December 2009 a man flying from Amsterdam, Netherlands, to Detroit, Michigan, tried to set off explosives hidden in his underwear shortly before the plane landed. Although he created a small fire, the explosives did not detonate. Passengers and crew members extinguished the fire and held the man for authorities. The incident prompted the TSA to greatly expand its use of whole-body imagers during airport screening. The imagers are more formally known as advanced imaging technology (AIT). The TSA reports in "Advanced Imaging Technology (AIT)" (February 12, 2014, http://www.tsa.gov/travelers-guide/advanced-imaging-technology-ait) that the imagers use millimeter wave technology. Millimeter wave imaging uses electromagnetic waves to create a three-dimensional image of the body and reportedly reveals any metal and nonmetal objects, including explosives, that are hidden beneath a person's clothing. The TSA indicates that as of 2014 it had deployed approximately 740 of the units at 160 airports.

At first, whole-body imaging raised the concerns of privacy advocates because the images revealed detailed features of the human body. After a public outcry the TSA implemented new software that incorporates a generic outline of the human body, rather than person-specific bodily features. Regardless, the effectiveness of the AITs remains controversial. Jane Merrick reports in "Are Planned Airport Scanners Just a Scam?" (Independent.co.uk, January 3, 2010) that private security experts do not believe that whole-body imagers would have revealed the explosives hidden in the underwear of the would-be Detroit bomber. Echoing this sentiment, the U.S. Government Accountability Office (GAO) acknowledges in *Aviation Security: TSA Is Increasing Procurement and Deployment of the Advanced Imaging Technology, but Challenges to This Effort and Other Areas of Aviation Security Remain* (March 17, 2010, http://www.gao.gov/

new.items/d10484t.pdf) that after scrutinizing the capabilities of the AIT technology "it remains unclear whether the AIT would have detected the weapon used in the December 2009 incident."

The TSA notes in "Advanced Imaging Technology (AIT)" that whole-body imaging is an optional screening procedure. Passengers can choose a physical pat down instead.

Another area of concern in aviation security is air cargo, such as packages, crates, and other items that are shipped by air. The TSA explains in "Programs and Initiatives: Air Cargo" (November 14, 2013, http://www.tsa.gov/stakeholders/programs-and-initiatives-1) that the Implementing the 9/11 Commission Recommendations Act of 2007 required that 100 percent of the cargo transported on commercial passenger aircraft be screened at a level of security equal to that used to screen passenger baggage by August 2010. Complete screening of domestic cargo was accomplished by the end of 2010. Screening of international cargo being shipped into the United States proved more difficult to achieve and the deadline was extended. However, efforts were greatly accelerated following incidents in October 2010, when bombs were hidden in cargo on planes bound from Yemen to the United States. The bombs were discovered and neutralized before reaching their destinations. By the end of 2012 complete screening of international cargo had been implemented.

The TSA also performs electronic screening of passenger luggage at U.S. airports. According to the GAO, in *Checked Baggage Screening: TSA Has Deployed Optimal Systems at the Majority of TSA-Regulated Airports, but Could Strengthen Cost Estimates* (April 2012, http://www.gao.gov/assets/600/590513.pdf), the TSA uses two types of screening equipment: explosives detection systems (EDS) and explosives trace detection (ETD) machines. The GAO states that EDS "use X-rays with computer-aided imaging to automatically recognize the characteristic signatures of threat explosives." ETD machines are described as machines that allow baggage screeners to use "chemical analysis to manually detect traces of explosive materials' vapors and residue."

Surface Transportation Security

The 9/11 terrorist attacks resulted in the tightening of security measures for the nation's aviation system. However, deadly terrorist attacks on passenger trains and subways in Spain, England, and India have raised concerns about the security of the U.S. surface transportation system. In September 2009 authorities arrested an Afghan man in the United States for allegedly plotting to set off bombs in the New York City subway. By that time many subway systems across the country had implemented new security measures, such as surveillance cameras and random checks of passenger bags, briefcases, baggage, and so on. Amtrak, a national passenger rail service owned by the U.S. government, had also implemented similar measures. In addition, the TSA launched in 2005 the Surface Transportation Security Inspection Program to inspect rail shipments at terminals and rail stations.

Port Security

The TSA notes in "Port and Intermodal" (August 5, 2014, http://www.tsa.gov/stakeholders/port-and-intermodal) that 99% of the U.S. overseas trade volume enters or leaves U.S. ports. Port security is a combined effort of private and government entities. At the federal level, the U.S. Coast Guard and the CBP play the major roles. The TSA operates the Transportation Worker Identification Credential (TWIC) program, which runs security checks and grants special identification cards to workers who have access to certain areas of ports and to off-shore facilities, such as off-shore oil rigs. The TWIC program was established following passage of the Maritime Transportation Security Act of 2002. The TSA (http://www.tsa.gov/sites/default/files/publications/pdf/twic/twic_dashboard_508_current.pdf) reports that as of July 2014 over 3 million workers had enrolled in the program.

Identifying Terrorists and Thwarting Their Movement

Another major component of homeland security is the collection of information about suspected and known terrorists. The U.S. government is aware that terrorists may use fraudulent identification documents to prevent being identified. In fact, the *9/11 Commission Report* indicated that some of the terrorists involved in the 9/11 attacks had fraudulent travel documents (e.g., passports) and state-issued identification documents (e.g., driver's licenses). In response, the federal government has initiated several programs that are designed to better identify people and to thwart the movement of people with terrorist ties.

REAL ID. The *9/11 Commission Report* recommended that the federal government "set standards for the issuance of birth certificates and sources of identification, such as drivers licenses." In response, Congress passed the Intelligence Reform and Terrorism Prevention Act of 2004, which was later superseded by the REAL ID Act of 2005. It called for all state-issued driver's licenses and other state-issued identification documents to meet specific federal standards for security and integrity by May 2008. The act has been extremely controversial for a variety of reasons. Some analysts have expressed concerns about privacy issues, and state legislatures have complained about the costs and difficulties of implementing the act.

The DHS did not release final regulations for the REAL ID program until January 2008, which left states little time to meet the original deadline. As a result, the federal government delayed the final deadline to the end of 2009. However, several states remained steadfastly opposed to the act. In "Real ID Act Might Cause Real Hassles for Travelers" (NPR.org, December 7, 2009), Brian Naylor reports that as of December 2009, 13 states had passed legislation prohibiting themselves from fully complying with the REAL ID Act due to "cost or privacy issues." In addition, the states disliked the extra bureaucratic procedures involved in the program and viewed it as an encroachment of the federal government into state rights. The DHS postponed the deadline to May 2011. Democratic politicians began pushing an alternative program called PASS ID that kept only some security measures of the REAL ID program and incorporated more privacy controls. However, PASS ID legislation failed to pass during the 111th session of Congress (January 2009–January 2011). States that had waited to implement the REAL ID program in the hopes that PASS ID was going to pass found themselves with little time to meet the looming deadline. The DHS extended the REAL ID deadline to January 2013 and then to April 2014. Daniel C. Vock notes in "REAL ID Is Slowly Changing State Drivers' Licenses" (USAToday.com, January 22, 2014) that as of January 2014 the final compliance deadline had been extended to 2016. At that time less than half of the states were in compliance with the program.

TERRORIST DATABASES AND WATCH LISTS. The No-Fly List and the selectee list are actually subsets of the Consolidated Terrorist Screening Database, which is maintained by the FBI's Terrorist Screening Center (TSC). This database is often referred to as the Terrorist Screening Database or the Terrorist Watch List. Creation of the database was authorized by President Bush in September 2003 through issuance of Homeland Security Presidential Directive 6 (http://www.fas.org/irp/offdocs/nspd/hspd-6.html).

Figure 5.3 shows the process by which individuals are nominated and accepted or rejected for inclusion in the database. Nominations can originate from federal agencies, such as the CIA, the FBI, the Defense Intelligence Agency, or the U.S. Department of State. The names are submitted to the National Counterterrorism Center (NCTC), which maintains the Terrorist Identities Datamart Environment (TIDE) database. NCTC analysts collect information about the nominated individuals and distribute the names of those believed to have a connection to international terrorism to the TSC. The TSC conducts its own screening process and accepted names are added to the Terrorist Screening Database. As shown in Figure 5.3, information in the database is then made available to various federal, state, and local agencies and to selected foreign governments.

FIGURE 5.3

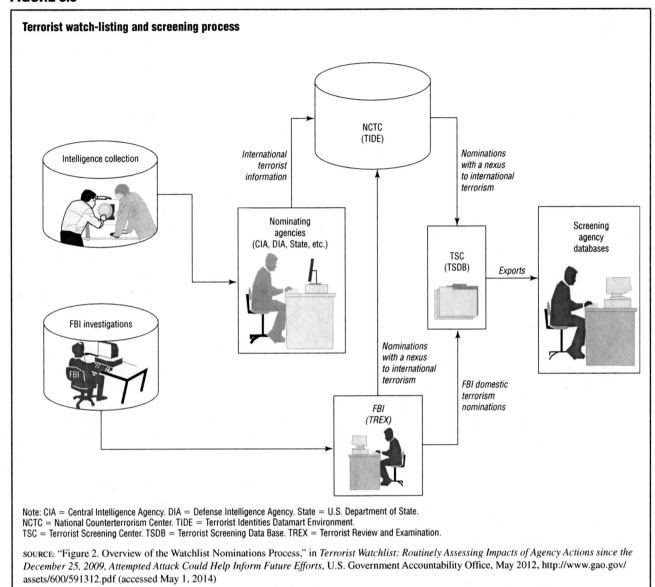

Terrorist watch-listing and screening process

Note: CIA = Central Intelligence Agency. DIA = Defense Intelligence Agency. State = U.S. Department of State. NCTC = National Counterterrorism Center. TIDE = Terrorist Identities Datamart Environment. TSC = Terrorist Screening Center. TSDB = Terrorist Screening Data Base. TREX = Terrorist Review and Examination.

SOURCE: "Figure 2. Overview of the Watchlist Nominations Process," in *Terrorist Watchlist: Routinely Assessing Impacts of Agency Actions since the December 25, 2009, Attempted Attack Could Help Inform Future Efforts*, U.S. Government Accountability Office, May 2012, http://www.gao.gov/assets/600/591312.pdf (accessed May 1, 2014)

PROTECT THE AMERICAN PEOPLE, CRITICAL INFRASTRUCTURE, AND KEY RESOURCES

Warning of Attacks

One of the tasks of the DHS is to operate a national warning system that keeps the public apprised about the nation's relative risk at any time to a terrorist attack. Prior to 2011, the Homeland Security Advisory System used a color-coded risk scheme to indicate risk. In April 2011 a new system called the National Terrorism Advisory System (NTAS) was implemented. According to the DHS, in "National Terrorism Advisory System" (2014, http://www.dhs.gov/files/programs/ntas.shtm), the new system relies on so-called alert bulletins that provide "timely, detailed information to the public, government agencies, first responders, airports and other transportation hubs, and the private sector." As of August 2014, no alerts had been issued under the new system; however, the DHS provides a sample NTAS alert at https://www.dhs.gov/sites/default/files/publications/ntas-sample-alert.pdf.

Critical Infrastructure and Key Assets

The federal government's overall strategy for protecting the nation's critical infrastructure and key assets was laid out in February 2003 in *National Strategy for the Physical Protection of Critical Infrastructures and Key Assets* (http://www.dhs.gov/xlibrary/assets/Physical_Strategy.pdf). This document outlined policy directives that the DHS used to develop a plan for infrastructure protection. As of August 2014, the most recently published plan was *National Infrastructure Protection Plan 2013: Partnering for Critical Infrastructure Security and Resilience* (2013, http://www.dhs.gov/sites/default/files/publications/NIPP%202013_Partnering%20for%20Critical%20Infrastructure%20Security%20and%20Resilience_508_0.pdf). The DHS defines critical infrastructure and

TABLE 5.3

Agencies responsible for critical infrastructure and key resources, 2014

Department/agency	Sector/subsector
Agriculture	Agriculture
	Food
Agriculture	Meat/poultry
Health and Human Services	All other
Treasury	Financial services (formerly banking and finance)
EPA	Water and waste water systems (formerly drinking water and water treatment systems)
Health and Human Services	Public health and healthcare
Defense	Defense industrial base
Energy	Energy[a]
Homeland Security	Transportation systems[b] (now includes postal and shipping)
Homeland Security	Information technology
Homeland Security	Communications
Homeland Security	Commercial nuclear reactors, materials, and waste
Homeland Security	Chemical
Homeland Security	Emergency services
Homeland Security	Dams
Homeland Security	Commercial facilities
Homeland Security	Government facilities (now includes national monuments and icons)
Homeland Security	Critical manufacturing

[a]While noted here as a single sector, in practice it is represented by two relatively separate sectors: electric power (except for nuclear power facilities); and the production, refining, and some distribution of oil and gas. The Department of Energy is the lead agency for both. However, the Department of Homeland Security (through the Transportation Security Administration) is the lead agency for the distribution of oil and gas via pipelines. Nuclear power is considered its own sector.
[b]While noted here as a single sector, Transportation includes all modes of transportation: rail, mass transit (rail and bus), air, maritime, highways, pipelines, etc. The Transportation Security Administration within the Department of Homeland Security, in collaboration with the Department of Transportation, is the lead agency for all but the maritime subsector, for which the Coast Guard, also within the Department of Homeland Security, acts as lead agency.
Note: EPA = Environmental Protection Agency.

SOURCE: John D. Moteff, "Table 2. Current Lead Agency Assignments," in *Critical Infrastructures: Background, Policy, and Implementation,* Congressional Research Service, February 21, 2014, http://www.fas.org/sgp/crs/homesec/RL30153.pdf (accessed May 1, 2014)

key assets as including "systems and assets, whether physical or virtual, so vital to the United States that the incapacity or destruction of such systems and assets would have a debilitating impact on security, national economic security, national public health or safety, or any combination of those matters."

Examples of critical infrastructure include sectors that are essential to survival (e.g., agriculture, food, and water) and those with economic, political, or social importance (e.g., the banking and chemical industries and the postal service). Infrastructure includes both distinct structures, such as buildings and dams, and the networks and components that make up the nation's telecommunications and cyber systems. Key assets include "individual targets" that are not essential or vital, but have national importance. The Statue of Liberty is a prime example. The DHS also includes high-profile events, such as the Super Bowl.

Table 5.3 indicates how the responsibility for protecting critical infrastructure and key resources is divided among several federal agencies.

Security against Catastrophic Threats

Catastrophic threats are those posed by weapons of mass destruction (WMDs). WMDs are unconventional weapons that use nontraditional means to cause destruction and death. This primarily includes nuclear technology or the release of chemical or biological agents. The major goals under this mission are to develop more effective detection and data-sharing techniques, preventive agents (such as vaccines), and antidotes and treatments to counter the risks posed by WMD attacks.

The Centers for Disease Control and Prevention (CDC) is a federal agency within the U.S. Department of Health and Human Services. Since its founding in 1946, the CDC has been responsible for protecting national public health, including the prevention and control of infectious diseases and other hazards. The CDC was tasked with preparing the United States for the health threats posed by WMDs following the 9/11 terrorist attacks.

CHEMICAL SECURITY. In "Chemical Security" (2014, http://www.dhs.gov/topic/chemical-security), the DHS notes that "the manufacturing, use, storage, and distribution of chemicals must be secured from threats including terrorism and accidents. Some chemical facilities possess materials that could be stolen and used to make weapons." Table 5.4 categorizes various hazardous chemicals by their toxicity. The chemical agents that are considered to be of greatest interest to terrorists are cyanide compounds (blood agents), mustard (a blister agent), and nerve agents, such as sarin, tabun, and VX. Videos recovered from terrorist training facilities in Afghanistan show dogs being killed in cyanide gas chambers. Cyanide compounds are easily available because they have a variety of commercial uses. Mustard gas is not commercially available, but is relatively easy to synthesize (produce) in a laboratory. Nerve agents are military-grade chemicals and thus are extremely difficult for terrorists to obtain.

Although these chemical agents are highly toxic, effective dissemination techniques have not yet been developed to make them strategically useful to terrorists. Airborne chemicals dissipate quickly unless they are in a confined space. Also, they may be detectable by human senses before reaching a lethal concentration. For example, hydrogen cyanide and cyanogen chloride have distinctive odors. It is likely that potential victims would flee the area before being overcome by such gases.

The DHS enforces the Chemical Facility Anti-Terrorism Standards (http://www.dhs.gov/chemical-facility-anti-terrorism-standards), which require covered chemical facilities to prepare assessments in which they identify any security vulnerabilities at their facilities and to develop and implement one of two types of plans: a Site Security Plan (SSP) or an Alternative Security Program

TABLE 5.4

Chemical agents, by category

Category	Description	Examples	
Biotoxins	Poisons that come from plants or animals	Abrin Brevetoxin Colchicine Digitalis Nicotine	Ricin Saxitoxin Strychnine Tetrodotoxin Trichothecene
Blister agents/vesicants	Chemicals that severely blister the eyes, respiratory tract, and skin on contact	Mustards Lewisites	Chlorarsine agents Phosgene oxime
Blood agents	Poisons that affect the body by being absorbed into the blood	Arsine Carbon monoxide Cyanide	Sodium monofluoroacetate (compound 1080)
Caustics (acids)	Chemicals that burn or corrode people's skin, eyes, and mucus membranes (lining of the nose, mouth, throat, and lungs) on contact	Hydrofluoric acid (hydrogen fluoride)	
Choking/lung/pulmonary agents	Chemicals that cause severe irritation or swelling of the respiratory tract (lining of the nose, throat, and lungs)	Ammonia Bromine Chlorine Hydrogen chloride Methyl bromide Methyl isocyanate Osmium tetroxide	Phosgene Phosphine Phosphorus, elemental, white or yellow Sulfuryl fluoride
Incapacitating agents	Drugs that make people unable to think clearly or that cause an altered state of consciousness (possibly unconsciousness)	BZ Fentanyls & other opioids	
Long-acting anticoagulants	Poisons that prevent blood from clotting properly, which can lead to uncontrolled bleeding	Super warfarin	
Metals	Agents that consist of metallic poisons	Arsenic Barium	Mercury Thallium
Nerve agents	Highly poisonous chemicals that work by preventing the nervous system from working properly	G agents (e.g., Sarin, Soman, Tabun)	V agents (e.g., VX)
Organic solvents	Agents that damage the tissues of living things by dissolving fats and oils	Benzene	
Riot control agents/tear gas	Highly irritating agents normally used by law enforcement for crowd control or by individuals for protection (for example, mace)	Bromobenzylcyanide Chloroacetophenone Chlorobenzylidenemalononitrile	Chloropicrin Dibenzoxazepine
Toxic alcohols	Poisonous alcohols that can damage the heart, kidneys, and nervous system	Ethylene glycol	
Vomiting agents	Chemicals that cause nausea and vomiting	Adamsite	

SOURCE: Adapted from "Chemical Agents, A to Z, by Category," in *Emergency Preparedness and Response: Chemical Emergencies*, Centers for Disease Control and Prevention, April 8, 2013, http://emergency.cdc.gov/agent/agentlistchem-category.asp (accessed May 6, 2014)

(ASP). As shown in Table 5.5, as of April 21, 2014, 4,133 facilities were covered by the standards. Nearly one-third (1,324) of them had submitted an SSP or ASP.

BIOLOGICAL SECURITY. Table 5.6 lists the biological agents and diseases that could be used in a terrorist attack. The agents are divided into three categories: bacterium, toxin, and virus. The Central Intelligence Agency explains in *Terrorist CBRN: Materials and Effects (U)* (May 2003, https://www.cia.gov/library/reports/general-reports-1/CBRN_threat.pdf) that anthrax and botulism are the diseases likely of most interest to terrorists. Anthrax is a bacterial disease caused by the *Bacillus anthracis* bacteria, with onset one to six days after exposure. There are two common routes of exposure: inhalation and cutaneous (through the skin). Inhaled anthrax is generally fatal unless antibiotics are given within the first few hours after exposure. Cutaneous anthrax is easily treated and rarely fatal.

Shortly after 9/11, several envelopes containing high-grade anthrax spores were discovered at various locations in the eastern United States. Five people died of inhalation

exposure and more than a dozen other people became sick but survived. The FBI suspected that the anthrax had originated at the U.S. Army Medical Research Institute in Fort Detrick, Maryland. The agency vigorously pursued one scientist from that facility, only to admit later that he was not the culprit. In July 2008 the FBI cleared the first suspect and paid him nearly $6 million to settle a lawsuit in which he claimed that the agency had violated his civil rights. A second scientist from the same facility, Bruce Ivins (1946–2008), was named the prime suspect in the case, but he committed suicide before being charged. In February 2010 the U.S. Department of Justice released *Amerithrax Investigative Summary* (http://www.justice.gov/archive/amerithrax/docs/amx-investigative-summary.pdf), which is a 96-page report that summarizes the FBI's case against Ivins and announces the case closed. The Department of Justice continues to maintain that Ivins was responsible for the 2001 anthrax attack.

Botulism is caused by the ingestion or inhalation of the *Clostridium botulinum* bacteria. The CIA reports that recovered terrorist training manuals have included

TABLE 5.5

Implementation of the Chemical Facility Anti-Terrorism Standards (CFATS) as of April 21, 2014

Tier*	Total # of facilities	Received final tier	Authorized SSPs and ASPs	Authorization inspection conducted	Approved SSPs and ASPs	Compliance inspections conducted
1	121	111	107	106	100	20
2	382	334	262	234	213	3
3	1,088	933	590	464	317	0
4	2,542	1,914	365	130	26	0
Total	**4,133**	**3,292**	**1,324**	**934**	**657**	**23**

*As of April 21, 2014.
SSP = Site Security Plan. ASP = Alternative Security Program.
Notes: Totals do not include facilities that are no longer regulated, but have received letters of authorization, authorization inspections, and/or approved SSPs/ASPs.

SOURCE: "CFATS Implementation Progress," in *Written testimony of NPPD Under Secretary Suzanne Spaulding and NPPD Office of Infrastructure Protection, Infrastructure Security Compliance Division Director David Wulf for a Senate Committee on Homeland Security and Governmental Affairs Hearing Titled "Charting a Path Forward for the Chemical Facilities Anti-Terrorism Standards (CFATS) Program,"* Department of Homeland Security, May 14, 2014, http://www.dhs.gov/news/2014/05/14/written-testimony-nppd-under-secretary-nppd-office-infrastructure-protection-senate (accessed May 25, 2014)

TABLE 5.6

Biological warfare agents

Agent	Possible means of delivery
Bacterium	
Anthrax	Aerosol
Brucellosis	Aerosol, expected to mimic a natural disease
Cholera	Sabotaged food and water supply; aerosol
Plague	Contaminated fleas, causing bubonic type, or aerosol, causing pneumonic type
Q fever	Dust cloud from a line or point source
Tularemia	Aerosol
Typhoid	Sabotaged food and water
Typhus	Contaminated lice or fleas
Toxin	
Botulinum	Sabotaged food and water supply; aerosol
Ricin	Aerosol
Virus	
Ebola	Aerosol; direct contact
Marburg	Aerosol; direct contact
Smallpox	Airborne
Venezuelan equine encephalitis	Airborne
Yellow fever	Aerosol

SOURCE: Adapted from "Table 7. Biological Warfare Agents," in *Homeland Security: First Responders' Ability to Detect and Model Hazardous Releases in Urban Areas Is Significantly Limited*, U.S. Government Accountability Office, June 2008, http://www.gao.gov/new.items/d08180.pdf (accessed May 25, 2014). Non-government data from Analytic Services, Inc. and Edgewood Chemical Biological Center.

procedures for producing small quantities of botulinum toxin. The onset of symptoms from botulism usually occurs two to three days after exposure and includes severe gastrointestinal illnesses.

Another biological agent of interest to terrorists is ricin, an extremely toxic agent that can be extracted from castor beans. Between 2011 and 2014 law enforcement officials prosecuted several Americans for conspiring to make ricin, possess it, or deploy it. A timeline of the cases is presented by CNN in "Ricin Fast Facts" (May 25, 2014, http://www.cnn.com/2013/05/31/us/ricin-fast-facts).

In 2011 four anti-government zealots in Georgia were arrested for plotting ricin attacks. Two were ultimately convicted on biological toxin charges while the other two pleaded guilty to lesser charges. In 2013 two separate batches of ricin-laced letters were sent to various public figures including President Obama. Two people were ultimately indicted for those incidents, which appeared to be motivated by personal grievances rather than by political ideologies. As of August 2014, both had pleaded guilty to the charges and one had been sentenced to 25 years in prison. Also in 2014 a Georgetown University student was arrested after he admitted making ricin in his dorm room. His motivations were unknown but in "Georgetown Student Charged with Possessing Ricin" (WashingtonPost.com, March 21, 2014), Justin Jouvenal and Matt Zapotosky report that the FBI did not believe the incident was terrorism-related. No one was sickened in any of these cases, because the ricin was in a crude form. Jouvenal and Zapotosky quote a researcher, who said, "It is relatively easy to make a crude version of ricin, but it is very difficult to make a good-quality, pure ricin protein."

CYBERSECURITY. Cybersecurity refers to safeguarding the nation's computer networks, data, and systems, including the Internet, from unauthorized access or hacking. The federal government's overall strategy for protecting these assets was described in February 2003 in *National Strategy to Secure Cyberspace* (https://www.us-cert.gov/sites/default/files/publications/cyberspace_strategy.pdf). Table 5.7 lists common sources of cyberthreats, such as hackers and terrorists. Table 5.8 lists common types of cybersecurity exploits. These exploits are tracked by the U.S. Computer Emergency Readiness Team (US-CERT), a division of the DHS. US-CERT also operates the National Cyber Awareness System (http://www.us-cert.gov/alerts-and-tips), which alerts the public about common cybersecurity threats.

TABLE 5.7

Sources of cyber security threats

Threat source	Description
Bot-network operators	Bot-net operators use a network, or bot-net, of compromised, remotely controlled systems to coordinate attacks and to distribute phishing schemes, spam, and malware attacks. The services of these networks are sometimes made available on underground markets (e.g., purchasing a denial-of-service attack or services to relay spam or phishing attacks).
Criminal groups	Organized criminal groups use spam, phishing, and spyware/malware to commit identity theft, online fraud, and computer extortion.
Hackers	Hackers break into networks for the thrill of the challenge, bragging rights in the hacker community, revenge, stalking, monetary gain, and political activism, among other reasons. While gaining unauthorized access once required a fair amount of skill or computer knowledge, hackers can now download attack scripts and protocols from the Internet and launch them against victim sites. Thus, while attack tools have become more sophisticated, they have also become easier to use.
Insiders	A disgruntled or corrupt organization insider is a source of computer crime. The insider may not need a great deal of knowledge about computer intrusions because his or her knowledge of a target system is sufficient to allow unrestricted access to cause damage to the system or to steal system data. The insider threat includes malicious current and former employees and contractors hired by the organization, as well as careless or poorly trained employees who may inadvertently introduce malware into systems.
Phishers	Individuals or small groups execute phishing schemes in an attempt to steal identities or information for monetary gain. A phisher may also use spam and spyware or malware to accomplish objectives.
Spammers	An individual or organization that distributes unsolicited e-mail with hidden or false information in order to sell products, conduct phishing schemes, distribute spyware or malware, or attack organizations (e.g., a denial of service).
Spyware or malware authors	An individual or organization with malicious intent carries out attacks against users by producing and distributing spyware and malware. Several notable destructive computer viruses and worms have harmed files and hard drives, and caused physical damage to equipment, including the Melissa Macro Virus, the Explore.Zip worm, the CIH (Chernobyl) Virus, Nimda, Code Red, Slammer, Blaster, and Stuxnet.
Terrorists	A terrorist seeks to destroy, incapacitate, or exploit critical infrastructures in order to threaten national security, cause mass casualties, weaken the economy, and damage public morale and confidence. The terrorist may use phishing schemes or spyware/malware in order to generate funds or gather sensitive information.

SOURCE: "Table 1. Sources of Cybersecurity Threats," in *Critical Infrastructure Protection: More Comprehensive Planning Would Enhance the Cybersecurity of Public Safety Entities' Emerging Technology*, U.S. Government Accountability Office, January 2014, http://www.gao.gov/assets/670/660404.pdf (accessed May 5, 2014)

TABLE 5.8

Types of cyber security exploits

Type of exploit	Description
Denial of service	An attack that prevents or impairs the authorized use of networks, systems, or applications by exhausting resources.
Distributed denial of service	A variant of the denial-of-service attack that uses numerous hosts to perform the attack.
Phishing	A digital form of social engineering that uses authentic-looking, but fake, e-mails to request information from users or direct them to a fake website that requests information.
Passive wiretapping	The monitoring or recording of data, such as passwords transmitted in clear text, while they are being transmitted over a communications link. This is performed without altering or affecting the data.
Trojan Horse	A computer program that appears to have a useful function, but also has a hidden and potentially malicious function that evades security mechanisms by, for example, masquerading as a useful program that a user would likely execute.
Virus	A computer program that can copy itself and infect a computer without the permission or knowledge of the user. A virus might corrupt or delete data on a computer, use an e-mail program to spread itself to other computers, or even erase everything on a hard disk. Unlike a computer worm, a virus requires human involvement (usually unwitting) to propagate.
Worm	A self-replicating, self-propagating, self-contained program that uses network mechanisms to spread. Unlike a computer virus, a worm does not require human involvement to propagate.
Exploits affecting the IT supply chain	The installation of hardware or software that contains malicious logic (like a logic bomb, Trojan horse, or a virus) or an unintentional vulnerability (the result of an existing defect, such as a coding error) or that may be counterfeited. A supply chain threat can also come from the failure or disruption in the production of critical product, or a reliance on a malicious or unqualified service provider for the performance of technical services.

Note: IT = information technology.

SOURCE: "Table 2. Types of Exploits," in *Critical Infrastructure Protection: More Comprehensive Planning Would Enhance the Cybersecurity of Public Safety Entities' Emerging Technology*, U.S. Government Accountability Office, January 2014, http://www.gao.gov/assets/670/660404.pdf (accessed May 5, 2014)

In May 2014 the U.S. government announced indictments against five members of the Chinese People's Liberation Army for cybercrimes against U.S. companies. According to Michael S. Schmidt and David E. Sanger, in "5 in China Army Face U.S. Charges of Cyberattacks" (NYTimes.com, May 19, 2014), the five members were charged with hacking into company networks to steal corporate secrets. Schmidt and Sanger state, "At the core of the indictment is the argument that while large countries routinely spy on each other for national security purposes, it is out of bounds to use state-run intelligence assets to seek commercial advantage." China and the United States have both accused each other of cyberspying and hacking into government networks related to national security.

SAFEGUARDING KEY PERSONNEL. As noted earlier, the U.S. Secret Service is responsible for protecting the president, vice president, and other designated individuals. In "Secret Service History" (2014, http://www.secretservice .gov/history.shtml), the agency notes that it was created in 1865 to combat counterfeiting. Later that century Secret Service agents began providing personal protection for the president. As of 2014, the Secret Service (http://www.secret service.gov/faq.shtml) included around 6,500 personnel. Its budget for FY 2014 was $1.8 billion. (See Table 5.1.) The agency expected to spend nearly $1.9 billion in FY 2015.

Beginning in 2012 the Secret Service experienced some highly publicized scandals that sullied its reputation. Jessica Durando reports in "3 High-Profile Secret Service Scandals in 3 Years" (USAToday.com, March 26, 2014) that the troubles started in April 2012, when President Obama was scheduled to attend a summit in Colombia. Before his arrival several off-duty Secret Service agents allegedly hired prostitutes and entertained them at the hotel where the agents were staying. Overall, more than a dozen employees were subsequently investigated for improper behavior related to the incident. The agency's director resigned in early 2013 and was replaced by Julia Pierson (1959–), the first woman ever to head the agency. Later that year a Secret Service supervisor made headlines for allegedly leaving a bullet in the room of a woman he had met in a hotel bar. Durando indicates that the agent "was pulled from his position" by the agency. In March 2014 three Secret Service agents were sent home after reportedly becoming intoxicated while in the Netherlands. The scandals have raised serious questions about the culture and management of the agency; however, as of August 2014, Pierson remained as its director.

RESPOND TO AND RECOVER FROM INCIDENTS

Emergency Preparedness

The DHS office of National Protection and Programs has programs and activities that are designed for emergency response professionals and the general public. At the professional level, the DHS offers training programs and grants for emergency planning.

For the general public, the DHS (2014, http:// www.ready.gov) provides information on how Americans should prepare for emergencies, including natural disasters and terrorist attacks. The Ready Campaign calls on every American to do four activities:

- Put together an emergency supply kit (see Table 5.9 for the suggested list of items)

- Prepare a family emergency plan that includes detailed instructions about how family members will communicate their whereabouts to each other if they become separated

- Stay informed about local conditions, the potential for emergency situations to develop, and the appropriate responses to take for particular emergencies

TABLE 5.9

Items recommended by the U.S. Department of Homeland Security for a basic emergency supply kit

A basic emergency supply kit could include the following recommended items:
- Water, one gallon of water per person per day for at least three days, for drinking and sanitation
- Food, at least a three-day supply of non-perishable food
- Battery-powered or hand crank radio and a NOAA weather radio with tone alert and extra batteries for both
- Flashlight and extra batteries
- First aid kit
- Whistle to signal for help
- Dust mask to help filter contaminated air and plastic sheeting and duct tape to shelter-in-place
- Moist towelettes, garbage bags and plastic ties for personal sanitation
- Wrench or pliers to turn off utilities
- Manual can opener for food
- Local maps
- Cell phone with chargers, inverter or solar charger

NOAA = National Oceanic and Atmospheric Administration.

SOURCE: Adapted from "Basic Disaster Supplies Kit," in *Ready: Build a Kit*, U.S. Department of Homeland Security, January 28, 2014, http://www.ready .gov/basic-disaster-supplies-kit (accessed May 5, 2014)

- Get involved in local community preparedness activities

Emergency Response

In any emergency, including a terrorist attack, the initial response is by local and state officials. These so-called first responders include police officers, firefighters, emergency medical technicians, hazardous materials response teams, rescue squads, bomb squads, officials with local and state emergency management agencies, and similar personnel.

FEDERAL ROLE. At the federal level the primary role of emergency preparedness and response is assumed by the Federal Emergency Management Agency (FEMA). FEMA became part of the DHS in 2003. FEMA personnel are dispatched following disasters (e.g., hurricanes and earthquakes) to provide large-scale services for displaced people. For example, after Hurricane Katrina hit the Gulf Coast in 2005, FEMA operated shelters and provided funds to victims who were left homeless by the devastation. The agency also offers training programs for first responders and helps local and state emergency management agencies prepare disaster and response plans.

Other DHS programs related to emergency preparedness and response are:

- National Disaster Medical System (http://www.phe .gov/Preparedness/responders/ndms/Pages/default .aspx)—this is a public-private system of hundreds of volunteer medical teams around the country. The system is overseen by FEMA and is designed to support local hospitals and emergency medical services in the event of a catastrophic disaster.

- Strategic National Stockpile—this is a national repository maintained by the CDC that includes large supplies of antibiotics, antidotes, and other medications, as well as medical and surgical supplies. According to the CDC, in "Strategic National Stockpile (SNS)" (July 10, 2014, http://www.cdc.gov/phpr/stockpile/stockpile.htm), one of the goals of the repository is to provide rapid delivery of medicine and medical supplies to disaster areas.

- Citizen Corps—this is a national system of volunteers trained to respond at the local level to terrorism events. A National Citizen Corps Council is overseen by the DHS and includes members representing various emergency response organizations and groups from the public and private sectors. A listing of all Citizen Corps around the country is available at http://www.ready.gov/citizen-corps.

HOMELAND SECURITY GRANT PROGRAMS

Acting through the DHS, the federal government supports state and local homeland security programs by issuing grants (funds designated for specific tasks or functions). The DHS notes in *FY 2013 Homeland Security Grant Program (HSGP)* (August 2013, http://www.fema.gov) that its FY 2013 security grants totaled $968.3 million. The three largest recipients were:

- Urban Areas Security Initiative—$558.7 million was allocated among 25 urban areas around the country

- State Homeland Security Program—$354.6 million was allocated among all 50 states, as well as the District of Columbia, Puerto Rico, American Samoa, Guam, Northern Mariana Islands, and the U.S. Virgin Islands

- Operation Stonegarden—$55 million was allocated among 19 border states and Puerto Rico

CHAPTER 6
COUNTRIES OF CONCERN

For much of its history, U.S. national security was focused primarily on other powerful nations. During the Cold War the Soviet Union and China amassed huge military forces and thousands of nuclear weapons. For decades the United States fought the spread of communism with diplomatic and economic means and through military engagements in Korea and Vietnam. The United States, however, never engaged in direct military conflict with the Soviet Union or China for fear of starting a nuclear war. Since the end of the Cold War, the threats posed by other nations to the United States have greatly diminished, but they have not disappeared.

Since 2001 the Gallup Organization has conducted occasional polls in which it asks Americans to name the one country they "consider to be the United States' greatest enemy today." In February 2014, 20% of the respondents named China, compared with 16% each for North Korea and Iran, 9% for Russia, and 7% for Iraq. (See Table 6.1.). Combined, these five countries account for two-thirds of the countries mentioned.

The U.S. government has provided information about the countries it believes pose a threat to national security in unclassified documents such as *Quadrennial Defense Review 2014* (March 2014, http://www.defense.gov/pubs/2014_Quadrennial_Defense_Review.pdf) from the U.S. Department of Defense and *Country Reports on Terrorism 2013* (April 2014, http://www.state.gov/documents/organization/225886.pdf) from the U.S. Department of State (DOS). In general, the U.S. government expresses the most alarm about nonallies that pursue weapons of mass destruction (WMDs) programs and/or provide aid to terrorists.

Chapter 7 examines the general steps the United States has taken to limit the proliferation (growth or multiplication) of WMDs including nuclear weapons. Although nearly all the nations of the world are party to international agreements regarding the development and spread of nuclear weapons, a handful of countries have refused to comply. India, Israel, Pakistan, and North Korea have all developed nuclear weapons outside of international agreements. The United States enjoys relatively good relations with these countries, except for North Korea, which is an old enemy from the Korean War (1950–1953). North Korea's nuclear weapons program is considered to be a major threat to U.S. national security.

The United States has also reacted strongly to efforts (or suspected efforts) by its nonallies to develop nuclear weapons. The Treaty on the Nonproliferation of Nuclear Weapons (NPT; 2000, http://www.un.org/en/conf/npt/2005/npttreaty.html) originally went into force in 1970 after being negotiated by the United Nations (UN). The United States and the Soviet Union were among the original signers of the treaty. It forbids countries with nuclear weapons from transferring nuclear weapons or related explosive devices "to any recipient whatsoever." No assistance can be offered to a nonnuclear weapon nation to manufacture or acquire the weapons. The parties to the treaty also agree to prevent "diversion of nuclear energy from peaceful uses to nuclear weapons" and to take measures leading toward nuclear disarmament. The International Atomic Energy Agency (IAEA) verifies that parties comply with the NPT.

In 2003 the concern that Iraq was developing nuclear weapons was a major factor in the United States' decision to invade that country and rout the Iraqi government from power. As explained in Chapter 3, U.S. officials ultimately learned their suspicions were incorrect: Iraq had not been actively developing nuclear weapons. With that threat out of the way, attention has turned to Iran and North Korea, countries with long histories of poor relations with the United States. In addition, Iran is also deemed a state sponsor of terrorism by the DOS. (See Table 6.1.) According to the DOS, in "State Sponsors of Terrorism" (2014,

TABLE 6.1

Trends in public opinion on the United States' greatest enemy, selected dates, 2001–14

WHAT ONE COUNTRY ANYWHERE IN THE WORLD DO YOU CONSIDER TO BE THE UNITED STATES' GREATEST ENEMY TODAY?

[Open-ended]

	2014 Feb 6–9	2012 Feb 2–5	2011 Feb 2–5	2008 Feb 11–14	2007 Feb 1–4	2006 Feb 6–9	2005 Feb 7–10	2001 Feb 1–4
China	20	23	16	14	11	10	10	14
North Korea/Korea (non-specific)	16	10	16	9	18	15	22	2
Iran	16	32	25	25	26	31	14	8
Russia	9	2	3	2	2	1	2	6
Iraq	7	5	7	22	21	22	22	38
Afghanistan	5	7	9	3	2	3	3	*
Syria	3	*	—	*	*	1	2	—
United States itself	2	1	2	3	2	1	2	1
Pakistan	1	2	2	2	*	*	*	—
South Korea	1	—	—	—	—	—	—	—
Saudi Arabia	1	1	1	1	3	1	2	4
France	*	—	*	*	*	1	2	—
Egypt	*	—	1	—	—	—	—	—
Venezuela	*	*	—	1	*	*	—	—
Japan	*	1	*	*	*	*	*	1
Cuba	*	*	*	*	—	*	*	2
Libya	*	*	—	—	—	—	*	4
Mexico	—	*	1	*	*	*	—	*
Yemen	—	*	1	—	—	—	—	*
The Palestinian Authority	—	—	*	—	—	*	*	1
Other	8	3	7	6	6	6	8	6
None (vol.)	2	1	1	2	1	1	2	2
No opinion	9	11	9	8	7	7	9	11

*Less than 0.5%
— = None

SOURCE: Jeff Jones and Lydia Saad, "14. What one country anywhere in the world do you consider to be the United States' greatest enemy today?" in *Gallup Poll Social Series: World Affairs—Final Topline*, The Gallup Organization, February 6–9, 2014, http://www.gallup.com/file/poll/167504/Americas_Greatest_Threat_140220%20.pdf (accessed May 5, 2014). Copyright © 2014 Gallup, Inc. All rights reserved. The content is used with permission; however, Gallup retains all rights of republication.

TABLE 6.2

Countries identified by U.S. government as state sponsors of terrorism, by date of designation

Country	Designation date
Cuba	March 1, 1982
Iran	January 19, 1984
Sudan	August 12, 1993
Syria	December 29, 1979

SOURCE: *State Sponsors of Terrorism*, U.S. Department of State, 2014, http://www.state.gov/j/ct/list/c14151.htm (accessed May 5, 2014)

http://www.state.gov/j/ct/list/c14151.htm), the countries listed in Table 6.2 have been "determined by the Secretary of State to have repeatedly provided support for acts of international terrorism." Until 2008 North Korea was also on the list of state sponsors of terrorism. As of 2014, the only other countries on the list were Cuba, Sudan, and Syria.

CHINA

China has become strong politically, militarily, and economically, and it strives to wield more diplomatic power in the world. Although the U.S. and Chinese governments enjoy relatively good relations, the U.S. public views China with unease. In February 2014 Gallup pollsters asked Americans to rank nine possible threats to U.S. interests in terms of their seriousness. Table 1.6 in Chapter 1 presents the results. More than half (52%) of those asked consider the economic power of China a "critical threat." Slightly less (46%) viewed the military power of China as a "critical threat." The latter opinion may be based on the enormous size of the Chinese military, which is the largest in the world. Table 6.3 is a ranking compiled by the DOS of national armed forces personnel based on the average annual number between 2000 and 2010. China, with nearly 2.3 million troops, easily holds the number-one spot. India and the United States, with approximately 1.4 million troops each, rank second and third, respectively. In contrast, the United States far surpasses China in military spending. (See Table 6.4.) Based on annual averages between 2000 and 2010, the United States spent $570 billion annually, compared with China, which spent $114 billion.

RUSSIA

Following the dissolution of the Soviet Union during the early 1990s, the United States and Russia enjoyed

TABLE 6.3

Top-25 nations in terms of armed forces personnel, annual average, 2000–10

[In thousands]

1	China, mainland	2,280
2	India	1,430
3	United States	1,420
4	Korea, North	1,170
5	Russia	1,050
6	Korea, South	691
7	Pakistan	594
8	Turkey	585
9	Iran	483
10	Vietnam	483
11	Burma (Myanmar)	475
12	Egypt	450
13	Indonesia	359
14	France	338
15	Colombia	336
16	China, Taiwan	312
17	Syria	310
18	Brazil	307
19	Thailand	288
20	Italy	287
21	Germany	266
22	Eritrea	254
23	Mexico	253
24	Japan	239
25	Ukraine	217

SOURCE: Adapted from "Table 1. Country Ratings and Trends," in *World Military Expenditures and Arms Transfers 2013*, U.S. State Department, 2013, http://www.state.gov/documents/organization/223436.xlsx (accessed May 6, 2014)

TABLE 6.4

Top-25 nations in terms of military spending, annual average, 2000–10

[In billions]

1	United States	$570.0
2	China, mainland	$114.0
3	Russia	$58.1
4	United Kingdom	$56.6
5	France	$51.8
6	Saudi Arabia	$40.7
7	Japan	$40.7
8	Germany	$38.3
9	Italy	$31.7
10	India	$29.9
11	Korea, South	$22.9
12	Brazil	$21.8
13	Turkey	$17.2
14	Australia	$15.1
15	Canada	$14.7
16	Spain	$13.9
17	United Arab Emirates	$12.3
18	Israel	$11.9
19	Netherlands	$9.8
20	Iran	$9.8
21	China, Taiwan	$7.9
22	Greece	$7.7
23	Colombia	$6.8
24	Pakistan	$6.3
25	Singapore	$6.1

SOURCE: Adapted from "Table 1. Country Ratings and Trends," in *World Military Expenditures and Arms Transfers 2013*, U.S. State Department, 2013, http://www.state.gov/documents/organization/223436.xlsx (accessed May 6, 2014)

relatively good relations for over a decade. The relationship has become strained in the 21st century for a variety of reasons, including Russian support for the Syrian government, which will be explored later in this chapter. Another troublesome issue has been Russian military incursions into neighboring countries that were once part of the Soviet Union. According to Eve Conant, in "Ethnic Russians: Pretext for Putin's Ukraine Invasion?" (NationalGeographic.com, May 2, 2014), the breakup of the Soviet Union left many "ethnic Russians" outside the borders of Russia in surrounding countries such as Georgia, Kazakhstan, and Ukraine. The Russian government has maintained close political and economic ties with these populations that, in some areas, vigorously oppose their national governments.

In 2008 Russian troops swept into the Georgian region of South Ossetia claiming that Georgian troops had attacked them and Russian citizens living there. The Russians seized control of South Ossetia and launched air raids against other parts of Georgia, evoking strong criticism from world leaders. Russian troops have since occupied South Ossetia and another Georgian region called Abkhazia. The Russian government officially considers them independent states, a designation that is disputed by the Georgian government and by most of the international community, including the United States.

In February 2014, after years of civil unrest, Ukraine experienced a revolution. Its pro-Russian president fled the country and was replaced by a pro-Western leader who was chosen by the Ukrainian parliament. The Russian government, led by President Vladimir Putin (1952–), denied the legitimacy of the new Ukrainian government. Since the breakup of the Soviet Union, Russia has kept a large naval fleet at Sevastopol, a Black Sea port on the southern end of the Crimean Peninsula in Ukraine. (See Figure 6.1.) Crimea also has a large ethnic Russian population. Pro-Russian militants with the alleged aid of the Russian military took control of Crimea after the Ukrainian revolution. In March 2014 a referendum was held in Crimea on politically reuniting the peninsula with Russia. The Russian government claims that more than 95% of the voters chose reunification. It has subsequently "annexed" the Crimean Peninsula, meaning that it has absorbed the territory as part of its own territory. The UN and numerous countries, including the United States, have denied the legitimacy of the referendum and Russia's annexation of Crimea. To punish Russia, President Barack Obama (1961–) has implemented economic sanctions against Russia, but has ignored calls from critics to take any kind of military response.

These events have seriously damaged U.S.-Russian relations and raise fears that Russia will seek to annex

FIGURE 6.1

Map of Ukraine, 2014

SOURCE: "Map of Ukraine," in "Europe: Ukraine," *The World Factbook*, Central Intelligence Agency, April 16, 2014, https://www.cia.gov/library/publications/the-world-factbook/geos/up.html (accessed May 8, 2014)

TABLE 6.5

Public opinion on the return of a Cold War with Russia, March 2014

DO YOU THINK THE UNITED STATES AND RUSSIA ARE HEADING BACK TOWARD A COLD WAR, OR NOT?

	% Yes, are	% No, are not
2014 Mar 22–23	50	43
1991 Feb 22	25	64

Note: The 1991 question used "Soviet Union" instead of "Russia" in the question wording.

SOURCE: Rebecca Riffkin, "Americans' Views about the Return of a Cold War," in *Half of Americans Say U.S. Headed Back to Cold War*, The Gallup Organization, March 27, 2014, http://www.gallup.com/poll/168116/half-americans-say-headed-back-cold-war.aspx (accessed May 26, 2014). Copyright © 2014 Gallup, Inc. All rights reserved. The content is used with permission; however, Gallup retains all rights of republication.

other areas with restive ethnic Russian populations. According to Conant, Putin signed a new law in April 2014 that makes it easier for people outside of Russia to be considered Russian citizens. The new law accommodates Russian-language speakers and people with ancestors who once lived in Russia. Some observers fear that the Russian government will use the law as an excuse to annex the territories of newly declared Russian citizens living in other former Soviet-bloc countries.

In March 2014 the Gallup Organization conducted a poll asking Americans if they believe the United States and Russia "are heading back toward a Cold War." Half (50%) of the respondents believe a Cold War is imminent. (See Table 6.5.) The same question was asked in early 1991, shortly before the breakup of the Soviet Union. At that time only 25% of respondents thought a resurgence of the Cold War with Russia was in the United States' future.

IRAN

Iran lies in a section of Asia known as the Middle East. The nation's capital is Tehran. (See Figure 6.2.) The Strait of Hormuz is a narrow waterway lying south of Iran that is the only connection between the Persian Gulf and the open ocean. This strait has great strategic importance to the United States as a passageway for oil exports from the region.

For centuries Iran was part of a series of empires and was called Persia by the outside world. In 1935 its name was officially changed to Iran. Beginning in 1941 the country was led by Shah Mohammad Reza Pahlavi (1919–1980). In 1979 the shah was overthrown by his people and forced to leave the country during a revolution that swept the Islamic cleric Ruhollah Khomeini (1902?–1989) into power. The country then adopted a

FIGURE 6.2

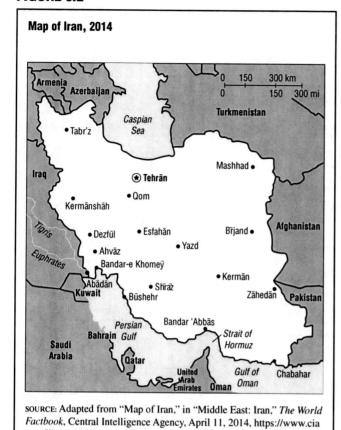

Map of Iran, 2014

SOURCE: Adapted from "Map of Iran," in "Middle East: Iran," *The World Factbook*, Central Intelligence Agency, April 11, 2014, https://www.cia.gov/library/publications/the-world-factbook/geos/ir.html (accessed May 5, 2014)

constitution. Khomeini initiated a cultural revolution that sought to remove influences of Western culture and instill conservative Islamic morals and customs. He served as Iran's supreme leader until his death in 1989, when he was replaced by Ali Khamenei (1939–).

Figure 6.3 shows the structure of the Iranian government. The supreme leader is considered Iran's spiritual leader and chief of state for life. Every four years or so the country elects government officials, including a president and members of the 290-seat Majles-e Khoebregan (the Iranian parliament). The most recent parliamentary elections were held in March 2012. A new president, Hassan Rouhani (1948–), was elected in June 2013. Although a cleric, he is considered to be relatively moderate compared with the ultraconservative Khamenei.

As shown in Figure 6.3, Iran has two main military branches: the regular military (i.e., army, navy, and air force), and the Islamic Revolutionary Guard Corps. The latter oversees the Basij and the Qods Force. In *Iran: U.S. Concerns and Policy Responses* (March 5, 2014, https://www.fas.org/sgp/crs/mideast/RL32048.pdf), Kenneth Katzman of the Congressional Research Service (CRS) describes the Basij as a "volunteer militia." The Qods Force conducts special operations and is believed to be highly trained. The DOS estimates that Iran has the ninth-

largest military force in the world based on annual averages between 2000 and 2010. (See Table 6.3.)

Table 6.6 provides vital statistics about Iran's geography, people, legal system, and economy. As of 2014, the population was estimated at 80.8 million people. More than 99% of the Iraqi people are Muslim, and they are overwhelmingly Shiite. This makes the country the undisputed Shiite power in the world. Iran is strong economically as measured by its gross domestic product (GDP; the total market value of final goods and services that are produced within an economy in a given year). Its GDP of $987.1 billion in 2013 was the 19th highest in the world. The country has substantial petroleum and natural gas resources. Its energy sector, however, has been hampered by international sanctions that will be described later in this chapter.

Past Foreign Relations

In 1979 President Jimmy Carter (1924–) allowed the ousted shah of Iran to enter the United States for medical treatment. The United States had supported the shah throughout his reign, even though his regime was considered to be brutal and corrupt by the Iranian people. The U.S. action incited radical elements within Iran who feared that the United States planned to reinstall the shah to power. Angry groups of students protested in the streets and seized the U.S. embassy in Tehran. Dozens of Americans were held hostage at the embassy for 444 days until their release in 1981.

Despite repeated demands from the U.S. government, Khomeini refused to intervene in the hostage crisis. During and after the Iranian Revolution, Khomeini often criticized the United States, referring to it as "the great Satan." Carter tried a variety of diplomatic and military options to release the hostages during the long ordeal, but none were successful. A rescue attempt by U.S. troops in 1980 ended in disaster when some of the helicopters accidentally crashed after secretly entering Iran. Eight U.S. servicemen were killed. The hostage release was ultimately achieved via diplomatic means. The hostage crisis severely damaged U.S. relations with Iran, and as of August 2014 the two countries had not restored diplomatic relations with each other.

The Iraqi president Saddam Hussein (1937–2006) launched an invasion of Iran in 1980. The resulting war lasted until 1988. In *Country Profile: Iraq* (August 2006, http://lcweb2.loc.gov/frd/cs/profiles/Iraq.pdf), the Library of Congress explains that the war was motivated by a variety of political, religious, and ethnic factors. However, eight years of bloody fighting produced no clear winner, so a cease-fire was finally negotiated.

Iran's Terrorist Connections

In 1984 the DOS first designated Iran as a state sponsor of terrorism because of Iranian support for organizations

FIGURE 6.3

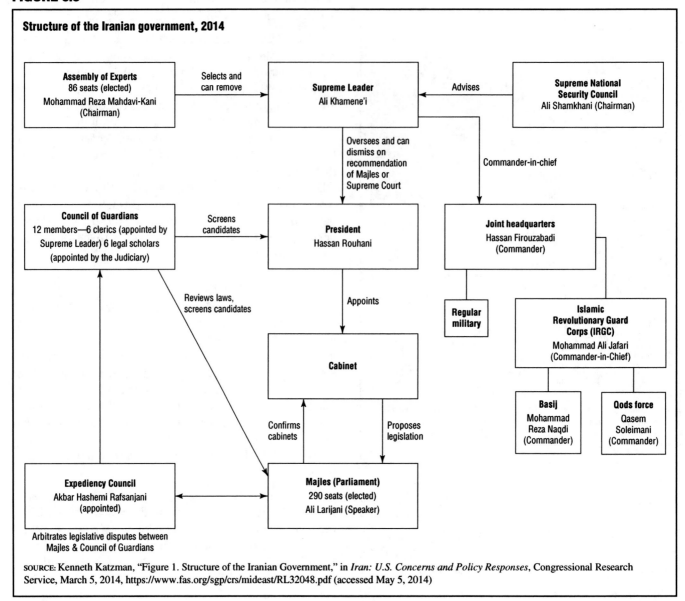

Structure of the Iranian government, 2014

SOURCE: Kenneth Katzman, "Figure 1. Structure of the Iranian Government," in *Iran: U.S. Concerns and Policy Responses*, Congressional Research Service, March 5, 2014, https://www.fas.org/sgp/crs/mideast/RL32048.pdf (accessed May 5, 2014)

TABLE 6.6

Statistics about Iran, 2014

Geographic area	636,372 square miles (1,648,195 sq. k)
Comparative size	Slightly smaller than Alaska
Population	80,840,713 (estimated 2014)
Ethnic groups	Persian 61%; Azeri 16%; Kurd 10%; Lur 6%; Baloch 2%; Arab 2%; Turkmen and Turkic tribes 2%; Other 1%
Religions	Muslim: 99.4% (Shia 90–95% and Sunni 5–10%); Other <1%
Languages	Persian (official) 53%; Azeri Turkic and Turkic dialects 18%; Kurdish 10%; Gilaki and Mazandarani 7%; Luri 6%; Balochi 2%; Arabic 2%; Other 2%
Number of provinces	31
Legal system	Religious legal system based on secular and Islamic law
Gross domestic product	$987.1 billion (estimated, in U.S. dollars), 19th highest in the world in 2013

SOURCE: "Middle East: Iran," in *The World Factbook*, Central Intelligence Agency, April 11, 2014, https://www.cia.gov/library/publications/the-world-factbook/geos/ir.html (accessed May 5, 2014)

such as Hamas, Hezbollah, and the Palestinian Islamic Jihad. Since then, the United States has imposed numerous restrictions on U.S. and international investments in Iran.

In *Country Reports on Terrorism 2013*, the DOS indicates that Iran has long supported international terrorist groups, particularly those targeting Israel and the United States. As noted in Chapter 3, Iran has strong ties with Hezbollah, which is based in Lebanon. According to the DOS, Iran has provided arms and "millions of dollars" to Hezbollah and has allowed "thousands" of Hezbollah fighters to come to Iran for paramilitary training. The DOS believes this training is provided by Iran's Qods Force, which is also accused of training, arming, and funding Shiite militant groups that targeted U.S. forces during the war in Iraq that began in 2003. The DOS also claims that Iran used the Qods Force and regional militant groups in 2013 "to implement foreign

TABLE 6.7

Summary of major United Nations (UN) sanctions on Iran's nuclear program as of 2014

Requires Iran to suspend uranium enrichment, cease construction of the heavy water reactor at Arak, and sign the Additional Protocol. (1737 and subsequent resolutions)
Prohibits transfer to Iran of nuclear, missile, and dual use items, except for use in light-water reactors. (All combined)
Prohibits Iran from exporting arms or WMD-useful technology. (1747)
Prohibits Iran from investing abroad in uranium mining, related nuclear technologies or nuclear capable ballistic missile technology. Prohibits Iran from launching ballistic missiles even
    on its own territory. (1929)
Freezes the assets of over 80 named Iranian persons and entities, including Bank Sepah, and several corporate affiliates of the Revolutionary Guard. (1737 and subsequent resolutions)
Requires that countries ban the travel of over 40 named Iranians.
Mandates that countries not export major combat systems to Iran. It did not bar sales of missiles not on the "U.N. Registry of Conventional Arms" (meaning that the delivery of the
    S-300 system, discussed above, would not be legally banned). (1929)
Calls for "vigilance" (a nonbinding call to cut off business) with respect to all Iranian banks, particularly Bank Melli and Bank Saderat. (1929)
Calls for vigilance (voluntary restraint) with respect to providing international lending to Iran and providing trade credits and other financing and financial interactions. (1929)
Calls on countries to inspect cargoes carried by Iran Air Cargo and Islamic Republic of Iran Shipping Lines—or by any ships in national or international waters—if there are indications
    they carry cargo banned for carriage to Iran. Searches in international waters would require concurrence of the country where the ship is registered. (1929)
A Sanctions Committee, composed of the 15 members of the Security Council, monitors implementation of all Iran sanctions and collects and disseminates information on Iranian
    violations and other entities involved in banned activities. A seven-member "panel of experts" is empowered (renewable each year) to report on sanctions violations and make
    recommendations for improved enforcement. The panel's reports are not officially published by the Sanctions Committee but are usually carried by various websites. Resolution 2105,
    adopted June 5, 2013, extended the mandate of the Panel of Experts until July 9, 2014. (1929)

Note: WMD = weapons of mass destruction.

SOURCE: Kenneth Katzman, "Table 6. Summary of Provisions of U.N. Resolutions on Iran Nuclear Program (1737, 1747, 1803, and 1929)," in *Iran: U.S. Concerns and Policy Responses*, Congressional Research Service, March 5, 2014, https://www.fas.org/sgp/crs/mideast/RL32048.pdf (accessed May 5, 2014)

policy goals, provide cover for intelligence operations, and create instability in the Middle East."

Iran's Nuclear Program

According to Sharon Squassoni of the CRS, in *Iran's Nuclear Program: Recent Developments* (September 6, 2006, http://www.fas.org/sgp/crs/nuke/RS21592.pdf), IAEA investigators discovered in 2002 that "significant" nuclear activities had been taking place in Iran of which the agency was not aware. This activity was a violation of the NPT that Iran had ratified in 1970. Iranian officials admitted they had been conducting undeclared activities and had obtained a so-called nuclear cookbook with instructions for producing nuclear weapon parts. The cookbook was allegedly created by the Pakistani scientist Abdul Qadeer Khan (1935–), who has been linked to many illicit transfers of nuclear technology to nonnuclear nations.

Squassoni notes that IAEA inspectors found two uranium enrichment facilities in Natanz, which is about 200 miles (320 km) south of Tehran. The World Nuclear Association explains in "Uranium Enrichment" (May 2014, http://world-nuclear.org/info/inf28.html) that natural uranium (U) consists mainly of two isotopes called U-235 and U-238. Isotopes are forms of a chemical element that contain the same number of protons, but different numbers of neutrons. It is the U-235 content that makes uranium useful in reactors and weapons. However, natural uranium contains less than 1% of U-235. Thus, uranium must be enriched to 3% to 5% of U-235 for use in common nuclear power reactors, to nearly 20% for use in certain nuclear research and development reactors, and to at least 90% for use in nuclear weapons.

In late 2003 Iran ceased some of its uranium enrichment activities and began negotiations with IAEA officials

and diplomats from three European Union (EU) countries: Germany, France, and the United Kingdom. However, negotiations broke down in August 2005, and Iran resumed operations and construction at its nuclear facilities. The IAEA reported Iran to the UN Security Council for violating the NPT. This triggered a series of UN resolutions that called on Iran to suspend its nuclear activities and begin cooperating fully with IAEA investigators. The major provisions of the key UN resolutions are summarized in Table 6.7.

The Status of U.S.-Iranian Relations

As noted earlier, the United States has had a contentious relationship with Iran since the 1979 hostage crisis. Numerous presidential executive orders and laws have been put into place in an effort to pressure Iran to change its behavior. The early measures focused only on Iran's involvement in international terrorism. However, once Iran's nuclear ambitions came to light, the U.S. government began an aggressive campaign of sanctions and urged its allies and the UN Security Council to do likewise. Israel, a strong American ally in the Middle East, went even further by publicly threatening to wage military strikes to prevent Iran from developing nuclear weapons. The two countries have an acrimonious relationship that has been aggravated by hostile anti-Israel statements made by Iranian leaders.

The U.S. government is worried that an Israeli air strike against Iran could evoke severe repercussions. In an attempt to avoid such action, the United States has reportedly worked closely with Israel to develop and deploy cyberweapons against the Iranian nuclear program. As explained in Chapter 1, cyberweapons rely on malicious software (malware) such as computer viruses or worms to disable or control enemy computer systems. Jim Finkle reports in "Researchers Say Stuxnet Was Deployed against Iran in 2007" (Reuters.com, February 26, 2013) that U.S. efforts in this regard date back to the administration of President George W. Bush (1946–), who was in office from January 2001 to January 2009. As early as 2007 a computer virus dubbed "Stuxnet" may have been secretly used to attack Iran's Natanz nuclear facility. A more robust version of Stuxnet developed during the first Obama administration was "discovered" by Internet experts in 2010, after it was inadvertently introduced to the Internet and infected computers around the world. According to William J. Broad, John Markoff, and David E. Sanger, in "Israeli Test on Worm Called Crucial in Iran Nuclear Delay" (NYTimes.com, January 15, 2011), Stuxnet is believed to have temporarily disabled approximately one-fifth of Iran's nuclear centrifuges. However, as of August 2014 neither the U.S. or the Israeli government had publicly admitted involvement in the cyberattacks.

Iraq, Iran's former enemy, has a large Shiite population. Since the pullout of U.S. troops from Iraq in 2011 the Iraqi government has forged ever closer ties with Iran, which is an unwelcome development for U.S. interests in the region. Obama has continued to use diplomatic measures such as economic sanctions to push Iran toward nuclear compliance. In 2012 the EU ratcheted up the pressure by banning all EU oil purchases from Iran. This drastic measure helped push Iran to enter a new round of international negotiations concerning its nuclear program.

Interim Agreement

In November 2013 representatives from Iran and six other nations (China, France, Germany, Russia, the United Kingdom, and the United States) reached an interim agreement on curbing some of Iran's nuclear activities and loosening some of the sanctions against the nation. In *Interim Agreement on Iran's Nuclear Program* (December 11, 2013, http://www.fas.org/sgp/crs/nuke/R43333.pdf), Kenneth Katzman and Paul K. Kerr of the CRS indicate the agreement was for a six-month period. Iran agreed to cease certain uranium enrichment activities and provide the IAEA with information about its nuclear program and greater access to its nuclear facilities. In exchange, several billion dollars of Iranian money that had been frozen in foreign accounts were to be released and Iran was to be allowed to conduct some foreign trade in petrochemicals, precious metals, and automobiles.

The interim agreement was met with skepticism and derision by some U.S. lawmakers and Israeli politicians. Parisa Hafezi and Justyna Pawlak note in "Breakthrough Deal Curbs Iran's Nuclear Activity" (Reuters.com,

November 24, 2013) that Israel condemned the agreement as a "historic mistake." The interim agreement went into effect in January 2014 and started a new round of negotiations aimed at producing a final agreement. As of August 2014, the talks were proceeding after the participating nations agreed to an extension of the original six-month deadline. Israel has continued to threaten military strikes against Iran's nuclear program; however, it is considered unlikely that Israel will take such a confrontational step while negotiations are under way.

NORTH KOREA

North Korea is a small country that sits on a peninsula along the coastline of East Asia. The nation's capital is Pyongyang. (See Figure 6.4.) North and South Korea were once a single country. Japan invaded Korea in 1905 and occupied it through World War II (1939–1945). Following the war the Allied powers split the Korea Peninsula into two countries, with the northern part falling under Soviet control and the southern part under U.S. control. In 1948 South Korea became an independent nation. North Korea was ruled by Kim Il Sung (1912–1994) from 1948 until his death in 1994. His son Kim Jong-Il (1942–2011) ruled until he died in December 2011, at which time his son, Kim Jong-Un (1983?–),

FIGURE 6.4

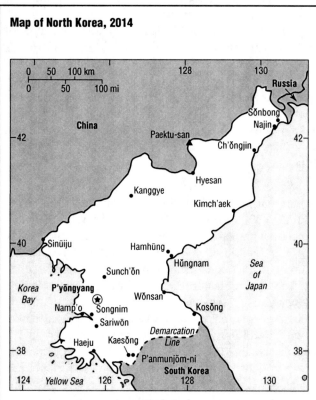

Map of North Korea, 2014

SOURCE: Adapted from "Map of North Korea," in "East and Southeast Asia: Korea, North," *The World Factbook*, Central Intelligence Agency, April 11, 2014, https://www.cia.gov/library/publications/the-world-factbook/geos/kn.html (accessed May 5, 2014)

TABLE 6.8

Top-25 nations in terms of military spending as a fraction of gross domestic product, annual average, 2000–10

1	Korea, North	19.7%
2	Eritrea	11.8%
3	Saudi Arabia	10.2%
4	Oman	10.0%
5	Israel	7.5%
6	Burma (Myanmar)	6.9%
7	Jordan	6.4%
8	Yemen	5.1%
9	United Arab Emirates	5.0%
10	Iraq	5.0%
11	Kuwait	4.9%
12	Syria	4.7%
13	Angola	4.6%
14	Lebanon	4.5%
15	Russia	4.4%
16	Burundi	4.4%
17	Singapore	4.4%
18	Djibouti	4.3%
19	Georgia	4.2%
20	Bahrain	4.2%
21	United States	4.2%
22	Sudan	4.0%
23	Vietnam	3.9%
24	Armenia	3.9%
25	Chad	3.8%

SOURCE: Adapted from "Table 1. Country Ratings and Trends," in *World Military Expenditures and Arms Transfers 2013*, U.S. State Department, 2013, http://www.state.gov/documents/organization/223436.xlsx (accessed May 6, 2014)

assumed power. He is a mysterious figure about whom little is known, even his age. Various media sources estimate him to be in his late 20s.

In *The World Factbook: North Korea* (June 20, 2014, https://www.cia.gov/library/publications/the-world-fact book/geos/kn.html), the Central Intelligence Agency (CIA) estimates North Korea's population was 24.9 million in 2014. The CIA describes North Korea as a "communist state one-man dictatorship." All of its political parties are controlled by the major party: the Korean Workers' Party. The CIA reports that decades of poor governance and economic mismanagement have rendered North Korea unable to feed many of its people. The population is highly dependent on international food aid and is believed to suffer from widespread malnutrition and poor living conditions. Much of the country's resources are devoted to maintaining its military. Table 6.8 provides ratios of military spending to GDP for 25 countries based on annual averages between 2000 and 2010. North Korea tops the list; it devoted 19.7% of its GDP to military expenditures. By comparison, the value for the United States was 4.2%. As shown in Table 6.3, North Korea has the fourth-largest army in the world based on annual averages between 2000 and 2010.

Past Foreign Relations

U.S. and allied forces under the UN went to war against North Korea during the early 1950s after North Korea invaded South Korea. North Korea was politically aligned with the Soviet Union and received help from the latter and from Chinese troops during the war. In 1953 a cease-fire agreement was reached that ended the armed conflict. Since that time an uneasy peace has been maintained along the 38th parallel (a line of latitude), which is the border separating North Korea from South Korea. North Korea has remained a communist nation. South Korea has become a democracy and is protected by UN troops (primarily U.S. forces).

During the war the United States imposed economic sanctions against North Korea that would last for decades. North Korea became highly dependent on its communist allies, particularly the Soviet Union and China, for foreign trade. The breakup of the Soviet Union during the early 1990s eliminated a major political ally and trading partner for North Korea; however, its close relationship with China has continued.

North Korea's Nuclear Program

Larry A. Niksch of the CRS notes in *North Korea's Nuclear Weapons Development and Diplomacy* (January 5, 2010, http://www.nkeconwatch.com/nk-uploads/nuclear weapons-1-5-10.pdf) that North Korea signed the NPT in 1985. Two years later it began operating a nuclear reactor near Pyongyang, ostensibly to produce electrical power. U.S. intelligence agencies, however, became suspicious that North Korea was producing nuclear weapons. The U.S. government was further disturbed by IAEA reports that North Korea was withholding data, being uncooperative, and threatening to withdraw from the NPT. In response, the United States threatened to bring new economic sanctions against North Korea through the UN. The two countries eventually negotiated the Agreed Framework (November 2, 1994, http://www.iaea.org/Publica tions/Documents/Infcircs/Others/infcirc457.pdf), which called for North Korea to remain a party to the NPT, to freeze its nuclear program, and to dismantle nuclear reactors under IAEA supervision in exchange for eased economic sanctions.

In 2002 the Agreed Framework fell apart after the United States accused North Korea of having operated since 1996 a secret program to develop nuclear weapons. North Korea responded by expelling IAEA inspectors and withdrawing from the NPT the following year.

FAILED NEGOTIATIONS. In 2003 the United States and North Korea began a series of negotiations that included high-ranking officials from South Korea, China, Japan, and Russia. The so-called six-party talks were initiated after the United States refused to hold bilateral (two-party) meetings with North Korea. Many negotiations were held in which virtually no progress was achieved in resolving the disputes at issue. Furthermore, the U.S. invasions of Afghanistan and Iraq in 2001 and

2003, respectively, made North Korea increasingly concerned about a military strike by U.S. forces. In 2003 North Korean officials publicly announced that the country had nuclear weapons. Subsequent announcements included hostile and threatening rhetoric toward the United States and South Korea.

In July 2006 the world was stunned when North Korea test-fired seven unarmed missiles toward the Sea of Japan to demonstrate its capabilities. One of the missiles was a Taepo Dong-2, which is thought to have a range of approximately 1,860 miles (2,990 km). That missile failed after approximately 40 seconds and fell into the sea. The other six missiles were short-range missiles. Japan and South Korea, in particular, are concerned about North Korea's missile capabilities. Both nations host large U.S. military bases, which could be targets for North Korean missiles in wartime.

North Korea received further international condemnation in October 2006, when it conducted an underground test of a nuclear weapon. The UN Security Council responded with Resolution 1718, which urged North Korea to resume the six-party talks and prohibited member nations from transferring to North Korea luxury goods and either money or technology that could support WMD development. U.S.–North Korean relations thawed in 2007, when the six-party talks resulted in a plan for North Korea to begin disabling its nuclear facilities in exchange for foreign economic and energy aid. In addition, the United States agreed to remove North Korea from the state sponsor of terrorism list. That removal occurred in 2008, after a verification program was established to confirm the declarations made by the North Korean government.

In April 2009 North Korea conducted another missile test. The UN promptly condemned the launch as a violation of Resolution 1718. North Korea responded by withdrawing from the six-party talks. It also expelled IAEA inspectors and U.S. technical experts who had been monitoring its nuclear activities and announced its intention to reactivate its nuclear facilities. In May 2009 North Korea disclosed that it had tested another nuclear weapon. The UN Security Council responded by further strengthening an arms embargo against North Korea. The country conducted additional missile tests throughout the remainder of the year. In November 2009 North Korea announced that it had successfully conducted experimental uranium enrichment.

In March 2010 a South Korean warship exploded and sank in the Yellow Sea, killing 46 people. North Korea was suspected of torpedoing the ship, although it denied doing so. Later that year North and South Korean forces exchanged fire for several hours after South Korean troops claimed they were fired upon while conducting military exercises.

Bilateral U.S.–North Korean negotiations resulted in an agreement in February 2012 that North Korea would cease projects related to long-range missiles, nuclear tests, and uranium enrichment in exchange for food aid from the United States. In addition, North Korea consented to IAEA inspections to verify the moratorium on its uranium enrichment activities. However, the agreement was short lived. In April 2012 North Korea launched what it said was a weather satellite; the rocket broke apart before reaching orbit. Alyssa Newcomb, Luis Martinez, and Martha Raddatz report in "North Korean Rocket Launch Fails: US Officials" (ABCNews.com, April 12, 2012) that experts "believed the satellite to be a cover in order to test a long-range missile." The U.S. government responded by refusing to uphold its end of the bilateral agreement.

Table 6.9 lists the status of North Korea's known nuclear power reactor projects as of 2013. Most of the projects were never completed; however, the reactor at Yongbyon is believed capable of producing weapons-grade plutonium. In 2013 North Korea conducted what it said was another underground nuclear test, prompting intense criticism and additional international sanctions against it. In March 2014 it test-launched what appeared to be two medium-range missiles. That same month the North Korean government announced its intention to conduct a "new form" of nuclear test. In "North Korea Vows to Use 'New Form' of Nuclear Test" (NYTimes.com, March 30, 2014), Choe Sang-Hun notes that international observers fear that North Korea may have developed a small nuclear device capable of being carried by an intercontinental ballistic missile. If so, this would greatly raise security concerns about North Korea, which continued to antagonize its neighbors and the United States. As of August 2014, the North and South Korean military forces had occasionally exchanged artillery fire with each other at sea. However, North Korea had not conducted any additional nuclear or missile tests.

OTHER COUNTRIES OF CONCERN

Although Iran and North Korea are considered to be the countries posing the most threat to U.S. national security, there are other countries of concern. These include three nations listed in Table 6.2 as state sponsors of terrorism: Cuba, Sudan, and Syria.

Cuba

Cuba is a small island lying between the Caribbean Sea to the south and the Gulf of Mexico and the North Atlantic Ocean to the north. (See Figure 6.5.) Cuba is only 90 miles (145 km) southeast of Key West, Florida. It is a communist state that was ruled for nearly five decades by one man: Fidel Castro (1926–). In February 2008

TABLE 6.9

North Korean nuclear power projects, 2013

Location	Type/power capacity	Status	Purpose
Yongbyon	Graphite-moderated Heavy Water Experimental Reactor/5 MWe	Currently shut-down; cooling tower destroyed in June 2009 as part of Six-Party Talks; estimated restart time would be 6 months; Re-start announced April 2013	Weapons-grade plutonium production
Yongbyon	Graphite-moderated Heavy Water Power Reactor/50 MWe	Never built; Basic construction begun; project halted since 1994	Stated purpose was electricity production; could have been used for weapons-grade plutonium production
Yongbyon	Experimental Light-Water Reactor/100 MWT (25–30 MWe)	U.S. observers saw basic construction begun in November 2010; Reactor dome emplaced on top of containment structure summer 2012	Stated purpose is electricity production; could be used for weapons-grade plutonium production
Taechon	Graphite-moderated Heavy Water Power Reactor/200 MWe	Never built; Basic construction begun; project halted since 1994	Stated purpose was electricity production; could have been used for weapons-grade plutonium production
Kumho District, Sinp'o	4 Light-water reactors/440 MW	Never built; part of 1985 deal with Soviet Union when North Korea signed the NPT; canceled by Russian Federation in 1992	Stated purpose is electricity production; could have been used for weapons-grade plutonium production
Kumho District, Sinp'o [KEDO Project]	2 Light-water reactors (turn-key)/ 1000 MWe	Never built; part of 1994 Agreed Framework, reactor agreement concluded in 1999; Project terminated in 2006 after North Korea pulled out of Agreed Framework	Electricity production

Notes: MW = million watts of heat. MWe = million watts of electricity per day. NPT = Nuclear Nonproliferation Treaty.

SOURCE: Mary Beth Nikitin, "Table 1. North Korean Nuclear Power Reactor Projects," in *North Korea's Nuclear Weapons: Technical Issues*, Congressional Research Service, April 3, 2013, https://www.fas.org/sgp/crs/nuke/RL34256.pdf (accessed May 5, 2014)

FIGURE 6.5

Map of Cuba, 2014

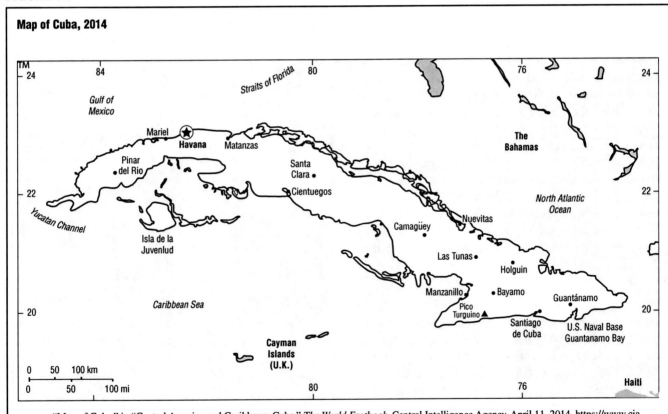

SOURCE: "Map of Cuba," in "Central America and Caribbean: Cuba," *The World Factbook*, Central Intelligence Agency, April 11, 2014, https://www.cia.gov/library/publications/the-world-factbook/geos/cu.html (accessed May 5, 2014)

he stepped down as Cuba's president because of ill health. His brother, Raúl Castro (1931–), officially became Cuba's leader.

Historically, Cuba enjoyed close economic and military ties to the Soviet Union. The demise of the Soviet Union during the early 1990s sent Cuba into a sharp economic recession from which it has never recovered. According to the CIA, in *The World Factbook: Cuba* (June 20, 2014, https://www.cia.gov/library/publications/the-world-factbook/geos/cu.html), the standard of living for the average Cuban was less in 2014 than it was before the loss of Soviet aid.

Cuba and the United States have had a contentious relationship since the time when Fidel Castro took power. In 1961 CIA-backed Cuban exiles attempted to invade Cuba and overthrow Castro. They were soundly defeated in a battle at the Bay of Pigs, a small bay on the southern coast of the island. The following year President John F. Kennedy (1917–1963) and the Soviet premier Nikita Khrushchev (1894–1971) faced off after U.S. intelligence agencies discovered that the Soviets had installed nuclear missile facilities in Cuba. After a suspenseful 12-day diplomatic standoff, the Soviets backed down and agreed to dismantle the facilities. The United States implemented the first of many economic sanctions against Cuba. With only a handful of exceptions, American citizens were forbidden to travel to Cuba. The United States issued an open invitation to Cuban citizens wanting to flee to the United States. Over the next four decades a succession of U.S. presidents openly expressed support for Cuban exiles and dissidents seeking to overthrow Castro's government.

During the 1970s relations thawed somewhat, and the United States opened an Interests Section office in the Swiss embassy in Havana, Cuba. However, in 1982 the DOS added Cuba to its list of state sponsors of terrorism. Then in 1996 the Cuban military shot down two U.S. civilian airplanes near Cuba, killing four people—all of whom were members of a Cuban American group opposed to the Castro regime. In retaliation, the United States imposed new economic sanctions against Cuba. After a hurricane struck the island in 2001, the United States sold food shipments to Cuba. However, relaxing all of the economic sanctions against Cuba was staunchly opposed by many conservatives in the U.S. government and by members of the politically powerful Cuban exile movement centered in Miami, Florida.

During his first administration, President Obama loosened some restrictions on travel, money transfers, and telecommunications between the United States and Cuba. However, relations between the two nations cooled in 2011, when Cuba sentenced Alan Gross (1949–), an American subcontractor, to 15 years in prison for allegedly spying on behalf of the U.S. government. Despite repeated requests from U.S. officials and politicians for his release, Gross remained imprisoned in Cuba as of August 2014.

Cuba's continued listing as a state sponsor of terrorism is increasingly under fire by critics who believe the listing is driven by politics rather than by national security concerns. In *Country Reports on Terrorism 2013*, the DOS only briefly mentions Cuba, noting that some former and current members of the Basque Fatherland Liberty terrorist organization were allowed to live in Cuba in 2013. That same year Raúl Castro announced that he planned to step down as president in 2018, following his second term in office. It remains to be seen how this development will affect U.S.-Cuban relations.

Sudan

Sudan is in the north-central part of the African continent. Its capital is Khartoum. (See Figure 6.6.) According to the CIA, in *The World Factbook: Sudan* (June 20, 2014, https://www.cia.gov/library/publications/the-world-factbook/geos/su.html), the ethnicity of the Sudanese population is mostly Sudanese Arab, and the predominant religion is Sunni Islam.

Sudan has a very troubled history. It became an independent state in 1956; however, it has suffered from decades of civil war, social unrest, and political instability. According to the CIA, the country's population was largely split between a northern region containing mostly Arabs and Muslims and a southern region containing mostly non-Arabs and non-Muslims. In 2005, after years of bloody civil war between the north and south, a peace agreement was reached that gave independence to the new nation of South Sudan in 2011. (See Figure 6.6.)

FIGURE 6.6

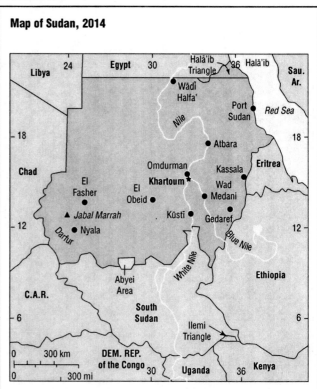

Map of Sudan, 2014

SOURCE: "Map of Sudan," in "Africa: Sudan," *The World Factbook,* Central Intelligence Agency, May 12, 2014, https://www.cia.gov/library/publications/the-world-factbook/geos/su.html (accessed May 25, 2014)

Meanwhile, a separate violent conflict has wracked the Darfur region of Sudan since 2003. The CIA notes that an estimated 200,000 to 400,000 people have died in the conflict, which has also displaced more than 2 million people. The Sudanese government's crackdown on rebels in Darfur has precipitated a humanitarian crisis and has been criticized by the international community as attempted genocide (the eradication of an entire group of people based on their nationality, ethnicity, religion, or race). In 2007 the UN Security Council authorized the deployment of a peacekeeping force in Darfur. The troops have been supplied by the African Union, which is a cooperative venture between several African nations.

In March 2009 the International Criminal Court (an international judicial body established in 2002) issued an arrest warrant for the Sudanese president Omar al-Bashir (1944–). He is wanted for war crimes and crimes against humanity that he allegedly committed in Darfur. In April 2010 al-Bashir won a new five-year term as Sudan's president in an election that international observers indicated was tainted by fraud.

U.S.-Sudanese relations have been poor for decades. The rift was deepened by U.S. support for Israel during the Six-Day War in 1967 and by the murders of American diplomats in Sudan during the 1970s and 1980s. In 1989 al-Bashir overthrew the existing ruler and installed a government known as the National Islamic Front. Al-Bashir is believed to have supported many terrorist organizations during the 1990s and provided a safe haven for notorious terrorists, such as Osama bin Laden (1957?–2011) and Abu Nidal (1937–2002). In 1993 the United States designated Sudan as a state sponsor of terrorism. Throughout the remainder of the decade the United States imposed ever-stricter economic and trade sanctions against Sudan. In 1998 U.S. missile strikes were conducted against targets in Khartoum in retaliation for Sudanese involvement in the bombings of U.S. embassies in Kenya and Tanzania.

The United States played a role in the 2005 peace agreement that helped South Sudan gain its independence, but has criticized Sudan for its crackdown on rebels in Darfur. In 2007 the U.S. government imposed new sanctions against Sudan for its actions in Darfur. In *Country Reports on Terrorism 2013*, the DOS provides a mixed analysis of Sudan's actions regarding terrorism, calling the Sudanese government "a generally cooperative counterterrorism partner." Although the DOS believes that al Qaeda members were in Sudan in 2013, the agency states that the Sudanese government "has taken steps to limit the activities of these elements, and has worked to disrupt foreign fighters' use of Sudan as a logistics base and transit point for terrorists going to Mali, Syria, and Afghanistan." However, the DOS notes that terrorist groups continued to operate in Sudan in 2013 and were believed to include Sudanese citizens.

Syria

Syria is a small Middle Eastern nation. Its capital is Damascus, which is located near the Lebanese border. (See Figure 6.7.) In 1946 Syria achieved independence after years of French rule. Decades of political instability and military coups culminated in 1970 with the assumption of power by Hafez Assad (1930–2000). According to the CIA, in *The World Factbook: Syria* (June 20, 2014, https://www.cia.gov/library/publications/the-world-factbook/geos/sy.html), Assad was a member of the Alawi minority, which is a religion distantly related to the Shia form of Islam. After his death in 2000, the presidency was turned over to his son, Bashar al-Assad (1965–), also an Alawi. The CIA describes the Syrian government as a "republic under an authoritarian regime."

FOREIGN RELATIONS. Syria and Israel have been enemies since the foundation of Israel in 1948 and have fought several wars. The most notable was the Six-Day War in 1967, during which Israel captured the Golan Heights. Israel has occupied this strategic piece of land along Syria's border with Israel ever since, deepening the divisions between the two countries. Syria has been on the U.S. list of state sponsors of terrorism since 1979,

FIGURE 6.7

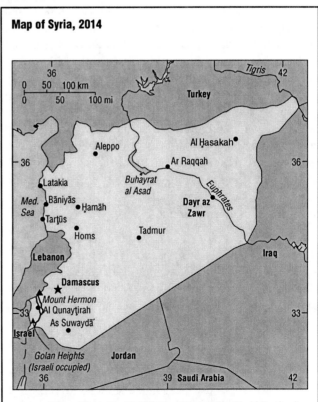

Map of Syria, 2014

SOURCE: "Map of Syria," in "Middle East: Syria," *The World Factbook*, Central Intelligence Agency, April 22, 2014, https://www.cia.gov/library/publications/the-world-factbook/geos/sy.html (accessed May 5, 2014)

primarily for its support of groups that conduct terrorist activities against Israel.

In 1976 Syria sent troops and intelligence personnel into neighboring Lebanon during the Lebanese civil war and began wielding considerable influence over Lebanese politics. In February 2005 Rafic Hariri (1944–2005), a former Lebanese prime minister, was assassinated. He had been openly criticizing Syria's military presence in Lebanon, and Syrian agents were suspected in his assassination. Two months later Syria withdrew its troops from Lebanon following intense pressure from the Lebanese people and the international community.

According to Jeremy M. Sharp of the CRS, in *Syria: Issues for the 112th Congress and Background on U.S. Sanctions* (April 28, 2011, http://fpc.state.gov/documents/organization/162748.pdf), the United States has maintained economic sanctions against Syria since the 1970s. U.S.-Syrian relations became particularly strained following the U.S.-led invasion of Iraq in 2003. U.S. officials accused Syria of allowing, and perhaps facilitating, the passage of militia fighters and arms across its border into Iraq to aid the insurgency against U.S. troops. Syria denied these claims. Other major issues have been Syria's continued "war of words" with Israel, its support for Hezbollah and Hamas (both of which are considered to be terrorist organizations by the United States), and its ties with Iran.

In 2007 the Israeli air force destroyed a complex that was believed to be a nuclear reactor under construction in northeastern Syria. Syria angrily denounced Israel and the United States for the raid and insisted that there were no nuclear activities at the complex. Syria is bound by the NPT, which it ratified in 1969. The IAEA reports in "Implementation of the NPT Safeguards Agreement in the Syrian Arab Republic" (February 18, 2010, http://www.isis-online.org/uploads/isis-reports/documents/IAEA_Report_Syria_18Feb2010.pdf) that the samples it collected at the bombed site in 2008 contained uranium particles "of a type not included in Syria's declared inventory of nuclear material."

In 2009 and 2010 Syria was implicated in several terrorist-related activities, including a series of bomb attacks in Iraq and transporting arms and missiles to Hezbollah. In February 2010 the Obama administration attempted to improve U.S.-Syrian relations by appointing Robert S. Ford (1958–) as the new U.S. ambassador to Syria. That position had been vacant since 2005. However, Ford left the country for his own safety in late 2011. The DOS (2014, http://damascus.usembassy.gov) notes that in February 2012 it suspended all operations at the U.S. embassy in Syria. In *Country Reports on Terrorism 2013*, the DOS indicates that in 2013 the Syrian government supported "a variety of terrorist groups affecting the stability of the region and beyond." Syria, like Iran, has strong ties with Hezbollah, and both nations are accused of providing political support and arms to Hezbollah.

REVOLUTION. The Arab Spring uprisings that began in 2010 swept dictators from power in four Middle Eastern countries. During the spring of 2011 simmering unrest in Syria also erupted into revolution. The events and their ramifications to U.S. interests are described in detail by Jeremy M. Sharp and Christopher M. Blanchard of the CRS in *Armed Conflict in Syria: U.S. and International Response* (July 12, 2012, http://fpc.state.gov/documents/organization/195385.pdf). According to Sharp and Blanchard, major antigovernment protests began in March 2011 after the government was accused of torturing children in Dara'a, a town in southern Syria. The government responded to the protesters with violent force, which only fueled public anger. Violence was initially limited to scattered pockets of resistance; however, by 2012 the government and opposition forces were engaged in an "all-out armed conflict."

Al-Assad's Alawite-dominated regime relies heavily on Iran, its closest ally, for political and military assistance. In addition, Russia, a long-time trading and political partner with Syria, has defiantly defended al-Assad. Sharp and Blanchard note that "Russian leaders would likely view the downfall of the regime as a serious blow to their diplomatic prestige and Middle Eastern/Mediterranean influence and military access." As a result, Russia has resisted international efforts to pressure al-Assad to step down and has blamed the rebels for inciting violence. Iran has done likewise and is believed to have provided al-Assad's regime with arms and other assistance. Iraq, another country with a Shia-dominated government, is accused of purposely allowing Iranian shipments to Syria to cross Iraqi territory and air space.

The opposition forces in Syria are largely Sunni and thus enjoy support from fellow Sunnis across the Middle East. At first, the U.S. government expressed support for the rebels. The Obama administration called for al-Assad to step down and provided some Syrian opposition forces with equipment, but not arms. However, the United States is concerned about the possible consequences of al-Assad's ouster. Syria has a large stockpile of WMDs, such as nerve gas and mustard gas, and is not a party to international agreements that ban WMD production. If he is ousted, the WMDs could fall into the hands of terrorist groups, the Iranian government, or other unfriendly parties.

After the revolution began the U.S. government became concerned that al-Assad would use WMDs against the rebels. In August 2012 President Obama (http://www.whitehouse.gov/the-press-office/2012/08/20/remarks-president-white-house-press-corps) responded to a reporter's question on this topic, noting, "That's an issue that doesn't just concern Syria; it concerns our close allies in the region, including Israel. It concerns us. We cannot have a situation where chemical or biological weapons are falling into the hands of the wrong people. We have been very clear to the Assad regime, but also to other players on the ground, that a red line for us is we start seeing a whole bunch of chemical weapons moving around or being utilized. That would change my calculus. That would change my equation." Some observers took Obama's "red line" statement to mean that he would use military force against the Syrian government if it used WMDs against its own people.

In August 2013 a Syrian government attack near Damascus was reported to have included chemical agents, prompting a UN investigation. In *United Nations Mission to Investigate Allegations of the Use of Chemical Weapons in the Syrian Arab Republic: Report on the Alleged Use of Chemical Weapons in the Ghouta Area of Damascus on 21 August 2013* (September 13, 2013, http://www.un.org/disarmament/content/slideshow/Secretary_General_Report_of_CW_Investigation.pdf), the UN concludes that "chemical weapons were used on a relatively large scale, resulting in numerous casualties, particularly among civilians and including many children." Based on sampling results, the UN believes the attack included sarin gas, a deadly nerve agent. The Obama administration also published a report on the incident based on intelligence it had gathered. In "Government Assessment of the Syrian Government's Use of Chemical Weapons on August 21, 2013" (August 30, 2013, http://www.whitehouse.gov/the-press-office), the Obama administration states, "The United States Government assesses with high confidence that the Syrian government carried out a chemical weapons attack in the Damascus suburbs on August 21, 2013. We further assess that the regime used a nerve agent in the attack." An estimated 1,429 people were killed in the attack, including at least 426 children.

Despite this revelation, Obama chose not to intervene militarily in Syria. He received some criticism for this stance in light of his "red line" speech the previous year. In May 2014 he defended his decision in a speech (http://www.whitehouse.gov/the-press-office/2014/05/28/remarks-president-west-point-academy-commencement-ceremony) at the U.S. Military Academy at West Point, New York. However, the president did indicate some willingness to intervene in the rebellion. He stated, "I will work with Congress to ramp up support for those in the Syrian opposition who offer the best alternative to

terrorists and brutal dictators." The reference to terrorists acknowledges that the rebellion has attracted many Islamist terrorists to Syria with their own agendas for overthrowing the al-Assad government. As such, the United States must be very cautious about which rebels it aids in Syria. There is a danger that any arms or other equipment provided to "moderate" rebels could fall into the hands of terrorists.

David E. Sanger reports in "Syria War Stirs New U.S. Debate on Cyberattacks" (NYTimes.com, February 24, 2014) that one option under consideration by the Obama administration is the use of cyberweapons. As noted earlier, it is believed the United States and Israel have deployed malware designed to sabotage Iran's nuclear program. According to Sanger, the U.S. government has developed a "battle plan" that includes cyberweapons that could disable computerized weapons systems employed by the Syrian military. If successful, this would provide a keen strategic advantage to rebel forces. Although the use of cyberweapons (rather than overt military force) by the United States has some advantages, it would also open the door for similar tactics by other nations. Sanger notes, "One of the central issues is whether such a strike on Syria would be seen as a justified humanitarian intervention, less likely to cause civilian casualties than airstrikes, or whether it would only embolden American adversaries who have themselves been debating how to use the new weapons."

The ongoing civil war in Syria also poses a threat to U.S. homeland security. There are fears that American sympathizers who have traveled to Syria to assist the rebels will be trained and indoctrinated by al Qaeda or other terrorist groups. These people could return to the United States and conduct terrorist attacks. In May 2014 an assailant in Belgium killed two Israeli tourists and a French citizen at a Jewish museum. Belgian authorities arrested a suspect who is believed to have traveled to Syria to aid the rebels there. According to Anne Penketh, in "French Suspect in Brussels Jewish Museum Attack Spent Year in Syria" (Guardian.com, June 1, 2014), authorities said the French suspect spent a year fighting with rebels in Syria. When he was captured, he allegedly had guns that were "wrapped in a white sheet scrawled with the name of the Islamic State of Iraq and the Levant." As explained in Chapter 3, this group is considered to be one of the most dangerous terrorist organizations to U.S. national security.

CHAPTER 7
PROLIFERATION OF WEAPONS

Proliferation means growth or multiplication. The proliferation of military weapons around the world is a national security concern for the United States. Military weapons fall into two broad types. Conventional armaments use chemically based explosive reactions to create death and destruction. The U.S. government strives to ensure that its military forces and those of its allies are heavily armed with conventional weapons. Unconventional weapons rely on nontraditional means, primarily nuclear technology or the release of chemical or biological agents. Small numbers of these weapons are capable of killing vast numbers of people; hence, they are called weapons of mass destruction (WMDs). The proliferation of WMDs is governed by many international agreements between countries. Therefore, the United States is most concerned about the acquisition and use of WMDs by terrorists and rogue nations (nations that ignore international restrictions on weapons proliferation).

ARMS AROUND THE WORLD

Numerous international organizations are devoted to reducing the proliferation of weapons worldwide. The United Nations (UN) is the prime example. It operates the UN Office for Disarmament Affairs, which promotes disarmament and the nonproliferation of conventional weapons and WMDs. Another relevant organization is the International Atomic Energy Agency (IAEA), which conducts inspection and verification services related to international nuclear weapons agreements. Private organizations that conduct research and/or provide educational resources related to nonproliferation include the Center for Arms Control and Non-proliferation (http://armscontrolcenter.org), the Vienna Center for Disarmament and Non-proliferation (http://vcdnp.org), and the European Union (EU) Non-proliferation Consortium (http://www.nonproliferation.eu).

Most nations of the world are heavily armed with conventional weapons. A handful of developed nations, including the United States, possess highly advanced conventional weapons that are enhanced by sophisticated technologies, such as laser guidance systems. The effectiveness of these weapons was first demonstrated by the U.S. military in 1991 during the Persian Gulf War against Iraq. Advanced weapons systems are very expensive. As shown in Table 6.4 in Chapter 6, the United States had the highest military expenditure of any country in the world between 2000 and 2010. Its average annual expenditure during this period was $570 billion.

The world's arms-producing industry is massive and mostly centered in the United States. The Stockholm International Peace Research Institute (SIPRI) is an international organization that conducts research on conflicts, arms, and arms control and proliferation. In *SIPRI Yearbook 2013: Armaments, Disarmament and International Security: Summary* (May 2013, http://www.sipri.org/yearbook/2013/files/SIPRIYB13Summary.pdf), the SIPRI estimates that sales of military-type arms and related services by the top-100 supplying companies in the world, excluding China, totaled $410 billion in 2011. Seven of the 10 largest producing companies were based in the United States, including the top two suppliers: Lockheed Martin and Boeing. The United States has a substantial defense industry that provides arms to the U.S. military and to allies in the rest of the world.

The U.S. Department of State (DOS) provides in *World Military Expenditures and Arms Transfers 2013* (2013, http://www.state.gov/t/avc/rls/rpt/wmeat/2013) information about international arms transfers between 2000 and 2010. The department defines arms as "military equipment and related services, including weapons of war, parts thereof, ammunition, support equipment, and other commodities designed for military use, as well as related services." As shown in Table 7.1, the DOS estimates that

TABLE 7.1

Arms delivery value by supplying country or region, 2000–10

[In billions of constant 2010 U.S. dollars]

Suppliers	Recipients	2000	2001	2002	2003	2004	2005	2006	2007	2008	2009	2010	Mean
World	World	87.7	90.1	90.3	97.2	101.7	106.5	111.8	105.7	124.6	143.2	152.3	110.1
United States of America	World	63.1	68.1	68.5	70.5	75.0	83.9	86.7	81.4	97.4	115.1	119.5	84.5
European Union (as of end of 2010)	World	13.8	10.9	11.1	14.8	14.3	12.5	13.2	12.1	13.0	14.0	15.0	13.1
• France	World	3.1	2.4	1.8	2.7	6.5	3.0	2.2	2.9	1.6	1.6	2.5	2.8
• Germany	World	1.7	0.9	1.5	2.3	2.4	2.1	2.4	3.2	3.8	3.9	3.4	2.5
• Italy	World	0.3	0.6	0.6	0.5	0.3	1.0	0.6	0.7	1.0	1.2	1.9	0.8
• United Kingdom	World	7.4	5.3	6.0	7.9	3.7	4.2	5.1	2.3	2.5	2.6	2.9	4.5
• Other E.U.	World	1.4	1.6	1.1	1.4	1.3	2.2	2.8	3.0	4.0	4.6	4.3	2.5
Russia	World	5.4	5.7	4.4	5.0	6.5	4.6	7.0	5.6	6.8	5.5	7.2	5.8
Other non-E.U. Europe	World	1.4	1.1	1.4	2.3	1.0	1.0	0.8	1.3	1.5	1.4	1.4	1.3
China	World	1.1	1.1	1.1	0.9	1.1	1.1	1.6	1.7	2.2	1.8	3.1	1.5
Other East Asia	World	0.6	0.8	0.5	0.3	0.4	0.7	0.5	0.5	0.4	0.5	0.7	0.5
Middle East	World	1.1	1.1	1.7	1.7	1.3	1.3	0.8	1.5	1.9	2.8	2.9	1.6
Others	World	1.2	1.3	1.7	1.6	2.1	1.5	1.2	1.6	1.5	2.2	2.5	1.7

Notes: Values are rounded to the nearest $0.1 billion ($100 million). Arms trade values include only trade among countries covered by World Military Expenditures and Arms Transfers (WMEAT) and unspecified or multinational entities. They exclude trade to and/or from lands not covered by WMEAT.

SOURCE: Adapted from "Table IV.a. Value of Arms Transfer Deliveries, 2000–2010," in *World Military Expenditures and Arms Transfers 2013*, U.S. State Department, 2013, http://www.state.gov/documents/organization/223437.xlsx (accessed June 6, 2014)

FIGURE 7.1

Breakdown of arms delivery value by supplying country or region based on average for 2000–10

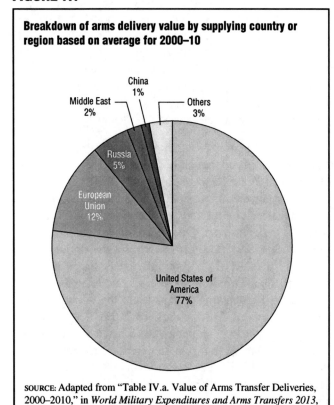

China 1%
Middle East 2%
Others 3%
Russia 5%
European Union 12%
United States of America 77%

SOURCE: Adapted from "Table IV.a. Value of Arms Transfer Deliveries, 2000–2010," in *World Military Expenditures and Arms Transfers 2013*, U.S. State Department, 2013, http://www.state.gov/documents/organization/223437.xlsx (accessed June 6, 2014)

breakdown of the trade by source country or region. The United States was the largest exporter, accounting for 77% of international arms transfers between 2000 and 2010. The European Union (12%) and Russia (5%) ranked second and third, respectively.

As shown in Table 7.1, the value of U.S. arms exports nearly doubled from $63.1 billion in 2000 to $119.5 billion in 2010. Some observers assert this increase was driven, in large part, by the foreign policy goals of President Barack Obama (1961–). For example, in "Obama Makes Arms Sales a Key Tool of U.S. Foreign Policy" (Forbes.com, January 2, 2012), Loren Thompson states, "The President and his advisors apparently have decided that well-armed allies are the next best thing to U.S. 'boots on the ground' when it comes to advancing America's global security interests."

MISSILES

One evolution in modern warfare has been the development of missiles that are self-propelled and guided (steered) toward their targets. Missiles fall into two broad categories: ballistic missiles and cruise missiles. Ballistic missiles are guided only during the initial portion of their flight. After that period the missiles go into free flight, during which they are totally under the influence of natural factors, such as gravity and wind. Cruise missiles are guided throughout their entire flight. In general, cruise missiles fly at low altitudes and with great precision. They may be guided by global positioning satellite data that are collected during flight.

In *Ballistic and Cruise Missile Threat* (May 2013, http://www.afisr.af.mil/shared/media/document/AFD-130 710-054.pdf), the U.S. Department of Defense (DOD)

international trade in arms grew from $87.7 billion in 2000 to $152.3 billion in 2010. These values are in constant 2010 dollars (i.e., assuming that the dollar had the same value each year as it did in 2010). The mean (average) annual value of international arms trade over this period was $110.1 billion. Figure 7.1 provides a explains that ballistic and cruise missiles can be armed with conventional or nonconventional warheads. Conventional warheads contain conventional explosives that detonate and provide "kill mechanisms." Nonconventional warheads come in two main types: WMDs and nonlethal warheads. WMDs include nuclear weapons and weapons that rely on chemical or biological agents. Nonlethal warheads are designed to "disable equipment rather than harm personnel"; for example, electromagnetic pulse weapons can disrupt or shut down electronic-based equipment.

The proliferation of missiles around the world, particularly those with great range (i.e., able to travel long distances), is of great concern to U.S. national security. The DOD states that "ballistic and cruise missiles present a significant threat to US and Allied forces overseas, and to the United States and its territories." As of 2014, only Russia and China possessed missiles of sufficient quality and range to significantly threaten U.S. interests. Sandra I. Erwin notes in "Proliferation of Cruise Missiles Sparks Concern about U.S. Air Defenses" (NationalDefenseMagazine.org, February 2013) that "the United States does not expect to be going to war against China or Russia, but the U.S. could in the foreseeable future have to fight other nations or non-state groups that are able to acquire missiles from those two powers."

Ballistic Missiles

In *Ballistic and Cruise Missile Threat*, the DOD classifies ballistic missiles into five categories:

- Short-range ballistic missile (SRBM)—range less than 621 miles (1,000 km)
- Medium-range ballistic missile (MRBM)—range of 621 to 1,864 miles (1,000 to 3,000 km)
- Intermediate-range ballistic missile (IRBM)—range of 1,864 to 3,418 miles (3,000 to 5,500 km)
- Intercontinental ballistic missile (ICBM)—range greater than 3,418 miles (5,500 km)
- Submarine-launched ballistic missile (SLBM)—any ballistic missile launched by a submarine regardless of maximum range

ICBMs and long-range SLBMs are of the most concern to U.S. national security. Table 7.2 shows characteristics of ICBMs deployed or being developed by Russia, China, North Korea, and India. According to the DOD, Russia has the largest supply of ICBMs outside the United States. The Russian arsenal includes more than 1,400 nuclear warheads on ballistic missiles that are believed capable of reaching the United States. The DOD notes, however, that "China has the most active and diverse ballistic missile development program in the world." The department estimates that by the late 2020s China will have more than 100 ICBM nuclear warheads capable of reaching the United States. North Korea and India have much smaller ICBM programs. Chapter 6 describes the North Korean missile program, which is particularly worrisome to the United States because of the poor relationship between the two countries.

TABLE 7.2

Characteristics of intercontinental ballistic missiles (ICBMs)

Missile	Number of stages	Warheads per missile	Propellant	Deployment mode	Maximum range (km)	Number of launchers[a]
Russia						
SS-18 Mod 5	2 + PBV	10	Liquid	Silo	10,000+	About 50
SS-19 Mod 3	2 + PBV	6	Liquid	Silo	9,000+	About 50
SS-25	3 + PBV	1	Solid	Road-mobile	11,000	More than 150
SS-27 Mod 1	3 + PBV	1	Solid	Silo & road-mobile	11,000	About 80
SS-27 Mod-2	3 + PBV	Multiple	Solid	Silo & road-mobile	11,000	About 20
New ICBM	At least 2	Undetermined	Solid	Road-mobile	5,500+	Not yet deployed
China						
CSS-3	2	1	Liquid	Transportable	5,500+	10 to 15
CSS-4 Mod 1	2	1	Liquid	Silo	12,000+	About 20
CSS-10 Mod 1	3	1	Solid	Road-mobile	7,000+	5 to 10
CSS-10 Mod 2	3	1	Solid	Road-mobile	11,000+	More than 15
North Korea						
Taepo Dong-2	2 or 3	1	Liquid	Fixed	5,500+	Unknown[b]
Hwasong-13	Undetermined	Undetermined	Undetermined	Road-mobile	5,500+	Unknown
India						
Agni V	3	1	Solid	Undetermined	5,000+	Not yet deployed

[a]The missile inventory may be much larger than the number of launchers; launchers can be reused to fire additional missiles.
[b]Launches of the TD-2 space vehicle have been observed from both east and west coast facilities.
ICBM = intercontinental ballistic missile. PBV = post-boost vehicle.
Note: All ranges are approximate.

SOURCE: "ICBM Characteristics," in *Ballistic and Cruise Missile Threat*, U.S. Department of Defense, Air and Space Intelligence Center, 2013, http://www.afisr.af.mil/shared/media/document/AFD-130710-054.pdf (accessed May 6, 2014)

TABLE 7.3

Characteristics of submarine-launched ballistic missiles (SLBMs)

Missile	Number of stages	Warheads per missile	Propellant	Submarine class	Maximum range (km)	Number of launchers
Russia						
SS-N-18	2 + PBV	3	Liquid	Delta III	5,500+	96
SS-N-23	3 + PBV	4	Liquid	Delta IV	8,000+	96
SS-NX-32 Bulava	3 + PBV	6	Solid	Dolgorukiy (Borey)	8,000+	16; Not yet deployed
				Typhoon		20; Not yet deployed
China						
CSS-NX-3/JL-1	2	1	Solid	XIA	1,700+	12; Not yet deployed
CSS-NX-14/JL-2	3	1	Solid	JIN	7,000+	12; Not yet deployed
India						
K-15	2	1	Solid	Arihart	700	12; Not yet deployed

SLBM = Submarine-launched ballistic missile. PBV = post-boost vehicle.
Note: All ranges are approximate.

SOURCE: "SLBM Characteristics," in *Ballistic and Cruise Missile Threat*, U.S. Department of Defense, Air and Space Intelligence Center, 2013, http://www
.afisr.af.mil/shared/media/document/AFD-130710-054.pdf (accessed May 6, 2014)

Table 7.3 shows characteristics of SLBMs deployed or being developed by Russia, China, and India. Only Russia has deployed SLBMs with ICBM-range capabilities (i.e., ranges greater than 3,418 miles [5,500 km]). The DOD indicates that Russia has "a substantial force" of submarines equipped with such missiles and is in the process of developing new and improved SLBMs. The department believes China has developed, but not yet deployed, an SLBM with an ICBM range. It notes that this weapon system will allow Chinese submarines "to target portions of the United States from operating areas located near the Chinese coast."

BALLISTIC MISSILE DEFENSE. As described in Chapter 1, since 1958 the United States and Canada have operated the North American Aerospace Defense Command (NORAD). NORAD's (2014, http://www.norad .mil/AboutNORAD/NORADHistory.aspx) primary mission is to provide aerospace warning and control for North America against hostile aircraft, missiles, and space vehicles. It utilizes a network of satellites and ground-based and airborne radar systems to detect these threats. During the Cold War NORAD's ability to detect incoming Soviet missiles would have given the United States time to warn the American public and to launch its own missiles in retaliation. This scenario never occurred. As military technology has advanced, the United States has developed weapons that are designed to intercept and destroy incoming ballistic missiles.

In February 2010 the DOD published the results of its first-ever *Ballistic Missile Defense Review Report* (http://www.defense.gov/bmdr/docs/BMDR%20as%20of %2026JAN10%200630_for%20web.pdf). At that time the DOD noted that only Russia and China had the capabilities to conduct "large-scale" ballistic missile attacks on U.S. territory. However, the department states,

"This is very unlikely and not the focus of U.S. [Ballistic Missile Defense] BMD." Of greater concern are so-called regional threats, primarily North Korea, Iran, and Syria, all of which have ballistic missiles that "threaten U.S. forces, allies and partners in regions where the United States deploys forces and maintains security relationships." U.S. relations with these countries of concern are described in detail in Chapter 6.

The United States has operated a BMD program since the 1980s. At that time the major threat to U.S. national security was the Soviet Union. In 1983 President Ronald Reagan (1911–2004) announced a new military venture called the Space Defense Initiative (SDI). The SDI planned to put a satellite shield in space to protect the United States from incoming Soviet nuclear missiles. Such a feat was well beyond the technical capabilities of the era. The media nicknamed the SDI the "Star Wars" project after the hit 1977 movie, which featured elaborate space weapons. The DOD began developing and testing interceptor missiles that were designed to intercept and destroy incoming ballistic missiles. By the early 1990s the Soviet Union had disintegrated into separate countries, including Russia, that were no longer directly hostile to the United States. However, the United States' BMD program continued to operate. A new concern became the proliferation of missiles around the world and their possession by terrorists and unfriendly nations. In 2002 the United States withdrew from the Antiballistic Missile Treaty of 1972. Forged with the Soviet Union (and later Russia), this treaty had strictly limited each nation's deployment of antiballistic missiles.

As of August 2014, the United States' BMD program was under the direction of the DOD's Missile Defense Agency (MDA). The MDA is developing and testing ground- and sea-based interceptor missiles and space-based

FIGURE 7.2

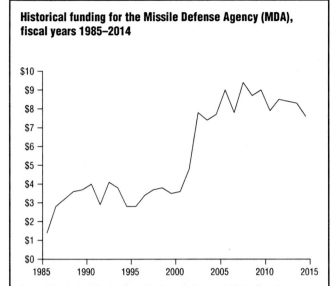

Historical funding for the Missile Defense Agency (MDA), fiscal years 1985–2014

Notes: Historical funding levels are for Strategic Defense Initiative Organization (SDIO), Ballistic Missile Defense Organization (BMDO), and MDA (Missile Defense Agency). The appropriation for fiscal year 2013 does not include the 9% across-the-board department wide sequestration cut. The Department cut $668 million, leaving $7.6 billion for fiscal year 2013 funding.

SOURCE: Adapted from "Historical Funding for MDA FY85-14," in *Funding Missile Defense*, U.S. Department of Defense, Missile Defense Agency, 2014, http://www.mda.mil/global/documents/pdf/histfunds.pdf (accessed May 6, 2014)

tracking systems. As shown in Figure 7.2, funding for the MDA in fiscal year (FY) 2014 was nearly $8 billion. By the end of FY 2014 the United States will have invested more than $165 billion in missile defense. According to the DOD, in "Department of Defense Briefing by Vice Adm. Syring on the Missile Defense Agency's FY 2015 Budget in the Pentagon Briefing Room" (March 4, 2014, http://www.defense.gov/Transcripts/Transcript.aspx?TranscriptID=5388), President Obama requested nearly $7.5 billion for the MDA in his proposed FY 2015 budget.

Figure 7.3 shows a typical ICBM engagement scenario for the BMD System. U.S. early warning sensors alert the system that a missile has been launched that is bound for territory defended by the United States. In response, a U.S. interceptor is launched that releases a "kill vehicle" designed to collide with the ICBM's warhead above the atmosphere, thus minimizing casualties and damage on the ground. The BMD System includes interceptor missiles that can be launched from the sea or from the ground to intercept threat missiles of various types. Some ground-based interceptor missiles are maintained at fixed locations called silos. Others, such as Patriot Advanced Capablity-3 (PAC-3) missiles, are transportable from place to place.

In the fact sheet "Ballistic Missile Defense Intercept Flight Test Record" (June 22, 2014, http://www.mda.mil/global/documents/pdf/testrecord.pdf), the MDA reports

that 65 of 81 hit-to-kill intercept attempts conducted since 2001 have been successful. A hit-to-kill intercept occurs when an interceptor missile collides with and destroys an airborne target.

Cruise Missiles

Cruise missiles are guided throughout their flight paths using highly sophisticated guidance systems. Christopher Bolkcom of the Congressional Research Service (CRS) explains in *Cruise Missile Defense* (March 15, 2007, http://assets.opencrs.com/rpts/RS21921_20070315.pdf) that cruise missiles can fly "low terrain-hugging" paths and can strike their targets with great accuracy. In *Ballistic and Cruise Missile Threat*, the DOD indicates that cruise missiles are typically categorized by mission (e.g., land-attack or antiship). They can be launched from the ground, air, or sea.

Andrew Feickert of the CRS notes in *Missile Survey: Ballistic and Cruise Missiles of Foreign Countries* (March 5, 2004, http://fpc.state.gov/documents/organization/31999.pdf) that during the early months of Operation Iraqi Freedom (the U.S.-led invasion of Iraq in 2003) the United States launched approximately 700 Tomahawk cruise missiles at Iraqi targets. U.S. defense officials claim that less than 10 of these missiles failed to hit their intended targets. The Iraqi military reportedly fired five cruise missiles at U.S. forces. According to Feickert, this was the first time in history that U.S. ground forces had been attacked by enemy cruise missiles.

CRUISE MISSILE DEFENSE. Ironically, the DOD notes in *Ballistic and Cruise Missile Threat* that the great success shown by the U.S. Tomahawk missiles has encouraged other countries to accelerate their development of cruise missiles. One factor is cost. Cruise missiles are much cheaper to deploy than a formidable manned air force, such as the United States'. According to Erwin, "Cruise missiles have been nicknamed a 'poor man's air force' as they could potentially undercut the military advantage of a much more powerful adversary such as the United States." The DOD admits that defending against this evolving threat is daunting because the missiles can fly at low altitudes, below the reach of conventional radar systems. In addition, some newer systems incorporate "stealth features" that make them even more difficult to detect.

Before 2006 the United States did not have a coordinated cruise missile defense (CMD) program because CMD efforts were conducted by the various military services. In 2006 CMD responsibility was given to the U.S. Strategic Command, which is headquartered at Offutt Air Force Base in Nebraska. The U.S. military is particularly worried about land-attack cruise missiles (LACMs). The DOD notes that LACMs are "highly effective weapon systems that can present a major threat

FIGURE 7.3

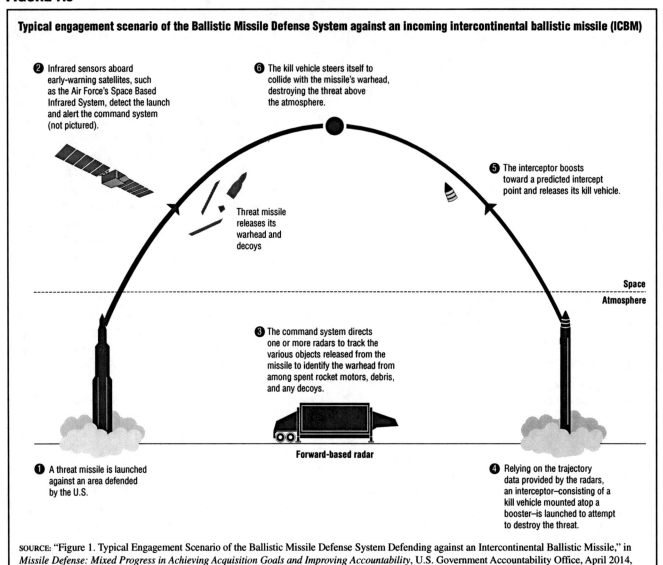

Typical engagement scenario of the Ballistic Missile Defense System against an incoming intercontinental ballistic missile (ICBM)

❷ Infrared sensors aboard early-warning satellites, such as the Air Force's Space Based Infrared System, detect the launch and alert the command system (not pictured).

❻ The kill vehicle steers itself to collide with the missile's warhead, destroying the threat above the atmosphere.

❺ The interceptor boosts toward a predicted intercept point and releases its kill vehicle.

Threat missile releases its warhead and decoys

Space
Atmosphere

❸ The command system directs one or more radars to track the various objects released from the missile to identify the warhead from among spent rocket motors, debris, and any decoys.

Forward-based radar

❶ A threat missile is launched against an area defended by the U.S.

❹ Relying on the trajectory data provided by the radars, an interceptor–consisting of a kill vehicle mounted atop a booster–is launched to attempt to destroy the threat.

SOURCE: "Figure 1. Typical Engagement Scenario of the Ballistic Missile Defense System Defending against an Intercontinental Ballistic Missile," in *Missile Defense: Mixed Progress in Achieving Acquisition Goals and Improving Accountability*, U.S. Government Accountability Office, April 2014, http://www.gao.gov/assets/670/662194.pdf (accessed May 6, 2014)

to military operations." However, the United States does have some CMD resources. The MDA (April 17, 2014, http://www.mda.mil/faqs.html) reports that the PAC-3 system, which is designed to defend against relatively low-flying SRBMs, can also intercept and destroy incoming cruise missiles.

CONVENTIONAL WEAPONS CONTROLS

The Convention on Prohibitions or Restrictions on the Use of Certain Conventional Weapons Which May Be Deemed to Be Excessively Injurious or to Have Indiscriminate Effects (2014, http://www.un-documents.net/cpruccw.htm) took effect in 1983. It restricts certain conventional weapons that are considered to have particularly horrific effects. The Convention on Conventional Weapons (as it is commonly called) originally had three protocols that covered weapons producing fragments not detectable in the human body by x-rays; land mines,

booby traps, and related devices; and incendiary weapons (weapons purposely designed to start fires or cause burns). In 1995 a fourth protocol was added to control the proliferation of laser weapons designed to permanently blind their victims. In 2003 a fifth protocol was added that requires bound parties to clear and destroy unexploded ordnances left over after a conflict has ended. As of August 2014, the United States was a party to all protocols of the convention.

The Wassenaar Arrangement on Export Controls for Conventional Arms and Dual-Use Goods and Technologies (2014, http://www.wassenaar.org) is a multilateral agreement established in 1996 that concerns the export of conventional weapons and dual-use (military and civilian) technologies that could pose a threat to a country's national security if they are acquired by that country's enemies. The end of the Cold War during the early 1990s precipitated the new agreement for which the stated purpose is to promote "transparency and greater responsibility in transfers of conventional arms and dual-use goods and technologies, thus preventing destabilising accumulations. Participating States seek, through their national policies, to ensure that transfers of these items do not contribute to the development or enhancement of military capabilities which undermine these goals, and are not diverted to support such capabilities." The United States is a party to the Wassenaar Arrangement.

In 2013 the UN (http://www.un.org/disarmament/update/20130402/ATTVotingChart.pdf) adopted the Arms Trade Treaty by a vote of 154 to 3. The three countries that voted against the treaty were Iran, North Korea, and Syria. As explained in Chapter 6, all three countries have been subject to UN sanctions related to arms transfers. According to the UN (2014, http://www.un.org/disarmament/ATT), "The treaty will foster peace and security by thwarting uncontrolled destabilizing arms flows to conflict regions. It will prevent human rights abusers and violators of the law of war from being supplied with arms. And it will help keep warlords, pirates, and gangs from acquiring these deadly tools." Fifty countries must ratify the treaty before it goes into effect. As of August 2014 (http://disarmament.un.org/treaties/t/att), it had been ratified by 44 countries. The U.S. secretary of state John Kerry (1943–) signed the Arms Trade Treaty in September 2013 on behalf of the United States. Under the U.S. Constitution a foreign treaty is not binding until it is ratified by a two-thirds majority vote in the U.S. Senate. As of August 2014, this vote had not occurred.

NUCLEAR WEAPONS

One legacy of the Cold War was the development and stockpiling of thousands of nuclear weapons by the United States and the Soviet Union. In 1961 the Soviets conducted nuclear tests in the atmosphere. The United States responded with its own atmospheric tests. The rest of the world watched uneasily as the two great superpowers seemed to edge closer and closer to a nuclear showdown. A crucial event in the nuclear arms race occurred in 1962: the Cuban missile crisis. U.S. intelligence agencies discovered the Soviets had installed nuclear missile facilities in Cuba, only 90 miles (145 km) from the U.S. coast. President John F. Kennedy (1917–1963) confronted the Soviets. He imposed a naval blockade around Cuba and demanded that the nuclear facilities be removed. After a suspenseful 12-day standoff the Soviets complied. It proved to be a turning point in the Cold War, as the two nations began negotiating treaties on limiting the testing and proliferation of nuclear weapons.

Nuclear Club

By 1964 there were five nations in the so-called nuclear club: the United States, the Soviet Union, the United Kingdom, France, and China. Before the end of the decade an important multilateral nuclear treaty had been signed by dozens of nations. The Treaty on the Nonproliferation of Nuclear Weapons (NPT; 2014, http://www.un.org/events/npt2005/npttreaty.html) acknowledged "the devastation that would be visited upon all mankind by a nuclear war" and included the following provisions:

- No transfer of nuclear weapons or nuclear-related technical assistance from a nuclear state to a nonnuclear state

- No manufacture of nuclear weapons by nonnuclear states or acquisition of the weapons or associated technologies from nuclear states

- Acceptance by nuclear states of safeguards overseen and verified by the IAEA to prevent conversion of peaceful nuclear energy projects to nuclear weapons development; these safeguards also apply to transfers of peaceful-purpose nuclear materials from nuclear states to nonnuclear states

The UN (http://disarmament.un.org/treaties/t/npt) indicates that as of 2014, 190 nations were parties to the NPT. They are required to provide the IAEA certain notifications about their nuclear programs and to allow IAEA inspection and verification of their nuclear activities. Failure to do so can trigger UN sanctions, as happened to Iran during the first decade of the 21st century.

As of 2014, India, Israel, North Korea, and Pakistan were not parties to the NPT. North Korea withdrew from the treaty in 2003, whereas the other three never became signatories. However, all four NPT outsiders have forged separate "safeguards" agreements with the IAEA in regards to certain aspects of their nuclear programs. For example, in 2009 India entered into a safeguards agreement (http://www.iaea.org/Publications/Documents/Infcircs/2009/infcirc754.pdf) that allowed the IAEA some oversight of its civilian nuclear program.

U.S.-Russian Nuclear Weapons Treaties

The United States and Russia have entered into bilateral (two-party) treaties related to nuclear weapons proliferation. As of August 2014, the most recent treaty was the New START Treaty, which became effective in February 2011. In the fact sheet "New START Treaty Entry into Force" (February 5, 2011, http://www.state.gov/r/pa/prs/ps/2011/02/156037.htm), the DOS notes that the treaty places specific limits on each country's number of warheads, launchers, and heavy bombers, as follows:

- Deployed strategic nuclear warheads—1,550

- Deployed and nondeployed strategic launchers and heavy bombers—800

- Deployed strategic launchers and heavy bombers—700

FIGURE 7.4

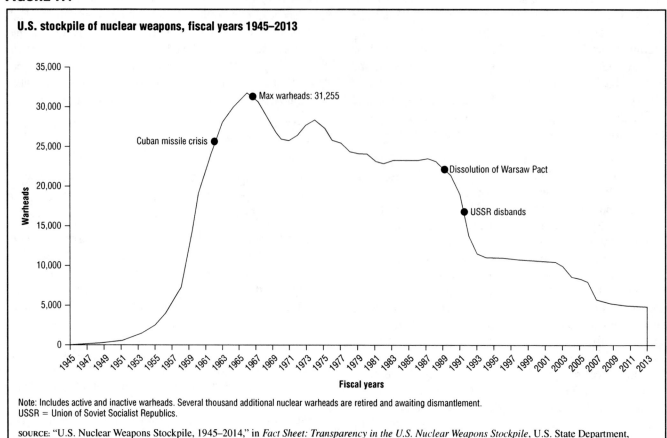

U.S. stockpile of nuclear weapons, fiscal years 1945–2013

Note: Includes active and inactive warheads. Several thousand additional nuclear warheads are retired and awaiting dismantlement.
USSR = Union of Soviet Socialist Republics.

SOURCE: "U.S. Nuclear Weapons Stockpile, 1945–2014," in *Fact Sheet: Transparency in the U.S. Nuclear Weapons Stockpile*, U.S. State Department, April 29, 2014, http://www.state.gov/documents/organization/225555.pdf (accessed May 6, 2014)

Although scaled deadlines are built into the treaty, all of the limits must be reached by February 5, 2018.

STOCKPILES AND DESTRUCTION. Figure 7.4 shows the U.S. nuclear weapons stockpile between FYs 1945 and 2013. (The federal government's fiscal year runs from October through September.) As of September 30, 2013, the total U.S. stockpile contained 4,804 warheads, including both active and inactive warheads. The United States dismantled 9,952 nuclear warheads between FYs 1994 and 2013. (See Table 7.4.) The DOS indicates in "Fact Sheet: Transparency in the U.S. Nuclear Weapons Stockpile" (April 29, 2014, http://www.defense.gov/news/d20100503 stockpile.pdf) that thousands more "retired" nuclear warheads are scheduled to be dismantled.

The breakup of the Soviet Union during the early 1990s into individual republics ended the Cold War but produced new security worries for the United States. In particular, the United States became concerned about the safety of the enormous stockpile of WMDs that the Soviets had accumulated. The new republics struggled economically after the breakup, stirring fears that WMDs or related technologies might be sold on the black market and end up in the hands of terrorists or rogue nations. In

TABLE 7.4

U.S. nuclear weapons dismantled by the U.S. Department of Energy, fiscal years 1994–2013

Department of Energy weapon dismantlements (Fiscal year 1994–2013)	
1994	1,369
1995	1,393
1996	1,064
1997	498
1998	1,062
1999	206
2000	158
2001	144
2002	344
2003	222
2004	206
2005	280
2006	253
2007	545
2008	648
2009	356
2010	352
2011	305
2012	308
2013	239
Total dismantlements	**9,952**

SOURCE: "Department of Energy Weapon Dismantlements (Fiscal Year 1994–2013)," in *Fact Sheet: Transparency in the U.S. Nuclear Weapons Stockpile*, U.S. State Department, April 29, 2014, http://www.state.gov/documents/organization/225555.pdf (accessed May 6, 2014)

1991 the Nunn-Lugar Act was spearheaded by Senators Sam Nunn (1938–; D-GA) and Richard G. Lugar (1932–; R-IN) to provide funding for the destruction of former Soviet missiles and chemical weapons and offer employment opportunities for former weapons scientists. The Cooperative Threat Reduction (CTR) office was created to implement the program, which was later taken over by the Defense Threat Reduction Agency (DTRA) within the DOD. In "Cooperative Threat Reduction Program" (2014, http://www.dtra.mil/Missions/Nunn-Lugar/Global CooperationInitiative.aspx), the DTRA indicates that CTR funding helped render Kazakhstan a nonnuclear weapons state in 1995, followed by Ukraine and Belarus in 1996.

During the first decade of the 21st century the program was expanded to include additional WMD concerns and nations outside of the former Soviet Union. By that time Russia and the former republics were much stronger economically, prompting calls within the United States to cease program funding in those regions. The original CTR program expired in June 2013.

The DTRA lists in "Nunn-Lugar CTR Scorecard" (May 31, 2013, http://dtra.mil/docs/system-documents/20130501_fy13_ctr-scorecard_slides_may13.pdf) the results achieved by the CTR program in the former Soviet republics and Albania through May 31, 2013. Substantial reductions were made when compared with the baseline amounts from 1994. Just over 82% of stockpiled warheads were deactivated and 71.9% of ICBMs were destroyed.

In June 2013 the DOS (http://www.state.gov/r/pa/prs/ps/2013/06/210913.htm) announced a new cooperative agreement with Russia regarding nuclear disarmament and security. The department notes that Russia will begin funding and conducting certain elements of the former CTR program. In "New U.S.-Russian Security Deal Greatly Scales Back Scope, Experts Say" (June 18, 2013, http://www.nti.org/gsn/article/new-us-russian-security-deal-greatly-scales-back-scope-experts-say), Douglas P. Guarino acknowledges the end of direct U.S. involvement in Russian WMD stockpile reductions. He indicates that some observers attribute the change "to Russia becoming increasingly reluctant to be perceived in recent years as a nation that is a proliferator or one that needs assistance."

As described in Chapter 6, pro-Russian militants with the alleged aid of the Russian military took control of the Crimean region of Ukraine after that nation experienced a revolution in February 2014. Subsequently, Russia moved to annex (absorb) Crimea as part of its territory. The events have negatively impacted the U.S.-Russian relationship. Some observers note the irony that the United States helped Ukraine rid itself of all nuclear weapons during the 1990s. For example, Michael Bowman quotes in "US

Lawmakers Worry Ukraine Crisis Will Impact Nuclear Proliferation" (VOANews.com, March 25, 2014) high-ranking U.S. lawmakers who fear the Russian annexation will dissuade other nations from reducing or eliminating their nuclear weapons stockpiles. Traditionally, the possession of nuclear weapons has been seen as a deterrent to aggressive foreign powers.

Nuclear Materials Security

In the United States the U.S. Department of Energy's National Nuclear Security Administration (NNSA) manages and ensures the security of the U.S. nuclear weapons stockpile. The NNSA's work took on extra significance in 2009, after President Obama made a pledge regarding WMDs. On April 5, 2009, in Prague, the Czech Republic, Obama (http://www.whitehouse.gov/the_press_office/Remarks-By-President-Barack-Obama-In-Prague-As-Delivered) stated: "So today I am announcing a new international effort to secure all vulnerable nuclear material around the world within four years. We will set new standards, expand our cooperation with Russia, pursue new partnerships to lock down these sensitive materials."

In *Securing Nuclear Materials: The 2012 Summit and Issues for Congress* (March 7, 2012, http://fpc.state.gov/documents/organization/187391.pdf), Mary Beth Nikitin of the CRS notes that in April 2010 Obama hosted the first Nuclear Security Summit, which was attended by the leaders of 47 nations. Subsequent summits took place biennially, most recently in March 2014 in the Netherlands. The Netherlands Ministry of Foreign Affairs (NMFA) notes in "Results of NSS 2014" (2014, https://www.nss2014.com/en/nss-2014/results) that 58 world leaders, including Obama, attended the summit. The summit participants presented progress reports (https://www.nss2014.com/en/nss-2014/reference-documents) that described their progress at achieving the three main goals of the summits:

- Reduce the worldwide amount of dangerous nuclear material, specifically highly enriched uranium. According to the NMFA, since 2009, 12 countries (Austria, Chile, the Czech Republic, Hungary, Libya, Mexico, Romania, Serbia, Taiwan, Turkey, Ukraine, and Vietnam) have removed all highly enriched uranium from their territories.

- Improve the security of all nuclear material and radioactive sources.

- Improve international cooperation, such as by conducting joint exercises, developing joint action plans, and supporting the security activities of other countries.

The Nuclear Threat Initiative (NTI) is a private nonprofit organization devoted to WMD nonproliferation. One of its projects is the Nuclear Materials Security

Index, which the NTI (2014, http://ntiindex.org/behind-the-index/about-the-nti-index) explains "was created to assess the security of nuclear materials around the world and to encourage governments to take actions and provide assurances about the security of the world's deadliest materials." As of August 2014, the most recent index report and data were released in January 2014 and were available online at http://ntiindex.org. The NTI uses the index to rate countries on their security activities related to weapons-usable nuclear materials. Each country is graded using a maximum score of 100. In *NTI Nuclear Materials Security Index: Building a Framework for Assurance, Accountability and Action* (2014, http://ntiindex.org/wp-content/uploads/2014/01/2014-NTI-Index-Report1.pdf), the NTI indicates that Australia received the highest score (92) in 2014, followed by Canada (88), Switzerland (87), Germany (85), and Norway (83). The United States ranked 11th with a score of 77.

RADIOLOGICAL WEAPONS

Radiological weapons are different from nuclear weapons. The latter use nuclear reactions to create a destructive force. Radiological weapons rely on conventional explosives to disperse radioactive materials into the air. Radiological dispersal devices are commonly known as dirty bombs. Although a dirty bomb does not have the destructive power of a nuclear bomb, it is an effective tool for creating terror. The detonation of a dirty bomb and the subsequent release of radiation could temporarily fool people into believing that a nuclear bomb has been detonated, leading to widespread panic.

The radioactive materials that can be used to manufacture a dirty bomb are widely found in industrial and medical equipment. Examples include low-level radioactive waste, such as protective clothing and shoe covers, tools and equipment, discarded reactor parts and filters, rags, mops, reactor water treatment residues, luminous dials, and laboratory and medical supplies. Sealed radiological sources are small sealed containers containing a radionuclide in solid or powder form. U.S. law requires that all sealed radiological sources be safeguarded by the licensees that use them. The Department of Energy is responsible for providing disposal for sources that are not needed anymore.

CHEMICAL AND BIOLOGICAL WEAPONS

Chemical and biological weapons are considered to be WMDs because relatively small amounts of the substances can expose large numbers of people to potentially lethal effects. The use of chemical weapons during warfare is not new. Jonathan Tucker describes in *War of Nerves: Chemical Warfare from World War I to al-Qaeda* (2006) their use by German forces during World War I (1914–1918).

In the spring of 1915 the German army reached a stalemate in Belgium against the Allied forces of France, Britain, and Canada. Both sides were huddled in trenches that crisscrossed the countryside. On April 22, German troops simultaneously opened more than 5,000 cylinders that contained chlorine gas. The wind blew the yellowish-green cloud across no-man's-land to the Allied trenches, where hundreds of soldiers were incapacitated almost immediately. The remainder of the troops fled in terror, many suffering from seared eyes and bronchial passages. At the time, Germany was a party to international treaties that prohibited the use of munitions to deliver chemical agents.

The horrors unleashed in the German attack led British forces to retaliate with chemical attacks of their own. Throughout the remainder of the war both sides employed toxic gases against one another with varying levels of success. The article "Gas Warfare" (January 15, 2000, http://www.worldwar1.com/arm006.htm) lists the chemical agents that were used during World War I. Public revulsion prevented the use of similar agents on the battlefield during World War II (1939–1945). They were employed by both sides during the Iran-Iraq War (1980–1988). The former Iraqi leader Saddam Hussein (1937–2006) was accused of using chemical weapons in 1988 against the minority Kurdish population in his own country. More recently in 2013, the Syrian government was found to have used chemical weapons against its own people. As described in Chapter 6, Syria has been roiled by a bloody civil war in which rebel groups are attempting to overthrow the government.

Chemical Weapons Controls

In 1997 the Chemical Weapons Convention (CWC) went into effect. It prohibits the development, production, stockpiling, and use of chemical weapons and includes a verification regime to ensure that certain chemicals are produced or traded only for peaceful purposes. According to the Organization for the Prohibition of Chemical Weapons (http://www.opcw.org/about-opcw/member-states), as of August 2014 there were 190 parties to the CWC, including the United States. As an original signatory to the CWC, the United States has committed to destroy 100% of its chemical weapons stockpile.

Several countries around the world are known to have developed chemical weapons at one time or another, including the United States. According to the U.S. Government Accountability Office (GAO), in *Chemical Demilitarization: Additional Management Actions Needed to Meet Key Performance Goals of DOD's Chemical Demilitarization Program* (December 2007, http://www.gao.gov/new.items/d08134.pdf), the U.S. stockpile included mustard gas and the nerve agents GB (also known as sarin gas) and VX. In "Closing U.S. Chemical Warfare Agent

Disposal Facilities" (April 29, 2014, http://www.cdc.gov/nceh/demil/closing_facilities.htm), the Centers for Disease Control and Prevention indicates that when the United States ratified the CWC in 1997, the nation's stockpile of chemical warfare agents totaled approximately 30,500 tons. By 2012 nearly 90% of the stockpile had been destroyed. As of August 2014, operations were ongoing at two sites—the Blue Grass Chemical Agent-Destruction Pilot Plant in Richmond, Kentucky, and the Pueblo Chemical Agent-Destruction Pilot Plant in Pueblo, Colorado—to destroy the remaining 2,700 tons of U.S. chemical warfare agents.

In May 2006 the GAO reported in *Cooperative Threat Reduction: DOD Needs More Reliable Data to Better Estimate the Cost and Schedule of the Shchuch'ye Facility* (http://www.gao.gov/new.items/d06692.pdf) that Russia once had the world's largest-known stockpile of chemical weapons. In 1992 Congress first authorized the DOD to assist the Russians in destroying their stockpile under the CTR program. This program is a high priority for the U.S. government because of the possibility of diversion and theft at the Russian storage facilities. The NTI notes in "Country Profile: Russia" (2014, http://www.nti.org/country-profiles/russia/chemical) that by September 2013 Russia had destroyed more than 76% of its stockpile and was expected to achieve 100% destruction by 2020.

Biological Weapons

The Convention on the Prohibition of the Development, Production, and Stockpiling of Bacteriological (Biological) and Toxin Weapons and on Their Destruction is commonly known as the Biological Weapons Convention (BWC). It went into effect in 1975 and prohibits the development, production, and stockpiling of biological weapons. According to the UN (2014, http://disarmament.un.org/treaties/t/bwc), 168 nations, including the United States, were party to the treaty as of 2014. Major BWC outsiders included Israel and North Korea.

The National Security Council (NSC) notes in *National Strategy for Countering Biological Threats* (November 2009, http://www.whitehouse.gov/sites/default/files/National_Strategy_for_Countering_BioThreats.pdf) that in the last two decades bioterrorism has become a "serious threat" to U.S. national security. In particular, the NSC reports that in 2001 coalition forces in Afghanistan uncovered a "significant body of evidence" that the terrorist group al Qaeda has been working to develop biological weapons.

The United States operates a biosecurity program to defend against bioterrorism and to counter any threats posed by biological weapons that might be held by foreign nations. In "Biosecurity" (2014, http://www.whitehouse.gov/administration/eop/ostp/nstc/biosecurity), the Office of Science and Technology Policy notes three key goals for the program:

- Biosafety—prevent the transmission of potentially harmful biologic agents from facilities (such as laboratories) to workers, other people, and the environment

- Laboratory biosecurity—prevent unauthorized possession, loss, theft, misuse, diversion, or intentional release of biological agents and toxins from laboratories

- Biodefense—prevent, detect, respond to, and/or recover from harm or damage caused by microorganisms and/or biological toxins to humans, animals, or the food supply.

CHAPTER 8

AMERICAN CIVIL LIBERTIES

Civil liberties (or civil rights) are individual rights that are designated by law. They are legal shields that protect citizens from abuses by their own government. Historically, times of war in the United States have produced situations in which the U.S. government has given national security concerns a higher priority than protection of the public's civil liberties. Most often, these transgressions have been instigated by the executive branch—the president and the departments and offices under his direct control. However, the framers of the U.S. Constitution included a system of checks and balances that allow individuals to challenge such transgressions in the courts. In addition, the Constitution's guarantee of freedom of speech allows the American press to publicize conflicts between the interests of national security and the protection of civil liberties. A debate over how best to balance these two important priorities has raged since the nation began and takes on new importance as the United States wages war once again.

HISTORICAL CONTEXT

In the United States the U.S. Constitution is considered to be the ultimate definer of Americans' civil rights. Times of war in the United States have often produced contentious debates over the proper balance between protecting national security and protecting civil liberties. History shows that some civil rights have not been honored by the U.S. government when the nation was threatened, a condition known by the Latin term *Inter arma enim silent leges*, which is popularly translated as "In times of war, the laws fall silent." These civil liberty conflicts most often involve individual rights that are protected by the First, Fourth, and Fifth Amendments of the Constitution:

- First Amendment—"Congress shall make no law respecting an establishment of religion, or prohibiting the free exercise thereof; or abridging the freedom of speech, or of the press; or the right of the people peaceably to assemble, and to petition the government for a redress of grievances."

- Fourth Amendment—"The right of the people to be secure in their persons, houses, papers, and effects, against unreasonable searches and seizures, shall not be violated, and no warrants shall issue, but upon probable cause, supported by oath or affirmation, and particularly describing the place to be searched, and the persons or things to be seized."

- Fifth Amendment—"No person shall be held to answer for a capital, or otherwise infamous crime, unless on a presentment or indictment of a grand jury, except in cases arising in the land or naval forces, or in the militia, when in actual service in time of war or public danger; nor shall any person be subject for the same offense to be twice put in jeopardy of life or limb; nor shall be compelled in any criminal case to be a witness against himself, nor be deprived of life, liberty, or property, without due process of law; nor shall private property be taken for public use, without just compensation."

The rights to free speech and peaceable assembly guaranteed by the First Amendment receive exceptional attention when they are exercised during wartime by people who are opposed to the government's actions. The protections afforded under the Fourth and Fifth Amendments relate to judicial procedures, legal due process, and privacy issues. A right to privacy is not specifically spelled out in the Constitution but is believed to result inherently if the government operates in accordance with the articles of the Constitution and respects the Bill of Rights.

Civil War: Suspension of Habeas Corpus

During the Civil War (1861–1865) President Abraham Lincoln (1809–1865) suspended the writ of habeas corpus (a legal procedure in which a court can order that a prisoner held by the government be presented to the court for determination if the imprisonment is legal or not). Article One of the Constitution allows such a suspension "when in cases of rebellion or invasion the public safety may require it." Lincoln's action allowed Union troops to detain Southern sympathizers and anyone else deemed to be a threat to public safety and hold them indefinitely. In addition, military commissions tried and convicted civilian detainees who were accused of crimes. Thus, martial law went into effect, meaning that the military took over powers normally held by the civilian law enforcement system.

The consequences of the suspension were highly controversial and led to a legal battle in the U.S. Supreme Court after the war ended. In the 1866 case *Ex parte Milligan* (71 U.S. 2), the court ruled that martial law cannot be imposed so long as civilian courts and governments are still in operation. In addition, any imposition of martial law must be confined to a limited area in which war is actually occurring. The Posse Comitatus Act of 1878 made it unlawful for the U.S. military to execute legal authority over civilians unless specifically authorized by the Constitution or an act of Congress. It should be noted that this prohibition does not apply to National Guard troops under state government command.

World War I: Free Speech?

The World War I era is associated with many serious conflicts between national security and civil liberties. Around the turn of the 20th century a number of movements associated with labor rights, anarchy, and socialism became active in the United States. Some elements of these groups incited violence and were considered subversive (advocating the overthrow of the government). As such, the nation was in a wary mood when World War I erupted in Europe in 1914.

The United States' entry into the war in 1917 was accompanied by the passage of several federal laws aimed at squelching what the government considered anti-American activities. The Espionage Act of 1917 and the related Sedition Act of 1918 included a variety of provisions that were designed to prevent the passage of national security information to the enemy. The acts also made it illegal for anyone to obstruct military recruiting or enlistment. Most troubling to civil libertarians were provisions in the Sedition Act that made it illegal to say or write anything "disloyal" about the U.S. government, Constitution, flag, or military forces. The act also prohibited any expression of resistance to the United States or support for its enemies. In other words, actions of dissent (disagreement with the government) were forbidden during the war.

The laws were used by the government against many socialists, anarchists, and other activists who waged a vocal antiwar campaign. In 1919 the Supreme Court heard a case involving a socialist who had mailed circulars to recent military draftees urging them to defy the government and oppose the draft system. In *Schenck v. United States* (249 U.S. 47), the court ruled in favor of the government and noted, "When a nation is at war many things that might be said in time of peace are such a hindrance to its effort that their utterance will not be endured so long as men fight and that no Court could regard them as protected by any constitutional right." Regardless, most of the provisions of the wartime acts were repealed during the 1920s.

World War II: Internment of Japanese Americans

One of the most often cited violations of American civil rights in wartime took place during World War II (1939–1945), when the U.S. government detained U.S. citizens of Japanese descent. In 1942 President Franklin D. Roosevelt (1882–1945) signed Executive Order 9066, which authorized the removal and internment of all people of Japanese descent living in California and in the western portions of Oregon and Washington. The military and civilian government decisions leading up to issuance of the executive order are described by Stetson Conn in "The Decision to Evacuate the Japanese from the Pacific Coast" (August 27, 1996, http://www.army .mil/cmh-pg/books/70-7_05.htm).

Conn notes that there was widespread and persistent paranoia among the U.S. population that Japanese American citizens had not been and would not be loyal to the United States. The National Archives and Records Administration explains in "Executive Order 9066: Resulting in the Relocation of Japanese (1942)" (2014, http://www.ourdocuments.gov/doc.php?doc=74) that approximately 122,000 people of Japanese descent were detained. Nearly 70,000 of them were U.S. citizens. The detainees spent the duration of the war in internment camps that were surrounded by barbed wire and patrolled by armed guards. Following the war, the detainees were released; however, many found it difficult to return to their previous homes and jobs.

In 1988 the Civil Liberties Act acknowledged that a "grave injustice" had been perpetrated on Japanese Americans during World War II by the U.S. government and offered a payment of $20,000 to each internee as restitution.

Cold War: McCarthyism

McCarthyism describes a phenomenon that occurred in the United States when intense paranoia about communism allowed civil liberties to be trampled in the interest of national security. The term is named after

Senator Joseph R. McCarthy (1908–1957; R-WI), who served in the U.S. Senate from 1947 until his death in 1957. Although the Soviet Union had been a U.S. ally during World War II, deep philosophical differences fostered a period of mutual distrust and animosity between the two nations after the war ended in 1945. In the United States many people believed the Soviets wanted to overthrow (subvert) the U.S. government and were being aided by American members of the Communist Party and sympathizers.

Congressional committees were formed to investigate alleged communist activities by Americans. People who refused to cooperate were sent to prison or, at the very least, lost their job and reputation. Their names were put on a so-called blacklist, which meant that businesses were afraid to hire them. McCarthy also began holding hearings and accusing fellow politicians of having communist sympathies. In "Censure of Senator Joseph McCarthy (1954)" (2014, http://eca.state.gov/education/engteaching/pubs/AmLnC/br60.htm), the U.S. Department of State (DOS) notes that McCarthy and his aides "made wild accusations, browbeat witnesses, destroyed reputations and threw mud at men."

In January 1954 McCarthy's hearings were televised for the first time. The DOS notes that "day after day the public watched McCarthy in action—bullying, harassing, never producing any hard evidence, and his support among people who thought he was 'right' on communism began to evaporate." The political tide turned against McCarthy, and in December 1954 the Senate passed a censure (official condemnation) of him for abusing his powers. The U.S. Supreme Court and state courts began ruling against the tactics that had been used on committee witnesses and government employees. Many rulings found that civil liberties had been violated during the anticommunist fervor.

Late 20th Century

The 1960s and early 1970s were a time of domestic strife in the United States. Many groups and movements actively protested against the government for various reasons, including opposing the Vietnam War (1954–1975) and advocating the enforcement of civil rights for minorities and women. Political and social activism became a common means of expressing discontent in public. Although some groups were openly subversive, many sought change through legal methods or civil disobedience (breaking civil laws in a nonviolent fashion, such as by trespassing or blocking traffic and refusing police orders to cease).

Chapter 2 describes the 17 federal agencies and departments that make up the U.S. intelligence community (IC). They include the Central Intelligence Agency (CIA) and the Federal Bureau of Investigation (FBI). The IC took a keen interest in the anti-establishment movement that flourished during the Vietnam War era. In their eagerness to protect national security, the agencies conducted activities that raised concerns about violations of the civil liberties of law-abiding Americans. Many of these secret activities were made public by journalists who were given insider information by whistle-blowers, mainly current or former IC employees who wanted to expose what they thought was wrongdoing.

During the 1970s intelligence activities of the CIA and the U.S. Department of Defense (DOD) came under fire when stories were published in the media about surveillance of U.S. citizens. In 1970 Christopher H. Pyle, a former intelligence officer in the U.S. Army, alleged that his agency had collected massive amounts of intelligence on Americans who were engaged in protest activities, primarily against the Vietnam War. Pyle also claimed that undercover army agents had been spying on protest groups since the 1960s. In 1971 burglars broke into an FBI office in Pennsylvania and stole hundreds of documents concerning the agency's domestic spying operations. The documents were then leaked to the press. They revealed that J. Edgar Hoover (1895–1972), the long-time head of the FBI, had conducted a massive surveillance program in which agents spied on Americans, including those engaged in peaceful war protests.

In 1974 Seymour M. Hersh stunned the nation when he alleged in "Huge C.I.A. Operation Reported in U.S. against Antiwar Forces, Other Dissidents in Nixon Years" (NYTimes.com, December 22, 1974) that the CIA had engaged in a "massive, illegal domestic intelligence operation" against antiwar protesters and other groups. Hersh claimed that the CIA had intelligence files on at least 10,000 U.S. citizens and had engaged in illegal surveillance activities, such as wiretapping and mail interdiction (secretly opening and reading mail sent to other people), since the 1950s. Spying on Americans was a direct violation of the CIA charter.

The allegations of wrongdoing against the IC during the 1970s resulted in congressional investigations led by Senators Sam J. Ervin (1896–1985; D-NC) and Frank Forrester Church III (1924–1984; D-ID). More questionable activities by the CIA were discovered, including attempts to assassinate foreign leaders in Chile, the Congo, Cuba, the Dominican Republic, and Vietnam. In response, President Gerald R. Ford (1913–2006) issued an executive order that banned the assassination of foreign officials.

The so-called Church Committee also investigated the activities of an obscure member of the IC: the National Security Agency (NSA). Formed in 1952, the NSA (November 5, 2009, http://www.nsa.gov/about/cryptologic_heritage/60th/index.shtml) evolved from the cryptographic (secret-code making and breaking) operations that the U.S. government conducted during World War II. The NSA was supposed to focus on foreign communications related to national security. However, in its 1976 report *National Security Agency Surveillance Affecting Americans* (http://www.intelligence.senate.gov/pdfs94th/94755_III.pdf), the Church Committee complained the "NSA has intercepted and disseminated international communications of American citizens whose privacy ought to be protected under our Constitution." The committee added, "Internal NSA directives now forbid the targeting of American citizens' communications. Nonetheless, NSA may still acquire communications of American citizens as part of its foreign intelligence mission, and information derived from these intercepted messages may be used to satisfy foreign intelligence requirements."

Public outrage about the multiple civil liberty violations brought to light by the congressional investigations led to passage of the Foreign Intelligence Surveillance Act of 1978. It established the Foreign Intelligence Surveillance Court (FISC) from which authorization must be obtained for the conduct of electronic surveillance or physical searches of people alleged to be acting on behalf of a foreign power to threaten U.S. national security. The FISC is described in detail later in this chapter.

NEW FOCUS ON THE NSA. During the late 1980s the NSA became the focus of investigative journalists. By that time the agency relied heavily on defense industry contractors, such as Lockheed Martin, for its workforce. The computer specialist Margaret Newsham, a former Lockheed employee, had worked at an NSA facility in England and claimed she helped develop a massive surveillance network called ECHELON. According to Patrick Radden Keefe, in *Chatter: Uncovering the ECHELON Surveillance Network and the Secret World of Global Eavesdropping* (2006), Newsham testified at a closed (secret) congressional hearing that ECHELON was being used to spy on Americans. She said she had personally listened to a telephone conversation of Senator Strom Thurmond (1902–2003; R-SC). Keefe notes that this allegation was reported in the newspaper the *Cleveland (Ohio) Plain Dealer*; the story, however, failed to gain widespread attention.

In 1998 the British journalist Duncan Campbell wrote "Somebody's Listening" (NewStatesman.com, August 12, 1998). Campbell claimed that following World War II five nations—the United States, the United Kingdom, Canada, Australia, and New Zealand (also known as the "five eyes")—agreed to form a massive signals intelligence network for the purpose of "global eavesdropping." Campbell alleged that the NSA's ECHELON system was targeting and intercepting domestic communications within the United Kingdom and the United States. Similar allegations appeared in the media over subsequent years, including in the 1996 book *Secret Power* by the New Zealand journalist Nicky Hager.

In 2000 the television news program *60 Minutes* also reported on domestic spying by the NSA. In "Ex-Snoop Confirms Echelon Network" (CBSNews.com, February 24, 2000), CBS News summarized the televised segment, which included interviews with Newsham and Mike Frost, a former Canadian intelligence agent, who claimed to have knowledge of ECHELON. CBS News notes that "on Feb. 23, [2000,] the European Parliament issued a report accusing the U.S. of using Echelon for commercial spying on two separate occasions, to help American companies win lucrative contracts over European competitors. The U.S. State Department denies such spying took place and will not even acknowledge the existence of the top secret Echelon project."

Despite the long-standing allegations about domestic surveillance being conducted by the NSA, the agency's activities failed to capture the public's attention until after the so-called War on Terror began.

THE WAR ON TERROR: NEW CONFLICTS ARISE

Since the terrorist attacks of September 11, 2001 (9/11), the United States has waged a new and completely different kind of war: a war against terrorism. In the intervening years Congress has passed new laws and amended old laws to give the executive branch special wartime powers. Critics complain these laws have been used to trample on American civil liberties. In response, numerous lawsuits have been filed, and the federal courts have considered the constitutional issues involved. These rulings and public opinion have reshaped executive powers as the War on Terror has proceeded.

PATRIOT ACT

The Uniting and Strengthening America by Providing Appropriate Tools Required to Intercept and Obstruct Terrorism (USA PATRIOT) Act of 2001—known simply as the Patriot Act—was passed by Congress in October 2001. Many of the provisions of the act deal with surveillance procedures and financial security enhancements that have implications for civil liberty issues.

The Patriot Act allows federal agents to obtain business records relevant to national security investigations without going through the grand jury process to obtain a subpoena. Instead, the request is made through the FISC, which can grant permission if the government meets certain criteria. Other components of the act facilitate information sharing and cooperation between different government agencies, increase the penalties for terrorist-related crimes, and designate new criminal offenses, such as harboring people who have committed or plan to commit terrorist acts.

FIGURE 8.1

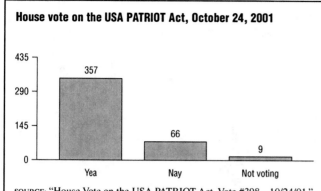

House vote on the USA PATRIOT Act, October 24, 2001

SOURCE: "House Vote on the USA PATRIOT Act, Vote #398—10/24/01," in *Passed by Congress*, U.S. Department of Justice, undated, http://www.justice.gov/archive/ll/subs/p_congress.htm (accessed May 7, 2014)

FIGURE 8.2

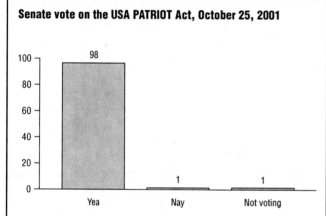

Senate vote on the USA PATRIOT Act, October 25, 2001

SOURCE: "Senate Vote on the USA PATRIOT Act, Vote #313—10/25/01," in *Passed by Congress*, U.S. Department of Justice, undated, http://www.justice.gov/archive/ll/subs/p_congress.htm (accessed May 7, 2014)

Controversy Erupts

At first, the Patriot Act was not considered to be highly controversial. In fact, it received overwhelming support in the U.S. House of Representatives (passing 357 to 66) and in the Senate, where only one senator out of 100 voted against it. (See Figure 8.1 and Figure 8.2.) The lone "nay" vote was cast by Senator Russ Feingold (1953–; D-WI).

Ever since its passage, however, the Patriot Act has been harshly criticized by groups, such as the American Civil Liberties Union (ACLU). Headquartered in New York City, the ACLU is a private nonprofit organization that is devoted to defending American civil liberties. In "National Security" (2014, http://www.aclu.org/national-security), the ACLU complains, "Over the last few years, the federal government has returned to the bad old days of unchecked spying on ordinary Americans, as part of a broad pattern of executive abuses that

FIGURE 8.3

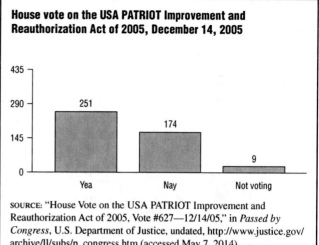

House vote on the USA PATRIOT Improvement and Reauthorization Act of 2005, December 14, 2005

SOURCE: "House Vote on the USA PATRIOT Improvement and Reauthorization Act of 2005, Vote #627—12/14/05," in *Passed by Congress*, U.S. Department of Justice, undated, http://www.justice.gov/archive/ll/subs/p_congress.htm (accessed May 7, 2014)

use 'national security' as an excuse for encroaching on our privacy and free speech rights without adequate—or any—judicial oversight."

Some cities and municipalities and even states have passed nonbinding resolutions expressing their opposition to certain provisions of the Patriot Act. The organization Bill of Rights Defense Committee claims in "Resolutions Passed and Efforts Underway, by State" (http://www.bordc.org/list.php) that as of August 2014, 414 resolutions had been passed.

Reauthorizations

Sixteen provisions of the 2001 Patriot Act were scheduled to sunset (automatically expire) in 2005. By that time civil liberty concerns about the act had been growing. In December 2005 the House voted 251 to 174 and the Senate voted 89 to 10 to renew the provisions with some modifications. (See Figure 8.3 and Figure 8.4.) The renewed act made permanent 14 of the original 16 sunset provisions and placed four-year sunset periods on the two remaining provisions (which concern surveillance techniques and the acquisition of business records). According to the U.S. Department of Justice (DOJ), in "Fact Sheet: USA Patriot Act Improvement and Reauthorization Act of 2005" (March 2, 2006, http://www.usdoj.gov/opa/pr/2006/March/06_opa_113.html), Congress added "dozens of additional safeguards to protect Americans' privacy and civil liberties" as part of the reauthorization. The renewed act also extended a provision of the Intelligence Reform and Terrorism Prevention Act of 2004 (IRTPA) that was scheduled to expire at the end of 2005. The so-called lone wolf provision concerned individual terrorists who are not linked to a foreign government or foreign terrorist organization.

In February 2010 the House voted 315 to 97 to renew (without change) the two expiring provisions of the Patriot Act and the expiring provision of the IRTPA

FIGURE 8.4

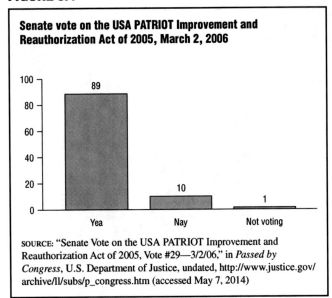

Senate vote on the USA PATRIOT Improvement and Reauthorization Act of 2005, March 2, 2006

SOURCE: "Senate Vote on the USA PATRIOT Improvement and Reauthorization Act of 2005, Vote #29—3/2/06," in *Passed by Congress*, U.S. Department of Justice, undated, http://www.justice.gov/archive/ll/subs/p_congress.htm (accessed May 7, 2014)

FIGURE 8.5

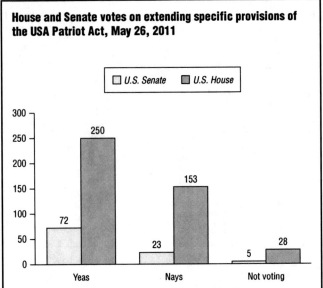

House and Senate votes on extending specific provisions of the USA Patriot Act, May 26, 2011

SOURCE: Adapted from "Final Vote Results for Roll Call 376," in *U.S. House of Representatives Roll Call Votes 112th Congress—1st Session (2011)*, U.S. House of Representatives, May 26, 2011, http://clerk.house.gov/evs/2011/roll376.xml (accessed May 7, 2014), and "Vote Counts," in *U.S. Senate Roll Call Votes 112th Congress—1st Session*, U.S. Senate, May 26, 2011, http://www.senate.gov/legislative/LIS/roll_call_lists/roll_call_vote_cfm.cfm?congress=112&session=1&vote=00084#top (accessed May 7, 2014)

TABLE 8.1

House vote on extending specific provisions of the USA Patriot Act, February 25, 2010

	Yeas	Nays	Not voting
Democratic	162	87	5
Republican	153	10	15
Independent	—	—	—
Totals	**315**	**97**	**20**

SOURCE: Adapted from "Final Vote Results for Roll Call 67," in *U.S. House of Representatives Roll Call Votes 111th Congress—2nd Session (2010)*, U.S. House of Representatives, February 25, 2010, http://clerk.house.gov/evs/2010/roll067.xml (accessed May 7, 2014)

through February 2011. As shown in Table 8.1, the extensions were widely supported by both Democrats and Republicans. The Senate approved the measure by a voice vote, meaning that it was not debated on the Senate floor. The three renewed provisions and their controversial features are as follows:

- Patriot Act Section 206—modifies the Foreign Intelligence Surveillance Act (FISA) to allow roving wiretaps. Roving wiretaps are authorized under U.S. criminal law, but require authorities to identify the targeted individual and the device, such as a cell phone, to be wiretapped. These requirements are not included in the FISA. In "Reform the Patriot Act" (2014, http://www.aclu.org/reform-patriot-act), the ACLU complains, "This provision is contrary to traditional notions of search and seizure, which require government to state with particularity what it seeks to search or seize."

- Patriot Act Section 215—modifies the FISA to allow the FBI to "make an application for an order requiring the production of any tangible things (including

books, records, papers, documents, and other items) for an investigation to protect against international terrorism or clandestine intelligence activities, provided that such investigation of a United States person is not conducted solely upon the basis of activities protected by the first amendment to the Constitution." Critics complain that the phrases "any tangible things" and "investigation to protect" are too broad and allow the government sweeping powers.

- IRTPA Section 6001—power to conduct surveillance of suspects who are not affiliated with a country or organization, provided the suspects are not U.S. citizens. Critics worry that the government might abuse this power to spy on people, such as protesters, who are not specifically linked to terrorism.

The three renewed provisions were later extended through May 2011. As the sunset deadline approached, some congressional members advocated amending the Patriot Act to include greater protections of civil rights. The fight was led by Democrats who found an ally in Senator Rand Paul (1963–; R-KY). David Welna explains in "Patriot Act Extension Came down to the Wire" (NPR.org, May 27, 2011) that Paul had "grave misgivings" about the extension and upset his party's top leaders by delaying its passage and proposing amendments to the act. The amendments were defeated, and the Patriot Sunsets Extension Act of 2011 passed readily. (See Figure 8.5.) The three disputed provisions of the Patriot Act/IRTPA were extended to May 2015.

FOREIGN INTELLIGENCE SURVEILLANCE COURT

As noted earlier, Congress passed the FISA in 1978, creating the FISC. The FISA stipulates that the government must obtain a special warrant from the FISC before conducting specific intelligence-gathering activities that are related to national security within the United States. The original act related primarily to electronic surveillance. The U.S. Supreme Court had made a ruling in 1972 in *United States v. United States District Court* (407 U.S. 297) that the executive branch cannot conduct domestic surveillance without a court order. Because national security issues typically involve top-secret information, the FISC was created as a judicial forum in which such information could remain secret.

Subsequent FISA amendments have allowed the executive branch to conduct covert "physical searches," access "tangible things" (e.g., business records), and use National Security Letters (NSLs). NSLs are letters used by intelligence agencies to request information (e.g., a suspect's credit card record from a financial institution). The recipient of an NSL does not have to comply with the request but must keep secret certain information about the request.

The FISC is a pool of 11 judges. According to the U.S. Code, Title 50, Section 1803 (2014, http://www.law.cornell.edu/uscode/text/50/1803), the judges are chosen by the chief justice (the head of the judicial branch of the federal government who presides over the U.S. Supreme Court). The FISC judges must be drawn from at least seven of the U.S. judicial circuits, and at least three of the judges must reside within 20 miles (32 km) of Washington, D.C. Each judge serves a maximum term of seven years on the FISC.

Judge Reggie Barnett Walton (1949–) explains in a letter (July 29, 2013, https://www.leahy.senate.gov/download/honorable-patrick-j-leahy) to Senator Patrick Leahy (1940–; D-VT), the chair of the Senate Committee on the Judiciary, that one of the 11 FISC judges is "on duty" for a week at a time. The on-duty judge can call on other FISC judges for assistance as needed. In addition, Section 1803 states that the court can meet en banc (including all the judges at once) under certain circumstances.

The workings of the FISC are described by the Federal Judicial Center (2014, http://www.fjc.gov/history/home.nsf/page/courts_special_fisc.html), an education and research agency for the federal courts. The process is as follows:

- A federal intelligence agency requests a warrant application
- The warrant application is drafted by attorneys at the NSA

- The application has to include certification from the U.S. attorney general that the target of the surveillance or search is a U.S. citizen or resident alien who "may be involved in the commission of a crime" or a foreign power or the agent of a foreign power
- The application is presented before the FISC
- If an application is denied, the government can appeal the decision to the Foreign Intelligence Surveillance Court of Review, which is presided over by three district or appeals court judges who are designated by the chief justice of the U.S. Supreme Court

The FISC is often called a "secret" court because much of its work is conducted in secrecy. The decisions of the court are based on classified information and are not released to the public. However, the FISA does require the U.S. attorney general to submit an annual report to Congress about the number of applications filed with the FISC and the number of orders issued by the court. The Federation of American Scientists, a nonprofit organization headquartered in Washington, D.C., maintains the website "Foreign Intelligence Surveillance Act" (2014, http://www.fas.org/irp/agency/doj/fisa), which provides copies of the annual reports. The first annual report is for 1979 and states that the FISC issued 207 orders that gave the government authority to use electronic surveillance as part of national security investigations.

As of August 2014, the most recent report (April 30, 2014, http://fas.org/irp/agency/doj/fisa/2013rept.pdf) provides information about FISC activities in 2013:

- The FISC reviewed 1,655 applications for authority to conduct electronic surveillance and/or physical searches.
- Most (1,588) of the applications included requests to conduct electronic surveillance.
- None of the applications were denied in full or in part.
- The FISC modified the proposed orders in 34 of the applications.
- The FISC approved 1,588 applications containing requests to conduct electronic surveillance.
- Another 178 applications were reviewed and approved by the FISC for access to certain business records for "foreign intelligence purposes." The FISC modified the proposed orders in 141 of these applications.

In addition, the FBI made 14,219 NSL requests concerning 5,334 different U.S. citizens in 2013. NSLs are not a new national security tool. Their use dates back several decades. However, critics complain that the Patriot Act greatly expanded the scope and conditions under which the government can issue the letters. NSLs do not require prior judicial approval. Until 2007 the FBI was able to impose a nondisclosure requirement (or "gag order") forbidding NSL recipients from discussing indefinitely the NSLs they received. In 2007 a federal court ruled that the gag order provision was unconstitutional. This ruling was upheld in 2008 by a federal appeals court, and the administration of President Barack Obama (1961–) did not appeal the decision to the U.S. Supreme Court.

WIRETAPPING WITHOUT FISC APPROVAL

In 2005 the *New York Times* published an article that accused the administration of President George W. Bush (1946–) of conducting wiretap operations without FISC approval. The media eventually began calling this practice warrantless wiretapping.

In "Bush Lets U.S. Spy on Callers without Courts" (NYTimes.com, December 16, 2005), James Risen and Eric Lichtblau allege that in early 2002 President Bush issued a secret executive order authorizing the NSA to bypass the FISC process for conducting domestic surveillance. Risen and Lichtblau estimate that the international phone calls and e-mails of "hundreds, perhaps thousands" of Americans had been monitored to search for links to international terrorism. They report that the government credited the surveillance program with uncovering several terrorist plots against targets in both the United Kingdom and the United States.

According to Risen and Lichtblau, the program was suspended temporarily in mid-2004 because of concerns about its legality. Reportedly, the suspension was spurred by a complaint from the federal judge overseeing the FISC. The program was "revamped" and continued to operate. Declan McCullagh indicates in "Attorney General: NSA Spy Program to Be Reformed" (CNET.com, January 17, 2007) that the U.S. attorney general Alberto Gonzales (1955–) announced in January 2007 that future electronic surveillance would be "subject to the approval of the Foreign Intelligence Surveillance Court." Thus, it is presumed that the practice of warrantless wiretapping ceased at that time.

Repercussions

Publicity about the warrantless surveillance program led to several repercussions for the Bush administration. One of the FISC judges resigned, supposedly to show his displeasure with the White House over the controversy. In 2006 the ACLU filed a lawsuit claiming that the surveillance program violated the First and Fourth Amendments of the Constitution and that President Bush had exceeded his authority under the separation of powers principles of the Constitution. The suit initially won in federal court, but was overturned on appeal. The ACLU asked the U.S. Supreme Court to reconsider the ruling, but the court declined to hear the case.

Numerous other lawsuits were filed against the federal government on behalf of clients alleging to have been the targets of warrantless wiretapping. DOJ officials with the Bush and Obama administrations had nearly all the cases dropped, arguing that the allegations could not be proven without the release of top-secret documents, which would harm national security. This argument is known in legal terms as the State Secrets Privilege.

However, one case did proceed to trial: *Al Haramain Islamic Foundation v. Obama* (Case No. 09-15266; originally filed in 2006 against the Bush administration). Carol D. Leonnig and Mary Beth Sheridan note in "Saudi Group Alleges Wiretapping by U.S." (WashingtonPost.com, March 2, 2006) that the suit alleged that the NSA conducted warrantless eavesdropping of conversations between people in Saudi Arabia and the United States. The federal government filed numerous motions to have the case dropped based on the State Secrets Privilege, but the motions were denied. In 2010 a federal judge in San Francisco ruled in favor of the plaintiffs and ordered the government to pay them damages and legal fees. However, that decision was reversed on appeal.

METADATA COLLECTION BY THE NSA

Metadata are data that describe other data. In 2006 media stories surfaced that the NSA had been collecting metadata about electronic communications made by Americans. In "NSA Has Massive Database of Americans' Phone Calls" (USAToday.com, May 11, 2006), Leslie Cauley reports that shortly after 9/11 the NSA began secretly collecting phone call data about "tens of millions of Americans." Cauley alleges that the agency was compiling a database of phone records to search for links to international terrorism. The collected information included the calling and receiving phone numbers and the call durations, but not the contents of the calls themselves. The NSA did not obtain warrants for the information but simply asked (and may have paid) telecommunications companies to cooperate.

Cauley's article led to media criticism of the telecommunications companies for complying with the NSA request, a claim that some of the companies subsequently denied. Dozens of class-action lawsuits were filed against telecommunications companies following the revelations. However, the cases were eventually stymied by provisions included in the FISA Amendments Act of 2008, which provides liability protection for companies that furnished assistance to the government in foreign intelligence collection activities in the past.

Edward C. Liu of the Congressional Research Service (CRS) explains in *Reauthorization of the FISA Amendments Act* (April 8, 2013, http://www.fas.org/sgp/crs/intel/R42725.pdf) that Congress added a section (Title VII) to the 2008 act that created "new separate procedures for targeting non-U.S. persons and U.S. persons reasonably believed to be outside the United States." In general, the new provisions release the government from the requirement for an individualized court order (i.e., specific to the target) to conduct surveillance on foreign people located outside the United States. Civil libertarians have complained that American phone calls and e-mails could be unintentionally intercepted as part of these surveillance efforts. Liu notes that several organizations challenged the constitutionality of the new provisions in court. A case brought by Amnesty International made it all the way to the U.S. Supreme Court, which ruled in *Clapper v. Amnesty International* (No. 11-1025 [2013]) that the organization did not have legal standing to challenge Title VII. Thus, the constitutional issues were not addressed by the court.

According to Liu, the new provisions covering U.S. citizens abroad generally continue previous FISA procedures, meaning that FISC authorization is required to target them. However, the standards for who can be targeted have been loosened. Previously, FISC applications required information about the facilities to be searched or subjected to electronic surveillance and how they were related to the targeted people. Also, U.S. citizens abroad could only be targeted if they were "linked to international terrorism or clandestine intelligence activities." The new FISA provisions do not contain these requirements.

In December 2012 President Obama signed the FISA Amendments Act Reauthorization Act of 2012, which extends Title VII of the FISA through December 2017.

Whistle-blowers or Traitors?

As noted earlier, there are allegations dating back to the late 20th century that the U.S. IC has spied on Americans. Since 9/11 and the beginning of the War on Terror more whistle-blowers have come forward with similar claims. Some of the most well-known individuals are:

- Russell D. Tice (1941–)—in "NSA Whistleblower Alleges Illegal Spying" (ABCNews.com, January 10, 2006), Brian Ross notes that Tice was a "longtime insider" at the NSA. Tice claims to be one of the sources for the 2005 *New York Times* article by Risen and Lichtblau, which revealed the U.S. warrantless wiretapping program. The NSA subsequently dismissed Tice for "psychological concerns," a charge he denies.

- Thomas Tamm (1952–)—the Public Broadcasting Service (PBS) program *Frontline* indicates in "United States of Secrets" (December 11, 2013, http://www.pbs.org/wgbh/pages/frontline/government-elections-politics/united-states-of-secrets/the-frontline-interview-thomas-tamm) that Tamm was a DOJ attorney from 2001 through 2003. He allegedly discovered

that the NSA was conducting warrantless wiretapping by bypassing the FISC. Tamm told *Frontline* that he leaked the information to Lichtblau in 2004. After the *New York Times* article was published in 2005, Tamm fell under suspicion. The FBI raided his home in 2007 and confiscated his family's computers and cell phones. Although he later had to testify before a grand jury, he was not charged with a crime.

- Mark Klein—according to *Frontline*, in "Spying on the Homefront" (May 15, 2007, http://www.pbs.org/wgbh/pages/frontline/homefront/interviews/klein.html), Klein was a computer technician for the telecommunications company AT&T for more than 20 years. He claims to have discovered "the whole flow of Internet traffic in several AT&T operations centers was being regularly diverted to the National Security Agency (NSA)." Klein went public with his allegations in 2006.

- Thomas A. Drake (1957–)—in "3 NSA Veterans Speak out on Whistle-Blower: We Told You So" (USAToday.com, June 16, 2013), Peter Eisler and Susan Page indicate that Drake was a senior NSA executive from 2001 until he resigned in 2008. During that time he raised concerns within the NSA and to the DOD and Congress about the agency's collection of "Americans' phone and internet records" and "also shared unclassified information with a reporter." The FBI raided his home in 2007, and he was indicted under the Espionage Act; however, the most serious charges were dropped. He ultimately pleaded guilty to a misdemeanor charge for which he was given probation and community service.

- William Binney—Eisler and Page report that Binney was a technical director at the NSA and retired in 2001 after nearly 40 years at the agency. He says he raised concerns to the DOD and Congress about the NSA's surveillance activities but to no avail. The FBI raided his home in 2007, but he was not charged with any crimes.

- J. Kirk Wiebe—according to Eisler and Page, Wiebe was a senior analyst at the NSA and retired in 2001 after more than 30 years of service. He worked with Binney at the NSA and joined him in airing concerns within the government about the agency's activities. His home was also raided by the FBI in 2007, but he was not charged with any crimes.

These whistle-blowers failed to capture widespread public attention, probably because they offered no proof or evidence of the practices that they alleged. This changed dramatically in 2013, when Edward Snowden (1983–) became perhaps the most notorious whistle-blower in U.S. history.

EDWARD SNOWDEN. As a young man in his 20s, Snowden worked for Booz Allen Hamilton, a contractor for the NSA. He became concerned about the agency's surveillance activities and downloaded more than a million documents from the NSA network before fleeing the United States in May 2013. Some of the classified information surfaced days later in the *Guardian*. Glenn Greenwald reports in "NSA Collecting Phone Records of Millions of Verizon Customers Daily" (Guardian.com, June 5, 2013) allegations (without naming Snowden) that the NSA collected telephone metadata about millions of U.S. customers of Verizon Communications. The online article includes a link (http://www.theguardian.com/world/interactive/2013/jun/06/verizon-telephone-data-court-order) to a "top secret" FISC order allegedly approving the collection activities. Greenwald notes, "The document shows for the first time that under the Obama administration the communication records of millions of US citizens are being collected indiscriminately and in bulk—regardless of whether they are suspected of any wrongdoing."

Although this claim echoes the one made by Cauley in 2006, Greenwald's inclusion of a supporting document and specific details made the story much more impactful. Over the following days additional revelations appeared in the *Washington Post* and the *Guardian*. On June 9, 2013, the *Guardian* released a video (http://www.theguardian.com/world/video/2013/jun/09/nsa-whistleblower-edward-snowden-interview-video) in which Snowden revealed himself as the source of the leaks and stated, "I don't want to live in a society that does these sort of things." At the time, Snowden was in Hong Kong. Within weeks the U.S. government had issued a criminal complaint (http://apps.washingtonpost.com/g/documents/world/us-vs-edward-j-snowden-criminal-complaint/496) charging him with theft of government property, unauthorized communication of national defense information, and willful communication of classified communications intelligence information to an unauthorized person. The latter two charges were brought under the Espionage Act of 1917.

Snowden disappeared from view before appearing in Russia. In "For Edward Snowden: Why Russia?" (CBSNews.com, June 24, 2013), Alexander Trowbridge notes that Russia and the United States do not have a formal extradition treaty, meaning that Snowden cannot be deported at the request of the U.S. government. In addition, Russia—under President Vladimir Putin (1952–)—and the United States do not have a particularly warm diplomatic relationship for a variety of reasons. Thus, Snowden became essentially untouchable to U.S. authorities, and as of August 2014 remained in Russia.

In the year following Snowden's departure from the United States, he leaked numerous documents to media contacts that produced headline stories around the world. Paul Szoldra briefly summarizes in "Snowden: Here's

Everything We've Learned in One Year of Unprecedented Top-Secret Leaks" (BusinessInsider.com, June 7, 2014) more than 100 revelations regarding spying by the U.S. and allied governments, particularly the other members of the five eyes. Some of the revelations proved especially embarrassing for the U.S. government, namely that the NSA eavesdropped on the communications of ordinary people and leaders of countries that are allied with the United States.

In some contexts, whistle-blowing is viewed in a positive light, especially when it exposes fraud or wasteful spending within a company or government agency. However, insiders who reveal information about the IC are more likely to be labeled as traitors who have betrayed their country. In addition, they face criminal charges under laws that specifically prohibit the sharing of intelligence with unauthorized people.

Snowden's actions spurred several notable U.S. lawmakers to publicly call him a traitor. Some even suggested that he should be tried for treason. According to Article Three of the U.S. Constitution, "Treason against the United States, shall consist only in levying war against them, or in adhering to their enemies, giving them aid and comfort." Throughout the course of U.S. history relatively few people have been convicted of treason, and none have been charged since the end of World War II; thus, it is unlikely that Snowden will face treason charges.

Among civil libertarians Snowden is viewed as a hero, or at least as a whistle-blower who deserves some consideration for exposing government wrongdoing. Some prominent people within the government, notably Senator Paul, have advocated leniency for Snowden. In "Rand Paul: Edward Snowden Deserves Leniency" (CBSNews.com, January 5, 2014), Jake Miller quotes Paul as saying, "Do I think that it's OK to leak secrets and give up national secrets and things that could endanger lives? I don't think that's OK. But I think the courts are now saying that what he revealed was something the government was doing was illegal."

Nevertheless, the Obama administration has maintained a tough line on Snowden. Executive branch officials have frequently urged him to return to the United States and face the consequences for his actions.

U.S. PUBLIC OPINION. Days after the first Snowden leaks were disseminated by the media the Gallup Organization conducted a poll to gauge public opinion on the issues involved. As shown in Table 8.2, a slim majority (53%) of those asked disapprove of the government's metadata collection activities. Just over one-third (37%) said they approve of the program, while 10% had no opinion on the matter. Democrats were more approving than Republicans or independents. Overall, 23% of the

TABLE 8.2

Public opinion on government surveillance program targeting telephone and Internet communications, June 2013

AS YOU MAY KNOW, AS PART OF ITS EFFORTS TO INVESTIGATE TERRORISM, A FEDERAL GOVERNMENT AGENCY OBTAINED RECORDS FROM LARGER U.S. TELEPHONE AND INTERNET COMPANIES IN ORDER TO COMPILE TELEPHONE CALL LOGS AND INTERNET COMMUNICATIONS. BASED ON WHAT YOU HAVE HEARD OR READ ABOUT THE PROGRAM, WOULD YOU SAY YOU APPROVE OR DISAPPROVE OF THIS GOVERNMENT PROGRAM?

	Approve	Disapprove	No opinion
National adults	37%	53%	10%
Democrats	49%	40%	11%
Independents	34%	56%	10%
Republicans	32%	63%	5%

SOURCE: Frank Newport, "As you may know, as part of its efforts to investigate terrorism, a federal government agency obtained records from larger U.S. telephone and Internet companies in order to compile telephone call logs and Internet communications. Based on what you have heard or read about the program, would you say you approve or disapprove of this government program?" in *Americans Disapprove of Government Surveillance Programs*, The Gallup Organization, June 12, 2013, http://www.gallup.com/poll/163043/americans-disapprove-government-surveillance-programs.aspx (accessed May 6, 2014). Copyright © 2013 Gallup, Inc. All rights reserved. The content is used with permission; however, Gallup retains all rights of republication.

TABLE 8.3

Poll respondents' reasons for approving or disapproving of government surveillance program targeting telephone and Internet communications, June 2013

ASKED OF THOSE WHO APPROVE: IS THAT MAINLY BECAUSE YOU DO NOT THINK THE PROGRAM SERIOUSLY VIOLATES AMERICANS' CIVIL LIBERTIES, (OR IS IT MAINLY BECAUSE) YOU THINK INVESTIGATING TERRORISM IS THE MORE IMPORTANT GOAL, EVEN IF IT VIOLATES SOME AMERICANS' CIVIL LIBERTIES?
ASKED OF THOSE WHO DISAPPROVE: DO YOU THINK THERE WOULD EVER BE CIRCUMSTANCES IN WHICH IT WOULD BE RIGHT FOR THE GOVERNMENT TO CREATE A DATABASE OF TELEPHONE LOGS AND INTERNET COMMUNICATIONS, OR WOULD IT NOT BE RIGHT FOR THE GOVERNMENT TO DO THIS UNDER ANY CIRCUMSTANCES?

	%
Approve of program	37
(Does not violate liberties)	11
(Terrorism more important)	23
(Unspecified)	4
Disapprove of program	53
(Are circumstances when it would be right)	21
(No circumstances when it would be right)	30
(Unspecified)	2
No opinion	10

SOURCE: Frank Newport, "Reasons for Approving/Disapproving," in *Americans Disapprove of Government Surveillance Programs*, The Gallup Organization, June 12, 2013, http://www.gallup.com/poll/163043/americans-disapprove-government-surveillance-programs.aspx (accessed May 6, 2014). Copyright © 2013 Gallup, Inc. All rights reserved. The content is used with permission; however, Gallup retains all rights of republication.

TABLE 8.4

Public concern about the federal government collecting data about their telephone calls or Internet communications, June 2013

IF YOU KNEW THAT THE FEDERAL GOVERNMENT HAD COMPUTERIZED LOGS OF YOUR TELEPHONE CALLS OR INTERNET COMMUNICATIONS STORED IN A DATABASE THAT IT USES TO TRACK TERRORIST ACTIVITY, HOW CONCERNED WOULD YOU BE THAT YOUR PRIVACY RIGHTS HAD BEEN VIOLATED—VERY CONCERNED, SOMEWHAT CONCERNED, NOT TOO CONCERNED, OR NOT CONCERNED AT ALL?

	Very concerned	Somewhat concerned	Not too concerned	Not at all concerned	No opinion
Jun 10–11, 2013	35%	22%	21%	21%	1%

SOURCE: Frank Newport, "If you knew that the federal government had computerized logs of your telephone calls or Internet communications stored in a database that it uses to track terrorist activity, how concerned would you be that your privacy rights had been violated—very concerned, somewhat concerned, not too concerned, or not concerned at all?" in *Americans Disapprove of Government Surveillance Programs*, The Gallup Organization, June 12, 2013, http://www.gallup.com/poll/163043/americans-disapprove-government-surveillance-programs.aspx (accessed May 6, 2014). Copyright © 2013 Gallup, Inc. All rights reserved. The content is used with permission; however, Gallup retains all rights of republication.

right," whereas 21% thought there "are circumstances when it would be right."

Gallup also asked poll participants their level of concern about their privacy rights if they knew that the government had computerized logs of their telephone calls or Internet communications. Just over half were either "very concerned" (35%) or "somewhat concerned" (22%). (See Table 8.4.) The remainder were either "not too concerned" (21%), "not at all concerned" (21%), or had no opinion (1%).

When asked specifically about Snowden, the American public was split. Overall, 44% of respondents thought it was "right" for him to leak the information to the media, while 42% thought it was "wrong." (See Table 8.5.) The remaining 14% did not have an opinion. Republicans were slightly more approving than independents or Democrats. The public showed a more favorable mind-set toward the media sources (the *Guardian* and the *Washington Post*) that first published the leaked information. More than half (59%) of those asked said the newspapers' actions were "right," whereas 33% said they were "wrong." (See Table 8.6.) The remaining 8% did not have an opinion. Independents were more approving than Republicans or Democrats.

PROGRAM CHANGES AND LAWSUITS. Snowden's revelations and public concerns about government surveillance spurred the Obama administration to make changes to the NSA programs involved. These developments are described by Edward C. Liu, Andrew Nolan, and Richard M. Thompson II of the CRS in *Overview of Constitutional Challenges to NSA Collection Activities and Recent Developments* (April 1, 2014, http://www.fas.org/sgp/crs/intel/R43459.pdf). They acknowledge that

total respondents favoring the program agreed with the statement that "investigating terrorism is the more important goal, even if it violates some Americans' civil liberties." (See Table 8.3.) Another 11% felt the program was okay because it "does not violate [Americans' civil] liberties." Of those who disapproved of the program, 30% said there are "no circumstances when it would be

TABLE 8.5

Public opinion on the appropriateness of the actions of Edward Snowden, June 2013

[ASKED OF A HALF SAMPLE] AS YOU MAY KNOW, A FORMER U.S. GOVERNMENT CONTRACTOR NAMED EDWARD SNOWDEN HAS CLAIMED TO BE THE SOURCE OF THE INFORMATION ABOUT THE GOVERNMENT PROGRAM REPORTED IN THE GUARDIAN AND WASHINGTON POST NEWSPAPERS. DO YOU THINK IT WAS RIGHT OR WRONG FOR HIM TO SHARE THAT INFORMATION?

	Right	Wrong	No opinion
National adults	44%	42%	14%
Democrats	39%	49%	12%
Independents	47%	41%	12%
Republicans	49%	38%	14%

SOURCE: Frank Newport, "[Asked of a half sample] As you may know, a former U.S. government contractor named Edward Snowden has claimed to be the source of the information about the government program reported in The Guardian and Washington Post newspapers. Do you think it was right or wrong for him to share that information?" in *Americans Disapprove of Government Surveillance Programs*, The Gallup Organization, June 12, 2013, http://www.gallup.com/poll/163043/americans-disapprove-government-surveillance-programs.aspx (accessed May 6, 2014). Copyright © 2014 Gallup, Inc. All rights reserved. The content is used with permission; however, Gallup retains all rights of republication.

TABLE 8.6

Public opinion on the appropriateness of newspapers publishing information provided to them by Edward Snowden, June 2013

[ASKED OF A HALF SAMPLE] AS YOU MAY KNOW, THE INFORMATION ABOUT THE GOVERNMENT PROGRAM WAS LEAKED TO THE GUARDIAN AND WASHINGTON POST NEWSPAPERS BY A FORMER U.S. GOVERNMENT CONTRACTOR. DO YOU THINK IT WAS RIGHT OR WRONG FOR THE NEWSPAPERS TO PUBLISH THAT INFORMATION?

	Right	Wrong	No opinion
National adults	59%	33%	8%
Democrat	54%	37%	9%
Independent	65%	30%	4%
Republican	58%	35%	8%

SOURCE: Frank Newport, "[Asked of a half sample] As you may know, the information about the government program was leaked to The Guardian and Washington Post newspapers by a former U.S. government contractor. Do you think it was right or wrong for the newspapers to publish that information?" in *Americans Disapprove of Government Surveillance Programs*, The Gallup Organization, June 12, 2013, http://www.gallup.com/poll/163043/americans-disapprove-government-surveillance-programs.aspx (accessed May 6, 2014). Copyright © 2013 Gallup, Inc. All rights reserved. The content is used with permission; however, Gallup retains all rights of republication.

the NSA has collected metadata on domestic and international telephone calls since 2001. This collection is believed to be allowed under Section 215 of the Patriot Act of 2001. The constitutionality of the program became a key focus during the summer of 2013, following Snowden's leaks.

Liu, Nolan, and Thompson explain that the NSA freely collects and retains metadata, but is subject to limitations when it wants to "search or make further use" of the metadata. They note that "these restrictions are not explicitly required by the statutory text of Section 215. Instead, they are delineated as part of the orders the FISC issues pursuant to Section 215." In January 2014 President Obama announced tighter restrictions on the NSA's ability to search the metadata. Specifically, some of the decision-making power formerly exercised by the NSA to justify metadata searches was turned over to the FISC. The FISC now has to approve a reason (which is based on "reasonable articulable suspicions" presented by the NSA) before the NSA can query the metadata, "except in cases of emergencies." In addition, Obama limited the number of "hops" that the NSA can make from a "seed" (a targeted telephone number). The first hop represents the people contacted by a seed. The second hop represents all the phone numbers called by those people, and so forth. Previously, the NSA could go three hops from a seed; the new rules allow only two hops.

The 2013 revelations about the NSA's metadata program prompted several lawsuits challenging its constitutionality. According to Liu, Nolan, and Thompson, two federal courts have issued conflicting rulings on the issue. In *ACLU v. Clapper* (959 F. Supp. 2d 724 [S.D.N.Y.

2013]), a federal judge dismissed the case, noting that the metadata is not protected by the Fourth Amendment. This decision was based on "third-party doctrine," a legal precedent that "a person has no legitimate expectation of privacy in information he voluntarily turns over to third parties." In this context, the "third parties" are the telecommunications companies. However, in *Klayman v. Obama* (No. 13-0881, 2013 WL 6598728), a judge found that metadata collection did constitute an "unreasonable search" under the Fourth Amendment. In both cases, the rulings were appealed. As of August 2014, the appeals had not been completed.

INTERNET DATA COLLECTION BY THE NSA

Another specific program revealed by Snowden involves NSA collection of Internet communications. Barton Gellman and Laura Poitras first provided details about the program based on Snowden's information in "U.S., British Intelligence Mining Data from Nine U.S. Internet Companies in Broad Secret Program" (WashingtonPost.com, June 7, 2013). According to Liu, Nolan, and Thompson, in 2001 the NSA "began acquiring Internet-based communications of overseas targets without the use of a traditional law enforcement warrant or an electronic surveillance order under Title I of FISA." As noted earlier, when the FISA was amended in 2008, Congress added Title VII, which allows the government to conduct surveillance on foreign people located outside the United States without obtaining an individualized court order (i.e., specific to the target).

Liu, Nolan, and Thompson indicate that through 2011 the NSA had collected 250 million Internet communications annually through the program. The vast majority

(91%) of the communications "were acquired 'directly from Internet Service Providers'" through a project called PRISM. The remaining communications were obtained through "upstream collection," meaning they were collected while in transit in cyberspace. The NSA's Internet communications program collects both metadata and the actual contents of the transmissions (e.g., e-mail texts). Liu, Nolan, and Thompson note that the Obama administration has admitted that "technical limitations" can result in the collection of communications "between persons located in the United States."

AMERICAN TERRORISM SUSPECTS

Chapter 9 discusses in detail the complex debate over the human and legal rights of the people who have been captured and detained by the United States since 2001, when the War on Terror began. The issue becomes even more complicated when suspects are U.S. citizens with constitutional rights, chiefly the right not to "be deprived of life, liberty, or property, without due process of law." A few days after the 9/11 attacks Congress passed the Authorization for Use of Military Force (AUMF; https://www.govtrack.us/congress/bills/107/sjres23/text#), which states: "The President is authorized to use all necessary and appropriate force against those nations, organizations, or persons he determines planned, authorized, committed, or aided the terrorist attacks that occurred on September 11, 2001, or harbored such organizations or persons, in order to prevent any future acts of international terrorism against the United States by such nations, organizations or persons."

Thereafter, terrorist suspects encountered outside the United States (e.g., in Afghanistan or Iraq) were legitimate targets of military action. Those who were captured were detained, primarily at the Guantánamo Bay detention facility, which is located within the U.S. naval base in Cuba. (See Figure 6.5 in Chapter 6.)

Habeas Corpus

In 2001 Yaser Esam Hamdi (1980–) was captured in Afghanistan and accused of being part of a Taliban military unit. He was initially imprisoned at the Guantánamo Bay detention facility, but was transferred to a U.S. brig in 2002, after authorities learned that he was a U.S. citizen. His father filed a petition for a writ of habeas corpus. The petition alleged that Hamdi was being held without access to legal counsel and without being formally charged with a crime. Although these conditions were allowed under the AUMF, they violated the U.S. Constitution. The conflict wound its way through the court system and eventually reached the U.S. Supreme Court. In June 2004 the Supreme Court ruled in *Hamdi v. Rumsfeld* (542 U.S. 507) in favor of Hamdi, finding that

although the military had the authority to detain him, he had the right as a U.S. citizen to contest his detention before a "neutral decisionmaker." Several months after the ruling, Hamdi was released without being charged.

Indefinite Detention

In *Hamdi v. Rumsfeld*, the U.S. Supreme Court recognized that the executive branch had the authority under the AUMF to hold detainees for the duration of the War on Terror. The AUMF applies to "covered persons." The National Defense Authorization Act for Fiscal Year 2012 was passed in December 2011 and provided the first legal definition for this term. There are two categories of "covered persons":

1. A person who planned, authorized, committed, or aided the terrorist attacks that occurred on September 11, 2001, or harbored those responsible for those attacks.

2. A person who was a part of or substantially supported al-Qaeda, the Taliban, or associated forces that are engaged in hostilities against the United States or its coalition partners, including any person who has committed a belligerent act or has directly supported such hostilities in aid of such enemy forces.

The law includes four possible dispositions for detainees, including trials and transfer of custody of foreign citizens to foreign governments. However, one disposition allows for "detention under the law of war without trial until the end of the hostilities authorized by the Authorization for Use of Military Force." This provision raises the specter that U.S. citizens can be seized by the U.S. military and held without trial indefinitely. After signing the law, President Obama issued "Statement by the President on H.R. 1540" (December 31, 2011, http://www.whitehouse.gov/the-press-office/2011/12/31/statement-president-hr-1540), in which he said, "I want to clarify that my Administration will not authorize the indefinite military detention without trial of American citizens." However, civil libertarians note that as long as the provision is the law of the land, future administrations might choose to use it against U.S. citizens.

Bob Van Voris notes in "Military Detention Law Blocked by New York Judge" (Bloomberg.com, September 12, 2012) that in January 2012 a group of writers and activists filed a lawsuit against the Obama administration regarding the new law. The plaintiffs feared they could be subject to detention under the second category of "covered persons" simply for their "speech and associations." A federal judge ruled in their favor; however, that decision was overturned on appeal. In April 2014 the U.S. Supreme Court refused to hear the case.

Drone Assassinations

As noted in Chapter 2, the CIA and U.S. military operate drone programs that have attacked and killed thousands of people, primarily in Pakistan and Yemen. Karen Deyoung and Sari Horwitz report in "U.S. to Reveal Justification for Drone Strikes against American Citizens" (WashingtonPost.com, May 20, 2014) that the government admitted in 2013 that it had killed four Americans with drones. However, only one of the people was specifically targeted: Anwar al-Awlaki (1971–2011), the suspected head of foreign operations for the terror group called al Qaeda in the Arabian Peninsula. The other three casualties, including al-Awlaki's teenaged son, were killed "incidentally."

According to Deyoung and Horwitz, the legal justification for assassinating the elder al-Awlaki was contained in a "secret 2011 memo." Reporters for the *New York Times* and the ACLU requested the memo under the Freedom of Information Act (FOIA). Originally passed in 1966, FOIA provides a means for people to access documents that are controlled by the federal government. The Obama administration fought the release of the memo in court and won, but that decision was overturned on appeal in April 2014. In "First Justice Department Memo on Killing Anwar Al-Awlaki" (NYTimes.com, August 15, 2014), Charlie Savage notes that as of August 2014, two memos had been released by the DOJ's Office of Legal Counsel regarding the matter. Both memos were in redacted form, meaning that the DOJ had omitted or blacked out information it considered secret.

In May 2013 the U.S. attorney general Eric Holder Jr. (1951–) sent a letter (http://www.nytimes.com/interactive/2013/05/23/us/politics/23holder-drone-lettter.html?_r=1&) to Senator Leahy to provide some of the justifications employed by the Obama administration for the drone assassinations of Americans. Holder notes the United States can use "lethal force in a foreign country" against U.S. citizens who are either senior leaders within al Qaeda and associated terrorist groups or "actively engaged in planning to kill Americans." The targeted individuals must be infeasible (not capable) to capture and deemed to pose an "imminent threat of violent attack" against the United States. The attack must be conducted "in a manner consistent with applicable law of war principles." As shown in Table 2.7 in Chapter 2, a Gallup Organization poll conducted in March 2013 found that 52% of respondents said the U.S. government should not use drones against U.S. citizens living abroad who are suspected terrorists. Another 41% thought the practice is acceptable, while 7% had no opinion on the matter.

CHAPTER 9
HUMAN AND LEGAL RIGHTS OF DETAINEES

The United States invaded Afghanistan in 2001 in response to the September 11, 2001 (9/11), terrorist attacks. This military campaign was part of a wider effort of the administration of President George W. Bush (1946–) called the War on Terror, which eventually included the invasion of Iraq in 2003. As of August 2014, the war in Iraq had officially ended, while the war in Afghanistan continued. The latter war has been nontraditional in that the United States has not fought against uniformed military forces officially representing a national government. This has confused the legal status of people who are captured and detained by U.S. military forces during the hostilities. Detainees are not considered soldiers, but civilians from various countries fighting for a common agenda or ideological purpose that the U.S. government defines as terrorism. As a result, a legal and political battle has raged within the United States over what kinds of human and legal rights should be afforded to detainees.

ENEMY COMBATANTS

Historically, the United States has treated enemy soldiers in accordance with specific humanitarian standards and international agreements, such as the Geneva Conventions. (See Table 9.1.) The Geneva Conventions prescribe minimum humanitarian standards for captured civilians and soldiers. Among other things, they prohibit torture and cruel, humiliating, and degrading treatment. Similar restrictions are proscribed in the United Nations (UN) Convention against Torture and Other Cruel, Inhuman, or Degrading Treatment or Punishment (http://www.ohchr.org/EN/ProfessionalInterest/Pages/CAT.aspx) to which the United States is a party. Likewise, U.S. behavior during wartime is governed by the War Crimes Act, which was signed into law in 1996 and amended in 1997. Basically, this act defines war crimes as violations of specific provisions of various international agreements, including the Geneva Conventions.

When the War on Terror began in late 2001, the Bush administration decided that most combatants fighting against the United States were not soldiers in the traditional sense but were war criminals. (Note that this distinction did not apply to the uniformed military forces of Iraq.) Captured nonsoldiers were not granted the protections afforded prisoners of war (POWs) under international law. In fact, captured combatants were called detainees, rather than POWs. President Bush made the decision that captured enemy civilians who were deemed terrorists were officially considered enemy combatants. This meant they left the realm of law enforcement and became legitimate targets of military action. In other words, terrorists could be killed outright by U.S. soldiers during the course of hostilities. Likewise, captured terrorists fell under military jurisdiction rather than under law enforcement jurisdiction and could be detained in military detention facilities.

The Bush administration also maintained that the Geneva Conventions are international treaties signed and ratified by nation-states. Because terrorist groups such as al Qaeda are private organizations, they cannot be party to the conventions. Foreign individuals fighting against the United States without official sanction from their governments also cannot be party to the conventions.

DETAINEES AND DETENTION FACILITIES

Since 2001 the United States has captured and detained thousands of enemy combatants at several detention facilities. The major detention facilities have included U.S. military prisons in Bagram, Afghanistan; Abu Ghraib, Iraq; and Guantánamo Bay, Cuba. The Guantánamo Bay detention facility is located within a U.S. naval base (known as GTMO in military terminology) in the southeastern corner of Cuba on land that has been leased by the United States from the Cuban government since 1903. (See Figure 9.1.) Every detention

TABLE 9.1

The Geneva Conventions

Part	Title	Treaty date	Ratified by U.S.	Scope
First Geneva Convention	Amelioration of the condition of the wounded in armies in the field	1949	1955	Concerns treatment of sick and wounded military forces and the neutrality of medical personnel assisting them
Second Geneva Convention	Amelioration of the condition of wounded, sick and shipwrecked members of armed forces at sea	1949	1955	Extends First Geneva Convention to naval warfare
Third Geneva Convention	Treatment of prisoners of war (POW)	1949	1955	Calls for humane treatment of POWs and all other combatants no longer active in hostilities
Fourth Geneva Convention	Protection of civilian persons in time of war	1949	1955	Governs the status and protection of civilian populations during wartime
Protocol I	Protection of victims of international armed conflicts	1977	No*	Protects people involved in battles for self-determination of their nations
Protocol II	Protection of victims of non-international armed conflicts	1977	No*	Protects people involved in internal national conflicts
Protocol III	Adoption of an additional distinctive emblem	2005	2007	Adds a new distinctive emblem called the red crystal

*The United States signed the protocol, but as of May 2014 had not ratified it. Other signatories that have not ratified the protocol are Iran and Pakistan.

SOURCE: Created by Kim Masters Evans for Gale, © 2014

FIGURE 9.1

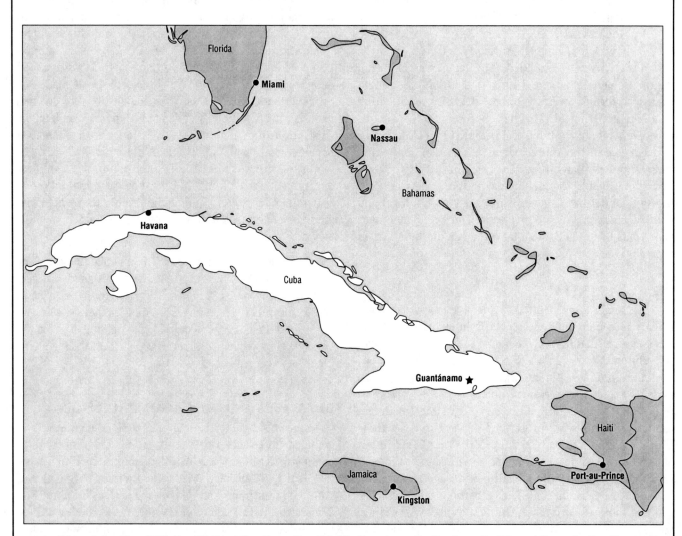

Location of U.S. Naval Station at Guantánamo Bay, Cuba

SOURCE: "Figure 1. Location of U.S. Naval Station at Guantánamo Bay, Cuba," in *Guantánamo Bay Detainees: Facilities and Factors for Consideration If Detainees Were Brought to the United States*, U.S. Government Accountability Office, November 2012, http://gao.gov/assets/660/650032.pdf (accessed May 7, 2014) facility has been plagued by accusations that its detainees have suffered mistreatment and even torture.

Abu Ghraib

Following the invasion of Iraq in March 2003, the U.S. military began using an existing prison in Abu Ghraib to detain prisoners. These included both enemy combatants and common criminals. In 2004 the media began reporting on digital photos taken by U.S. soldiers at Abu Ghraib that showed prisoners posing in sexually explicit positions and enduring humiliating and abusive treatment. Many of the photos included smiling U.S. soldiers posing with the prisoners.

The photos caused an uproar around the world and inflamed anti-American sentiment, particularly among Muslim populations. A series of investigations was launched by U.S. officials. Eventually, the *Final Report of the Independent Panel to Review DoD Detention Operations* (http://www.defenselink.mil/news/Aug2004/ d20040824finalreport.pdf) was issued in August 2004 by the Independent Panel to Review DOD Detention Operations, a group created by the U.S. secretary of defense Donald H. Rumsfeld (1932–). The panel concluded that "acts of brutality and purposeless sadism" had been committed at the detention facility by both military police and military intelligence personnel. The panel found that the abuses depicted in the photographs were conducted primarily for the entertainment of the U.S. personnel involved and were not part of interrogation procedures. In fact, the victims in the photographs were not intelligence targets but civilian or criminal detainees. Eventually, 11 U.S. soldiers were convicted of crimes related to the abuse of detainees at Abu Ghraib.

Interrogation Techniques

Confusion about appropriate interrogation techniques among U.S. military personnel in Afghanistan and Iraq was well documented in the panel's final report. Table 9.2 lists interrogation techniques that were approved by U.S. Department of Defense (DOD) officials at one point or another between 2002 and 2004 for use on enemy combatants at the GTMO detention facility.

The techniques in use during much of 2002 came from the *U.S. Army Field Manual* dating from 1992. In December 2002 Rumsfeld approved additional, more intense techniques for use under certain conditions and with his express approval on specific detainees at the GTMO detention facility. Many of these techniques lost their approval only a few weeks later in January 2003, after concerns were raised about their legality by military legal experts. U.S. officials later learned that the December 2002 list of interrogation techniques was widely circulated in Afghanistan and Iraq and that some commanders mistakenly assumed it applied to detainees under all circumstances.

In April 2003 the list was revised again, reauthorizing two of the more intense techniques and authorizing three new techniques known as environmental manipulation (such as exposure to loud music), sleep adjustment (changing the regular sleeping hours of a detainee; this technique does not include sleep deprivation), and false-flag (fooling a detainee into believing that he is being questioned by a representative from another country, typically a Muslim country).

James Risen, David Johnston, and Neil A. Lewis report in "Harsh C.I.A. Methods Cited in Top Qaeda Interrogations" (NYTimes.com, May 13, 2004) that after 9/11 the Central Intelligence Agency (CIA) began using "harsh" interrogation methods against detainees considered to be "high-level leaders and operatives of Al Qaeda." They describe an interrogation technique called "waterboarding," in which detainees are strapped to a board and lowered under water to make them believe they might drown.

Office of the Inspector General Report

In *A Review of the FBI's Involvement in and Observations of Detainee Interrogations in Guantanamo Bay, Afghanistan, and Iraq* (October 2009, http://www.justice .gov/oig/special/s0910.pdf), the U.S. Department of Justice's (DOJ) Office of the Inspector General (OIG) summarizes its findings regarding the observations and participation of Federal Bureau of Investigation (FBI) agents in detainee interrogations conducted at detention facilities in GTMO, Afghanistan, and Iraq between 2001 and 2004. The OIG reviewed relevant documents, interviewed over 200 witnesses, and surveyed more than 1,000 FBI agents as part of the investigation. The report is unclassified, but redacted, meaning that parts of it are blacked out or omitted to protect national security interests.

The OIG acknowledges that FBI agents witnessed interrogation techniques "that caused them concern." Questions and protests made by FBI agents in the field to the interrogators "sometimes resulted in friction between the FBI and the military." This was particularly true at the GTMO detention facility, where FBI agents reported serious concern about military interrogation techniques that were used against certain "high-value" detainees, including Mohammad al-Qahtani (1979–). Al-Qahtani is believed to have been involved in the planning of the 9/11 terrorist attacks. FBI agents complained that in late 2002 and early 2003 al-Qahtani was subjected to many "aggressive techniques," including being put on a leash and forced to do dog tricks, held in "stress positions," having women's underwear put on his head, and ordered to pray to an idol shrine. The OIG finds

TABLE 9.2

Department of Defense-approved interrogation techniques for Guantánamo Bay detainees, 2004

Interrogation techniques	FM 34–52 (1992) Jan 02–01 Dec 02	Secretary of Defense approved tiered system 02 Dec 02–15 Jan 03	FM 34–52 (1992) with some Cat I 16 Jan 03–15 Apr 03	Secretary of Defense memo 16 Apr 03–present
Direct questioning	X	X	X	X
Incentive/removal of incentive	X	X	X	X
Emotional love	X	X	X	X
Emotional hate	X	X	X	X
Fear up harsh	X	X	X	X
Fear up mild	X	X	X	X
Reduced fear	X	X	X	X
Pride and ego up	X	X	X	X
Pride and ego down	X	X	X	X
Futility	X	X	X	X
We know all	X	X	X	X
Establish your identity	X	X	X	X
Repetition approach	X	X	X	X
File and dossier	X	X	X	X
Mutt and Jeff				X*
Rapid fire	X	X	X	X
Silence	X	X	X	X
Change of scene	X	X	X	X
Yelling		X (Cat I)	X	
Deception		X (Cat I)		
Multiple interrogators		X (Cat I)	X	
Interrogator identity		X (Cat I)	X	
Stress positions, like standing		X (Cat II)		
False documents/reports		X (Cat II)		
Isolation for up to 30 days		X (Cat II)		X*
Deprivation of light/auditory stimuli		X (Cat II)		
Hooding (transportation & questioning)		X (Cat II)		
20-interrogations		X (Cat II)		
Removal of ALL comfort items, including religious items		X (Cat II)		
MRE-only diet		X (Cat II)		X*
Removal of clothing		X (Cat II)		
Forced grooming		X (Cat II)		
Exploiting individual phobias, e.g. dogs		X (Cat II)		
Mild, non-injurious physical contact, e.g. grabbing, poking or light pushing		X (Cat III)		
Environmental manipulation				X
Sleep adjustment				X
False flag				X

*Techniques require SOUTHCOM approval and SECDEF notification.
Notes: MRE=meal, ready to eat. FM=field manual. Cat=category.

SOURCE: "Evolution of Interrogation Techniques—GTMO," in *Final Report of the Independent Panel to Review DoD Detention Operations*, U.S. Department of Defense, August 2004, http://www.defenselink.mil/news/Aug2004/d20040824finalreport.pdf (accessed May 25, 2014)

that FBI complaints to the DOD about the legality and effectiveness of these techniques were never officially addressed.

In total, more than 200 FBI agents who visited the GTMO detention facility reported witnessing or hearing about "harsh" interrogation techniques used by the military. Some of these techniques were in violation of DOD regulations effective at the time. A smaller unnamed number of FBI agents reported similar problems in Afghanistan. Over 300 FBI agents reported observing or hearing about "harsh" interrogation techniques used by the military on detainees in Iraq. One hundred and twelve of the agents personally observed these techniques. However, the OIG notes that the "vast majority" of FBI agents stationed at GTMO, Afghanistan, and Iraq reported neither observing nor hearing about harsh interrogation techniques.

New Detainee Rules

By 2005 continued allegations and reports about detainee mistreatment had become a major problem for the U.S. government. In December 2005 Congress passed the Detainee Treatment Act of 2005. The new law outlaws torture or cruel and inhuman treatment of detainees by military and civilian federal agencies. It requires that military interrogators use only interrogation techniques that are listed in the *U.S. Army Field Manual*, which adheres to the requirements of the Third Geneva Convention for the treatment of POWs.

In September 2006 the DOD issued Directive 2310.01E (http://www.defense.gov/pubs/pdfs/Detainee _Prgm_Dir_2310_9-5-06.pdf), which calls for all detainees to be treated in accordance with humanitarian standards, including the Geneva Conventions. That same month

TABLE 9.3

List of detainee treatments specifically prohibited by U.S. Army Field Manual, 2006

<u>Section 5-74</u>
Specifically prohibited treatments under all circumstances:

Forcing an individual to perform or simulate sexual acts or to pose in a sexual manner.
Exposing an individual to outrageously lewd and sexually provocative behavior.
Intentionally damaging or destroying an individual's religious articles.

<u>Section 5-75</u>
Specifically prohibited treatments during interrogations:

Forcing the detainee to be naked, perform sexual acts, or pose in a sexual manner.
Placing hoods or sacks over the head of a detainee; using duct tape over the eyes.
Applying beatings, electric shock, burns, or other forms of physical pain.
"Waterboarding."
Using military working dogs.
Inducing hypothermia or heat injury.
Conducting mock executions.
Depriving the detainee of necessary food, water, or medical care.

SOURCE: Adapted from "Cruel, Inhuman or Degrading Treatment Prohibited," in *FM 2-22.3 (FM 34-52) Human Intelligence Collector Operations*, U.S. Army, September 2006, https://rdl.train.army.mil/catalog/view/100.ATSC/10492372-71C5-4DA5-8E6E-649C85E1A280-1300688170771/2-22.3/toc.htm (accessed May 7, 2014)

the U.S. Army released a new version of the *U.S. Army Field Manual*, known as *FM 2-22.3 (FM 34-52) Human Intelligence Collector Operations* (http://www.fas.org/irp/doddir/army/fm2-22-3.pdf). The new manual prohibits cruel, inhuman, and degrading treatment of detainees. Specific prohibitions on the treatment of detainees are listed in Table 9.3.

Secret CIA Prisons Acknowledged

Risen, Johnston, and Lewis report that after 9/11 the CIA began operating a secret detention system that housed up to 20 high-level detainees. Furthermore, the CIA refused to allow independent observers or human rights groups access to the prisoners. Dana Priest provides more detail about this program in "CIA Holds Terror Suspects in Secret Prisons" (WashingtonPost.com, November 5, 2005). The prison system allegedly included facilities in several countries in eastern Europe and Thailand and was conducted with the cooperation of those governments. Priest claims that CIA interrogators were allowed to use "enhanced interrogation techniques," such as waterboarding, that are prohibited by international law and the U.S. military.

According to Adam Liptak, in "Interrogation Methods Rejected by Military Win Bush's Support" (NY Times.com, September 8, 2006), President Bush admitted in a September 2006 speech that the CIA had been operating secret overseas prisons. However, he denied that the detainees had been tortured, claiming they had been subjected to techniques that "were tough, and they were safe and lawful and necessary." All the detainees were believed to have been transferred to military control.

In July 2007 President Bush issued Executive Order 13340, which required CIA interrogators to use interrogation techniques on terror suspects in accordance with the Geneva Conventions. Later that year the director of the CIA admitted that videotapes of some detainee interrogations had been destroyed by the agency.

Redefining War Crimes

In October 2006 Bush signed the Military Commissions Act of 2006 (MCA of 2006). Michael John Garcia of the Congressional Research Service describes the effect of the new law on the War Crimes Act and the Detainee Treatment Act of 2005 in *The War Crimes Act: Current Issues* (October 2, 2006, http://fpc.state.gov/documents/organization/75257.pdf). According to Garcia, the MCA of 2006 criminalized only certain "grave breaches" of the Geneva Conventions regarding the treatment of captured individuals. The act also specifically provided a statutory defense for U.S. personnel accused of crimes against detainees under the War Crimes Act. The defense was that the personnel were operating with the authorization of the administration and under the reasonable belief that their actions were lawful.

Analysts believe that passage of the law was driven by fears within the Bush administration that officials could be held legally culpable for the alleged mistreatment of detainees. Calls for such prosecutions were being made publicly, such as by Amnesty International (AI), a London-based private independent group concerned with human rights. The UN Committee against Torture was also highly critical of U.S. government actions regarding detainees.

Public Opinion on Detainee Treatment

Darren K. Carlson of the Gallup Organization reports in *Public Believes U.S. Government Has Tortured Prisoners* (November 29, 2005, http://www.gallup.com/poll/20170/Public-Believes-US-Government-Has-Tortured-Prisoners.aspx) that in November 2005, 74% of Americans believed U.S. troops and government officials had tortured prisoners in Iraq and in other countries, whereas 20% believed torture had not taken place. Carlson notes that this poll was conducted only weeks after President Bush and Porter J. Goss (1938–), the director of the CIA, had assured the American public that prisoners in the War on Terror were not being tortured.

During the same poll respondents were asked about their willingness to have the government torture known terrorists with details about future terrorist attacks. Carlson notes in *Would Americans Fight Terrorism by Any Means Necessary?* (March 1, 2005, http://www.gallup.com/poll/15073/Would-Americans-Fight-Terrorism-Any-Means-Necessary.aspx) that this same question was asked by Gallup pollsters in October 2001 (only weeks after the

9/11 terrorist attacks) and in January 2005. In all three polls a majority of the respondents opposed the use of torture to obtain vital information about future attacks. In November 2005, 56% of those asked had this viewpoint, compared with 38% who were willing to use torture.

U.S. Senate Committee on Armed Services Report

In December 2008 the U.S. Senate Committee on Armed Services published its findings after conducting a lengthy investigation of detainee treatment. In *Senate Armed Services Committee Inquiry into the Treatment of Detainees in U.S. Custody* (http://www.gwu.edu/~nsarchiv/torturingdemocracy/documents/20081211.pdf), the committee outlines the Bush administration's decisions and policies that ultimately influenced the treatment of detainees.

In particular, the committee focuses on interrogations that employ Survival Evasion Resistance and Escape (SERE) techniques. The DOD's Joint Personnel Recovery Agency (JPRA) conducts training classes known as SERE schools, in which U.S. military personnel are trained to withstand interrogation techniques that are forbidden by the Geneva Conventions. The students (who volunteer for the training) are subjected to interrogation methods that include "stripping students of their clothing, placing them in stress positions, putting hoods over their heads, disrupting their sleep, treating them like animals, subjecting them to loud music and flashing lights, and exposing them to extreme temperatures." The committee notes that some SERE schools in the past also included waterboarding. All the forbidden techniques are based, in part, on the techniques that were used by Chinese interrogators on U.S. POWs during the Korean War (1950–1953). The purpose of the SERE schools is to expose students to interrogation techniques to which they might be subjected if captured by an enemy that does not adhere to the Geneva Conventions and to help them to withstand the techniques.

The committee finds that after the War on Terror began, "senior government officials" began asking the JPRA for training not on how to withstand the illegal techniques, but on how to administer them to detainees. The committee points out, however, that the JPRA personnel who teach these techniques in SERE schools are not trained interrogators—that is, they have not been trained in how best to obtain reliable and useful information from prisoners. Nevertheless, the JPRA was actively involved in detainee interrogations for at least two years at the request of senior U.S. officials. At the same time, senior lawyers within the Bush administration and the DOD were writing legal opinions "justifying the legality of the techniques."

The committee notes that in September 2002 officials at the GTMO detention facility specifically asked for permission from Rumsfeld to use SERE interrogation techniques on detainees. In December 2002 Rumsfeld authorized the use of most, but not all, of the requested SERE techniques on GTMO detainees based on recommendations from William J. Haynes II (1958–), the general counsel for the DOD. The committee finds that other senior legal officials within the DOD, particularly the chief counsels for the U.S. Army, the U.S. Air Force, the U.S. Navy, and the U.S. Marine Corps, had expressed serious reservations about the effectiveness and legality of the techniques. In addition, the committee claims that "Rumsfeld authorized the techniques without apparently providing any written guidance as to how they should be administered." Nevertheless, SERE trainers were dispatched to GTMO, and interrogators there began using the techniques. The committee notes that allegations of detainee mistreatment were soon raised by some DOD personnel and FBI agents at the facility.

In January 2003 Rumsfeld reversed his earlier decision and withdrew his approval for use of the SERE techniques at the GTMO detention facility. However, his December 2002 memorandum had already been widely distributed to military officers in Afghanistan and Iraq, who believed that the SERE techniques had Rumsfeld's express support. SERE trainers were summoned to those countries, and SERE techniques were subsequently used on detainees, including those at the Abu Ghraib detention facility in Iraq. In 2004 public allegations about detainee mistreatment led senior DOD officials to cancel all future plans for SERE training for the purpose of detainee interrogation.

The committee concludes that "the abuse of detainees in U.S. custody cannot simply be attributed to the actions of 'a few bad apples' acting on their own. The fact is that senior officials in the United States government solicited information on how to use aggressive techniques, redefined the law to create the appearance of their legality, and authorized their use against detainees. Those efforts damaged our ability to collect accurate intelligence that could save lives, strengthened the hand of our enemies, and compromised our moral authority."

The Obama Administration

During his 2008 presidential campaign, Senator Barack Obama (1961–) pledged to end interrogation techniques considered to be torture and to close the GTMO detention facility. On January 22, 2009—two days after his inauguration as president—Obama issued three executive orders regarding detainee treatment. Overall, the standards of the Geneva Conventions became the minimum standards for detainee treatment. Despite intense pressure from within his party and from human rights groups to prosecute Bush administration officials for sanctioning harsh interrogation techniques, Obama decided not to pursue legal action against them.

Senate Select Committee on Intelligence Investigation

In 2009 the Senate Select Committee on Intelligence (SSCI) began an investigation of the interrogation techniques used by the CIA during the Bush administration. In "Public Feud between CIA, Senate Panel Follows Years of Tension over Interrogation Report" (WashingtonPost.com, March 12, 2014), Greg Miller and Adam Goldman note that the investigation was driven by SSCI members who were "outraged by the revelation that CIA officers had destroyed videotapes of some of those early [interrogation] sessions." The CIA provided the committee with digital access to millions of its internal documents via a three-part computer network. One part of the network was accessible only by the CIA, the second part was accessible only by the SSCI, and the third part was a shared space that both sides could access.

In March 2014 Senator Dianne Feinstein (1933–; D-CA), the chair of the SSCI, publicly accused the CIA of secretly searching some of the committee members' computers. The CIA countered that the committee had somehow obtained agency documents that were not on the shared space of the computer network. The implication was that SSCI members had perhaps hacked into the CIA side of the network to obtain the documents. The CIA forwarded its concerns to the FBI for an investigation of possible wrongdoing, a move that greatly angered Feinstein. According to Miller and Goldman, numerous other problems have plagued the investigation, including fighting between the Republican and Democratic committee members. In fact, the Republican members wound up abandoning the investigation over concerns about the lack of CIA cooperation and fears that the committee's report "would be shaped by political interests." The final report, which contained more than 6,000 pages, was completed in 2013. Miller and Goldman claim the report is "a damning chronicle" of the CIA's interrogation program and that the agency provided the SSCI a "lengthy" rebuttal of the report objecting to "many of its findings." In April 2014 the SSCI voted to release parts of the report, specifically the executive summary and conclusions. However, the final decision lies with the Obama administration.

Greg Miller reports in "CIA Director John Brennan Apologizes for Search of Senate Committee's Computers" (WashingtonPost.com, July 31, 2014) that the FBI closed its investigation in July 2014 "after finding insufficient evidence that either side had committed a crime." However, an internal CIA investigation conducted by the agency's Inspector General revealed that five CIA staffers had improperly searched the SSCI's portion of the network. As a result, the CIA director John Brennan (1955–) publicly apologized to Feinstein and other congressional leaders. As of August 2014, the committee's report had not been released to the public.

LEGAL RIGHTS OF ALIEN DETAINEES

Besides the controversy over detainees' human rights, there is also debate concerning their legal rights. These two types of rights are intertwined. For example, the Geneva Conventions prohibit countries at war from subjecting captured individuals to criminal punishments, including executions, that are conducted without due legal process. This provision (http://www.un-documents.net/gc-1.htm) specifically requires that defendants receive "all the judicial guarantees which are recognized as indispensable by civilized peoples."

The U.S. Constitution sets forth many judicial guarantees and legal rights for U.S. citizens. As explained in Chapter 8, conflicts between legal rights and national security concerns often arise during wartime. This has certainly been the case for U.S. citizens who have been detained during the War on Terror. The issue is even more complicated for alien (noncitizen) detainees. Controversy rages over what, if any, legal rights inherent to the U.S. justice system should be afforded to alien detainees.

In general, the debate has centered around four issues:

- Indefinite detention without trial—the right to a trial is protected by the U.S. Constitution.

- The right to habeas corpus—this is a legal procedure in which a court can order that a prisoner held by the government be presented to the court for determination if the imprisonment is legal or not. In "Habeas Corpus" (2014, http://www.law.cornell.edu/wex/habeas_corpus), the Cornell University Law School notes that the U.S. Constitution does not create the right, but presents the narrow conditions under which the right can be suspended. Thus, a habeas corpus right was already recognized to exist. Over time, the right has become engrained in U.S. federal laws.

- Trial by military commissions rather than by civilian courts—the use of military commissions (tribunals) during wartime has historical precedent. In *Ex Parte Quirin* (317 U.S. 1 [1942]), the U.S. Supreme Court decided that President Franklin D. Roosevelt (1882–1945) had the authority to convene a military tribunal to try eight civilian Germans who had entered the United States to commit sabotage during World War II (1939–1945). Six of the men were ultimately executed by electric chair.

- Trying detainees that have been tortured—under U.S. law information that is obtained via torture from a criminal suspect is not admissible in court. In fact, torture is forbidden under the U.S. Constitution's prohibition against "cruel and unusual punishment."

Legal Basis and Controversies

In September 2001 Congress passed the Authorization for Use of Military Force (AUMF; https://www.govtrack.us/congress/bills/107/sjres23/text), which enabled the president "to use all necessary and appropriate force" against accused terrorists. These so-called war powers extend through the duration of the U.S. War on Terror. However, unlike previous wars with defined beginning and ending dates of hostility, the War on Terror has turned into an indefinite war with no clear ending point. Also, in November 2001 President Bush signed the military order Detention, Treatment, and Trial of Certain Non-citizens in the War against Terrorism (http://www.law.cornell.edu/background/warpower/fr1665.pdf), which granted him power to determine whether a captured person was a member of al Qaeda and had committed terrorist acts. It also stated that military commissions would be used to try unlawful enemy combatants captured during the War on Terror.

RASUL V. BUSH. In June 2004 the U.S. Supreme Court issued a ruling concerning the legal rights of foreign detainees. Fourteen alien detainees at the GTMO detention facility had filed a petition in a U.S. district court challenging the legality of their detention. They claimed they had never been charged with a crime, permitted to have legal counsel, or provided access to the courts. The district court considered the petition a request for habeas corpus and dismissed it because this right had previously been deemed not to extend to aliens detained outside "United States sovereign territory." However, the U.S. Supreme Court overruled the district court, ruling in Rasul v. Bush (542 U.S. 466) that the Guantánamo Bay Naval Station is under the "complete jurisdiction and control" of the United States. This ruling precipitated the filing of dozens of habeas corpus petitions on behalf of GTMO detainees.

In July 2004 the DOD announced in the press release "Combatant Status Review Tribunal Order Issued" (http://www.defenselink.mil/releases/release.aspx?releaseid=7530) the creation of a Combatant Status Review Tribunal (CSRT) process for detainees held at the GTMO detention facility. The DOD defined the CSRT "as a forum for detainees to contest their status as enemy combatants."

The Detainee Treatment Act

The Detainee Treatment Act of 2005 is described by Garcia in Boumediene v. Bush: Guantanamo Detainees' Right to Habeas Corpus (September 8, 2008, http://fas.org/sgp/crs/natsec/RL34536.pdf). According to Garcia, the act eliminated the jurisdiction of federal courts to consider habeas corpus petitions by aliens who challenged their detention at the GTMO detention facility. The U.S. Court of Appeals for the District of Columbia Circuit (the D.C. Appeals Court) was granted sole jurisdiction over the review of determinations made by CSRTs and military commissions. In other words, the act made clear that alien combatants who are detained outside the United States do not have constitutional rights. It also stripped the courts of jurisdiction to hear habeas corpus petitions from detainees.

Hamdan v. Rumsfeld

In June 2006 the Supreme Court ruled in Hamdan v. Rumsfeld (548 U.S. 557) that U.S. law did not allow military commissions such as those created by President Bush's 2001 military order. In addition, Garcia explains in Boumediene v. Bush: Guantanamo Detainees' Right to Habeas Corpus that the court ruled that the stripping of habeas corpus rights enacted through the Detainee Treatment Act of 2005 did not apply to alien combatants who had habeas corpus petitions pending when the law was passed. Congress responded with the MCA of 2006. It established procedures for the use of military commissions to try alien detainees and specifically stripped habeas corpus rights from alien combatants in both pending and future cases. In March 2007 the Australian David Hicks (1975–) was the first GTMO detainee sentenced under the MCA of 2006. Detained since 2002, Hicks was charged with many serious crimes, including attempted murder and conducting terrorist acts for the Taliban in Afghanistan. He ultimately pleaded guilty to only one charge (providing material support for terrorism) and was turned over to Australia to serve the remaining nine months of his sentence.

In July 2007 the DOD issued the memorandum "Application of Common Article 3 of the Geneva Conventions to the Treatment of Detainees in the Department of Defense" (http://www.defense.gov/pubs/pdfs/DepSecDef%20memo%20on%20common%20article%203.pdf). The DOD ordered all of its personnel to treat detainees in accordance with Common Article 3 of the Geneva Conventions. Common Article 3 prohibits "the passing of sentences and the carrying out of executions without previous judgment pronounced by a regularly constituted court affording all the judicial guarantees which are recognized as indispensable by civilized peoples." This article was interpreted to mean that detainees have a legal right to challenge their detention.

Boumediene v. Bush

In June 2008 the U.S. Supreme Court ruled in Boumediene v. Bush (553 U.S. ___; combined with Al Odah v. United States) that alien enemy combatants detained at the GTMO detention facility do have the constitutional privilege of habeas corpus. Garcia describes this ruling in detail in Boumediene v. Bush: Guantanamo Detainees' Right to Habeas Corpus. According to Garcia, the court found unconstitutional the section of the MCA of 2006 that stripped the courts of jurisdiction to hear pending and future habeas corpus petitions.

Obama's Executive Orders

As noted earlier, in January 2009 President Obama issued three executive orders (13491, 13492, and 13493) dealing with detainees. One of the orders (13492) called for a "prompt and thorough review" of each individual's circumstances and legal status and the closure of the GTMO detention facility within one year or upon finalization of the dispositions of all the detainees.

The Guantanamo Detainee Review Task Force issued a report in January 2010 specifying on a case-by-case basis which GTMO detainees should be prosecuted, which should be released, and which should be detained without trial. In "Justice Task Force Recommends about 50 Guantanamo Detainees Be Held Indefinitely" (WashingtonPost.com, January 22, 2010), Peter Finn notes that human rights groups are opposed to detainees being held indefinitely without trial. However, the Obama administration reportedly believes that such detainees are "dangerous to release but unprosecutable because officials fear trials could compromise intelligence-gathering and because detainees could challenge evidence obtained through coercion."

Military Commissions Act of 2009

In late 2009 Congress passed the Military Commissions Act of 2009 (MCA of 2009). The law provides the authority for military tribunals or commissions to try "alien unprivileged enemy belligerents." It also details the makeup and activities of the military commissions and specifies particular legal rights for the detainees. One notable provision forbids the use against the accused of statements obtained "by the use of torture or by cruel, inhuman, or degrading treatment," as defined by the Detainee Treatment Act.

Trying Detainees in Civilian Courts

In 2009 President Obama tried unsuccessfully to move to the federal court in New York City the trials of five GTMO detainees with ties to the 9/11 attacks. The city's mayor and other officials raised concerns about the tight security measures that would be required.

Also in 2009 Ahmed Khalfan Ghailani (1974–) was transferred from the GTMO detention facility to the federal court in New York City for trial on charges that he participated in the 1998 terrorist bombings of the U.S. embassies in Nairobi, Kenya, and Dar es Salaam, Tanzania. His trial took place in 2010. According to Benjamin Weiser, in "Detainee Acquitted on Most Counts in '98 Bombings" (NYTimes.com, November 17, 2010), Ghailani faced 280 charges of conspiracy and murder but was convicted of only one count of "conspiracy to destroy

government buildings and property." The judge disallowed some key testimony against the defendant because the information had been obtained during torture. Ghailani, who was captured in Pakistan in 2004, had allegedly spent five years in a "black site" (a secret overseas prison operated by the CIA) and at the GTMO detention facility. His acquittal on all but one of the serious charges against him fueled criticism of Obama's desire to try other GTMO detainees in civilian courts.

In March 2011 Obama announced that in the future the U.S. government would use military commissions to try GTMO detainees. Although he also called for more detainees to be prosecuted in U.S. criminal courts, when appropriate, analysts indicate that this is not likely to happen.

Since 2009, Congress has passed laws thwarting efforts by the Obama administration to move detainees from Cuba to the United States. As of August 2014, the most recent prohibitions were included in the National Defense Authorization Act for Fiscal Year 2014, which was passed in December 2013. The law funds the DOD for fiscal year 2014 (October 2013 to September 2014) and includes special provisions devoted to U.S. counterterrorism activities. (See Table 9.4.) Among other things, the law prohibits the use of DOD funds for the transfer or release of detainees from the GTMO detention facility to the United States. It also prohibits the use of DOD funds to construct or modify detention facilities within the United States that might be intended to house GTMO

TABLE 9.4

Counterterrorism sections of the National Defense Authorization Act for Fiscal Year 2014

Section	Title
Sec. 1031.	Clarification of procedures for use of alternate members on military commissions.
Sec. 1032.	Modification of Regional Defense Combating Terrorism Fellowship Program reporting requirement.
Sec. 1033.	Prohibition on use of funds to construct or modify facilities in the United States to house detainees transferred from United States Naval Station, Guantanamo Bay, Cuba.
Sec. 1034.	Prohibition on the use of funds for the transfer or release of individuals detained at United States Naval Station, Guantanamo Bay, Cuba.
Sec. 1035.	Transfers to foreign countries of individuals detained at United States Naval Station, Guantanamo Bay, Cuba.
Sec. 1036.	Report on information relating to individuals detained at Parwan, Afghanistan.
Sec. 1037.	Grade of chief prosecutor and chief defense counsel in military commissions established to try individuals detained at Guantanamo.
Sec. 1038.	Report on capability of Yemeni government to detain, rehabilitate, and prosecute individuals detained at Guantanamo who are transferred to Yemen.
Sec. 1039.	Report on attachment of rights to individuals detained at Guantanamo if transferred to the United States.

SOURCE: Adapted from "Subtitle D—Counterterrorism," in *National Defense Authorization Act for Fiscal Year 2014*, U.S. Government Printing Office, December 2013, http://www.gpo.gov/fdsys/pkg/CPRT-113HPRT86280/pdf/CPRT-113HPRT86280.pdf (accessed May 7, 2014)

detainees. Overall, the act helps ensure that the GTMO detention facility will remain in operation indefinitely.

National Defense Authorization Act for Fiscal Year 2012

As explained in Chapter 8, the National Defense Authorization Act for Fiscal Year 2012 was passed in December 2011. It provided the first legal definition for "covered persons" under the AUMF and listed four possible dispositions for them:

- Detention under the law of war without trial until the end of the hostilities authorized by the AUMF.

- Trial under chapter 47A of title 10, United States Code (as amended by the Military Commissions Act of 2009 [title XVIII of Public Law 111-84]).

- Transfer for trial by an alternative court or competent tribunal having lawful jurisdiction.

- Transfer to the custody or control of the person's country of origin, any other foreign country, or any other foreign entity.

In "Guantanamo Bay: What Happens When Detainees Held for Years Get Out?" (CNN.com, June 4, 2014), Greg Botelho and Faith Karimi note that the GTMO detention facility once held 770 detainees; by May 2014 that number had dwindled to 154 detainees. Thus, more than 600 detainees had left the detention facility.

Every six months the Office of the Director of National Intelligence (ODNI) submits to Congress a report regarding the dispositions of GTMO detainees. As of August 2014, the most recent report was published in March 2014 and provided data through January 14, 2014. In "Summary of the Reengagement of Detainees Formerly Held at Guantanamo Bay, Cuba" (March 5, 2014, http://www.dni.gov/files/documents/Newsroom/Reports%20and%20Pubs/GTMO.pdf), the ODNI notes that nine detainees died while at the GTMO detention facility, one detainee (Ghailani) was transferred to New York for trial, and 614 detainees were transferred to foreign custody or control. Of the latter number, 104 detainees (16.9%) were confirmed as having reengaged (returned to terrorist activities). Twenty of that number subsequently died and 27 were recaptured. Thus, 57 former detainees were actively reengaged in terrorism. Another 74 detainees (12.1%) released to foreign countries were suspected of reengaging. Two of that number subsequently died and 24 were recaptured. This left 48 former detainees suspected of actively reengaging in terrorism. Overall, 29% of the 614 GTMO detainees transferred to foreign custody were confirmed or suspected of reengaging. The ODNI notes that reengagement is most likely when detainees are transferred to "countries with ongoing conflicts and internal instability as well as active recruitment by insurgent and terrorist organizations."

As described in Chapter 4, in June 2014, five GTMO detainees—all Taliban members—were released in a trade for Bowe Bergdahl (1986–), a U.S. soldier. He had been held prisoner in Afghanistan since 2009. The five detainees were transferred to the custody and control of Qatar, which promised to keep them from leaving the country for at least one year. Critics of the prisoner swap fear that the Taliban members will reengage in terrorism.

THE TRIALS OF THE 9/11 DETAINEES. Five of the most notorious detainees at the GTMO detention facility are accused of direct involvement in the 9/11 terrorist attacks. Chief among them is Khalid Shaikh Mohammed (1964–). He has been in U.S. custody since 2003 and is believed to be the primary planner behind the attacks. The article "Khalid Sheikh Mohammed Guantanamo Hearing Gets Chaotic Start" (BBC.com, May 6, 2012) notes that "CIA documents confirm that he was subjected to simulated drowning, known as waterboarding, 183 times." Mohammed and four alleged accomplices were originally charged with murder and terrorism in 2008, but those charges were dropped when the Obama administration attempted unsuccessfully to switch them to criminal court jurisdiction in New York City. In June 2011 the charges were refiled.

In May 2012 the five men had an arraignment hearing at the GTMO detention facility, during which the formal charges against them were presented. The hearing was raucous. Peter Finn describes in "9/11 Detainees Work to Disrupt Opening of Arraignment at Guantanamo Bay" (WashingtonPost.com, May 5, 2012) the unruly behavior of the detainees as an attempt to "make every effort to disrupt and delay the proceeding." The detainees were at times noncommunicative and at other times loud and quarrelsome with the military judge. None of the detainees officially entered a plea at the hearing. As of August 2014, their trial dates had not been set. It remains to be seen if their harsh treatment during detention will become an issue during the trials.

CHAPTER 10
U.S. RELATIONS WITH THE ISLAMIC WORLD

Terrorism became a serious threat to U.S. national security after World War II (1939–1945). The vast majority of terrorist acts committed against Americans during this period were perpetrated by Muslims, or at least by people who claim to be acting in accordance with Islamic principles. This raises troubling issues about the nature and future of relations between the United States and Muslims around the world. Do terrorists who claim to be Muslims represent the true spirit of Islam, or are they rebels and rogues who have hijacked the religion for their own violent purposes? How deep are the ideological and political divides between the Islamic and non-Islamic world? Can they be bridged?

WHAT IS ISLAM?

Islam translates into English as "submission" and advocates submission to God by its followers. As described in Chapter 1, Muslims believe that during the seventh century the angel Gabriel revealed God's messages to the prophet Muhammad (c. 570–632). Those messages were eventually written down to form the Koran, Islam's holy book.

Sharia is the body of Islamic law and is based on the Koran. It covers all aspects of life, rather than just matters of a legal nature. The hadith are also important to Muslims. They are a collection of Muhammad's sayings and actions that help Muslims follow a way of life (called Sunna) modeled after Muhammad and based on the Koran.

The Council on American Islamic Relations (CAIR) notes in "Islam Basics" (2014, http://www.cair.com/american-muslims/about-islam.html) that there are five pillars of Islam:

- Declaration of faith—a person becomes a Muslim by declaring the following: "There is no deity but God, and Muhammad is the messenger of God"

- Obligatory prayers—Muslims are required to pray five times per day at set times

- Zakat—this is charitable giving to those in need

- Fasting—Muslims fast from sunrise to sunset during the Islamic lunar month called Ramadan if they are physically able to do so

- Hajj—this is a pilgrimage to Mecca, a sacred site in Saudi Arabia, that all Muslims are supposed to make at least once during their lifetime if they are physically and financially able to do so

Islam recognizes many prophets from the Judeo-Christian tradition, including Abraham (c. 1996–c. 1821 BC), Jacob (1838?–1689 BC), Moses (c. 1392–c. 1272 BC), David (1000–c. 960 BC), and Solomon (985?–925? BC). Unlike Christians, Muslims believe that Jesus (4? BC–AD 29?) was a prophet rather than a divine messiah. Islam lacks a centralized leadership. There is no single religious leader (such as the pope in Roman Catholicism) who speaks on behalf of all Muslims. In fact, there is not even a structured hierarchy. Islam esteems many respected elders, learned men, and Islamic scholars, some of whom have titles such as mufti (judge) or sheikh (sheik). Prayer, worship, and other religious activities often take place at mosques, which are meeting places for Muslims.

The Diversity of Islam

Different people practice Islam in different ways around the world. While they agree on certain core tenets, they may diverge over many other aspects of their faith. In some cases they may disagree so strongly that one group will not recognize another as being Muslim at all. In this, Islam is no different than any other active and widespread faith or ideology. For example, there are many differences among those who call themselves Christians.

There are two main sects within Islam: Sunni and Shia. Their followers have historical disagreements about issues related to governance and theological interpretations. However, there are also differences among Muslims that center around social, moral, and political issues. These will be explored in more detail in this chapter.

THE ISLAMIC WORLD

There are various estimates of the number of Muslims in the world. The Pew Research Center estimates in *The Future Global Muslim Population Projections for 2010–2030* (January 2011, http://www.pewforum.org/uploadedFiles/Topics/Religious_Affiliation/Muslim/FutureGlobalMuslimPopulation-WebPDF-Feb10.pdf) that in 2010 there were 1.6 billion Muslims, which accounted for 23.4% of the total world population of 6.9 billion. The four countries with the largest Muslim populations in 2010 were Indonesia, Pakistan, India, and Bangladesh. Each contained more than 148 million Muslims.

According to Pew, the Muslim population is forecast to increase at approximately twice the rate of the non-Muslim population between 2010 and 2030. By 2030 the Muslim population is projected to be 2.2 billion, or 26.4% of the world's total population.

Pew estimates that the sectarian breakdown of Muslims in 2010 was 87% to 90% Sunni and 10% to 13% Shia. This breakdown is expected to continue through 2030. As of 2010, the countries with the largest Sunni-majority populations were Egypt, Indonesia, Bangladesh, and Pakistan. In all these nations Sunnis accounted for more than 87% of the Muslim population. The countries with the largest Shia-majority populations in 2010 were Iran, Azerbaijan, Bahrain, and Iraq. At least two-thirds of the Muslims in these nations were Shiites.

HISTORICAL CONTEXT FOR U.S. RELATIONS

The roots of U.S.-Muslim relations can be traced back to medieval clashes between the Islamic world and the European kingdoms. In 1096 armies of Christian European knights and soldiers began the first of what would later be called the Crusades. These were military campaigns waged against Muslim forces in the Middle East. In 1099 the European armies captured Jerusalem, only to lose it in 1187 to Muslim forces led by Saladin (c. 1138–1193), a renowned figure in Islamic history. In 1192 Saladin and King Richard I (1157–1199) of England signed a treaty agreeing that Jerusalem would remain under Muslim control but Christian pilgrims would be allowed to visit the city. Crusaders captured the city again in 1229 only to lose it to the Muslims for the last time in 1244.

Within Western history and literature, the Crusades have become highly romanticized adventures that focus on the feats of King Richard I and the European knights. By contrast, the Islamic world regards the Crusades as a brutal invasion by European nations. Peter Ford reports in "Europe Cringes at Bush 'Crusade' against Terrorists" (CSMonitor.com, September 19, 2001) that President George W. Bush (1946–) was chastised by Muslims after the September 11, 2001 (9/11), terrorist attacks for referring to U.S. retaliation as a "crusade" against terrorism. For Americans, it was a clue that events centuries old still resonate with many Muslim people.

Colonial Resentment

Following World War I (1914–1918) several Middle Eastern territories fell under colonial rule. These included Iraq and Palestine, which were under the administration of Great Britain, and Syria and Lebanon, which were under the administration of France. All nations but Palestine eventually achieved their independence. The lack of an official homeland for the Palestinians became a major point of contention in the Middle East.

Even before the war, most Muslim nations had been under European control at one time or another. Great Britain, France, and Italy all had colonies in the Middle East and/or North Africa during the 1800s and early 1900s. Even nations that were not colonized experienced some level of protection or influence by European powers, particularly Great Britain. The major exception is Saudi Arabia, which has been under continuous Muslim control for centuries.

By the 1950s most Muslim countries had achieved their independence. However, resentment about colonial rule and interference still plays a major factor in Middle Eastern politics. Although the United States did not exist at the time of the Crusades and was not a colonial power in the Middle East like its European allies, it must still contend with old grievances in the region.

IDEOLOGICAL DIFFERENCES

In many cases, there are deep differences between the Islamic and non-Islamic world regarding political, social, and moral ideologies. These differences typically relate to one key point: the role of religion in a nation's government and legal system. Most Islamic nations strongly intertwine their religious beliefs into their mode of governance and rule of law. This is not true in much of the non-Islamic world, particularly Western nations that champion the separation of church and state.

Political and Legal Systems

Many Muslims feel that Islam should influence all aspects of society. They see it as a method for living life, governing nations, and maintaining law and order. For example, Saudi Arabia uses the Koran and Sunna as its constitution. Some governments in the Middle East are more secular (not controlled by religion) than others, with Turkey being considered the most secular nation in the region.

Many Muslim-majority countries are ruled by autocrats (rulers with vast or unlimited power). These include kings in monarchies in which rule remains in the royal family. Examples include Saudi Arabia, Jordan, Morocco, and Kuwait. Several Islamic countries have less autocratic forms of government, including Indonesia and Egypt.

Muslim nations allow various degrees of democratic representation. In 2005 and 2011 Saudi Arabia conducted limited municipal elections; however, only men were allowed to vote and run for office. The Saudi government has promised that women will be allowed to vote and run for office in the planned 2015 elections. Iran has elections that determine the nation's president and legislative members. Turkey is often heralded as the most democratic nation in the Muslim world.

SHARIA. Toni Johnson and Mohammed Aly Sergie of the Council on Foreign Relations explain in "Islam: Governing under Sharia" (July 25, 2014, http://www.cfr.org/religion/islam-governing-under-sharia/p8034) that Sharia means "path" in Arabic. It is based on the Koran, the Sunna, interpretations by legal scholars, and "the consensus of the Muslim community." Sharia basically provides a legal code for dealing with both criminal and civil matters, such as marriage, divorce, and inheritance. Sharia is applied in varying degrees in Muslim countries. Johnson and Sergie note that Saudi Arabia's legal system strictly adheres to Sharia, but that other Muslim-majority nations have a two-part system that includes both secular and Sharia courts. The secular courts deal with criminal matters, whereas the Sharia courts oversee civil matters (e.g., family law).

Criminal punishments under Sharia can be notoriously brutal, including amputations, flogging, and death by stoning for certain crimes. In "Hadd" (2014, http://www.oxfordislamicstudies.com/article/opr/t125/e757), the Oxford Dictionary of Islam explains that the six most serious crimes under Sharia—apostasy (rejecting one's religion), drinking intoxicants, highway robbery, illicit sexual relations, making unproven accusations of illicit sex, and theft—are "considered to be against the rights of God." The fixed harsh punishments for them are called "hudud" and are derived from the Koran and the hadith. For example, apostasy and having illicit sexual relations are both punishable by death. Some Muslim countries allow stoning as a means of capital punishment, whereas others do not. There are strict requirements for the kinds of evidence that can support hudud charges, making them difficult to prove. Johnson and Sergie note that the harsh punishments are seldom used and serve more as a deterrent to criminal behavior. However, incidents in which the

punishments are used or proscribed capture keen public attention and condemnation, particularly in the West.

Some countries with large Muslim-minority populations allow Islamic (Sharia) courts to hear cases involving family law. These nations include India, Israel, and the United Kingdom. In the United States there has been vocal opposition to what some people consider "Sharia creep" into Western legal systems. However, it is important to note that the United States already has religious tribunals and courts that handle some issues related to family law and business matters. These forums provide people with a voluntary option for arbitration (the settling of disputes with the help of an impartial third party) in accordance with their religious beliefs. Examples include rabbinical tribunals used by Orthodox Jews and diocesan tribunals used by Roman Catholics. Parties unhappy with the rulings can take their cases to civil courts if the issues involved are also covered by secular law.

According to Pew, in "State Legislation Restricting Use of Foreign or Religious Law" (April 8, 2013, http://www.pewforum.org/2013/04/08/state-legislation-restricting-use-of-foreign-or-religious-law), between 2010 and 2012 legislators in 32 states introduced bills "to restrict the circumstances in which state courts can consider foreign or religious laws in their decisions." Six states—Arizona, Kansas, Louisiana, Oklahoma, South Dakota, and Tennessee—enacted the laws; however, Oklahoma's law was later overturned. It specifically prohibited Sharia law and was found unconstitutional. Critics claim the legislative trend is driven by anti-Muslim sentiment and unfounded fears that Sharia law could usurp secular laws in the United States.

In 2014 Brunei, a tiny country in Southeast Asia, became the first nation in that region to add Sharia criminal law to its existing legal system. The move was widely criticized by international human rights groups. In Beverly Hills, California, protesters marched at two prominent hotels owned by Brunei to express their displeasure. Several organizations that were scheduled to hold conferences at the hotels canceled their reservations. Celebrities including Jay Leno (1950–) and Ellen Degeneres (1958–) called on people to boycott the hotels.

Tolerance for Other Religions

Religious tolerance (the tolerance of a government and its people toward religions other than any official or majority religion) is a controversial topic in U.S. relations with Islamic nations. In the Western world religious tolerance is generally favored as a means to further social harmony. This is not the case in much of the Muslim world, where strict adherence to religious traditions and teachings requires complete devotion to the Islamic faith.

Many Muslim-majority nations have declared Islam their official religion in their constitutions. The constitutions of some Islamic countries also allow, in theory, for freedom of other religious beliefs and expressions. This is true for Egypt and Iran. However, the protections of these freedoms may be limited or even nonexistent in practice. Extremely conservative Muslim nations, such as Saudi Arabia, do not provide any legal rights for people to practice a religion other than Islam. In fact, the public practice of a non-Islamic religion is forbidden by law. Likewise, converting from Islam to another religion is considered to be a crime in some predominantly Muslim countries.

Sudan is a Muslim-majority country. In 2014 Meriam Yehya Ibrahim Ishag (1987–) was found guilty of apostasy and illicit sexual relations. She was sentenced to 100 lashes followed by death by hanging. Ishag, a Christian, was born to a Muslim father, which the court considered as proof that she was a Muslim. As a result, she was accused of leaving Islam. She had married a Christian man and was pregnant with their second child at the time of the trial. This precipitated the illicit sexual relations charge. Ishag could have avoided the apostasy conviction by renouncing her Christian faith, but she refused to do so. There was an international outcry of criticism following her sentencing. The U.S. secretary of state John Kerry (1943–) called for leniency for her and for Sudan to abandon laws prohibiting Muslims from converting to other faiths. Ishag was released from prison after her case was heard by Sudan's appeals court; she and her family moved to the United States.

Freedom of Speech

Freedom of speech is another highly regarded principle in Western democracies. As such, Western speakers and writers feel free to openly discuss matters of religion, including matters that relate to Islam. This has led to clashes with Muslims who hold many subjects within Islam to be so sacred or sensitive that they must be discussed in a manner deemed respectful. In addition, most Muslims consider it blasphemous to visually depict God or the prophet Muhammad in any media, including artwork.

In 1988 the Indian-born writer Salman Rushdie (1947–) published in Great Britain *The Satanic Verses*, which included dreamlike sequences involving Muhammad and the Koran. The book sparked outrage among many Muslims who felt it was blasphemous. The following year Ruhollah Khomeini (1902?–1989), the supreme leader of Iran, issued a fatwa (religious edict) that called on Muslims around the world to kill Rushdie. The author was forced to go into hiding. The incident severely strained Iran's relations with other nations, particularly Great Britain, which severed diplomatic ties with Iran.

During the late 1990s moderates within the Iranian government downplayed the fatwa. However, Iran took a conservative turn in 2005 and the fatwa was reaffirmed. Mia de Graaf reports in "Iranian Mullah Revives Death Fatwa against Salman Rushdie over Satanic Verses 25 Years after It Was Issued" (DailyMail.co.uk, February 16, 2014) that as of 2014 the fatwa against Rushdie was still upheld by the Iranian clergy.

The provocative 10-minute film *Submission: Part 1* was released in 2004 in the Netherlands. It included several naked women with verses from the Koran written on their bodies. The film was a commentary on the alleged mistreatment of women in Islamic society. Its release led to the murder of its director, Theo van Gogh (1957–2004; a descendant of the painter Vincent van Gogh [1853–1890]), by Mohammed Bouyeri (1978–), a man of Moroccan Dutch descent who was affiliated with Islamic extremists.

Another freedom of speech furor erupted in 2005, when the Danish newspaper *Jyllands-Posten* published a series of comic strips that featured Muhammad as a character. One of the drawings depicted Muhammad wearing a turban with a bomb underneath it. Muslims reacted with anger. Dozens of people were killed in riots across the Middle East, and Scandinavian embassies and diplomatic offices in the region were attacked and set on fire. The newspaper received many bomb threats, and the comic strip artists had to go into hiding for fear of their lives. Several Muslim countries initiated an economic boycott of Danish goods.

The publication of the comics (or cartoons as they were called in Europe) and the resulting fury sparked a debate across Europe about the freedom of expression. Within a few months the newspaper issued a formal apology. However, in "Why I Published Those Cartoons" (WashingtonPost.com, February 19, 2006), Flemming Rose, the editor who had published the comics, defends his decision. He argues that the newspaper had a tradition of using satirical drawings to lampoon public figures, even religious ones. He rejects calls for self-censorship by the media to prevent insulting Muslims, noting that "if a believer demands that I, as a nonbeliever, observe his taboos in the public domain, he is not asking for my respect, but for my submission. And that is incompatible with a secular democracy."

The furor over the comics did not subside. According to Souad Mekhennet and Alan Cowell, in "Qaeda Group Says It Bombed Embassy" (NYTimes.com, June 6, 2008), 17 Danish newspapers republished the comics in February 2008 "as a statement of solidarity and press freedom." The republication reportedly followed the arrest of three Muslims for plotting to kill one of the cartoonists. Several months later, in June 2008, a suicide car bomber attacked the Danish embassy in Islamabad,

Pakistan, killing six people. The terrorist group al Qaeda claimed responsibility for the attack as an act of revenge for the Danish comics.

Frank Jordans reports in "Muslim Countries Seek Blasphemy Ban" (Associated Press, November 23, 2009) that in 2009 Islamic nations began campaigning the United Nations (UN) for an international treaty to "protect religious symbols and beliefs from mockery." The Organisation of Islamic Cooperation (OIC) was behind the initiative. As of 2014, the OIC (http://www.oic-oci.org/oicv2/page/?p_id=52&p_ref=26&lan=en) included 57 nations. The OIC proposal faced stiff opposition from Western democracies, such as the United States, that value freedom of speech. However, Jordans notes that the OIC and its member states believed the ban would further human rights, the way that laws against racism protect the human rights of minority races.

In September 2012 another furor erupted over the free speech issue after an anti-Islamic video made in the United States was posted on the Internet. The 13-minute video *Innocence of Muslims* was described by various media sources as amateurish or crudely made. In "Man Tied to Anti-Islam Video Held on Probation Charge" (NYTimes.com, September 27, 2012), Brooks Barnes states that the video "depicts the Prophet Muhammad as a buffoon, a womanizer and a child molester." It first appeared in English in June 2012 on YouTube (a video sharing website) and was then translated into Arabic and "uploaded several more times."

Many people in the United States first became aware of the video on September 11, 2012, when it triggered violent protests at U.S. embassies in Egypt and Yemen. That same day the U.S. ambassador to Libya and three of his staffers were killed in Libya. The killings were at first blamed on video protesters; however, blame soon shifted to Libyan militias with ties to terrorism. (See Chapter 3 for details on the Libyan attack.) U.S. officials, including President Barack Obama (1961–) and the U.S. secretary of state Hillary Rodham Clinton (1947–), strongly condemned the video, but that did little to quell outrage in the Muslim world. Barnes notes that a Pakistani cabinet minister offered a $100,000 reward "for the death of the person behind the video." Again, there were calls from Muslim nations for an international ban on blasphemy. Google, Inc., the owner of YouTube, refused to remove the video; however, it did block access to the video in certain countries.

In late September 2012 Nakoula Basseley Nakoula (1957–), the purported maker of the video, was arrested in Los Angeles, California, for violating the terms of his probation on a 2010 bank fraud charge. In November 2012 he was sentenced to a year in prison, but was released 10 months later.

Public Relations

Despite the ideological differences between Islamic and non-Islamic nations, fairly good relations exist between the two at the government-to-government level. For example, the United States has good relations with Saudi Arabia, which is an extremely conservative Muslim country that allows virtually no democracy, religious tolerance, or freedom of speech. Likewise, the United States enjoys good foreign relations with the governments of most other Muslim-majority countries. However, as noted earlier the governments of many of these countries are autocratic and suppressive, rather than democratic, in nature. Thus, the actions of the government may not represent the general will of the people.

The Israeli-Palestinian conflict is described in detail in Chapter 1. Both sides believe they hold historical rights to the land now known as Israel. The United States has been a close ally of Israel since the latter's creation in 1948. U.S. political and financial support for Israel over the decades is a source of deep resentment among the predominantly Muslim peoples of the Middle East. The 2001 invasion of Afghanistan and the 2003 invasion of Iraq (both Muslim-majority countries) significantly degraded opinions of the United States in Islamic countries. President Bush became very unpopular in the Muslim world because his administration's War on Terror was seen as an attack on Islam. However, Muslim public opinion about the United States improved slightly with the advent of the Obama administration. President Obama has ties to the Islamic world: his father was born into a Muslim and Christian family, and when Obama was a boy he lived in Indonesia, a Muslim-majority country.

There is no doubt that influencing international opinion in favor of the United States is a very difficult task. Thomas L. Friedman observes in *Longitudes and Attitudes: Exploring the World after September 11* (2002), "Since the end of the cold war anti-Americanism has overtaken soccer as the world's favorite sport." U.S. politicians and reporters often refer to the effort to make Muslim opinions more favorable toward the United States as "winning hearts and minds." Since the 9/11 terrorist attacks the United States has made the spread of democracy among Muslims, and especially in the Middle East, an important priority. After invading Afghanistan in 2001 and Iraq in 2003 the United States helped devise new, democratic constitutions for those nations. It has also pushed for democratic-style governments in other autocratic countries in the Middle East.

As described in Chapter 2, the U.S. Department of State (DOS) conducts programs of public diplomacy in an attempt to influence the attitudes and behaviors of people around the world. As part of this effort the U.S. government finances radio and television networks to counter what it considers to be misinformation disseminated about the United States by the state-run media in many Middle Eastern countries. Radio Sawa, an Arabic-language radio station that plays pop music, news, sports, and other programs, was launched in 2002. Alhurra Television provides commercial-free Arabic-language news and feature stories throughout the Middle East. Radio Free Europe/Radio Liberty broadcasts in eastern Europe and central and southwestern Asia in 28 languages and is available over the radio, television, and Internet. In 2003 the DOS provided millions of dollars for the new magazine *Hi* that was designed to reach the teenage populations of Arabic countries. Its sales were dismal, and the program was suspended in late 2005.

Middle Eastern youth, particularly boys, are the primary target of U.S. information campaigns. It is hoped that the information will help counteract the radical version of Islam that is associated with some Islamic religious schools called madrassas. These boarding schools are financed by wealthy Muslims and provide room and board for poor children (mostly boys) throughout the Islamic world. The educational studies are devoted almost exclusively to the Koran and Sharia. There are believed to be thousands of madrassas throughout the Middle East. The National Commission on Terrorist Attacks upon the United States notes in *The 9/11 Commission Report* (July 2004, http://www.9-11commission .gov/report/911Report.pdf) that some of these schools "have been used as incubators for violent extremism." According to Philippa H. Stewart, in "Can Madrassas Help Developing Countries?" (Aljazeera.com, March 13, 2014), as of 2014 at least 20,000 madrassas were operating in Pakistan with an estimated 2 million to 3 million students.

Foreign Aid

Another key element of U.S. public diplomacy is foreign aid. Providing food, money, and other aid to struggling countries has been a hallmark of U.S. foreign policy since the end of World War II. Under the Marshall Plan billions of dollars went to European countries to help them rebuild infrastructure and industries that were devastated during the war. The money helped ensure political stability, stave off communist interference, and create trading partners for the United States.

Muslim-majority countries have been the beneficiaries of U.S. foreign aid in the past. These countries received new emphasis when the War on Terror (later the Overseas Contingency Operations) began in September 2001. As shown in Figure 1.1 in Chapter 1, Muslim-majority countries, such as Afghanistan, Iraq, Egypt, Jordan, and Pakistan, were among the top recipients of U.S. economic and military assistance in fiscal year 2012.

AMERICAN PUBLIC OPINION ABOUT ISLAM AND MUSLIMS

Public opinion polls conducted in the United States by the Gallup Organization reveal negative feelings among Americans about Islam relative to other religions. In *In U.S., Religious Prejudice Stronger against Muslims* (January 21, 2010, http://www.gallup.com/poll/125312/ Religious-Prejudice-Stronger-Against-Muslims.aspx), Gallup reports that more than half (53%) of the respondents in a poll that was conducted between October and November 2009 expressed unfavorable views about Islam. In contrast, Buddhism, Judaism, and Christianity were viewed much more favorably. In addition, 43% of those asked admitted having "feelings of prejudice" toward Muslims. Only 14% to 18% expressed prejudiced feelings toward Christians, Jews, or Buddhists.

Pew also gauges U.S. public opinion regarding Islam and Muslims. As described in Chapter 3, in May 2013 two young Muslim men allegedly set off bombs along the finish line of the Boston Marathon that killed three people and injured more than 200 others. Soon afterward, Pew polled Americans about possible connections between Islam and violence. The results were reported in "After Boston, Little Change in Views of Islam and Violence" (May 7, 2013, http://www.people-press.org/ 2013/05/07/after-boston-little-change-in-views-of-islam-and-violence). The Pew pollsters asked respondents whether they agreed or disagreed with the statement: "Islam is more likely than other religions to encourage violence among its believers." More respondents disagreed (46%) than agreed (42%) with this statement. In general, the results mirrored those obtained in previous polls dating back to 2002, in which 25% to 45% of respondents agreed with this statement.

MUSLIMS WITHIN THE UNITED STATES

The United States has a relatively small population of Muslims. Because the U.S. Census does not ask people about religious affiliation, there is no official count by the U.S. government. However, various private groups have published estimates. For example, Pew estimates in *The Future Global Muslim Population Projections for 2010–2030* that the Muslim population in the United States was around 2.6 million in 2010, or approximately 0.8% of the total U.S. population. By contrast, CAIR estimates in "Islam Basics" the number was 6 million to 7 million in 2014.

Islamophobia?

Since the 9/11 attacks Muslims within the United States have faced heightened scrutiny (and hostility) from people who are concerned about the terrorist threat posed by some individuals and groups that claim to represent

Islamic interests. The fear and general ill will directed toward Muslims, or people perceived to be Muslims, has been dubbed Islamophobia by the media.

The U.S. government considers hate crimes to be crimes motivated by an offender's personal prejudice or bias against a victim. In *Confronting Discrimination in the Post-9/11 Era: Challenges and Opportunities Ten Years Later* (October 19, 2011, http://www.justice.gov/crt/publications/post911/post911summit_report_2012-04.pdf), the U.S. Department of Justice (DOJ) notes there was a sharp uptick in anti-Muslim hate crimes in 2001. The DOJ states, "The first threats of violence and acts of violence against people perceived to be Arab, Muslim, Sikh, and South Asian occurred within hours of the 9/11 attacks. The violence intensified for the next three weeks, eventually tapering off but never falling below the levels documented before 9/11."

Muslims have also encountered stiff resistance to their efforts to build or expand mosques within the United States. One case in particular made national headlines. A Muslim group aroused great controversy in New York City when it announced plans to build a mosque and Islamic community center within two blocks of "ground zero," the former site of the World Trade Center buildings that were destroyed in the 9/11 attacks. Critics protested that the project was disrespectful to the thousands of people who died in the attacks, whereas supporters touted the project as a forum for moderate Muslims to practice their faith and build relationships in the community. Despite fierce opposition, the center opened in late 2011.

Radicalization of U.S. Muslims

As noted in Chapter 3, since 2009 the United States has seen a dramatic increase in terrorism charges against people who were either born in the United States (i.e., "homegrown" suspects) or had become U.S. citizens. Many of these suspects converted to Islam from other religions and/or became radicalized—meaning that they embraced a very radical Islamic view that condones violence. In "Attorney General's Blunt Warning on Terror Attacks" (ABCNews.com, December 21, 2010), Jack Cloherty quotes the U.S. attorney general Eric Holder Jr. (1951–) as saying: "The threat has changed from simply worrying about foreigners coming here, to worrying about people in the United States, American citizens—raised here, born here, and who for whatever reason, have decided that they are going to become radicalized and take up arms against the nation in which they were born."

In 2011 Representative Peter T. King (1944–; R; NY) chaired the U.S. House of Representatives Committee on Homeland Security. He decided to hold a series of hearings around the country regarding the extent and threat of radicalization of U.S. Muslims. The results were reported in *Committee on Homeland Security: "The American Muslim Response to Hearings on Radicalization within Their Community"* (June 20, 2012, http://homeland.house.gov/sites/homeland.house.gov/files/06-20-12-Report.pdf). Table 10.1 summarizes the committee's major findings. The committee concludes that "the increasing frequency of Muslim-Americans becoming radicalized is an alarming trend and a great concern for U.S. national security." The committee offered no potential solutions or recommendations to counter the problem of radicalization and

TABLE 10.1

Findings of U.S. House hearings on the radicalization of Muslim Americans, June 2012

Hearing #1: "The extent of radicalization in the American Muslim community and that community's response."

Finding #1: The radicalization of Muslim-Americans constitutes a real and serious homeland security threat.
Finding #2: There is not enough Muslim-American community cooperation with law enforcement.
Finding #3: There is a need to confront the Islamist ideology driving radicalization.

Hearing #2: "The threat of Muslim-American radicalization in U.S. prisons."

Finding #4: The radicalization of prison inmates to an extremist form of Islam is a significant problem, which can often manifest once radicalized prisoners are released.
Finding #5: The radicalization of prison inmates is often precipitated by the presence of radical clergy or extremist materials within the prison.

Hearing #3: "Al-Shabaab: recruitment and radicalization within the Muslim-American community and the threat to the homeland."

Finding #6: There are direct ties between Al-Shabaab and Al Qaeda and its affiliates, and Al-Shabaab recruits are often indoctrinated into Al Qaeda's ideology and network.
Finding #7: More than 40 Muslim-Americans radicalized and recruited by Al-Shabaab may pose a direct threat to the national security of the United States and its allies.
Finding #8: The committee's hearings on the radicalization of Muslim-Americans have empowered Muslims to effectively address this issue.

Hearing #4: "Homegrown Terrorism: The threat to military communities inside the United States."

Finding #9: The terrorist threat to military communities is severe and on the rise.
Finding #10: The "insider" threat to military communities is a significant and potentially devastating development.
Finding #11: Political correctness continues to stifle the military's ability to effectively understand and counter the threat.
Finding #12: The administration chose political correctness over accurately labeling and identifying certain terrorist attacks appropriately, thereby denying Purple Hearts medals to killed and wounded troops in domestic terror attacks.

SOURCE: "Committee Findings," in *Committee on Homeland Security: "The American Muslim Response to Hearings on Radicalization within Their Community,"* U.S. House of Representatives, Committee on Homeland Security, June 20, 2012, http://homeland.house.gov/sites/homeland.house.gov/files/06-20-12-Report.pdf (accessed May 25, 2014)

FIGURE 10.1

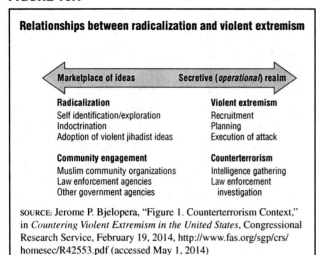

Relationships between radicalization and violent extremism

Marketplace of ideas   Secretive (*operational*) realm

Radicalization	**Violent extremism**
Self identification/exploration	Recruitment
Indoctrination	Planning
Adoption of violent jihadist ideas	Execution of attack
Community engagement	**Counterterrorism**
Muslim community organizations	Intelligence gathering
Law enforcement agencies	Law enforcement
Other government agencies	investigation

SOURCE: Jerome P. Bjelopera, "Figure 1. Counterterrorism Context," in *Countering Violent Extremism in the United States*, Congressional Research Service, February 19, 2014, http://www.fas.org/sgp/crs/homesec/R42553.pdf (accessed May 1, 2014)

stoked fierce criticism for holding the hearings in the first place. Laurie Goodstein reports in "Muslims to Be Congressional Hearings' Main Focus" (NYTimes.com, February 7, 2011) that King's hearings "provoked an uproar from both the left and the right. The left has accused Mr. King of embarking on a witch hunt. The right has accused him of capitulation for calling Muslims such as Representative Keith Ellison, Democrat of Minnesota, to testify while denying a platform to popular critics of Islamic extremism." Criticism was particularly acute from some elements within the Muslim American community, which feared that the hearings encouraged Islamophobia.

Jerome P. Bjelopera of the Congressional Research Service examines the relationship between radicalization and violent extremism in *Countering Violent Extremism in the United States* (February 19, 2014, http://www.fas.org/sgp/crs/homesec/R42553.pdf). As shown in Figure 10.1, radicalization occurs within a "marketplace of ideas." Bjelopera notes that as Muslims become radicalized, "they do not necessarily commit crimes." If they do become operational terrorists, then any successful plots they conduct may spur additional radicalization. He points out, however, that successful counterterrorism efforts may "discourage radicalizing individuals within the marketplace of ideas from eventually embracing violent acts of terrorism as an ultimate goal." Bjelopera urges counterterrorism officials to interact with the Muslim community at large to help prevent terrorism recruitment. Examples of such interactions and efforts by U.S. government agencies are shown in Figure 10.2.

FIGURE 10.2

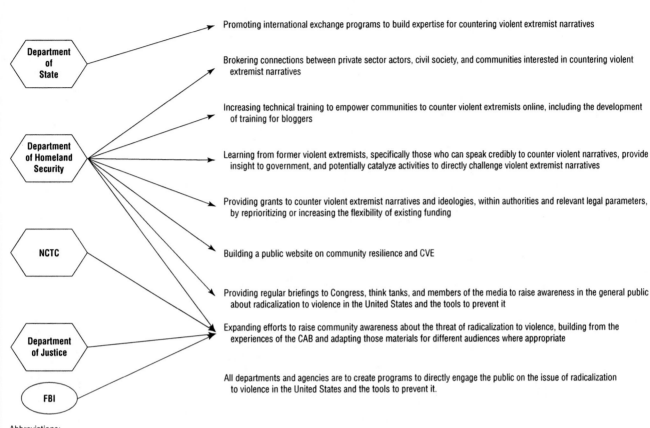

Lead agencies tasked with countering violent extremist propaganda while promoting U.S. ideals

Department of State

Department of Homeland Security

NCTC

Department of Justice

FBI

Promoting international exchange programs to build expertise for countering violent extremist narratives

Brokering connections between private sector actors, civil society, and communities interested in countering violent extremist narratives

Increasing technical training to empower communities to counter violent extremists online, including the development of training for bloggers

Learning from former violent extremists, specifically those who can speak credibly to counter violent narratives, provide insight to government, and potentially catalyze activities to directly challenge violent extremist narratives

Providing grants to counter violent extremist narratives and ideologies, within authorities and relevant legal parameters, by reprioritizing or increasing the flexibility of existing funding

Building a public website on community resilience and CVE

Providing regular briefings to Congress, think tanks, and members of the media to raise awareness in the general public about radicalization to violence in the United States and the tools to prevent it

Expanding efforts to raise community awareness about the threat of radicalization to violence, building from the experiences of the CAB and adapting those materials for different audiences where appropriate

All departments and agencies are to create programs to directly engage the public on the issue of radicalization to violence in the United States and the tools to prevent it.

Abbreviations:
CVE—Countering Violent Extremism.
NCTC—National Counterterrorism Center.
FBI—Federal Bureau of Investigation.
CAB—Community Awareness Briefing, developed in 2010 by NCTC.
Notes: The text in Figure 4 shifts to the present progressive tense, as does the text in the SIP related to the future activities and efforts for Objective 3.
SIP = Strategic Implementation Plan for Empowering Local Partners to Prevent Violent Extremism in the United States (December 2011).

SOURCE: Jerome P. Bjelopera, "Figure 4. Lead Agencies and Their 'Future Activities and Efforts' for SIP Objective 3, Countering Violent Extremist Propaganda While Promoting U.S. Ideals," in *Countering Violent Extremism in the United States*, Congressional Research Service, February 19, 2014, http://www.fas.org/sgp/crs/homesec/R42553.pdf (accessed May 1, 2014)

IMPORTANT NAMES
AND ADDRESSES

American Civil Liberties Union
125 Broad St., 18th Floor
New York, NY 10004
(212) 549-2500
URL: http://www.aclu.org/

Amnesty International USA
Five Penn Plaza, 16th Floor
New York, NY 10001
(212) 807-8400
FAX: (212) 627-1451
E-mail: aimember@aiusa.org
URL: http://www.amnestyusa.org/

**Centers for Disease Control and
Prevention**
1600 Clifton Rd.
Atlanta, GA 30329-4027
1-800-232-4636
URL: http://www.cdc.gov/

Central Intelligence Agency
Office of Public Affairs
Washington, DC 20505
(703) 482-0623
FAX: (571) 204-3800
URL: http://www.cia.gov/

**Congressional Research Service
Library of Congress**
101 Independence Ave. SE
Washington, DC 20540
URL: http://www.loc.gov/crsinfo/

Council on American Islamic Relations
453 New Jersey Ave. SE
Washington, DC 20003
(202) 488-8787
FAX: (202) 488-0833
URL: http://www.cair.com/

Defense Threat Reduction Agency
8725 John J. Kingman Rd., Stop 6201
Fort Belvoir, VA 22060-6201
(703) 767-5870
1-800-701-5096

FAX: (703) 767-4450
E-mail: dtra.publicaffairs@dtra.mil
URL: http://www.dtra.mil/

Electronic Privacy Information Center
1718 Connecticut Ave. NW, Ste. 200
Washington, DC 20009
(202) 483-1140
FAX: (202) 483-1248
URL: http://www.epic.org/

Federal Bureau of Investigation
J. Edgar Hoover Bldg.
935 Pennsylvania Ave. NW
Washington, DC 20535-0001
(202) 324-3000
URL: http://www.fbi.gov/

Federal Emergency Management Agency
500 C St. SW
Washington, DC 20472
(202) 646-2500
URL: http://www.fema.gov/

International Atomic Energy Agency
Vienna International Centre
PO Box 1001400
Vienna, Austria
(011-43-1) 2600-0
FAX: (011-43-1) 2600-7
E-mail: Official.Mail@iaea.org
URL: http://www.iaea.org/

International Committee of the Red Cross
19 Avenue de la paix
CH 1202
Geneva, Switzerland
(011-41-22) 734-60-01
FAX: (011-41-22) 733-20-57
URL: http://www.icrc.org/eng

Joint Chiefs of Staff
1400 Defense Pentagon
Washington, DC 20301-1400
URL: http://www.dtic.mil/jcs

Missile Defense Agency
5700 18th St., Bldg. 245
Fort Belvoir, VA 22060-5573
E-mail: mda.info@mda.mil
URL: http://www.mda.mil/

**National Consortium for the Study of
Terrorism and Responses to Terrorism**
8400 Baltimore Ave, Ste. 250
College Park, MD 20740
E-mail: infostart@start.umd.edu
URL: http://www.start.umd.edu/

National Guard
111 S. George Mason Dr.
Arlington, VA 22204
(703) 607-2584
URL: http://www.nationalguard.mil/

National Security Agency
(301) 688-6524
FAX: (301) 688-6198
E-mail: nsapao@nsa.gov
URL: http://www.nsa.gov/

North Atlantic Treaty Organization
Rue Léopold 31000
Brussels, Belgium
(011-32-2) 707-41-11
URL: http://www.nato.int/cps/en/natolive/
index.htm

**Office of the Director of National
Intelligence**
Washington, DC 20511
(703) 733-8600
URL: http://www.dni.gov/

Transportation Security Administration
601 S. 12th St.
Arlington, VA 22202
(571) 227-2829
1-866-289-9673
E-mail: TSA-ContactCenter@dhs.gov
URL: http://www.tsa.gov/

United Nations
First Avenue at 46th St.
New York, NY 10017
URL: http://www.un.org/

U.S. Agency for International Development
Ronald Reagan Bldg.
Washington, DC 20523-0016
(202) 712-4810
FAX: (202) 216-3524
E-mail: pinquiries@usaid.gov
URL: http://www.usaid.gov/

U.S. Air Force
Office of the Secretary of the Air Force
Public Affairs Resource Library
1690 Air Force Pentagon
Washington, DC 20330-1670
(703) 571-2784
1-800-423-8723
URL: http://www.af.mil/

U.S. Army
Media Relations Division
Office of the Chief of Public Affairs
1500 Army Pentagon
Washington, DC 20310-1500
URL: http://www.army.mil/

U.S. Citizenship and Immigration Services
425 I St. NW
Washington, DC 20536
1-800-375-5283
URL: http://www.uscis.gov/portal/site/uscis

U.S. Coast Guard
2100 Second St. SW
Washington, DC 20593
URL: http://www.uscg.mil/

U.S. Customs and Border Protection
1300 Pennsylvania Ave. NW
Washington, DC 20229
(202) 325-8000
1-877-227-5511
URL: http://www.cbp.gov/

U.S. Department of Defense
1400 Defense Pentagon
Washington, DC 20301-1400
(703) 571-3343
URL: http://www.defense.gov/

U.S. Department of Energy
1000 Independence Ave. SW
Washington, DC 20585
(202) 586-5000
URL: http://energy.gov/

U.S. Department of Homeland Security
Washington, DC 20528
(202) 282-8000
URL: http://www.dhs.gov/

U.S. Department of Justice
950 Pennsylvania Ave. NW
Washington, DC 20530-0001
(202) 514-2000
E-mail: AskDOJ@usdoj.gov
URL: http://www.justice.gov/

U.S. Department of State
2201 C St. NW
Washington, DC 20520
(202) 647-4000
URL: http://www.state.gov/

U.S. Department of the Treasury
1500 Pennsylvania Ave. NW
Washington, DC 20220
(202) 622-2000
FAX: (202) 622-6415
URL: http://www.treasury.gov/

U.S. Government Accountability Office
441 G St. NW
Washington, DC 20548
(202) 512-3000
E-mail: contact@gao.gov
URL: http://www.gao.gov/

U.S. Marine Corps
Director of Public Affairs
2 Navy Annex
Washington, DC 20380-1775
(703) 614-1034
URL: http://www.marines.mil/

U.S. Navy
Chief of Information
1200 Navy Pentagon
Washington, DC 20350-1200
URL: http://www.navy.mil/

White House
1600 Pennsylvania Ave. NW
Washington, DC 20500
(202) 456-1111
URL: http://www.whitehouse.gov/

RESOURCES

Several government agencies and organizations provided resources for this book. The U.S. Government Accountability Office (GAO) is the investigative arm of Congress and posts its many publications online. GAO reports on national security, weapons of mass destruction, and federal government agencies and spending were invaluable. The Congressional Research Service (CRS) is a division of the Library of Congress and publishes regularly updated reports on U.S. policies and laws and other issues of interest to members of Congress. CRS reports on foreign policy and civil and human rights were a major source of information for this book.

Other government agencies and offices consulted during the compilation of this book include the Broadcasting Board of Governors, the Central Intelligence Agency, the Federal Bureau of Investigation, the Library of Congress, the Missile Defense Agency, the Nunn-Lugar Cooperative Threat Reduction Program, the Office of the Coordinator for Counterterrorism, the U.S. Agency for International Development, the U.S. Department of Defense, the U.S. Department of Energy, the U.S. Department of Homeland Security, the U.S. Department of Justice, the U.S. Department of State, the U.S. Department of the Treasury, the U.S. House of Representatives' Committee on Homeland Security, the U.S. National Counterterrorism Center, and the White House. The latter provided national strategy and planning documents, budgetary information, and the text of presidential speeches and executive orders.

Commissions appointed by U.S. presidents, Congress, or agency heads have produced reports on topics related to national security. The Central Intelligence Agency's *World Factbook* provides a wealth of information about countries around the world and is updated frequently. Other valuable resources in the intelligence community are the National Counterintelligence Executive and the Office of the Director of National Intelligence.

The following news organizations and outlets were useful for providing timely features about national security: ABC News, Associated Press, BBC News, CBS News, CNN.com, National Geographic, *New York Times*, Reuters, *Time*, *USA Today*, *Wall Street Journal*, and *Washington Post*.

Private domestic and international organizations that provided information for this book include the American Civil Liberties Union, Amnesty International, the Arms Control Association, the Council on American Islamic Relations, the Council on Foreign Relations, the Electronic Frontier Foundation, the Electronic Privacy Information Center, the Federal Judicial Center, the Federation of American Scientists, the International Committee of the Red Cross, the National Conference of State Legislatures, the Nuclear Threat Initiative, the Organisation of Islamic Cooperation, the Pew Research Center, the United Nations, and the World Nuclear Association. As always, much thanks to the Gallup Organization for its insightful articles and poll results.

INDEX

L

9 781573 026468